MUSIC FOR LISTENERS

das due vivens
hostia ze teutsch
ajunuth

De lebendes oblat purivut vnde lebeny |

In dem allem opfer hat/gat ein end gegebn/durch dich

auch wart der maiestat/lob in preis gegebn/durch dich

auch die kirchen stat/schon benant vnd erbin Aue vas de

sensstikait/schrein di suessen hymme/durchn lust vnd biume

waid/hímmels smachs begir im Merlichait vnd besinhait

Music
FOR LISTENERS

WILLIAM THOMSON

State University of New York at Buffalo

PRENTICE-HALL, INC., Englewood Cliffs, New Jersey 07632

Library of Congress Cataloging in Publication Data

THOMSON, WILLIAM, date
  Music for listeners.

  1. Music—Analysis, appreciation. I. Title.
MT6.T48M9   780'.15   77-8049
ISBN 0-13-608026-X

10 9 8 7 6 5 4 3 2 1

PRENTICE-HALL INTERNATIONAL, INC., *London*
PRENTICE-HALL OF AUSTRALIA PTY. LIMITED, *Sydney*
PRENTICE-HALL OF CANADA, LTD., *Toronto*
PRENTICE-HALL OF INDIA PRIVATE LIMITED, *New Delhi*
PRENTICE-HALL OF JAPAN, INC., *Tokyo*
PRENTICE-HALL OF SOUTHEAST ASIA PTE. LTD., *Singapore*
WHITEHALL BOOKS LIMITED, *Wellington, New Zealand*

THIS BOOK is dedicated to Arrand, Beth, Bob, Chet, Dave, Grant, Jody, Louis, Mickey, Norman, Robert, Sam, Thane, Vincent, Warren, and Wiley, who made the CMP era memorable.

CONTENTS

PART **II**

**MUSIC FOR LARGE
INSTRUMENTAL GROUPS**

PART **III**

VOCAL MUSIC

PART IV

THE CONCERTO

PART **V**

SOLO AND CHAMBER MUSIC

PART **VI**

JAZZ

PART **VII**

**ART MUSIC OF TWO OTHER
CULTURES, JAPAN AND INDIA**

PREFACE

This book is for anyone who wants to know more about music and wishes to develop deeper satisfaction from listening. It is not a history of music, although you will find many pages that weave an historical scene around the pieces discussed, nor is it a theory of music, although those kinds of information are very much in evidence in all the descriptive essays about musical properties and particular compositions. It is a guide to experiencing music in ways that can make this art a more prominent and gratifying aspect of your life.

Try to imagine a day when you haven't heard some kind of music. You may decide the notion is unthinkable—unless you live in utter seclusion. Whether by choice or by chance, music surrounds us. We worship, we war, we love, we work, we play, and we relax to the strains of some kind of sound stimulation. And thus it has been since history began.

You may well ask such questions as: "Having spent these years surrounded by music, why read a book about it?" "What is one to learn that hasn't been known before? Why not just spend the time listening to more music?" After all, a book *about* music is at best a second-hand source of musical pleasure. Similarly, a book about swimming can't provide the basic fun of "getting wet."

And yet, books can help us gain insights that years of listening might never provide. In fact, reading about music is just another path to enjoying it more, one way of sharing the experience. If you and I both listen to Mozart's *G Minor Symphony* we are left with our individual experiences;

but if we discuss our impressions about the work, then there is a good chance we can fill in gaps in each other's pleasure and understanding. Consequently, we will both get more from Mozart the next time we listen.

Although a book is necessarily a one-sided conversation—with the author doing all the talking—this is the basic thrust of the book.

ORGANIZATION

The central core is a collection of 39 compositions about which we can feel some excitement and wonderment. Each composition is discussed in detail to whet your interest and guide your understanding. And since music is created within a society by real people, each of these discussions is introduced by an essay about some of the social, political, religious, artistic, professional, and personal events that surrounded the work's creation—its *background*.

Before getting into this core of 39 compositions, our first six chapters plow the ground. Their function is to establish common paths for our later discussions. In these chapters the listener's awareness of basic properties is developed, so that one can proceed quickly in an understanding of how music is organized and how one might best approach it and talk about it with others. But even in these first chapters, reading without listening will prove to be empty. Every idea touched upon is meaningful only in terms of *how it sounds in music*. And thus, we turn constantly to musical examples to drive home a point.

MAIN GOAL OF THE BOOK

Our experiences of music are what we make of them—they can be superficial or deep, highly intellectual or supercharged with emotion (or both). There is no shortage of music to fit any response we can muster, from the idle tapping of a foot to the brainiest analysis. The long-play recording has placed a bountiful choice of music within immediate reach. Simply by entering a record store we can choose a culture, a century, a composer, or a particular performer. Within a few steps we can sample a rock opera, a Bach fugue, an Indian rāga, a country blues, or a French love song of the fourteenth century. Our problem is not variety; rather, it is making the most of what we have at our fingertips.

Our goal in this book, therefore, is to establish a perspective for comprehending and enjoying music, one that can be expanded and sharpened by talking about it, not merely by listening to it. Even though the listening is more important than the talking, nevertheless, having one without the other robs us of much of the enjoyment, and prolongs the journey as well.

Knowing a piece of music is much like knowing a person. It is one thing to observe and respond to skin-deep qualities. It is quite something else to make contact with the inner life—those deeper traits that make one person (or one composition) unique and prized. We seek this latter kind of knowing.

An in-depth knowledge of a musical composition is not easy. Even Leonard Bernstein, one of the most gifted musicians of all times, acknowledges that "Music is hard." He means that getting "inside" a piece of music requires more than a passive hearing of its sounds, more than tapping one's foot to its pulse. He elaborates by saying that music

> ... may be easy to take, or pleasant to hear for many people; it may evoke fanciful images in the mind, or bathe in a sensuous glow, or stimulate, or soothe, or whatever. But none of that is listening.*

These pages are meant to help you become a listener of the kind Bernstein had in mind. Don't settle for less.

William Thomson
BUFFALO, NEW YORK

---

*In *The Infinite Variety of Music,* pp. 19–20.

ACKNOWLEDGMENTS

Writing a book involves an author directly or indirectly with many others. A number of writers could be mentioned because their ideas have left indelible marks on my own. More direct aid came from various friends and colleagues. Some read the growing manuscript, others patiently discussed points of view and intricacies of organization with me. Among these were John Bloom, James Anthony, Robert Rainier, Walter Kaufmann, Dizzy Gillespie, Donald Erb, Mildred Trevett, William Kraft, Karen Ervin, Ira Cohen, and Donald Booth. I should also like to thank Bud Therien, Jeff McCartney, and Fred Bernardi of Prentice-Hall.

The most notable help of all was the role of omniscient counsel played by my wife, Betty, who possesses that infinite patience required by mates of perennial authors.

My sincere thanks to them all.

In addition, I am indebted to the publishers for permission to quote from or use the following material:

ALI AKBAR COLLEGE OF MUSIC: photos of Indian players with their instruments by Betsey Bourbon. BELWIN MILLS PUBLISHING CORP.: Hindemith, *Kleine Kammermusik* (for Wind Quintet), Op. 24, No. 2, Movement 2 (Walzer), measures 1-6, and Movement V, measure 5; Hindemith, *Theme and Four Variations (The Four Temperaments) for Piano and Strings,* Theme, measure 1, and First Variation, first six measures; Penderecki, *Stabat Mater* (for Three Mixed Choruses a capella), measures 58-63 and 86. THE BETTMAN ARCHIVE, INC.: pictures of Brahms, Robert and

Clara Schumann, Mozart with his father and sister, De la Pierce and band, and Hindemith conducting. BOOSEY AND HAWKES, INC.: excerpts from Bartok, *Concerto for Orchestra and Mikrokosmos;* excerpts from Copland, *Billy the Kid* and *Clarinet Concerto.* FRANK COOPER: photograph of a harpsichord constructed by Stephen Wessel that is a replica of the double manual instrument of 1623. CULVER PICTURES, INC.: pictures of Louis Armstrong, J. S. Bach, Bela Bartok, Hector Berlioz, F. Chopin, Claude Debussy, Benny Goodman, Charles Ives, Martin Luther, Mozart, Palestrina, Charlie Parker, Pope Gregory I, St. Thomas Church, Leipzig, Bessie Smith, and John Philip Sousa. PETER HASTINGS (CLEVELAND COMMERCIAL STUDIOS): photos of the Cleveland Orchestra and of solo pianist, G. Szell, conducting. Indiana University School of Music: photos of a dance scene from a production of *Eugene Onegin* and of Giovanni's house from a production of *Don Giovanni.* WILLIAM KRAFT: excerpt from his own *Encounters IV* (for Tape, Trombone, and Percussion). KATHY LIBRATY: photos of Japanese players and their instruments. NEW DIRECTIONS PUBLISHING CORP.: poetry by Federico Garcia Lorca as used in composition by George Crumb in *Ancient Voices of Children.* YOSHIHISA OSHIDA: photos of traditional Japanese instruments. C. F. PETERS CORPORATION: excerpts from Crumb, *Ancient Voices of Children.* THEODORE PRESSER COMPANY: excerpts from Erb, *Concerto for Solo Percussion and Orchestra;* excerpts from Persichetti, *Divertimento for Band,* Op. 42; and excerpts from Rochberg, *Twelve Bagatelles for Piano.* ROYAL HAWAIIAN BAND: photo of Royal Hawaiian Band at Iolani Palace Grounds in Honolulu. SUMMY-BIRCHARD COMPANY: Mildred J. Hill and Patty S. Hill, "Happy Birthday to You." YASUHARU TAKAHAGI: photos of traditional Japanese instruments. Universal Edition: Berg, *Violin Concerto (Violinkonzert),* Movement I, measures 24-27, 114, 115, 137, 139, and 213-221; Webern, *Symphony,* Opus 21, Movement II, measures 1-11.

MUSIC FOR LISTENERS

I

MUSICAL
PROPERTIES

I

MUSIC:
THE ART OF SOUND,
SPACE, AND TIME

Books of this kind often begin with some lofty question like "What is music?" We shall bypass any such speculations. You wouldn't be reading this now if you didn't already have a pretty good idea of what music is. Our answer might very well be that given by Louis Armstrong many years ago, when a woman asked the great jazz trumpet player, "Mr. Armstrong, what is jazz?" The irrepressible Satchmo retorted, "M'am, if ya gotta ask the question, there ain't no use in me tellin' ya."

Whatever its source or style, whatever its source of appeal, music is the *sound* art. Once we have valued a pattern of sounds for its own sake, a musical event has occurred. One main point of our study will be to develop an understanding of just what the composer does when he wrenches our attention away from the non-music world and engages us in his own world of interesting sounds.

MUSIC'S EVOCATIVE POWER

These patterns of sound that we call *music* are not just "interesting" from an intellectual point of view. They also can produce within us emotions of varying degrees and kinds. The way we respond to them is controlled mainly by the particular music we are hearing, but also by our individual personalities and past experiences. There are compositions that make us feel somber or sad (like funeral marches or dirges). And there are still other compositions that, no matter what our current state of mind, make us feel light-headed and joyful.

Illustration 1.1 While music can take place anywhere, the modern concert hall is specially designed to accommodate attentive listening. Severance Hall is the home of the Cleveland Orchestra, shown here with the late George Szell conducting to a capacity audience.

Yet, in spite of its many powers, music cannot refer to other things in the same way that painting and sculpture can. On its own, music cannot tell us a story (although it can confirm a plot described for us in words). Music can't depict a worldly event (although it can undergird an event with an appropriate mood if, as in ballet or in the movies, the event is represented pictorially).

To understand better what music does and how it does it, we must first establish a common perspective about some very general musical properties. We already have mentioned sound *patterns*, and this is crucial. The single isolated sound is not a likely object of our attention for very long.

Our car's horn may blast an especially provocative tone, but it isn't music. The tinkle of our spoon against a wineglass may provide a simple pleasure, but it doesn't rise to the level of music. And sometimes even the traffic on the street outside our window weaves an engaging web of sounds. Yet we find it difficult to hear these sounds in and for themselves, apart from the procession of vehicles that makes them. They don't quite make it *as music*.

MUSIC'S THREE BASIC DIMENSIONS

Music is a very special mixture of sounds. It possesses an integrity rarely found in the random sounds of the world. It is sounds organized in special ways. Every statement we might make about its organization demands some direct or indirect reference to one of three essential dimensions: *sound*, *space*, and *time*.

The first of these dimensions refers to the inherent qualities of *sound* itself, the individual sound bits that make up any musical pattern. *Space* refers here to the high-low aspect of the pattern, and *time* has the same meaning we associate with the later-earlier and longer-shorter events of everyday life.

So space and time are the boundaries within which the sound patterns of music reside. True, that single blast of the automobile horn remains just a honk; but if joined by other horns in a series of blasts, it just might rise to the level of what we might call *music*. In a nutshell, then, music consists of sounds that maneuver in time and space, in ways that create intellectually and emotionally stimulating patterns. We can isolate some aspects of these three dimensions of sound/space/time to better understand how they apply to any musical experience.

MUSIC AS THE SPACE-TIME ACTION OF SOUNDS

Perhaps our use of the term "space" needs some more explanation. In this case it doesn't refer to the geographical location of sounds but to *our sense of* their high-low placement. This is a kind of space defined by the difference, for example, between the high pitch of the soprano voice and the low pitch of the bass voice, or by the contrast in "depth" of that car horn and the tinkling wineglass.

The extent or breadth of musical space is determined by the apparent distance between highest and lowest pitches that make up any sound pattern. The sound-space available from a symphony orchestra seems boundless when compared with the sound-space of the folksinger and his guitar. The sound-space activated by a modern piano is far greater than that of the pennywhistle.

Composers often use this high-low difference of pitch to form the shape of their music as it progresses in time. That is, the sound patterns they *create* maneuver within different ranges of pitch at different times. For instance, the early sounds of a composition might lie within a relatively low pitch area; a shift to higher levels might then occur in contrast to the earlier parts; and a return to the low pitch area of the beginning might end the piece.

A short piano piece by Claude Debussy, "The Little Shepherd" ("Le petite berger"), does just about what we have described. In terms of its space and time characteristics, we might say that it begins with a melody that dips to a low point, rises to a highest point at about three-quarters of its course, then returns to one of the low points heard earlier.

We can make a "map" of this overall shape that looks like Example 1.1.* Here the highest and lowest pitches of "The Little Shepherd" are marked by the upper and lower extremities, and the total time of the piece is bounded by the double bars.

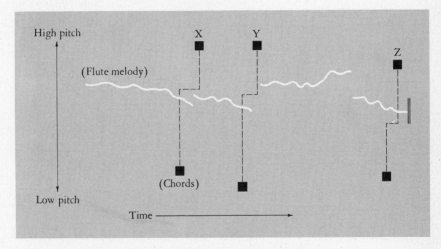

Example 1.1   Space-time mapping of "The Little Shepherd," Debussy

The advantage of this kind of elemental *map* is its ability to show in a glance some of the larger features of a whole composition. It cannot reveal details, nor can it reflect the charm or mood of the music. But it can depict basic shape, which is our main interest for the moment.

Note in the map of Example 1.1 that the music is punctuated at three points by rather low and high sounds. (They are indicated as *x, y,* and *z.*) Within the areas between these points the melody moves in a relatively confined space. It dips to its lowest point just before *y* and rises to its highest just before *z.* Filling sound-space in these different ways helps music to project a sense of motion and, toward the end of "The Little Shepherd," a sense of finality.

The same kind of high-low shaping occurs in far more involved music than Debussy's little piano work. Samuel Barber's Adagio for Strings is an instructive example worth hearing. It moves with a placid

---

*This composition can be found in the composer's collection of piano works called *Children's Corner Suite,* which he wrote for his young daughter.

motion within relatively low pitch levels in its beginning minutes. It then begins a gradual growth that reaches a tense point of climax at a very high pitch level. This is followed by a rapid decay to a point of rest at a low pitch level.

A mapping of the overall pitch-shape of a work like Barber's "Adagio for Strings" might look something like Example 1.2,* where line patterns are only rough approximations of the actual sounds.

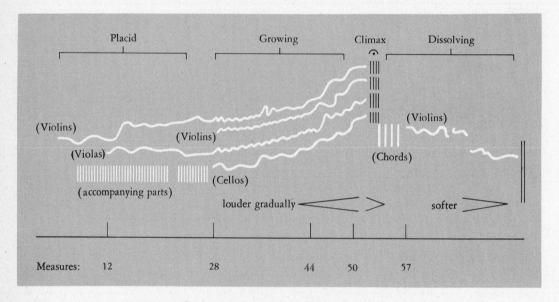

Example 1.2   Space-time mapping of "Adagio for Strings," Barber

Observe that the mounting tension you hear after the beginning passages is partly caused by the rise in pitch and growth in loudness to a highest point. This is a good example of one musical dimension (loudness) reinforcing another (pitch).

Even short melodies usually exhibit the same kind of high-low distribution that gives the listener a sense of overall shape. Most of the folk songs, hymns, and communal songs we hear consist of a stanza repeated several times. In that respect they cut a rather static pattern in musical space. But the stanza by itself almost always outlines a small-scale shape, or "contour," that depends on contrasts of high and low pitches.

A song such as Kathy Moriarty's "Just Keep on Moving" contains this kind of melodic shaping.

---

*Measure numbers are shown at the base line of the map only as relative reference to the time dimension. The measure in musical notation is the space between two vertical bars (*bar lines*) which divide the staff.

Example 1.3 Melody of one verse, "Just Keep on Moving"

(phrase 1)
And here at work   I   just   keep on   mov - ing;

(2)
Just keep pre - ten - ding to   ev - - 'ry   one,

(3)
You nev - er touched me   and   reached such a   lost   heart.

(4)
Tru - ly the words   are you   nev - er   knew   me.

As with all folksongs, the melody and the "meaning" of "Just Keep on Moving" are both derived from a text. The words tell about the disappointment of a love that never was and the disappointed one's attempts to hide feelings of rejection. But aside from the story unfolded, the melody's tones shape contours that project a musical form. A map of one stanza is shown in Example 1.4.

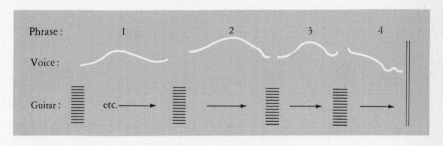

Example 1.4 Mapping of the melody, "Just Keep on Moving"

The space-filling motion of this folk song has the following characteristics:

1   A low opening arch pattern;
2   Repetition of the arch at a slightly higher pitch level;
3   Repetition of the same arch, same level as in #2;
4   A final sweep from the higher pitch level to the lower level of the beginning phrase, and thus an ending gesture.

Sing through one verse of "My Country, 'tis of Thee" and you can hear a melodic shape similar to that of "Just Keep on Moving."

9

MUSICAL STYLE AND THE SOUND/SPACE/TIME DIMENSIONS

If we surveyed the music of different cultures and historical periods, we would find that some music covers a very broad pitch span, while other music operates within a narrow band. A child's song might cover no more than three different pitches quite close together, while a composition for solo flute could span more than ten times as much space. A symphony might span twenty-five times as much.

Modern musical instruments make available a far greater breadth of musical space than was dreamed possible by musicians of earlier times. Even so, most of them provide a band of pitch that covers only the lower reaches of human hearing.* The chart in Example 1.5 gives a rough notion of the pitch resources of modern musical instruments as they compare with the human hearing range, which is about 18 to 18,000 cycles per second. (The *cycles per second* rate refers to how rapidly something is vibrating to make a particular pitch.)

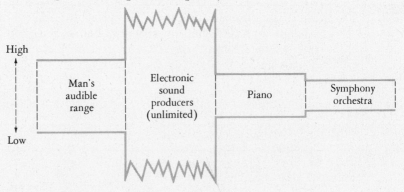

Example 1.5 A comparison of pitch ranges of modern instruments and human hearing

We can say with some accuracy that the history of music reflects an ever-expanding universe of the three dimensions of sound, space, and time. Compositions have gradually become longer; they have made use of a continually enlarged vocabulary of sounds; and the higher-lower limits of pitch-space have expanded from generation to generation.

This brings us to a final point: how a musical passage might contain successive shifts from low to high and from thick to thin. Composers sometimes create these shifts suddenly to produce a particular sense of

---

*Modern electronic sound producers, or "synthesizers," can create sounds as low and as high as we can hear—and even beyond.

drama. For some composers such dramatic gestures are a major feature of the way a musical passage unfolds in time. The introductory passage of Beethoven's Piano Sonata Opus 13 (the *Pathetique*) is masterful in the way it creates an effect of expectancy. It develops this effect largely by rapid shifts from low to high and from thick to thin sounds. We have reproduced the notation of this passage in Example 1.6. If possible, listen to it played and compare the mapping of Example 1.7 with what you hear. (Note that the bracketed areas *w*, *x*, *y*, and *z* on the mapping correspond to the areas so denoted on the printed music.)

Example 1.6   Introduction, Piano Sonata Op. 13, Beethoven

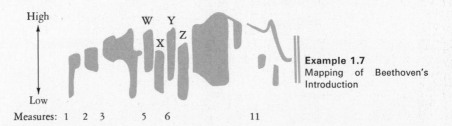

Example 1.7
Mapping of Beethoven's Introduction

In this passage a chain of steps from low to high occurs within the first four measures. After this (at *w* in our mapping) a series of brief high-low statements begins a buildup that doesn't subside until the final three measures. The highest point is reached in measure 9.

The overall effect of Beethoven's Introduction is quite different from that of music in which a narrow band of pitch is maintained rather uniformly over a period of time. Beethoven's passage reveals one of the ways composers can use musical space to suggest an emotional state, in this case one of mounting tension and expectancy.

To summarize our discussion of the three musical dimensions, we first might recall that sounds bounded in time and space form the irreducible conditions of music. We hear an infinite variety of different patterns fashioned within these basic dimensions. If a composer is skillful, his patterns will catch our fancy, leading us to cherish what we hear.

One of the ways the composer organizes music is by placing sounds in contrasitng levels of high and low. Some music operates within a uniformly thin band of pitch; other music extends from the very depths to the heights of available pitch. And often composers will inject a sense of shape or suggest emotion in their music by following one passage of sound with a lower or higher level of sound.

These are extremely simple and general ways of talking about music. They also are quite fundamental, and thus important for a listener.

WRITTEN MUSIC

Before our study progresses further, we can offer one aid for your subsequent reading: how to decipher musical notation. Our discussion will not enable you to read music as well as a musician, but you should be able to follow the basic signs and symbols. This will help you understand some of the ideas and terms that can ease your comprehension of the music you hear. (If you can read music fairly well already, consider skipping this section.)

Music notes are the written "alphabet" of a two-dimensional language. Placed in relationships to one another within the five lines and spaces of the musical staff, they represent the time and space dimensions we discussed earlier.

Pitch
Representation

The five-line staff is a simple grid that indicates relative pitch level. The higher a pitch, the farther toward the top of the staff that pitch appears. Thus you would hear the series of notes shown in Example 1.8 as a progression of successively lower pitches.

Example 1.8 Pitch representation by notes

Particular pitch levels are assigned to staff lines and spaces by *clef signs*. Some of the clef signs you might see in printed music are shown in Example 1.9. We indicate the pitch reference for each one, but you need not remember this aspect for all of the clefs.

Example 1.9 Clef signs

The most common clef, the treble clef, assigns still a different pitch "meaning" to the five lines and spaces of the staff. Its graceful lower curves encircle the line that represents the note *g*.

Example 1.10 The treble clef

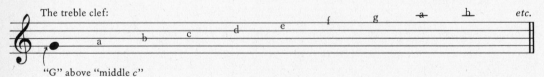

The music part read by a pianist or organist usually is notated in both the highest and lowest clefs, treble and bass. This provides a wide expanse of pitches within a relatively limited space on music paper. Listen to Example 1.11 played at a piano and note the broad coverage of pitch afforded by these two sets of five staff lines. Two notes (the first and the fifth) are placed on *ledger lines,* which extend above or below the staff.

Example 1.11   The Great Staff (treble and bass combined)

(treble clef)

(bass clef)

We shall discuss note names and other aspects of pitch notation and terminology in further detail later. For the present our goal is recognition of how the notes we see are made to correspond to the pitches we hear. This high/low aspect of musical notation is probably easier to grasp than the next we shall discuss, which has to do with the time dimension.

Time Representation

Traditional music writing uses different kinds of notes to signify different sound durations. For instance, the notes used in Example 1.11 have black note heads and simple vertical stems: ♩, ♩ , and so on. They are all of the same relative duration. Each is called a *quarter note.*

Since musical rhythms usually consist of different durations, other note values than the quarter are required. Using the quarter note as our reference, we can relate some other notes to it as follows:

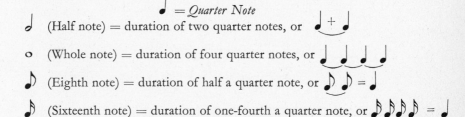

This aspect of notation is easy to understand but difficult to incorporate into the actual act of reading. Getting used to the relative durations of such strange markings as ♩ ♫♫ ♩ ♫ and so on is one of the problems musicians must cope with in the very beginning of their careers.

You can test your own fluency in rhythms by reading the durations shown next. The task can be simplified if you will tap a pulse that corresponds to the quarter notes. (One pulse = one quarter note.) We have shown the quarter notes below our rhythm, making it easier to keep up with the changing note values. (Sing any pitch that feels comfortable to your voice.)

Frequently in music you will see notes followed by dots, such as ♩. or ♩. . The dot prolongs the duration of the note it follows by one-half. That is, while a half note equals two quarters tied together (♩ = ♩♩), a dotted half note equals three (♩. = ♩♩♩).

Together, note values and their placement in the musical staff provide the coordination of time and pitch that are the basis of music writing. A familiar tune like "America the Beautiful" should seem rather easy to read if you keep in mind the way the two coordinates operate together.

Example 1.12 "America the Beautiful," first phrase

(A - mer - i - ca)

Or try reading the next melody. With some patience you should be able to discover what it is.

Example 1.13 Familiar tune

We shall add to your understanding of rhythmic notation as our study demands. In Chapter 3, for example, we shall discuss tempo, meter, and phrase, all of which are represented in notation by particular signs or words. But even that will only tap the most fundamental information about reading music.

2

MUSICAL FORM:
THE BIG PICTURE

Musicians use special words to describe the ways sounds are organized in space and time. For instance, they refer to *melody* when a pattern consists of pitches in succession. When different pitches are sounded together (i.e., simultaneously), they call the resulting sound *harmony*.

There are still other kinds of patterns sounds make when they occur in succession, or together, or both. There are *rhythm and texture*, and the most inclusive of all, *form*. Since this last property is the most general, we shall discuss it first.

THE LARGE PATTERNS OF FORM

The form of any object—be it a building, a statue, or a musical composition—depends upon everything that contributes to its shape. But we usually think of the gross shape, the general outline, when we refer to form. The form of a face is not changed by a freckle. Nor is the form of a cathedral marred when a pigeon lands on its roof. It is the big parts that give these objects their form.

When we talk about musical form, we usually mean the way a whole composition is shaped in relatively large blocks of time. The graphs in Chapter 1 of Samuel Barber's Adagio for Strings and Debussy's "The Little Shepherd" represent what we mean by form. A part of a composition's effect on us depends on how its large parts hang together. Random sounds on the city street don't add up to a pattern, nor do the hungry cries of animals in a zoo project a design. To produce an impression of

17

coherence—a belonging together—sounds must be organized in ways that create unity.

Most music contains *repetition* (which unifies), *contrast* (which adds variety), and *alteration* (which both unifies and varies). You can find all three of these kinds of processes playing lesser and greater roles in musical forms.

But what is it that is repeated? What is contrasted? What is altered in shaping a musical form? A true answer would have to be an evasive "Many things!" In Chapters 3, 4, 5, and 6 we shall discuss some of the properties that play prominent roles in musical organization. They are rhythm, melody, harmony, and texture. And frequently we shall note how various aspects of sounds themselves, particularly their loudness and timbre,* help to partition off the parts that make up a musical form.

For now let us get a better idea of the kinds of schemes these ingredients are molded into by composers. There are really only four basic types. They are *strophic, additive, return,* and *processive.*

STROPHIC FORMS

If you have ever sung (or heard sung) a song of several stanzas, you know what strophic form is like. Church hymns, patriotic songs, and most folk songs fit this description. They consist of a long musical pattern—a single melody—that is repeated for each verse of text. We could call this kind of form *repetitive.* Musical tradition provides the word *strophic*; the original unit and each of its repetitions are called *strophes.*

Strophic form can produce dull music, but there usually are circumstances that help hold our interest. Most compositions in this form are songs, so the words of their texts provide a sense of change or progress that is lacking in the music. A folk ballad like Buffy St. Marie's "Johnny Be Fair" tells an engaging tale of disappointment, for example. The unfolding tale relieves the monotony we might feel from hearing the same music repeated several times without conspicuous changes.

ADDITIVE FORMS

The direct opposite of strophic form is just what its name suggests: different patterns following, one after another. In an additive form nothing is repeated; no early part of the composition returns later. This is not a plentiful form in our musical world. Without repetitions or returns, music would risk sounding like the babbling of an idiot, whose words don't add up to make sentences.

---

*Timbre (pronounced *tam'ber* or even *tim'ber*) is the word we shall use to denote the quality or "color" of any sound.

Illustration 2.1 Compared with the building shown in Illustration 2.2, this apartment's face is a study in extreme unity. Its four dominant parts are the repetition of a single shape creating an architectural *strophic form*.

And yet some music unravels as a chain of ever-different links, with sound providing its only source of unity. The influence of the music of other cultures during the past decade has caused some composers of the West to take notice of the artistic possibilities of additive forms. Even some ancient dance music is of this type, and it is usually called "through-composed."

Illustration 2.2 This urban apartment row shows the essential ingredient of additive form: its face is divided by four parts, each slightly different from the others.

RETURN FORMS

Most of the music we hear is of this third type. In it a later section of a composition returns to a musical pattern heard earlier, after intervening patterns have supplied contrast. There might be one return or several returns; there are many variants of the return form. Because of the abundance of music that is shaped in this way, we shall discuss particular examples of it presently. Its counterpart in architecture is readily demonstrated in Illustration 2.3.

Illustration 2.3
If we call the left spire of this 19th century building *A* and the lower middle portion *B*, then the right spire is the "return of *A*." You can see the same kinds of symmetry in the lower structure (*B*) by itself. *Return form* dominates the entire building.

PROCESSIVE FORMS

Suppose we sound a musical pattern, then repeat it many times but alter it slightly with each repetition. If we do this effectively we can achieve the delightful goal of having something different and yet always the same. A paradox! But it is possible in music. Let us explain through a simple parallel.

Joe was our childhood friend. We are therefore very familiar with both his appearance and his personality. We run into him one day on the college campus, three years after high school. He is older, he is dressed differently, and now he wears glasses. But without a doubt, it's still "the same old Joe." Five years pass. Joe brushes past us in a hotel. He is heavier, he has exchanged his campus jeans for a business suit, and his once abundant hair is considerably thinner. But enough remains to clinch the recognition. The aging process, the changed surroundings, and the camouflage of clothing are never enough to hide the *basic Joe*.

And so it is with processive forms, whose overall course is steered by some kind of musical process. If you have already heard Samuel Barber's Adagio for Strings, recall how it unfolded as a succession of four musical conditions: *Calm. . Growth. . Climax. . Resolution*. Each of these conditions was different from every other, and yet all bore an indelible kinship. A *process* is the work's main feature. A theme is established; it begins a process of growth; it reaches a point of climax; it resolves to a quiet ending.

We shall discuss other, sometimes quite different, examples of processive form in later pages. Most are not as easy to hear as a succession of partitioned sections like the strophic, additive, or return types. Yet some combine one of these other types with processive features. And this alone suggests that our four basic form-types are not enough: we need a fifth possibility to explain the forms of all music.

HYBRID FORMS

The overall forms of many compositions are not so simple that they fit neatly into the strophic, additive, return, or processive molds. Some works—and this is particularly true of art music—combine at least two of these principles in the way their sound patterns are shaped in time.

This is especially true of the return and processive types. These two frequently are blended together in a single composition. It also is true of some music in which the strophic principle seems to play a guiding role, yet the main pattern is so overlaid with additive features that its repetitions go almost unnoticed.

SUMMARY OF THE BASIC FORM-TYPES

You may find it easier to remember these four form principles as sets of alphabetic symbols. For instance, if we let each letter represent the full duration of each large musical pattern, then the strophic form can be represented as a design of $A\ A\ A\ A$.

Using this generalized kind of representation, additive forms can be thought of as a scheme of $A\ B\ C\ D\ E$. Return forms assume a succession like $A\ B\ A$ or $A\ B\ A\ C\ A$, and processive is best symbolized by $A^1\ A^2\ A^3\ A^4$. Each successive section in this last one is marked by some manner of alteration or development applied to the recurring pattern that forms the nucleus of the piece.

Now that we have general guides for understanding form, we can continue our discussion by examining a few compositions that illustrate some of the more common schemes we have talked about. In doing this we shall attend constantly to the musical properties like melody and harmony that play leading roles in shaping sounds into a particular form.

TERNARY FORM: A RETURN TYPE

Listen to the second movement* (*Giuoco delle coppie*) of the Concerto for Orchestra by Béla Bartók. As you listen, keep one main goal in mind: try to recognize the largest sections that shape the whole movement. Don't read the comments that follow before listening, unless you are willing to deprive yourself of the joy of discovering this movement's form on your own.

Heard only once, the movement may seem so loaded with interesting patterns of sound that it is difficult to distinguish an overall shape. A second hearing should make clear that a decisive contrast occurs around the midpoint. Following this second large section there is a return to the same kinds of patterns heard in the beginning. Let us see what is the nature of these patterns and how the composer has created a form of *ternary* (three-part) outline. We might speak of this as an $A\ B\ A$ form, or as *Exposition–Contrast–Return*.

As a total movement, the most definite difference comes when several musical properties change at the same time. This event is symbolized by the B in our mapping in Example 2.1. Perhaps the tally-sheet

---

*When a large composition consists of several separate and distinct parts, these parts usually are called "movements." Performers usually pause briefly between the movements of a composition.

synopsis can best reveal the most obvious large-scale features of the movement.

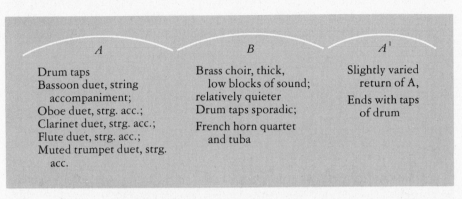

A	B	A¹
Drum taps	Brass choir, thick,	Slightly varied
Bassoon duet, string	low blocks of sound;	return of A,
accompaniment;	relatively quieter	Ends with taps
Oboe duet, strg. acc.;	Drum taps sporadic;	of drum
Clarinet duet, strg. acc.;	French horn quartet	
Flute duet, strg. acc.;	and tuba	
Muted trumpet duet, strg.		
acc.		

Example 2.1 Mapping of Concerto for Orchestra, Second Movement, Bartók

One curious thing about this movement is the brevity of its middle section (*B*) in comparison with the two *A* sections that frame it. This middle section also is a more unified series of events than its companions.

The title of the movement is *Giuoco delle coppie,* which in Italian means "playing of couples." And this is one of the main points of the two outer *A* sections: the playing of five different couples of instruments in succession, led off by a couple of bassoons. Variety is provided by these changes of timbres, and by the changing melodies and harmonies. The sense of variety that prevails in these outer sections ceases at midpoint when the brass instruments take over. The relative sameness of this middle section—its slower pace, quieter sounds, and singularity of rhythm—helps this shorter passage to balance, in effect, the longer companion passages. In a way, it is a "breathing spot" between the more active beginning and ending sections. Its difference helps to dramatize further the return effect of *A* when it follows.

You will find similar conditions in other ternary forms, whether they occur in a popular song, a classical minuet and trio, or in a military march.

THE RONDO: A HYBRID RETURN FORM

Since music stretches out in time, it is only natural that composers have developed forms that provide an effect of unity in the midst of variety.

If the principle of return is extended so that two or more returns occur, the result is called a *rondo*.

The origins of the rondo lie within social dances. In a round dance there is usually an exchange between the whole group and a soloist. If the group in such a dance repeats the same pattern several times around a soloist's pattern, the total form might be represented as the following:

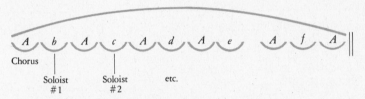

Example 2.2   Form-plan for a Round Dance

As a musical outline we can show these events as $A B A C A D A$. In other words, a recurring musical pattern provides a successional unity that is divided by several contrasts. A hybrid return form is produced. It combines the *additive* principle (the $B C D$) with the *return* principle (in the $A A A A$ recurrences).

The modern rondo is not associated with a chorus and soloist. It usually is a buoyant work played by instruments. In the absence of a group-soloist division of forces, other properties must provide the elements of contrast and return. Although some rondos do make use of a large body contrasted with a soloist (or a small soloistic group), many must depend upon melodies, rhythms, textures, harmonies, and timbres to project the contrast and return conditions we have discussed.

One composition you can hear that retains a group-solo contrast is the third movement of Beethoven's Concerto for Violin and Orchestra in D Major. It is far more sophisticated than a round dance; it reinforces its sectional differences with different melodies, rhythms, textures, harmonies, and loudnesses.

Listen to Beethoven's third movement several times. Make your own mapping of it as soon as you have grasped its sectional plan; then consider the following questions:

1   How many large sections form the work?
2   How are sections contrasted? What is different about each?
3   When patterns return, do they return in exactly the same way? For instance, does the beginning section always return in the same fashion or is it changed in character or length?
4   Near the end of this movement the violinist plays a *cadenza*, which is an extended virtuosic passage played solo. In view of the musical passages

that have gone before, does the cadenza lead us to anticipate the end of the movement?

5   How is the cadenza related to patterns heard in earlier sections?

Other rondos you hear might differ in many ways from Beethoven's, and yet all will in some way contain the same kind of multiple contrasts and returns. Try at least one of the following, making your own mapping to provide a reference for thinking back through the music.

J. S. Bach: "Gavotte en rondeau" from Sonata No. 3 for Unaccompanied Violin

S. Barber: Mvt. II, Sonata for Piano, Op. 26

B. Bartok: Mvt. IV, Concerto for Orchestra
              Mvt. IV, Music for Strings, Percussion and Celesta

L. v. Beethoven: Mvt. IV, Sonata for Piano, Op. 2, No. 2
                   Mvt. III, Symphony No. 7, Op. 92

F. Chopin: Mazurka in B♭ Major, Op. 7, No. 1

D. Milhaud: Mvt. V, Suite Francaise

W. Piston: Mvt. III, Sonata for Violin and Piano
              Mvt. III, String Quartet No. 1

THEME AND VARIATIONS: A STROPHIC-PROCESSIVE FORM

Many works from the history of Western art music conform to our definition of the processive type. Some are wholly processive, while others only partially manifest the conditions that are typical of the type. In later chapters we shall discuss a number of works that contain different kinds of processes.* For the present we shall investigate two particular examples of the processive type. As you will see, both bear elements of the strophic type as well.

The basis of a theme and variations piece is simple. An initial musical passage of unique properties—the *theme*—is exposed. This is followed by a succession of separate units (often separated with short pauses) of the same or nearly the same length as the theme. These successive units, or *variations*, retain some similarities with the theme, yet they are distinctly different in one or several ways. Like our hypothetical friend "Joe," they change without losing their fundamental ties with their prototype, which is the theme.

In some theme-and-variation pieces each variation bears obvious links with its theme. Others may be composed in a way that makes their kinship next to impossible to detect. This confusion usually can be cleared

---

*The Bach G minor Fugue discussed in Chapter 29, for example, and the several sonata-forms in the symphonies and chamber music of Haydn, Mozart, and Beethoven.

by listening several more times. There are composers, however, who seem to go out of their way to make relationships puzzling. This is not the case with our first example.

The blues of Negro origin is a kind of lamentation about life (usually about lost love). It also is a very simple variation form, a set plan known to all jazz musicians. Listen to Lightnin' Hopkins or Billie Holliday sing the blues (or Louis Armstrong or Miles Davis *play* the blues) and you will hear an age-old musical process: variations on a theme.

When it is sung, the text verses of the conventional blues follow a three-part form of *A A B* (or sometimes *A A' B*). Note how a single verse of one such blues piece, the *Rainy Day Blues* of Lightnin' Hopkins, unfolds this three-part scheme.

A   Lawd I'm jes sittin' down here thinkin',
       What am I gonna do on this rainy day.

A   Yes, I'm jes sittin' down here thinkin',
       What am I gonna do on this rainy day.

B   Well it don't look like the clouds ever
       Were gonna let the sun shine another day.

In almost all blues songs, this kind of *A A B* verse is set to a series of chords. This series—the twelve-bar blues progression—is diagrammed in Example 2.3 as a succession of measures. It consists of two basic kinds of chords: one kind projects an effect of repose while all others project non-repose. We shall use the symbol ○ to represent repose and ✕ to represent non-repose in our diagram.* The repose chord is also called *tonic* or *key center*.

In listening to any genuine blues, you will find it easy to keep up with the chord changes by noting that the first of the three phrases begins and ends with the repose chord (○). Both the middle and the final phrases begin with non-repose chords (✕).

There are many variants of this chord series that accompanies the "basic blues." In fact, there are about as many variants as there are different performers of the blues. And yet its essential scheme of three phrases provides the formal base for any performer's rendition. Like the English sonnet or the Japanese *haiku*, the blues is a set scheme within which artists can realize their poetic-musical statement. In this respect, every blues performance is an additional variation on the prototype theme.

---

*A more precise version of the blues progression appears on page 61. For the present we should point out that the symbol ✕ does not always represent the same chord; it represents *any chord other than the tonic chord*.

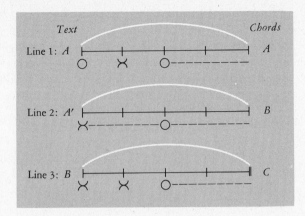

Text   Chords

Line 1: *A*   *A*

Line 2: *A'*   *B*

Line 3: *B*   *C*

Example 2.3
Correspondence of chords and text in the blues

Air with Variations for harpsichord by G. F. Handel

The blues' harmonic plan *as theme* functions much as the theme in compositions called "Theme and Variations." This latter form has been popular with composers since the seventeenth century. We shall use an example from the early eighteenth century for an introductory look into this form.

Illustration 2.4
This beautiful two-manual harpsichord was built recently by Stephen Wessel, yet it is an exacting copy of an original instrument constructed in 1623. Its two keyboards are controlled by small hand levers (called *stops*) rather than by foot pedals.

The Air with Variations by George Frederic Handel has a brief theme—or *air*—that sets the scene for its ensuing five variations. Each of these five variations bears a close relationship with the air, although each is different in a number of ways. We shall discuss only the air and the first two variations; our remarks about the first two will hold true for all five.

Example 2.4   Air with Variations: Air and Variations 1 and 2 only

The series of chords Handel uses is in some ways simpler than the blues progression. Although it contains more actual chord changes, its fundamental shape is a two-part (or *binary*) pattern. The first part beings and dwells on the tonic chord (the repose chord, ◯). Then it closes with a non-repose chord. Its second half beings with the non-repose chord (◯) and moves back to close on tonic. (The air is repeated, as are the two parts of each variation.)

In this scheme harmony provides a sense of openness, or motion, in the middle (between the two parts). Closure comes at the end of the

Example 2.5 Chordal basis of the Air, phrases 1 and 2

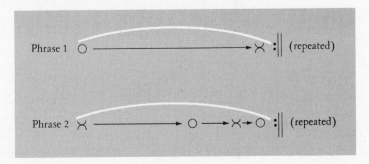

second part. The same scheme is repeated in each variation, so it forms a main thread of similarity between the air and each of its five variations.

Melody provides still another thread of continuity; usually the same basic up-and-down paths can be heard running through most of the variations, in spite of the other ways they are different from the air. We shall discuss this property of melodic contour in Chapter 4, but a brief look at it here is worth our time.

Similarity of Melodic Motion in the Air and Variations

Although Variation 1 consists of faster motion than the air, the rapid articulations of its highest part nonetheless outline the same path: it rises gently, then falls rapidly at the end. If we compare the detailed outlines of the air with its first two variations, we can see even more clearly a remarkable duplication of underlying motion, in spite of distinct surface differences.

In their details, these three contours are quite different. Yet they each harbor a fundamental outline of gentle arching from pitch to pitch, up to a high point that is the same (the note *G*) in all three patterns. They then fall to a point at the end of the arch that is lower than the beginning. So in spite of their apparent differences, each variation shares with the air a common chord series and conforming melodic shape. In a set of variations composed fifty years after this—say by Mozart or Haydn—there would be even more obvious melodic similarities.

Example 2.6 Comparisons of melodic contours, first phrases only

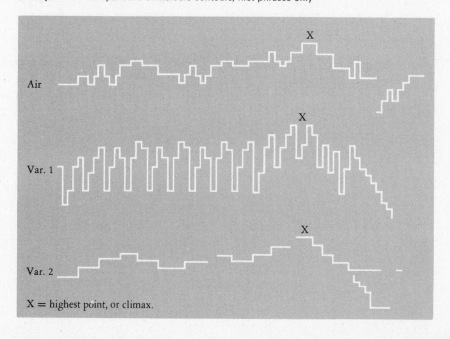

Air

Var. 1

Var. 2

X = highest point, or climax.

We shall attend to other examples of large-scale forms in subsequent chapters. A chief point of understanding for any musical composition is how its large sections relate one to another to satisfy a listener's sense of order.

MUSIC MAPPING

We have called our diagrams of the compositions we have discussed *maps*. Although you probably think of maps as representations of geographical areas, they often are used to serve other functions. We could make mappings of the human circulatory system, areas of the brain, the stars in the sky, or the chain of command in the U.S. Army just as well as we could map urban Chicago. Each map would be a "picture" of the way various elements are related.

Maps are incomplete pictures. In fact, their value lies in their ability to display only the most important elements of whatever they represent: they are simplified pictures of reality. Old maps of buried treasures—the kind that ignite our adventurous spirits—are good examples of how crude a map can be and still provide an adequate picture. Modern cartographers might find them wholly inadequate for their purposes, but for pirates they functioned admirably.

Conductors need a precise and elaborate mapping—the musical score—to conduct their orchestras through a symphony. On the other hand, the ordinary listener can profit from a mapping that rises only to the level of the pirate's map. These are the kinds of pictorial diagrams you can rely on in thinking through and discussing the compositions you study. Mappings need display only the most basic features of a musical landscape; it can be your pleasure when listening to observe the rich details that flesh out the broad outlines and make the music come alive.

Practice making your own maps for compositions you want to know. Since you will be more responsive to some musical elements than to others, you should expect your maps to differ in some respects from another person's. They should be personal chartings of the "terrain" observed, so they can be different and still be accurate guides. The main judgment of any map is how meaningful it is for *you,* how effectively it can help you to "think through" the composition it represents without actually listening to it again. (At the same time, don't expect any mapping to make much sense to you if you have not heard the work at least once!)

There are some fundamental rules of map-making. These rules must be kept simple or you will find that you won't be able to hear what you map or map what you hear.

1   Do as little note-taking as possible while actually listening. Develop the habit of recall; think back through a composition just as it ends, notating the basic features from memory.

2   Space the elements in your map to correspond with the time relationships in the music. For example, if you are mapping a piece that consists of three large sections whose relative durations are *long, short,* and *long,* your map should reflect this. The way you do it might follow one of the modes shown in our next example.

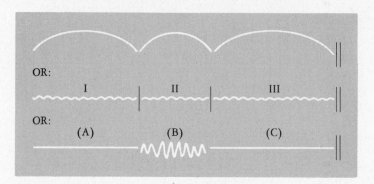

Example 2.7   Three ways of mapping relative section lengths

3   Use words, special signs, or spacings to represent the high-low (pitch) aspects of a piece when these seem important. For instance, if the composition represented in our previous examples consisted of mainly high sounds in the short section and mainly low sounds in the longer sections, your map might take on the shape of one of the following (or perhaps something of all three).

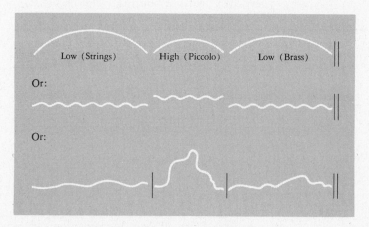

Example 2.8   Representation of pitch-space in maps

4   Add details to your map each time you hear the composition, but don't overload the picture. Add them only to the degree that they are needed to guide you through the music.

5 Improve your map each time you listen to the composition. Make realignments and additions or deletions that help it to correspond more faithfully with what you hear. In this way your map is a developing chart; it should grow more accurate with each observation.

A hypothetical mapping might go through the following stages before it becomes a useful guide.

Stage 1: Listening carefully

Stage 2: Listing of main parts

Quiet/jumpy melody—clarinet and trumpet/Soft violins . . . drums toward end/

Stage 3: Addition of some details, sectioning

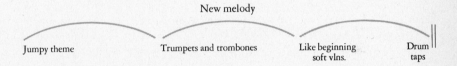

New melody

| Jumpy theme | Trumpets and trombones | Like beginning soft vlns. | Drum taps |

Stage 4: Realignments of sections as necessary, more precision

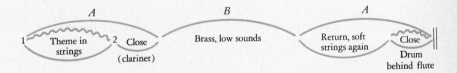

| | *A* | *B* | *A* | |
| 1 | Theme in strings | 2 Close (clarinet) | Brass, low sounds | Return, soft strings again | Close Drum behind flute |

By the end of stage 4 you should have a fairly reliable guide for the composition. You may have to hear the piece several times just to complete stage 2, but each new stage will find you with a better sense of what the work is all about, its particular beauty, and its special emotional message. These are the most important goals of your listening. The map is only your guide.

Before moving on to subsequent chapters, listen to at least two compositions—of any style—that you have heard before. Make your own map of each to help you think back through the form of the work. Once you have a good "picture" of the composition, decide what form type (*return, additive, strophic, processive,* or *hybrid*) it seems to fit best. This exercise with familiar music will make your subsequent encounters with unfamiliar music more rewarding.

3

RHYTHM:
THE ARTICULATION OF TIME

The punch line of the old Gershwin song "I Got Rhythm" suggests the elemental importance of rhythm in music. If you can respond to sounds as they articulate time—if you can *feel* musical motion—then "Who could ask for anything more?"

Maybe Gershwin's lyric overstates the case a bit, but there can be no question that rhythm is music's basic force. Our muscles yield readily to its sounds. We tap our feet, nod our heads, wave our arms, and sway our torsos. We can imagine even more athletic movements when the music is appropriately active.

The power of musical rhythm has been recognized from ancient times, and it casts its spell on the more sophisticated listener of today as readily as it did upon our remote ancestors. We don't always display our responses with the fervor of more primitive people, but this only proves our ability to repress these urges in favor of more socially acceptable behavior.

LEVELS OF RHYTHM

If *rhythm* refers to the way sounds articulate time, then we must recognize that this property occurs at more than one level of musical structure. Just as one man can be uncle, father, husband, and child, the *rhythm* of a musical passage refers to more than one kind of relationship. We can use a sample melody everybody knows to illustrate what is meant by these several "levels of rhythm."

Example 3.1 "Happy Birthday"

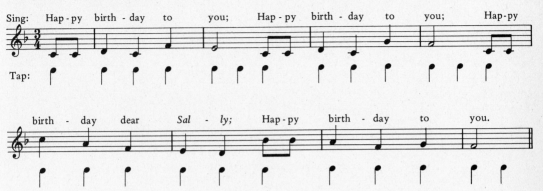

Sing through this song several times as you follow the notes, even if you can't actually *read* music. Once you can scan the notation as you sing, tap the notes shown below the melody. These coincide with the *pulse* of the song's rhythm. Now let us examine four kinds of rhythm that occur together in this melody.

Pulse

The simplest level is the pulse you tapped. It moves steadily as a kind of gauge for the other levels, which contain longer patterns. It is a *rhythm*, for it is an articulation of time.

Phrase

The next level of rhythm contains longer patterns. It is the *phrase*, and its units divide this melody into four parts. Sing the song once again and notice that the arrangement of text lines in Example 3.2 reveals the structure of this longer rhythm.

Example 3.2 Phrase structure of "Happy Birthday"

Phrase 1: "Happy birthday to you;

Phrase 2: "Happy birthday to you;

Phrase 3: "Happy birthday dear Sally;

Phrase 4: "Happy birthday to you.

The melodic pattern groups its sounds in a way that marks off each phrase. In this melody a longer sound coincided with the word "you" in phrases 1, 2 and 4; these act as the arrival points for the pattern, the *cadences*. Even the space-motion of the melody reinforces this rhythmic grouping. As Example 3.3 shows, each phrase is distinguished by its high/low pattern.

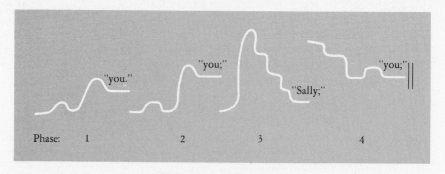

Example 3.3 Contours of the four phrases in "Happy Birthday"

Meter

Another kind of rhythm lies in between the pulse and phrase levels of this song. Called *meter*, it is a grouping of pulses into units of accented and unaccented parts. You can recognize it by exaggerating the accents of some words as you sing the song. In this respect it corresponds to the poetic meter of the words themselves. As you sing the song one final time, stress syllables as they are marked in the following:

Happy BÍRTH-day to YÓU;

Happy BÍRTH-day to YÓU;

Happy BÍRTH-day dear SÁL-ly;

Happy BÍRTH-day to YÓU.

Meter:

If you can tap the pulses while singing in this exaggerated way, you will find that the stresses you sing occur in patterns of three: *three ONE two three ONE two three ONE two three*, and so on. And this makes the meter of the song a *triple*, or three-pulse meter.

Melodic Rhythm

Pulse, phrase, and meter are periodic rhythms; they consist of the same unit lengths repeated over and over again (at least in most music). A fourth kind of rhythm—and this is the one we usually refer to as *the rhythm*—consists of a variety of unit lengths. It is formed by the separate tones in a melody. In "Happy Birthday" this melodic rhythm consists of the pattern:

It can be illustrated as longs and shorts of durations by dashes: _ _ _ _ _ _ _ _ _ _ _ _ ——. Together with pulse, meter, and phrase, the melodic rhythm completes the total rhythmic structure of a melody. It is these four rhythms in their totality that we respond to when we say we "hear the rhythm of the music."

KINDS OF METER

Triple Meter

Other melodies may have the same meter as "Happy Birthday" but consist of quite different melodic rhythms. The song illustrated in Example 3.4 has triple meter, but its melodic rhythm cuts a pattern all its own.

Example 3.4   "Lullaby," J. Brahms, Op. 39 No. 15

The next series of examples shows still other melodies (most of them well known) that are in triple meters. The numbers above their notation serve as a guide to your tapping while you sing.

Example 3.5   "Blow the Man Down," traditional folk song

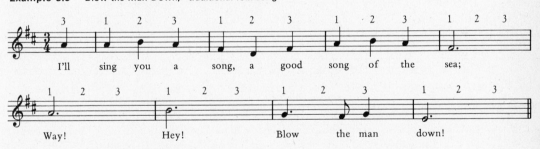

Example 3.6   "Star-Spangled Banner"

Duple Meters

All marches in some way project a meter that matches the left-right, left-right movement of marching feet. The result is a pattern of *ONE-two*,

ONE-*two*—a *duple meter*. Any music that projects its rhythms in groupings of twos is said to be in a duple meter.

Example 3.7 shows three melodies that look quite different, yet all are alike in that they are in duple meters. Note that each bears a different set of numbers as a *meter signature*, yet the numbers that appear above the notation reveal the two-by-two pattern that forms each measure. If you know these melodies, sing them while tapping the two-pulses for each measure.

Example 3.7   Melodies in duple meters

a.   "Skip to My Lou," folk song

b.   "America the Beautiful"

c.   "Farmer in the Dell"

Composite Meters

Music composed primarily for listening does not have to conform to the restrictions imposed on marches and dances. It is free to move within whatever rhythms the composer's imagination might produce. While most music does move in meters of twos or threes, some does not. If we call "two meters" *duple* and "three meters" *triple*, we might call these other meters *composite*, for they consist of mixtures of twos and threes (or threes and twos). Perhaps an example will make this seem less strange.

The "Mexican Hat Dance" from Aaron Copland's *Billy the Kid* ballet moves within this kind of composite pattern. Its measures can be broken down into patterns of 2 + 3. The principal melody of the piece is illustrated in the dash-graph of Example 3.8. Note that it establishes a grouping of unequal lengths, a *short-long* pattern that imparts a refreshing lilt to this music.

Example 3.8 "Mexican Hat Dance" and its rhythms

As in most music, there are pulses you might feel in addition to this *short-long* pattern. You might, for example, tap rapid strokes that correspond to the five separate pulses of the whole measure. Or you might even adopt a much slower tap that is equal to the duration of five pulses joined together. This would correspond to a pulse-per-measure.

Experiment with each of these possibilities while listening to "Mexican Hat Dance" to decide which best expresses the flow of this melody to you. Whatever your decision, it will in some way conform to the groupings of five we have shown, except for those occasional spots (where our graph shows a *short-short* pattern) where there is a deviation from fives.

Other composite meters are produced from similar groupings of unequal units. A seven meter, for instance, would result from the following kinds of flow:

short—short—long:

short—long—short:

long—short—short:

Lots of music from South America, or music inspired by South American dances like the rhumba, consists of a meter of *long-long-short* units as expressed in the following:

ABSENCE OF PULSE, METER, OR PHRASE

Most music we hear contains the three rhythmic levels of pulse, meter, and phrase. It is rare to find music that is not organized with at least one of these time-tracks as its main rhythmic ingredient. The chants of early Christian music we discuss in Chapter 16 project strong phrases, a relatively steady pulse, but no sense of meter.

Rhythmic Density

A lot of recent music, particularly music created by electronic synthesizers, lacks pulse and meter both. Rhythmic shape comes instead from changes of *rhythmic density*. That is, a passage of relatively sparse articulations might be followed by a passage of more abundant articulations.

This is really a more primitive way of organizing musical time. It occurs in older music too, music that contains pulse and meter as its principal organizing means. But this factor of rhythmic density is usually hidden when pulse and meter are present. Perhaps you can recall a composition you know that at some point rises to a high level of excitement, a climax. In doing this, several musical properties of the piece undergo changes: loudness increases, the pitch level rises, and the texture of sound thickens.

At this point we might retrace some earlier steps. We might call attention to the interaction of sound events of large and small dimension that create the sense of motion we feel upon hearing music. In some music we can be aware of only relatively slow or fast articulations. These articulations resist our attempts to hear them as a pattern of weak and strong pulses—as meter. But in most music the very basis of onward flow is rooted in the way pulses join together into *strong-weak* or *long-short* patterns, creating the kind of duple, triple, or composite meters we discussed.

TEMPO

The rate at which a musical passage unfolds is called its *tempo*. Tempo is not the same as rhythmic density; a musical passage can contain a high rhythmic density yet move at a slow tempo. It also can consist of relatively sparse articulations and yet move at a rapid tempo.

The two rhythms shown next illustrate the difference between tempo and rhythmic density. Both are to be performed at the same pulse rate

Example 3.9   Difference between tempo and rhythmic density

(or *tempo*), yet example *b* has greater density (more articulations per pulse) than *a*.

We usually associate tempo with pulse rate. The faster we tap in response to music, the faster its tempo is said to be. It is this sense of forward motion, and its relative pace, that we first encounter as one of the emotion-provoking elements in any piece of music.

There is a fundamental association of rapid motion with gaiety and ease, slow motion with sadness and labored movement. Other musical properties like harmony and timbre can alter the strength of these associations, of course. But aside from conflicting feelings affected by any other musical property, tempo has this power to channel our emotional states in response to music.

FINDING THE PULSE

Although it usually is easy to identify the tempo of a piece—at least in terms of relative slowness or fastness—it sometimes is not easy to agree on exactly what is the fundamental pulse. When we hear some music for the first time, what we tap for a pulse is a bit open to choice. The apparent pulse may be so ploddingly slow that we find it more comfortable to think in terms of divided pulses. In this way we can imagine a four-part division (*One-and-two-and*) within a two-pulse pattern of ONE-two, ONE-two. Or the same condition might prevail within a meter of threes, in which a *ONE-two-three* is divided into *ONE-and-two-and-three-and*, which actually makes a six-pulse meter.

Furthermore, to the sound of most music we can clap or tap at more than one pulse rate and respond accurately to its rhythm. In one case we may be "keeping time" with the actual pulse; in another case we may be "keeping time" with the meter unit, or measure. We might generalize, then, by noting that in some music a *most plausible* pulse is accompanied by other *less plausible* pulses. This is true because, as we mentioned earlier, there are several levels of rhythm, each of which might catch our attention.

When we speak of pulse in music we usually refer to this most evident rate, that which best enables us to respond to music's rhythms. There seems to be an area of pulse rates which we find most comfortable or convenient for gauging the rate of musical motion. We usually choose one that falls within this range.

FINDING THE METER

It is usually possible to discover the meter of a work by listening carefully and tapping out possible measures. Because of the occasional uncertainty about pulse we have just mentioned, this process sometimes must be a "hit-or-miss" one. When attempting to decide whether a passage is in duple, triple, or some form of composite meter, follow the procedure outlined next.

1   Tap or clap any regular pulse that seems to fit the flow of the music.
2   Now tap only the pulse of the pattern tapped for step #1 that seems to represent the accent (or "grouping") pulse.
3   Tap the regular pulses again (those of #1), but this time count aloud, calling the accented pulse "one," and continuing with successive numbers until "one" returns.
4   If a "one-two" or a "one-two-three" pattern does not emerge after several tries, two alternatives may be attempted. Seek another rate of regular pulse, or try groupings consisting of composite patterns such as *long-short*, *short-long*, *long-long-short*, and so on.

Don't despair if you have difficulty in determing the meter of any work. Too much emphasis can be placed on this kind of recognition; you can respond with deep feeling and understanding to a composition without knowing what its actual meter might be called. Knowing such information can make communication with others more fluent and precise, however, and it is to satisfy this need that we attend to it here.

The list of compositions that closes this chapter contains music particularly suitable for hearing the various rhythmic components of pulse, meter, phrase, rhythmic density, and tempo. In listening to any or all of these, arrive at some conclusions about the following:

1   How would you describe the tempo? Fast? Slow? Moderate?
2   Demonstrate (by tapping) the most plausible pulse.
3   What is the meter? Is it duple, triple, or composite? Or does the music seem to be non-metric?
4   Does rhythm seem to play a big role in shaping the whole piece, in terms of contrasts in tempo, rhythmic density, or meter? Is the pulse always clear, or is it sometimes vague?

Pieces in Duple Meters
L. Bernstein: "Tonight" from *West Side Story*.
F. Chopin: Prelude No. 20 in C minor.
F. J. Haydn: Mvt. IV of Symphony No. 101 in D major ("Clock").
Mozart: "Theme" from Theme and Variations, Mvt. I, in Piano Sonata in D major, K. 284.
Wm. Schuman: Mvt. III ("Chorale") from Symphony No. 3.

Pieces in Triple Meters
J. S. Bach: "Invention in D minor" from Fifteen Two-part Inventions.

L. v. Beethoven: "Minuetto," Mvt. II, from Piano Sonata in F minor, Op. 2, No. 1.

L. Bernstein: "I Feel Pretty" and "One Hand, One Heart," from *West Side Story*.

R. R. Bennett: Dance No. IV from *Suite of Old American Dances*.

J. Brahms: Intermezzo in A major, Op. 118, No. 2.

Chopin: Mazurka No. 5 in B♭ major, Op. 7.

Vivaldi: Mvt. II from Concerto for Violin and Orchestra in E, Op. 8, No. 1.

Pieces in Composite Meters

B. Bartók: "Dance in Bulgarian Rhythm No. 150" from *Mikrokosmos*, Volume VI.

L. Bernstein: "Maria" from *West Side Story*. (Although notated as a duple meter, the song's *actual flow* is composite: *long-long-short*.)

D. Brubeck: "Blue Rondo a la Turk" from *Time Out* album. (Beginning and ending sections are in composite meter; middle is in duple.) The composite meter is $2 + 2 + 2 + 3$.

A. Copland: "Mexican Hat Dance" from *Billy the Kid*.

D. Ellis: "The Great Divide" from *Don Ellis at Fillmore* album.

Mussorgsky: "The Great Gate of Kiev" from *Pictures at an Exhibition*.

Meterless Music

O. Coleman: "Congeniality" from *The Shape of Jazz to Come*.

M. Davidovsky: *Electronic Study No. 2*.

C. Debussy: Opening of Prelude to *The Afternoon of a Faun*. (Although notated with a meter signature, this flow of sounds projects no overall sense of meter.)

Gregorian Chant: Any recording made by the Monks of Solesmes.

E. Rudnik: *Dixi* from *Electronic Music, Vol. IV*.

4

MELODY:
PITCH AND RHYTHM
COORDINATED

"It's a tune of some kind!" most people would reply when asked, "What is music?" And melody probably is the most memorable property of music. It can be hummed or whistled or its rhythm tapped out in the privacy of one's own recollections, long after the original sounds have died away.

Aside from this well-known hangover effect, melody is indeed a powerful part of music. It usually is the pattern we are most aware of hearing. It is what seems to express emotional content most directly. And its role in concert music is as central as it is in folk music, in jazz, or in the latest pop hit.

MELODIC PROPERTIES

If we wished to describe the face of one friend to another friend, we probably would rely on toting up separate features that make the face unique. We first would describe separate properties like nose, mouth, coloring, jaw, and eyes that shape the total face. If we transfer this approach to melody we can recognize four features as defining properties: *contour, rhythm, tonality,* and *form.*

We discussed the main aspects of rhythm in Chapter 3, and form in melody is not notably different from the four form-types we discussed in Chapter 2, except that the sections of a melody are shorter than those in the form of a whole work. So we can turn our full attention to contour and tonality as the main features of our present discussion of melody.

Melodic Contour   When a string of tones of different pitch is heard, a melodic contour is the result. In Chapter 3 we noted how contours and rhythms in "Happy Birthday" interact to project a four-phrase form. Our concern now is with the various qualities of contours we can find in melodies. The contour of our "Star-Spangled Banner," for instance, is rather jagged and spacious. It skips a lot and covers a wide pitch-space in a relatively brief time. Compared to the melody of "America," its shape is erratic and disjunct.

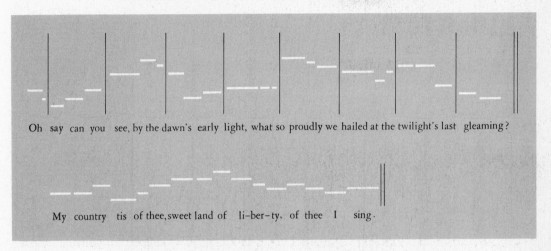

Example 4.1 Melodic contours of the "Star-Spangled Banner" and "America"

Contour offers us one way of defining a melody, then, both in terms of its tone-to-tone motion (whether *conjunct* or *disjunct, smooth* or *jagged*), and in terms of its overall shape in time. This latter facet can be seen more clearly in the melody of Example 4.2.

Example 4.2   Main theme of Mvt. IV, Oxford Symphony, Haydn

If we graph the pitch motion of this melody, its arch-like contour is even more obvious. Notice that our line-replica of this melody in Example 4.3 represents only the main up-down sweep rather than note-to-note details.

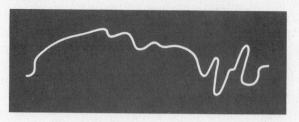

Example 4.3
Generalized contour of the Haydn melody

In contrast to the Haydn melody, the next forms a contour of rapid sweeps through a wide pitch-space. Even more than the *Star-Spangled Banner*, it covers its broad range by successive skips, which add up to a decidedly disjunct path.

Example 4.4a   Opening melody, Piano Sonata in F minor, Opus 2, No. 1, L. v. Beethoven

Example 4.4b   Generalized contour of the same melody.

Not all melodies have such pronounced up-or-down contours. Some even hover within a tight little orbit, lacking any strong direction up or down. These kinds of melodies consist of frequent returns to a single pitch that serves as a kind of rallying point for all other pitches. This is the case in both of the melodies illustrated next.

Example 4.5   Theme from Mvt. I, Symphony in D minor, C. Franck

1st mvt., 3rd Theme

Example 4.6 Theme from *Stabat Mater*, K. Penderecki

Still other melodies embody considerable up-and-down motion, yet they too lack the forward propulsion of downward or upward thrust. They consist of interior "mini" contours. They are not as a consequence "bad" or "ineffective" melodies. They merely lack strong overall contour. The Beethoven melody illustrated next is of this type. It is from the rondo we discussed in Chapter 2.

Example 4.7a Main theme, Mvt. III, Violin Concerto in D major

Example 4.7b
Generalized contour of the same melody

Tonality in Melody   Tonality resides not only in melody. It also is a product in most music of the whole musical substance. We already have hinted at its nature in our discussion of musical form. There we adopted two symbols to represent opposing conditions of harmony, those of repose (◯) and non-repose (⤬).

These two conditions are fundamental to almost all of the music we hear. Tonality is such a significant ingredient in this repose-non-repose condition that it was the chief issue of a musical revolution initiated during the early part of the twentieth century by the composer Arnold Schoenberg. This composer departed radically from tradition by doing away with tonality, or pitch focus, as a property in his compositions.

Unlike melodic contour, tonality cannot be shown as a graph; unlike form, it cannot be represented as an organization plan. It cannot be pointed to in a musical score as a "thing." As we suggested earlier, it is a result of the way pitches relate to one another. It is one of the ways the pitch-space of sound can be organized, just as meter is one way of organizing the time dimension.

In discussing the blues earlier we observed that a series of chords performs an important role in shaping the sections of a form. In the blues, for example, three different chords in a particular order provide a substructure over which melodies are woven. This series of chords channels the progression of sounds in time. Just as the progression of chords in blues begins and ends with a chord of repose, most melodies begin and end with a pitch that projects the same quality. This single pitch—the *focal pitch*—can produce for that melody an effect of resolution, of ending, that no other pitch can produce.

This is a curious phenomenon. It is not unlike the kind of focus we can see in most paintings or drawings. In this sense, tonality is the *perspective* of music. We must hasten to add that a lot of modern music does not incorporate tonality, just as a lot of modern painting does not incorporate linear perspective.

We can draw an analogy—strained yet revealing—between the *pitch focus* of the melody by Beethoven illustrated in Example 4.7 and the *spatial focus* we see in the print by Bernard Buffet reproduced in Example 4.8. In the melody it is pitches, related one to another in time, that bring about the centrality of the note *D* for the entire melody. In Buffet's print it is lines and their directional forces that bring about the focus on the tiny house. The abstraction in Example 4.9 is provided to dramatize this visual focus.

 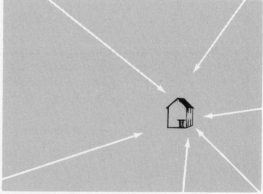

Example 4.8   (Left) *Rue de Banlieue*, Bernard Buffet
Example 4.9   (Right) Abstraction of *Rue de Banlieue*

If you don't completely grasp what is meant by tonality (or *pitch focus*), sing or play through one verse of the song "Joy to the World." As a reminder, the melody and words are reproduced in Example 4.10. The designated notes will be referred to in our ensuing discussion.

Example 4.10 "Joy to the World"

Isaac Watts (1674–1748)   George F. Handel (1685–1759)

This is a simple melody. One of the reasons for its simplicity is the direct way it establishes a pitch focus around the note *D*, its beginning and ending pitch. How does it do this? We might enumerate the causes, for they are true for many other melodies too.

1   The melody's contour is framed by its beginning pitch *D* and the pitch of the same name (a lower *D*) at the end. That is, the whole melody lies within the pitch-space, or interval, bounded by two pitches of the same name. (Such an interval is called an *octave*.*) They help to define their melody's tonality.

2   The last pitch is *D* and the first pitch is *D*. These time boundaries—first and last—of any melody impart an importance to the pitches that occupy those locations.

3   The pitch *D* also occurs frequently within the interior of this melody. Notice how it ends the downward motion of the first line on the word "Come." Also note how it ends the following upward motion on the word "king," and then how the same pitch occurs in two other locations in this area (these are marked D^4 and D^5).

4   And finally, the last melodic pattern repeats the *D–D* pitch frame established earlier by leaping upward (at D^6), just before the rise to the concluding *D*.

---

*The term *octave* refers to the eight lines and spaces of the musical staff which separate a pitch and its duplicate name at a higher or lower level.

All of these reinforcements of the pitch *D* in "Joy to the World" make it that melody's central tone. It is the melody's *tonic*, or *tonal center*. In this melody it represents what we mean by *pitch focus*.

Not all melodies circumscribe a pitch frame so tenaciously. And yet the melodies of pop songs, folk songs, songs of social and religious utility, and most of the melodies of Western concert music possess the pitch focus that we have observed in "Joy to the World."

Some melodies make their tonal orientation immediately and indelibly clear. The melody from Beethoven's Violin Concerto we discussed earlier is a good example of this kind of clarity. The symbols that appear below it in Example 4.11 show the same kind of repose and non-repose features we illustrated in our earlier discussion of the blues progression.

Example 4.11   Repose and non-repose background in Beethoven's melody.

And yet many melodies achieve a portion of their charm through a less obvious kind of pitch focus. Some produce a slightly equivocal condition, never making their tonic really clear. When this happens, accompanying harmonies (if there be any) sometimes provide the pitch focus lacking in the melody by itself. This is the case with the next melody of Example 4.12. Only its final pitch provides a conclusive clue as to its tonic.

Example 4.12a   Chanson "Allon, Gay, Gay" by G. Costeley

melody alone:

Example 4.12b   Same melody with chords

same melody with chords:

51 MELODY: PITCH AND RHYTHM COORDINATED

Modulation

Although most melodies begin and end with the same tonic pitch, some shift to another tonic within interior phrases. This process of shifting focus is called *modulation*. It occurs as a significant feature in whole compositions as well as just in melodies. One way a composer suggests tension and resolution through his music is to modulate from an initial key, then create a sense of resolution by returning to that initial key.

In melody a modulation usually occurs within an interior phrase; an ensuing phrase reestablishes the original tonic. Example 4.13 shows a melody that begins with the pitch *A* as tonic. In measure 9 the melody replaces *A* with *F♯* as tonic, with a return to tonic *A* in measure 14. Listen to the melody to see if you can hear the shift in tonal center that takes place in measure 9.

Example 4.13 A modulating melody, F. Chopin

A more startling kind of shift can be seen in the next melody. Here the initial tonic of *C* is replaced in measure 12 by *E*. Again, the first tonic returns for the last phrase of the melody.

Example 4.14 Another modulating melody, J. Strauss

change of tonic

(E = tonic)

Whatever the nature of a particular modulation, it provides tonal variety. In some melodies the change occurs abruptly when a previous phrase is shifted (transposed) up or down to another pitch level. This occurs in the melody of Example 4.15, where the first phrase has the tonic C. The second phrase is almost an exact duplication of the first, but it is transposed to a slightly lower pitch level so that G is now tonic.

Example 4.15 Modulation by transposition, Russian folk song

(tonic = C)   (tonic = G)

Just as we can describe a melody by its contour (or lack of contour), we also can characterize it by the quality of its tonality. Since this property depends to a great extent on the listener's ability to hear it—something that can improve with repeated hearings—we are not talking about a simple kind of "yes or no" experience. The truth of the statement "The pitch D is the tonic of the melody in Example 4.10" is not as easily verified as the truth of the statement "Austin is the capital of Texas."

In some melodies tonality is very clear. And then in other melodies tonality is ambiguous or not even present. The melodies in the next three examples correspond to each of these three conditions. Listen to each

Example 4.16 Main melody of Mvt. II, Surprise Symphony, F. J. Haydn
(clear tonality : tonic is C)

played by a piano (or any suitable musical instrument) to determine that the first is clearly tonal (with *C* as tonic), the second is ambiguous (maybe *C* is its tonic), and the third lacks a pitch focus.*

Example 4.17 "Theme" of Theme and Four Variations (*The Four Tempera-ments*), P. Hindemith (ambiguous tonality: is it *C*?)

Example 4.18 Opening of Mvt. II, Symphony, Op. 21, A. Webern (no tonality)

SUMMARY OF MELODY

With contour and tonality we have two important ways of describing any melody. They are only two of many. We also can note for any particular melody what timbres form it—the shrill high notes of a trumpet or the low resonance of a flute. Or we can describe a melody's relative loudness and the way its parts add up to a form. If these are not sufficient, we also can describe its rhythms, in terms of tempo, pulse, meter, and rhythmic density.

These are the main properties that describe the kinds of patterns we call *melodic*. The presence of all does not thereby ensure a beautiful, a striking, or a moving melody. The absence of any one (or even several) does not ensure a bad melody. But one or more of these must be present for a succession of sounds to create what we can call *melody* in the first place.

---

*Music that lacks pitch focus of the kind we have described is sometimes called *atonal* or *atonical*.

5

HARMONY:
MIXTURES OF SOUND IN TIME

For those who think melody is almost synonomous with music itself, harmony is only a kind of shadowy backdrop. This isn't a bad metaphor for a lot of music; many compositions are little more than melodies with inconsequential chords in support. Yet harmony can be a crucial shaping force and a rich source of emotional content, even when it enacts a supportive role. There is music in which it is the foreground element, melody playing the secondary role. There is even music in which there is no melody to speak of.

Our goal now is to gain some insight that will enable us to understand better how musical tones are mixed together to make chords, which themselves are the individual building blocks of harmony.

HARMONIC DENSITY

If we poise our forearm just above the keys of a piano and drop it firmly to strike the keys, we produce a *chord*. The result may not sound like Beethoven; by definition, however, tones sounding together make a chord. But how does this chord—our forearm "blob"—differ from the chords a blues singer strums on his guitar? In other words, what are the defining characteristics of one chord that enable us to compare it with a different chord?

First there is *harmonic density*. This aspect of a chord is determined by the number of different *pitch classes* it contains. All of the separate pitches we can hear from low to high belong to one of twelve "classes of pitch." These class names (or *note* names) are A, B, C, D, E, F, G, or the sharp or flat alteration of one of these (like $F\sharp$ or $B\flat$). Just as Albert Einstein was a member of the class of human males, the C in about the middle of the piano keyboard is a member of the pitch class of all C's. So while our dense forearm chord might contain as many as twenty-eight different *pitches*, it can contain no more than twelve *pitch classes*.*

Example 5.1 Forearm chord played at the piano

(all black and white keys)

Calling this thick mass of sound a "chord" may seem wholly capricious at first, and yet its sound might be exactly appropriate in a particular musical passage. Chords of this kind are called *tone clusters*. They occur frequently in the music of a number of recent composers. Observe the content of the chord sung on the word "Christe" in Example 5.2. It consists of every available pitch between the lowest bass voice and the highest soprano. Like our forearm chord, it contains all twelve pitch classes of the chromatic scale.

Such a dense harmonic block is a far cry from the kind of chord we might hear in the music of Bach or Louis Armstrong. Their music (and most of the music of our history) contains chords that, by and large, are made of no more than three or four different pitch classes.

And so these more familiar kinds of chords are distinguished from the tone clusters of Penderecki† and our forearm chord in being of considerably less density. Within music there is a continuum from chords of two pitch classes (called *diads*) to chords of the kind we have seen in Penderecki's *Stabat Mater*. The chords that form the familiar harmonies of pop music, classical music, and traditional jazz have, on the average, harmonic densities of from three to five.

---

*If you play from lower to higher (or vice versa) on each of twelve successive black and white keys of the piano, you will hear the *chromatic scale*. This is just one series of all twelve pitch classes.

†Pronounced *Pender et'-ski*

Example 5.2
Excerpt from "Complaceam Christe," *Stabat Mater*, K. Penderecki

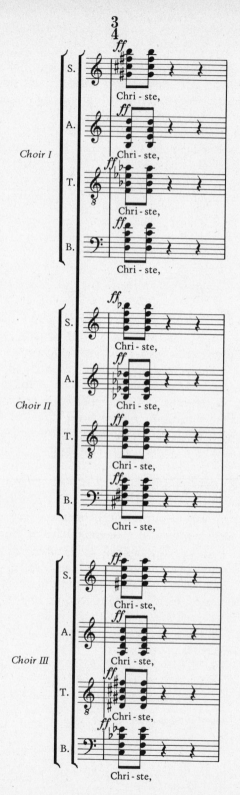

HARMONIC SONANCE

Another property we can mention in defining harmony is *sonance*. Like temperature, sonance is a neutral concept. The range of temperature runs from hot to cold; the sonance range extends from *con*-sonant to *dis*-sonant. Generally speaking, a more dense chord is also a more dissonant chord. That is, more pitch classes sounding together will produce a chord that is more complex, less stable, more dissonant. (And for some ears it will be less pleasant to hear as a sound by itself.)

And yet chords do not have to contain many different pitch classes to be relatively dissonant; harmonic sonance is not completely equatable with harmonic density. Sonance is the quality affected by what relationships, or *intervals*, are formed between the pitches that make a chord.

Some pitch intervals have a relatively intense sound (more dissonant), while others strike our ears as comparatively relaxed in effect (more consonant). You need not know all of the intervals that can be produced by the twelve pitch classes of music, but you can get a good idea of what we mean by interval quality if you listen to the three shown in our next example played on the piano.

Example 5.3 Pitch intervals of different sonance

Major 3rd   Perfect 5th   Major 7th

Next, study the series of chords shown in Example 5.4. These represent a range from more consonant to more dissonant. Listen to these chords played on a piano and you will understand better how different chords can be defined in terms of their sonance.

Example 5.4 A continuum of chords: more consonant to more dissonant

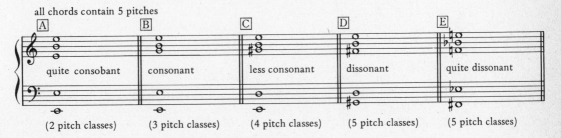

all chords contain 5 pitches

A	B	C	D	E
quite consobant	consonant	less consonant	dissonant	quite dissonant
(2 pitch classes)	(3 pitch classes)	(4 pitch classes)	(5 pitch classes)	(5 pitch classes)

A work called *The Unanswered Question*, by the late American composer Charles Ives, is unique in the way it mixes quite consonant chords with relatively dissonant ones. The more consonant chords of this work contain an average of only three pitch classes, and the more dissonant contain only four. But if you listen to Ives's piece you will detect a great gulf between the sonance values of the two kinds of chords.

In this composition a string choir (violins, violas, cellos, and basses) is pitted against the sounds of a solo trumpet and a flute quartet. These three forces—strings, trumpet, and flutes—portray a programmatic idea. The string chords represent the bleak quiet of the ages. The trumpet intones what Ives called "the perennial Question of Existence," and the flutes scurry around in search of an answer to this question.*

This music consists, then, of three distinct layers of sound. Two of them (trumpet and flute quartet) are carefully organized to clash with the string choir, which forms a ghostly background that prevails to the end. Flutes play dissonant chords; strings play consonant chords.

Most compositions do not combine separate strands of consonance and dissonance in quite this way. Usually the sum total of any texture will be either relatively consonant or relatively dissonant.

You can compare the chords played by the strings in *The Unanswered Question* with those played by the flutes by studying the notated chords in Example 5.5, playing them (or listening to another person play them) at a piano or organ. The more grating sound of the flute chords becomes apparent when they are played in the reduced versions, which reveal more clearly the relationships of their pitches.

---

*We shall discuss this composition more fully in Chapter 12.

Example 5.5 Chords of strings and flutes in *The Unanswered Question*

Typical chords played by strings:

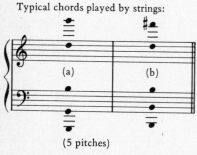

(5 pitches)

reduced to pitch classes:

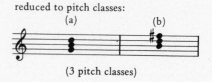

(3 pitch classes)

Typical chords played by flutes:

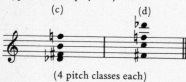

(4 pitch classes each)

Music in which consonances are the harmonic staple can be found in any hymn book or in the chords of rock music. These chords usually contain only three different pitch classes, so they are called *triads*. And most choral music of early history contains relatively consonant chords of the same kind. The next illustration shows only a brief segment of a composition of the Renaissance (1450–1600), with a commentary about the pitch content of each chord. This is music of low harmonic density and low sonance.

Example 5.6 Fantasia for Lute, L. de Milan (first 8 measures)

chords:

(all major and minor triads, except one dyad)

(dyad)

Example 5.7 "From the Diary of a Fly," first two measures

Allegro ♩ = 146

pp

reduction:

At the other end of the sonance spectrum, many recent compositions, like Penderecki's *Stabat Mater*, contain chords of consistently high dissonance. In such music every chord consists of either a great number of pitch classes or else a few pitch classes which form dissonant relationships.

An example that is quite different from the Penderecki and Ives compositions is the engaging piece by Béla Bartók called "From the Diary of a Fly."* In it you will find chords of very low density (only two pitch classes) but rather high dissonances. Since this beginning passage is easily

*From *Mikrokosmos*, Volume VI, page 9.

played at the piano, you might find the right keys and experiment with the sounds. Or ask a friend to play them for you.

Like Ives's *The Unanswered Question*, the title of this piece suggests something that is extra-musical, a "program" or "story." In making the composition live up to images of what we might expect from the diary of a pesky fly, the composer employs some rather obvious musical properties in special ways. Note particularly its light texture and its relatively high, thin sounds. And note also the sharp articulations—a kind of "pecking" effect—produced by the pianist's light jabs at the keys. (This is called *staccato*.) But of greatest interest to us for the moment is the prevailing dissonance produced by pitches that are quite close together. This is evident from the beginning, when the two strands of the texture lie only a half-step apart. This is the *harmonic* way Bartók's piece suggests the flitting memoirs of a bothersome fly.

HARMONIC PROGRESSION

Thus far we have discussed harmony only in terms of the single harmonic unit, the chord. A more complete picture of harmony demands some attention to the way chords occur in successions, the way one chord relates to another. Clearly, most music does not consist of just one chord repeated continuously. Usually, two or more chords are strung one after another to produce a sense of motion, the ebb and flow of repose and non-repose. We shall restrict our discussion here to the very simplest kinds of chords in the most rudimentary kinds of successions, the basis of what is usually called *tonal harmony*.

Harmonic
Progression in the
Twelve-bar Blues

We introduced the blues progression in Chapter 2 as a three-phrase series consisting of repose and non-repose chords. We can introduce the notion of harmonic progression by developing our discussion from that basic information.

Blues is tonal music. One cause of its tonality is its employment of a set of three basic chords, one of which functions as its tonic chord. (Recall the pitch focus we discussed in melody? Replace a single pitch class with a single chord as a focal point and the notion of a tonic *chord* will be clear.)

The tonic chord dominates the blues progression. It is the first heard, it is the terminating chord of each of the three phrases, and it usually is a more consonant chord than the two other chords. (This last characteristic depends, of course, on who is playing the blues!)

The notation in Example 5.8 shows reduced versions of these three chords that form the blues harmonic progression, as it might be played with an *F* chord as the tonic. The same set of chords could be transposed to other pitch levels to provide the same progression in a different key.

Example 5.8 The three chords of the basic blues progression

If we deploy these three chords in certain locations within the three-phrase scheme of the blues, we have the harmonic basis of that form.

Harmonic
Functions in
Tonal Music

The scheme in Example 5.9 is a simplified version of what musicians elaborate when they play the blues. Each artist adds his or her own favored decorations, and yet any true blues retains the polarity of these three chords: *tonic* (or the I chord), *subdominant* (or the IV chord), and *dominant* (or the V chord).* The same three chord functions serve as the harmonic underpinnings in much of the music composed since about 1450.

Example 5.9 Harmonic progression of the twelve-bar blues

Listen to the next two short pieces while following the notation in Examples 5.10 and 5.11. Although the second example contains only two pitches sounding at any one moment, the composer has created the parts in such a way that they project the chords designated. The main point of this listening exercise is to develop your ability to detect changes from one chord unit to another, noting how these coincide with the flow of the melody.

---

*The tonic chord is the ◯ chord of our earlier discussion. The subdominant and dominant chords were previously represented by the single non-repose sign, ⋈ .

Example 5.10 "Have You Ever Seen a Lassie?" (traditional song)

Chords: I   I   V   I   I   I   V   I
(key of F)

Example 5.11 "Dance," L. v. Beethoven

Chords: I (O)   I   V   V
(key of D)

I (O)   I   V (✗)   I (O)

In tonal music the tonic chord provides the effect of harmonic repose. For this reason it is usually the chord that ends a composition, just as the tonic pitch usually ends a melody. All other chords project varying degrees of non-repose.

The harmonies that fill in this scheme of repose and non-repose are usually of uniform density and sonance. Rarely does a composer shift back and forth between extremely dissonant and extremely consonant chords. (Ives is one notable exception!) But these norms of harmonic quality do change from century to century. In some cases they change from composer to composer.

EVOLUTION OF HARMONY FROM CONSONANT TO MORE DISSONANT

It is not a distortion to view the history of Western art music as a gradual evolution from more consonant to more dissonant harmonies. Listen to the five excerpts shown in Examples 5.12–16 as a kind of capsule review of this evolution. Our main point is to make a comparison of the sonance

Example 5.12 Organum in the style of Perotin (thirteenth century)

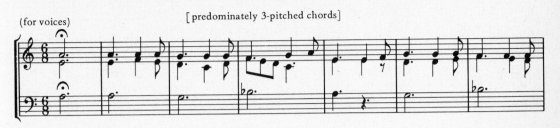

Example 5.13 Theme and Variations, A. de Cabezon (sixteenth century)

and density of chords that occur in these passages, which date from a scattering of times in history. In terms of harmonic density, this selection reveals a gradual increase from chords of two pitch classes to chords of from six to twelve pitch classes. And sonance increases from the very consonant sounds of the thirteenth century to the relatively dissonant sounds of the twentieth century.*

---

*Perform each excerpt on the piano in order to focus on harmonic content. Only the Hindemith and Rochberg works were meant for that instrument.

Example 5.14 "Prelude," *Tristan und Isolde*, R. Wagner (nineteenth century)

(predominantly 4-pitched chords)

Example 5.15 "Variation 1," Theme and Four Variations, P. Hindemith (twentieth century)

[predominantly 4- and 5-pitched chords]

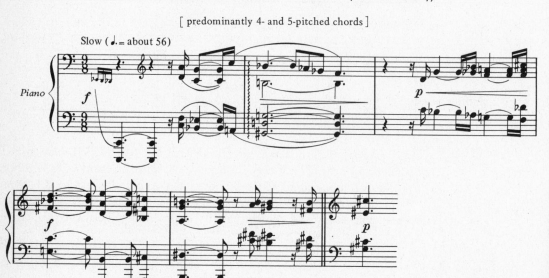

Example 5.16 "Bagatelle No. 1," Twelve Bagatelles for Piano, G. Rochberg
(twentieth century)

Don't conclude that all recent music makes use only of highly dissonant chords. In fact, some composers of contemporary music have retained in their harmonic palette the kinds of chords we can hear in Wagner's "Prelude" (Example 5.14). And much of the electronic music composed during the past fifteen years consists of even sparser harmonic combinations. As a generalization, however, we can let stand our remark that music has moved gradually toward the dissonant side of the sonance scale since early medieval times (around 800 A.D.).

SUMMARY OF HARMONY

In concluding this introductory discussion, let us recall the three main aspects of harmony that determine its character. First is the property of harmonic density, which refers to how many different pitch classes fill in the single chord. Related, yet clearly separable from density, is sonance. Any chord consists of two or more pitch classes, and the relationship borne by these pitch classes—their intervallic quality—determines the relative consonance and dissonance of the whole chord.

We have suggested that it is misleading to speak of dissonance and consonance as if they are absolute terms. Such judgments as "This is a dissonant chord" or "That is a consonant chord" must in the end be understood as purely relative expressions. More meaningful would be

"This is a more dissonant chord than that," or "The chords of 1925 jazz music are more consonant than the chords in Arnold Schoenberg's music."

And finally, the relationships formed by a series of chords, as they succeed one another in time, create an overall character that we usually have in mind when we speak of the "harmony of music." Most of the music we hear employs a limited harmonic vocabulary. It is a vocabulary consisting of only two or three different chords of relatively low sonance, and these are couched within relationships that project a clear sense of tonality. A lot of music departs from this narrow vocabulary. We shall discuss these instances as they arise in the later parts of our study.

6

TEXTURE:
THE BLEND OF RHYTHM,
HARMONY, AND MELODY

We already have used the word *texture* a number of times, assuming all the while that it would have adequate meaning where it appeared. It is a kind of catch-all word in musicians' vocabularies, but it usually has one of two tightly defined uses. These are our current concern, for they can shed light on the way sounds are mixed to make music.

TEXTURE AS SPATIAL DISTRIBUTION OF SOUND

Earlier we used the word *texture* to refer to one thing: how the highs and lows of sound can be put together to make thick or thin, dense or sparse combinations. The effect of a musical passage is considerably affected by whether its strands of sound are spread far apart in pitch or packed close together. (We heard the latter disposition in Bartók's "From the Diary of a Fly.") And furthermore, given three or more simultaneous melodic layers within a composition, it is important whether these layers are equidistant from one another.

To make this last point more concrete, imagine a composition composed for a chorus of voices. Let us note, then, some of the ways these voices might be deployed together in musical space. We shall refer to the separate parts as *soprano, alto, tenor,* and *bass.*

One kind of spacing our hypothetical voices might assume would be thin and uniform (i.e., about equally spaced). The parts would lie close together and at about the same distances from each other.

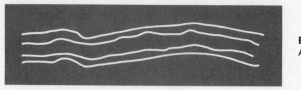

Example 6.1
A thin, uniform texture

In musical notation such a texture would look something like the following:

Example 6.2   An example of the texture represented in Ex. 6.1

Another possibility would be a relatively wide spacing, but one that still retains approximately equal interval distances between the adjacent strands.

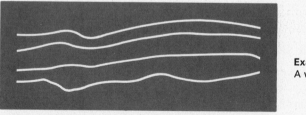

Example 6.3a
A wide, uniform texture

Example 6.3b   Musical example of the same texture

These two kinds of spacings are the norms of musical texture, but they by no means exhaust all possibilities. The following graphs and notated examples show some additional types that we frequently hear. The accompanying titles should suffice as descriptions of each.

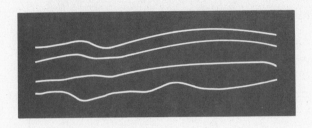

Example 6.4a
Wide, gapped texture; two middle parts coupled

Example 6.4b   Musical example of the same texture

Example 6.5a
Wide, gapped texture; two pairs of coupled voices

Example 6.5b   Musical example of the same texture

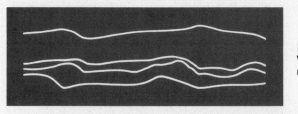

Example 6.6a
Wide, gapped texture; separated upper part

Example 6.6b   Musical example of the same texture

These five examples of texture should provide a helpful reference for the many ways the pitch space of music might be sliced by four participating parts, whether they be played by instruments or sung by voices. This is one meaning of *texture*. It is an important aspect any composer controls when he composes music.

TEXTURE AS INTERACTION OF PARTS

The way parts (or "voices") are combined from high to low is not difficult to understand. Another meaning of texture is a bit more complicated. It has to do with the relative prominence of the individual strands, as they operate together within the unfolding music.

Homophonic
Texture

We already have discussed a number of compositions that consist of a single prominent melody accompanied by one or more instruments. The kind of texture produced by this melody-accompaniment interaction is called *homophonic*. It consists of a single dominating pattern (a melody) that is thrust into relief over a less prominent background of sounds. If we represented this kind of texture graphically it would look somewhat like the following:

Melody:

Accompaniment:

Example 6.7b Musical example of the same texture

The several strands of such a texture might move together rhythmically, their spatial distributions looking like those illustrated in Examples 6.1 and 6.3a. In such cases, the prominence of any one strand—"the melody part"—might be determined by one or more factors: by that part's greater loudness, by its more interesting melodic contour, or by its position at the top of the sound combination. In distinguishing this type from the melody-accompaniment type, we sometimes use the word *melorhythmic*, sometimes *familiar style*.

The songs of the folk singer are clear examples of melody-accompaniment textures, but one can find the same types in concert music. It would seem that the notion of foreground-background, or melody-accompaniment, is basic to all music-making.

The next example shows a homophonic texture in which four voices move in relative uniformity, without projecting a sense of great separation between melody and accompaniment. It is a vocal work from the early eighteenth century, a setting of a Lutheran song, or *chorale*. In this texture the tune lies in the soprano part at the top. The remaining parts thicken musical space with their lines, enhancing but not competing with the primacy of the tune. The opening of this chorale is notated in Example 6.8 to show the distribution of parts as they appear in the chorus score. If possible, sing it with a group to become more familiar with its sound. If this is not possible, listen to a recorded version of the chorale.

Example 6.8 First phrase, Verse 7, *Christ lag in Todesbanden*, J. S. Bach

Verse VII. (Chorale)

Polyphonic Texture

When a texture contains more than one strand of melodic prominence it is called *polyphonic*. The term itself literally means "many sounds." For musicians it refers to a texture in which several melodic patterns may catch the listener's attention. In many polyphonic textures one part still dominates, and yet the remaining parts have contours and rhythms that are engaging in their own right.

Round songs like "Frère Jacques" and "Row, Row, Row Your Boat," are well-known examples of polyphony. In these songs the texture is produced by successive imitations of the same melody. The same procedure abounds in sophisticated concert pieces like fugues. In fact, the term *fugal* refers to a string of imitative responses to a single melodic pattern. A polyphonic texture is not necessarily made of imitations. Many passages that are polyphonic consist of quite independent lines, each unfolding its own unique contours and rhythms.

Example 6.9 shows a set of three textures, all of which contain the same top part and the same basic harmonic scheme. All three differ, however, in the way separate strands relate to each other. Excerpt *a* shows a homophonic setting; notice that sustained chords form its accompanying harmonies. Excerpt *b* also is homophonic, but here a single strand outlines the same chords heard in Excerpt *a*. Excerpt *c* is different in a basic way. It is polyphonic because its lower strand cuts a definite contour and rhythm of its own. This lower line even bursts forth at times to claim attention away from the top line.

Example 6.9a, b and c   Two homophonic textures and one polyphonic texture using the same melody and harmony

a. Homophonic setting of a J. S. Bach melody: sustained chords

b. Homophonic setting: broken chords

c. J. S. Bach, Polyphonic setting

Any number of separate parts might participate in a polyphonic texture. As you might expect, however, there is a saturation point. Beyond that point a composer risks confusing his listener. For this reason, most polyphonic textures consist of no more than two or three truly separate and individual parts. Even in those cases, as we said earlier, one part frequently enjoys a more prominent status than the others.

Like the terms consonance and dissonance, polyphony and homophony are not absolute terms. A precise definition of just *how* individualized the strands of a texture must be in order to qualify as polyphonic is beside the point. Bertrand Russell once posed the question "How many hairs can a man have on his head and still be called bald?" Our question, "Where lies the dividing line between polyphonic and homophonic textures?" is equally difficult to answer. Our only conclusion can be, of course, that such definitions defy precision. Some textures lie in between. Others will be definitely homophonic or polyphonic.

Heterophonic Texture

A third kind of musical texture is unique because it is an unusual crossing of mere melody (which would be a *monophonic* texture) and polyphony. Imagine two jazz performers playing the same tune simultaneously. If one or both embellish this tune with their own ornamentations, the result is *heterophonic texture*.

Heterophony is rare in the art music of the Western world. It flourishes in the native music of some Eastern cultures such as those of Indonesia and Japan, and it occurs on occasion in American jazz idioms like New Orleans style. The recent strong influence of the Orient on the West has led to its use in some of the works of art music composers. We shall discuss incidences of heterophony in a piece composed by the American

Illustration 6.1 Heterophonic texture is standard in the music of a traditional Japanese ensemble. This San-Kyoku (or trio) ensemble consists of shamisen, koto, and shakuhachi.

Illustration 6.2 A New Orleans jam session of today is not much different from its counterpart of the early 1900s. This seven-piece band contains the favored instruments of tradition—including even the female piano player.

composer George Crumb in Chapter 22, as well as in the music of Japanese gagaku in Chapter 39.

We mentioned earlier that heterophony is rarely found in music of the West. But the next illustration shows a relatively clear case of mutual dependence between the melodic parts, in spite of abundant independence at times. In this example (which you should try to hear performed at the piano or by a pair of intruments) the correspondence of the two lines is apparent on the first pulse of almost every measure. Asterisks (*) mark locations where note duplications occur (always an octave apart), and a set of dotted lines in measure eleven marks where both lines are more dependent than usual.

Example 6.10 English dance from the thirteenth century, "Stantipes"

TEXTURE AND MUSICAL STYLE

In the final pages of Chapter 1 we discussed how a composition's filling out of sound-space is one determinant of musical style. There we were most concerned with high-low distributions of sound, the way different composers might control the band of pitch provided by the instruments for which they were composing. Now we can speak in more specific terms about the way these bands of pitch might be organized within themselves. This also controls the musical message transmitted by the composer to his listener. We shall be brief in our comments, trusting that all of the compositions you hear later will provide a more enduring understanding of texture.

Most of the music we hear daily, the songs of love and pain and hope that dot the scene of any age, is homophonic. Art music also favors the homophonic texture. You will find it plentiful in the music of every composer from the ninth century to the present.

But composers of art music work from more than one bag of textural tricks. Their training and sharp insight enable them to create musical events of great variety; they utilize a wide range of textural types in their compositions. We can find in the music of J. S. Bach some of the most compelling musical experiences imaginable: some involve polyphony, others are as simply homophonic as the catchiest pop composition. And yet Bach's own time in history (early eighteenth century) is remembered as one of the great ages of polyphonic music. The music of Giovanni

Palestrina (sixteenth century) likewise contains simple homophony along with intricately woven polyphony. His age, like Bach's, is generally acknowledged as one of the golden ages of polyphony.

There have been composers since Bach and Palestrina who were skilled at making compelling musical statements from interweaving melodies. In fact all of the most effective composers of history have employed a polyphonic texture in their music when it best suited their expressive needs.

In addition to contrasting melodies, timbres, harmonies, and loudnesses, contrasting textures provide still another way for the composer to shape his music into sound images of expressive power for listeners. We'll encounter these successions of differing textures in most of the works we discuss in later chapters.

PART II

MUSIC FOR LARGE INSTRUMENTAL ENSEMBLES

INTRODUCTION

Now we change the thrust of our interest. The musical properties we talked about in the foregoing chapters—timbre, form, rhythm, melody, harmony, and texture—remain as basic guides for our discussions. But the focus of the next thirty-four chapters shifts to individual compositions and their composers. Each of these works can provide a wealth of musical satisfaction, as well as sound, space, and time characteristics you by now should find familiar.

This second part, Chapters 7 through 15, covers a variety of large instrumental works composed between 1792 and 1961. The selection favors orchestral music, although one work, by Vincent Persichetti, is performed by wind band. Our coverage of worthy composers is only barely representative. The particular works have been selected because they represent some of the best ensemble music of our heritage, and, as a group, they suggest a chain of musical development over a period of one hundred and seventy years.

Although these nine works in Part II are introduced in chronological order, this need not keep you from studying them in another sequence. Information exposed in an earlier chapter is helpful in some instances for understanding works discussed later, but those few cases should raise no insurmountable obstacles. The glossary at the end of this volume, or a suitable music dictionary, can provide minimal information as needed.

In your approach to each new composition, read the background material first. This should provide you with some perspective on the composer, the cultural influences of his life, and the broader forces at work in the composition itself. Then listen to the music once or twice for a grasp of its main features, its dominant sounds. Only then should you read the discussions that deal with its form and musical details. Use these discussions as guides for later hearings, moving back and forth between music and text until you feel that you know the work well. Most important, make your own mapping of each piece as you listen.

THE LARGE INSTRUMENTAL ENSEMBLE

The large ensembles of Western art music have evolved during the past three hundred years. Like the melodic, rhythmic, and harmonic characteristics of music, the sound-makers themselves change through the ages.

Cleveland Orchestra, Lorin Maazel conducting. Photo by Peter Hastings.

The orchestra a composer used in 1603 was radically different in size and constitution from the orchestra a composer utilizes in 1977. The evolution of the intervening years has led to an ever greater array of sound sources, their increasing power as a combined unit coupled with increasing variety of nuance.

In following our discussions you will find it helpful to remember the basic instrumental families and their individual members. Our listing includes instruments found in standard modern ensembles, with the important reminder that groups of earlier times normally consisted of reduced variety as well as numbers. We shall mention these differences as they arise in our discussions of particular compositions.

MODERN ORCHESTRA	MODERN WIND BAND
Woodwinds	*Woodwinds*
Piccolo (1)	Same complement as the orchestra but with addition of:
Flute (2)	
Oboe (2)	1. far more clarinets of assorted sizes
English horn (1)	2. Choir of saxophones: alto, tenor, baritone, and bass
Clarinet (2)	
Bass clarinet (1)	
Bassoon (2)	
Contrabassoon (1)	
Saxophones only for particular compositions	
Brass	*Brass*
Trumpet (3–4)	Same complement as the orchestra but with addition of:
Horn (also called French horn) (4)	
Trombone (3)	1. Cornets (at least 4)
Tuba (1)	2. Baritone Horn, or "euphonium" (2)
	3. Several tubas
Strings	*Strings*
Violins (20–30, divided as *1st and 2nd Violins*)	No strings except one or two double basses. Piano and harp are used rarely.
Violas (10)	
Cellos (10)	
Double Basses (8–10)	
Harp (1–2)	
Piano (as required)	
Percussion	*Percussion*
Timpani, or "kettledrums" (4, with one player)	Same complement as the orchestra.
Snare, tenor, and bass drums	
Any other conceivable instrument that is struck to make a sound	

The numbers of individual instruments in a wind band are less standardized than they are in the symphony orchestra. You might hear a college wind band, for example, that contains ten flutes or twenty trumpets and equally expanded numbers of other instruments.

(a)

(b)

(c)

(a) Violin (Patricio Cobos)
    Viola (Pamela Benjamin)
(b) Cello (Luca Dicecco)
(c) Bass (Paul Schmidt)

(d)

(e)

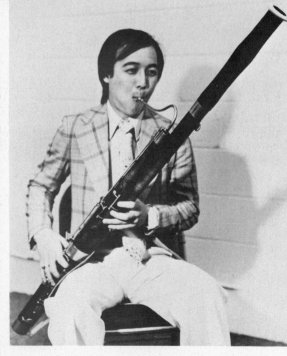

(f)

(g)

(d) Flute (James Pellerite)
(e) Oboe (Nora Post)
(f) Bassoon (Richard Hoteke)
(g) Trumpet
(h) Horn
(i) Timpani

(h)

(i)

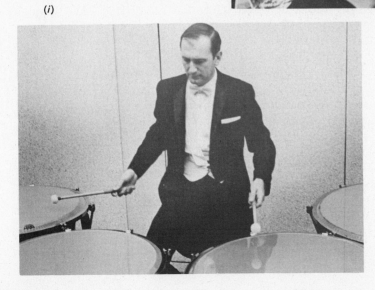

7

SYMPHONY NO. 94 IN G MAJOR ("Surprise Symphony")

Franz Josef Haydn (1732–1809)

BACKGROUND

Haydn* did not singlehandedly create the symphony. But the more than one hundred works he produced in that form went far in establishing symphonic dimensions, even up into the twentieth century. He worked for many years as court composer and musical director for the estate of Prince Nicholas Esterhazy. His everyday duty was to make music to accompany many forms of entertainment. As something of a musical celebrity late in life, he was able to command the patronage of one of the great impresarios of the day, J.P. Salomon. Within this professional whirlwind of playing, conducting, and composing, the symphony was Haydn's principal large-scale vehicle for musical expression.

Haydn's position in the Esterházy court placed him forty miles southeast of Vienna, which at that time was the musical center of Europe. He was in contact at various times with the younger Wolfgang Amadeus Mozart and Ludwig van Beethoven.† The three shared a healthy exchange of musical knowhow. (Haydn even taught Beethoven for a short time.) His music after 1785 reveals clearly some imprint of the genius of Mozart, who in that year was twenty-nine. But it was Haydn, more than any other composer, who contributed most of the characteristics of what we call today the "Viennese classical style."

---

*Pronounced as *High'dn*
†*Mote'zart* and *Bay'toh-ven*

In order to gain some perspective on the *Surprise* Symphony and other symphonies of the same period, it might be helpful to itemize, according to the properties we discussed in Chapters 2–6, the main characteristics. Many of these remarks pertain to chamber music of the classical period as well.

Map of Europe

CHARACTERISTICS OF THE SYMPHONY

Form

Most of the forms are of the return type, yielding a calculated balance and unity. Although there are a number of different overall designs incorporated in each of the four movements of symphonies, they almost all contain single or multiple returns. One exception is the theme and variations. But even in this processive form there usually is a return to the melodic, textural, and timbral features of the theme itself. This creates a sense of return for the whole movement. In general, forms are clear and easy to follow. Distinct contrasts separate large sections because of simultaneous changes of theme, texture, tonality, and timbre.

Most symphonies consist of four movements. Although a variety of instrumentation and form can be found in all of Haydn's symphonies (written over a thirty-eight-year period), they usually display the following characteristics:

FIRST MOVEMENT. Rapid tempo, sometimes with a slow introduction. The shape is usually that of an elaborate return plan that also has processive features in its middle section. This is called *sonata form*. The processive aspect occurs within the *Development* section, where melodies exposed earlier are "processed" in a dramatic way. The return aspect is provided by the *Recapitulation* section, where themes return in much their original shape.

The mapping shown next is a generalized representation of the events that occur in a typical sonata form.

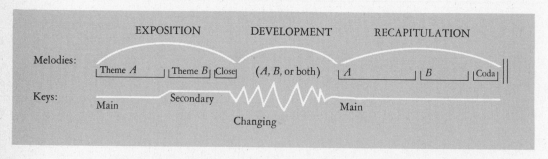

Example 7.1 Outline of Classical Sonata-Form

There usually are many cues that reveal how a particular first movement fits (or does not fit) this generalized plan. Note that our mapping deals with only two aspects, melodies (themes) and keys. You will become familiar with other relevant aspects as we discuss specific compositions that are cast in sonata form.

SECOND MOVEMENT. Slow tempo, usually a simple return form (*A B A*), although sometimes theme and variations. In late Mozart symphonies the second movement might even be a slow sonata form.

THIRD MOVEMENT: Medium fast, usually a return form of *A B A* called *Minuet* and *Trio*. In this dance-like movement the order is *Minuet–Trio–Minuet*, thus creating the ternary form.

FOURTH MOVEMENT: Fast tempo, either a rondo or a sonata form; sometimes (especially with Haydn) a mixture of both.

Melody

The dominating property of music of this period (roughly 1750–1820) is melody. The tunefulness of Haydn's music makes it exemplary in this respect. Melody dominates; it is always present and is one of the obvious agents by which the music is organized into formal sections. The melodies are contoured, possessing clear shapes of rise and fall, frequently in arch-like patterns. They also project a clear sense of tonality, establishing pitch focus within their first few notes. One way composers frequently extend a brief pattern into a complete melodic phrase is by sequence. In a sequence a motif is repeated successively at different pitch levels. The following passage contains a typical sequence from the music of Haydn.

Example 7.2   Melodic sequence, first main theme, Mvt. 1

Rhythm

Again, simplicity is the key word. It is supremely easy to tap a steady pulse to this music. Its meters move in clear duple or triple groupings. Syncopation occurs frequently, but usually in ways that do not mask the normal rhythmic flow. There is not always the "perpetual motion" one can hear in the music composed earlier in the eighteenth century, but tempo and pulse usually remains constant within a movement. A frequent rhythmic jolt in Haydn's music is provided by the "Grand Pause." This is a point at which sound ceases abruptly for a full measure, providing a dramatic gesture of expectancy.

Most notable in the Viennese style is the sing-song quality of melodic rhythms. That is, phrases almost always consist of duplex, or two-by-two arrangement. The theme of the second movement of the *Surprise* Symphony is an admirable example of this kind of balanced and predictable organization.

Example 7.3 Phrase structure, second theme, Mvt. II

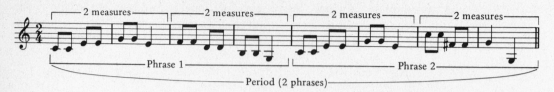

This same pattern is then repeated, forming a section of two balanced parts. And thus every level of structure in the opening of the theme is organized in units of equal lengths, each of a two-plus-two arrangement.

Texture

Homophony is the reigning texture in this music. Its accompanied melody offers a marked change from the polyphony favored by the composers of Bach's generation. There are indeed exciting and complex passages of melodic imitation. Both Haydn and Mozart composed some of the most masterful polyphony to be found in any music. And yet these passages are not the norm. They supply dramatic change from the homophony that is the textural staple of the times.

Most important is the matter of textural clarity—*transparency of texture*, as it has been called by many writers. That is, parts are blended together within the musical fabric so that each is neatly separate, and yet all are unified by a common harmonic basis.

Contrasts of texture partition off sections of overall form. A new musical section normally is characterized by a narrower or wider, denser or sparser texture than that of the preceding section. Sometimes these contrasts are great, such as the rich sound of the whole orchestra yielding to a single flute melody accompanied only by violins. These textural contrasts sometimes occur within sections also, separating thematic events on a smaller scale.

Timbre

The sound of the classical orchestra is distinctive. It consists mainly of the string body (dominated by violins), with a prominent supporting role played by the woodwinds. Flutes, oboes, and bassoons provide the main contrast with strings, as well as frequent reinforcement of parts played by violins, violas, and cellos.

Trumpets in the orchestra (for Haydn there were two) do little more than provide support. They frequently play the same patterns as the timpani (at a higher pitch, of course), while their mellower brethren the horns* provide sustained tones for background. Within the orchestra these brass members rarely supply truly melodic interest beyond infrequent martial flourishes from the trumpets.

---

*When we identify instruments as *horns*, we refer to what many people call *French horns*.

Harmony

This is *tonal music* of the simplest kind. Movements normally begin and end in the same key. All except the second movement are usually pitched in the same key. There are tonal diversions within movements, shifts to other keys for brief periods that provide an atmosphere of tonal variety. But the prevailing musical flow is solidly entrenched in the tonic key. This is what is meant by titles like Symphony in G or Sonata in B♭.

The harmonies of the Haydn–Mozart style are appropriate to a music in which melody reigns supreme. Chords are decidedly consonant, their densities confined to three or four pitch classes. Even when only two voices sound together, the melodic patterns themselves imply a harmonic unit. High degrees of dissonance occur only as a product of melodic patterns that brush against the consonant chord tones.

An elemental feature in many passages is what amounts to a basic two-chord harmonic scheme. Around this set of two basic chords other chords may (or may not) be woven. On these terms the interplay of tonic (I) and dominant (V) chords is a principal structural feature. This in itself provides a large measure of the music's tonal simplicity. In some passages the tonic-dominant alternation occurs as a mere succession of chords; in other passages it acts as the organizing thrust for an entire phrase. This latter condition prevails in the simple theme of the second movement. Example 7.3 shows the chordal flow in that melody, which we illustrated earlier.

Example 7.4   Tonic-dominant polarity (I–V) in the theme of Ex. 7.2

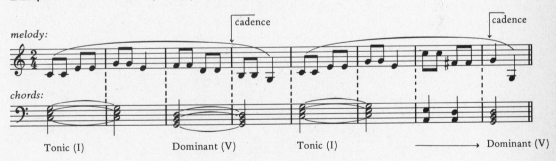

The same kind of polarity occurs between whole sections. A first theme in a major key is followed by a second theme in the key that is in the dominant relation (interval of a fifth above). We shall note this relationship several times within the *Surprise* Symphony. A similar polarity operates when the first key is minor. Then the key of the next theme is usually that of the relative major, as illustrated in Example 7.5.

Example 7.5   Usual key relationships in classical symphonies

If first tonic chord is Major,

G major

second section will be in the key of the *Dominant* (V)

D major

If first tonic chord is minor,

g minor

second section will frequently be in the key of *relative* Major (III)

major

To make more concrete the harmonic conventions of Haydn's period, the next example shows the kind of major and minor scales that represent the basic pitch material of the times. The principal chords that dominate the harmonic palette appear to the right of the scales.

Example 7.6a and 7.6b   Major and minor scales and chords derived from them

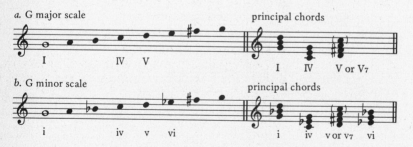

a. G major scale   principal chords

I   IV   V   I   IV   V or V₇

b. G minor scale   principal chords

i   iv   v   vi   i   iv   v or v₇   vi

Passages at variance with this slightly oversimplified description of tonality and harmony do occur. The Development sections of movements in sonata form usually abound in rapid changes of key, undermining the more placid and settled key unity of the Exposition and Recapitulation sections. This is one way the Viennese composer could create contrasts of tension and relaxation in his music.

THE SURPRISE SYMPHONY: GENERAL CHARACTERISTICS

This work was composed for a concert in London in March, 1792, for which J. P. Salomon had invited Haydn to be guest composer and conductor. (He was billed for these concerts as "The World's Greatest Composer.") The symphony's "surprise" is the unexpectedly loud chord within the opening of the otherwise calm second movement. It isn't much of a surprise for those of us today who lack the expectations of symphonic movements shared by concert-goers of 1792. Haydn is reported to have remarked, with characteristic wit, that "There all the ladies will scream."

The instrumentation is typical of symphonies composed before Mozart first used clarinets in his symphonies. It consists of duets of flutes, oboes, bassoons, horns, and trumpets, a pair of timpani (kettledrums), and the string section passed on from the early eighteenth-century orchestras of Bach and Handel. By this time the harpsichord no longer provides the accompanying parts that had prevailed in orchestral works of the first half of the century.

True to form, Haydn's Symphony No. 94 is in four movements. Their order and individual characters are typical of symphonies of the Viennese group of composers as a whole, and the moods of the work are wholly consistent with others of the time. It is tunefully buoyant, rhythmically vivacious in every part. Even the slow movement (the second) was delegated by the composer to project his most dolorous sympathies.

Haydn's orchestra at the Esterházy estate boasted a normal force of from twenty-five to thirty instrumentalists, the exact number depending on how many amateurs among the estate's guests might join in for a performance. (Some of the nobility were remarkably accomplished performers.) The London orchestra for which the *Surprise* was composed probably contained no more than thirty-five players, the extras beefing up the string section. This still was a far cry from the ninety or more musicians who populate our major orchestras today, and conductors who care about authenticity of performance use a reduced force when playing Haydn and Mozart symphonies.

Movement I:
Adagio cantabile;
Vivace assai

This movement is a relatively straightforward sonata form. The qualification "relatively" is applied only because the contrast between the first and second themes in the Exposition is not overwhelming. There is a definite key change prior to the second theme's entrance, and there is a distinctly new rhythmic lilt. But there is no corresponding textural contrast, and the melodic contour does not offer a bold departure from that of the first theme.

A simple mapping of the movement shows its main parts. Observe the double-dot sign. This denotes repetition of the Exposition, a common

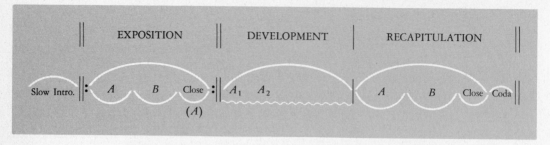

Example 7.7   Form of the first movement

practice in performances of the eighteenth century that sometimes is ignored today.

The introduction to this movement is a dignified "call and response" between woodwinds and strings. It is a simple and direct opening gesture in slow triple meter. It bears no thematic relationship with the remainder of the symphony. The fast section opens with the first violins sounding the beginning of the first main theme, now a fast triple rhythm accompanied only by a bare line in the second violins. The melody is notable because it begins with a simple sequence like that we illustrated in Example 7.1.

The remaining portion of the first theme, *A*, contains an interplay, typical of the openings of classical symphonies, between orchestral texture (*tutti*) and smaller combinations of instruments. The similarity between this series of thick and thin, loud and quiet contrasts and those found in the orchestral music of the late Baroque period (Bach's time) suggests a holdover from that earlier period. In the Haydn Symphony, separate themes are played by the light textures (the more tuneful falling sequence) and the full ensemble.

The most engaging feature at the outset of the *B* theme in this movement is its syncopated rhythm. Here the strings accent notes in a way that contradicts the normal rhythmic flow, as illustrated in Example 7.8.

Example 7.8   Syncopation in the first movement, theme *B*

The key has changed to *D* major (dominant key) just before this syncopated pattern establishes the second section's beginning. It persists to the end of the Exposition section, where an ending gesture on a single bare pitch is made by violins alone. At this point the orchestra either proceeds into the Development section or else repeats the Exposition, beginning just after the Introduction. (This decision is made by the individual orchestra conductor.) A closing theme, as tuneful as the *A* theme, provides a closing pattern for this first large section of the form.

The Development section merits some attention because it is important for us to discover some of the processes that make such a musical passage *developmental*. In this movement development begins with the return of the head motif from the *A* theme. But circumstances have changed: now the motif becomes a fragment from which the total melodic life of the texture is formed. Even this unit is further fragmented, a reduced version now becoming the melodic building block. These chains of fragments flesh out a continuing melodic line. They are passed from high to low pitch by the strings and woodwinds, a shifting harmonic scheme rendering a kaleidoscopic image of changing sound. And thus a known musical quantity, the melodic motif of *A*, itself split amoeba-like into a new motif, is transformed through its association with a new set of harmonies. It is *developed*.

The result is a musical section that contrasts with Exposition and Recapitulation, primarily through its greater tension. This tension is a product of rapid changes marked by greater uncertainty. As in any human situation, a rapid play of events creates an excitement we don't feel when only one idea or mood dominates a scene.

The hubbub and tension of the Development are replaced by the more settled character of the Recapitulation. It projects a sense of return to "normalcy." Here the *A* theme returns in its original key and texture and, except for a high flute that doubles the violins, it is a return to the earlier pitch location of the theme. A genuine return has been accomplished; this resolution is even further reinforced because the remaining portions of the Recapitulation remain within the same key, the tonic key of *G* major.

You will note in Example 7.7 that the *A* theme returns once more after the *B* theme has sounded in the Recapitulation. This final return is just another example of the classic composer's penchant for "rounding off" a movement's form. The music then proceeds through the closing theme and an extended passage that forms the final *coda*, or closing gesture.

Movement II: Andante

We illustrated earlier the usual symmetrical unit-structure of classical melodies by citing the first two phrases of this movement. Its simple two-by-two balance serves admirably as the theme for a set of four variations.

These variations never move far afield from the theme itself; the ways Haydn varies materials are typical of his style. He relies mainly on fashioning each new little section from its parent theme, using textural overlay and embellishing rhythms. An almost exact replica of the theme can be heard in Variations 1 and 3. Even the coda of the whole movement is a remodeling of the theme's first phrase into a passage that suggests imminent finality.

Because of this fondness for staying close to the theme, the *processive* qualities in this theme-and-variations form are overshadowed by elements of *return*. The overall shape of the theme is shown in Example 7.9. Its two-part, or *binary*, design consists of only two melodic patterns, *a* and *b*.

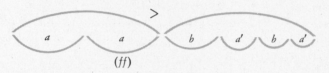

(ff)

Example 7.9
Form of the Theme, second movement

Variation 1: Here the theme's melody is overlaid with rapid figures from violins and flute.

Variation 2: Now a shift to minor key for the first few measures. Melodies are rapid figures turned around the main pitches of the theme. This variation is cast in the same basic phrases as the theme, yet a short bridge into *Variation 3* is played by violins alone. Relatively broad and dense textures prevail in this variation.

Variation 3: Now back in a major key. Rapid articulation of the theme's melody alternates with statements of the theme in its original state, accompanied by running patterns of flute and oboe. A lighter texture here contrasts with the heaviness of Variation 2.

Variation 4: The heaviest texture of the movement occurs in the opening of this variation. Woodwinds, brass, and even timpani intone the theme while violins add breathless figurations. The second *a* of this section drops to a lighter texture to sound a varied statement of the theme by violins. The full orchestra returns for a regal completion of the *b a'*, *b a'* second half.

At the end of Variation 4 a typical Haydnesque mini-drama is enacted. The final chord of the variation, always a chord of repose in preceding sections, is now anything but terminal in its effect. This brief surprise provides a momentary tinge of bewilderment, promising the listener that the ensuing coda will be all the more final.

Movement III: Menuetto

The throbbing duple meter of the second movement is replaced with an equally relentless triple meter, the characteristic rhythm of the minuet. This movement is a prime example of ternary form; it reveals as forcefully as a movement could the affinity for formal balance that is typical of the Viennese classic style. Note even the contrast-return ordering within the *Menuetto* and the *Trio* parts.

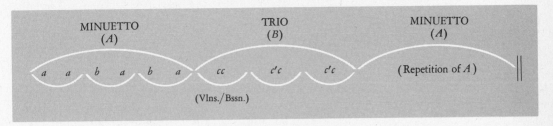

Example 7.10   Form of the Minuetto and Trio

This is good-humored music that rocks along at a pace quite removed from the delicate strains of a genuine minuet-for-dancing. A slightly comical event occurs within the *Menuetto* section at the seam between *b* and the restatement of *a*. Here a brief hesitation is created by widely separated imitations of flute/oboe and bassoon/cello. It slyly hints that these parts were "left over" from the preceding excitement; now the players regroup for another go at the main melody.

Movement IV:
Allegro di Molto

The fourth movement is normally the finale of the classic symphony, so its essence is usually that of flourishing release, a galloping race to the finish. Its mood and structure are more akin to that of the first movement. Its form is sometimes sonata form, sometimes rondo. Haydn cleverly combines the features of both in this movement.

As the mapping of Example 7.11 shows, returns to the main theme within the middle area negate a developmental atmosphere. Since these recurrences are in the tonic key (*G major* for the *Surprise* Symphony), and since their texture and timbre identify fully with the original theme, they suggest a stability that doesn't fit with the normal conditions of a Development section.

Example 7.11   Form of the fourth movement

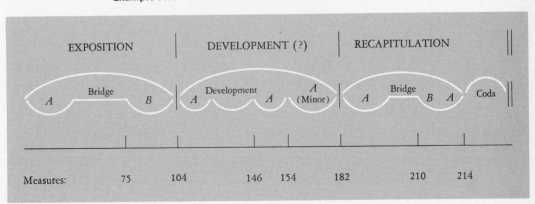

What prevents our calling this an unqualified sonata form? Mainly the unvaried returns of the *A* theme in the middle section. Each of these returns is followed by passages that suggest developmental action (temporary changes of key, rapid shifts of melodic figures). But then things settle once again into the stability that the next returning *A* theme provides. As is common in a Recapitulation section, the *B* theme recurs now in the tonic key, rather than in the dominant, as in the Exposition section. But listening carefully, you may note a curious thing about this theme each time it is heard in both the Exposition and Recapitulation: Haydn has cleverly accompanied it with a rhythm we associate with the beginning of the *A* theme. In this way he brings a degree of melodic unity to the section that is exceptional: it occurs where contrast is expected.

8

SYMPHONY NO. 5
IN C MINOR, OPUS 67

Ludwig van Beethoven (1770–1827)

BACKGROUND*

The succession of three classical period composers—Haydn, Mozart and Beethoven—provides a lesson in the changing economics of music as well a collection of great symphonies. The composer-as-individual did not achieve prominence outside the domain of the church until the seventeenth century. A rising middle class and the dispersal of religious rule begun by the Protestant Reformation created a new social base for musical performances. At first the moneyed aristocracy, then gradually the public-at-large, became this base.

By Haydn's day the musician was employed by a court or a church, but sometimes the religious music establishment was difficult to differentiate from its secular counterpart. Haydn was retained for most of his productive years by the Esterházy family, and his fame and fortune were strengthened by his forays into the broader world of concertizing, such as his trips to London for the impresario Salomon. The public concert was a growing phenomenon that provided fame and fortune for the foremost performers and composers.

Mozart, Haydn's younger contemporary, was essentially a public performer. The darkest times of his short life (1756–1791) stemmed from fruitless attempts to gain a secure post equal to his talents. He worked

---

*Further discussion of Beethoven can be found in Chapter 34.

himself to death fulfilling commissions for works—operas and symphonies as well as a variety of trivia—to be performed for civic presentations. Among aristocratic circles he was a "public personality" in the way a television actor or professional football player might be today.

Beethoven completed the eighteenth-century transformation of the professional composer. His livelihood came from commissions from wealthy patrons and box office receipts of public concerts (some of which he sponsored himself). For the first time in the history of Western art music, the composer was now a solitary figure, depending on his creative prowess without benefit of corporate subsidy. As he began to earn an income from a variety of sources, his social position rose to that of public hero rather than mere courtly employee or panderer to a single patron's tastes.

THE COMPOSER'S LIFE

No composer was better suited, musically or by temperament, to represent this new status of liberation than was Beethoven. A product of his times, which saw the rise of the French Revolution, he was an unquestioning believer in "equality and fraternity" for all mankind. He bore these burdensome dreams as though they were his personalized cross of penance.

Born in 1770, Beethoven was Haydn's contemporary for almost forty years. The work of that great elder statesman of music was his professional point of departure. Like Haydn, his development as a composer was slow. Had he died at thirty-five like Mozart, his music would be remembered today more as a promise of talent rather than as the fulfillment of greatness.

His father, Johann, was a drunken schemer, a singer of minor roles in the civic choir and opera of Bonn, Germany. Struggling to support seven children, he happened on the notion that young Ludwig could be shaped into a child prodigy like Mozart, perhaps to become a breadwinner for this hapless clan. By the time his son was six he was playing rather formidably on the piano and violin; by 1778 he was launched in his first public recital. (Father Johann added a characteristic Hollywood flair to this touching scene by claiming that his *Wunderkind* was two years younger than his true age.)

But alas, father Johann was not the teacher and promoter Mozart's father had been, and son Ludwig did not have the astonishing talent of the young Wolfgang. The anticipated public splash came off more as a tinkle. The foremost gain of Ludwig's first recital was Johann's wise turn to other teachers for continued instruction for his son. Only in 1780 did his hope of success seem fulfilled when the next of a long line of teachers proved to be effective. He was the local court organist, Christian Neefe. Neefe introduced Ludwig to the music of Bach and provided a more substantial musical foundation for the boy than old Johann and his cronies could muster. By the time Ludwig was fourteen he was made Neefe's assistant at a salary half that of his father's.

Probably the biggest event in Beethoven's youth came in 1787 when, on his first trip to Vienna, he met Mozart. Then at the height of his creative powers, Mozart praised the younger man's playing, which even then must have been phenomenal. But this fortunate contact could not be used to advantage, for Beethoven's only source of income was in Bonn, where he also had to shoulder the economic and moral responsibility for his family. In 1789 he even became the legal head of this unit, publicly acknowledging the irresponsibility of his pitiful father.

Move to Vienna   While still living in Bonn, Ludwig made contact with the music of his time by playing viola in the municipal orchestra. In 1792 Haydn passed through the city, returning from his first London tour. His reponse to Beethoven's music was encouraging enough to justify a move to Vienna to study with this greatest of living composers. Ludwig's wealthy friends interceded with the Elector to secure financial help, and thus he left Bonn for what would become his permanent home.

The teacher-student relationship between Haydn and Beethoven was not smooth. Their vastly different temperaments led to a break, a touchy emotional event slightly relieved by Haydn's departure on a second London tour. Beethoven claimed that he learned nothing from his studies with Haydn, and this may be true. But the mark made by the elder composer's music is quite another matter.

Beethoven was a rousing success in Vienna. He met people who treasured his musical talents and who could in turn reward those talents. They provided commissions and the kind of word-of-mouth fame so critical for the success of one whose fortunes depended upon box office acceptance. His life was a social whirl, replete with successions of brief love affairs and friendships with the aristocracy of a Vienna in its worldly glory.

Those local events were punctuated by occasional forays into neighboring countries for concerts of his own music. In this way he was indeed a late-blooming Mozart, enjoying considerable successes in Germany, Hungary, and Czechoslovakia as well as Austria. In 1815 he was even granted tax-free status in Vienna—"freedom of the city"— and was allowed the use of the public hall for concerts whose revenues were his own.

But worldly success was not the balm it could have been for a less disturbed personality. His family's lingering tragedies, his emotional inability to continue a lasting love attachment with a woman, and, most of all, a rapidly developing deafness shut out the sense of fulfillment made possible by his professional conquests. In the truest sense of the term, Beethoven was "fashionable," yet he also was frequently at the point of personal despair.

Evolution of Beethoven's Style

His early compositions are essentially chips off the old Haydn-Mozart block. In 1802, however, a turn toward a unique, more personal style came with his announcement that "I am not satisfied with my work thus far. From here on I'll take a new path." This new path is most evident in the highly charged atmosphere his works manifest after that date, an electrifying tension rarely found in the music of earlier composers.

The change is perhaps most evident in the increased length of his compositions. His Symphony No. 3 (called the *Eroica*), for instance, lasts about forty-six minutes. But also evident is the obvious tension suggested in his later music by sudden contrasts of texture, loudness, and pitch. Here the composer is not just creating fetching sound patterns: he is consciously transmitting emotional states to his audience through his music. We saw one example of this emoting in the beginning of his Pathetique Sonata, Example 1.5, where high/low pitch contrasts shape the musical flow.

Like the later works of Haydn and Mozart, Beethoven's music displays a debt to J.S. Bach, particularly in his most mature compositions. From 1823 his piano sonatas and string quartets abound in polyphonic elaborateness. But in these works contrapuntal complexity is not just laid over traditional forms. These works fly the coop of sonata form and other of the formal details observed by his predecessors. For this reason many people have considered these later compositions "difficult," even proof that the embittered composer indeed was hopelessly deaf. But such an evaluation implies that composers should not seek their own paths, that the individual creator has no right to tamper with the ways and means imposed by the past. In Beethoven's tamperings one can view the bared roots of modern music and our acceptance of the individual voice—indeed of our demand for originality in any artistic product.

Unhappy Final Years

It is ironic that Beethoven's fatal illness was contracted in helping the son of his dead brother Karl, a helpless boy who had become the composer's legal ward in 1820. This maladjusted young man attempted suicide in the summer of 1826. Ludwig fled to the country in early autumn, dragging Karl along in an attempt to revitalize him and their family tie. While there he attempted to convince his younger brother, Johann Beethoven, that he should make their nephew his heir. His pleading was in vain. Ludwig rushed in a huff back to Vienna in an open carriage during early December. The inclement weather brought on a fever, and he was bedridden from then until March 26, 1827, when he died.

Concert Fashions of the Times

Our own ideas about what makes a "proper" symphonic concert are jolted when we read about the conditions under which some acknowledged "masterpieces" were first performed. Many of these concerts were as long, as improvised, and as fitful as a modern rock concert. The public unveiling of the Fifth Symphony, for example, was enough to scare away the most devoted music lover. The total concert lasted four hours. It included two new symphonies (Fifth and Sixth), an operatic "scene" for soprano and orchestra, selected parts from a new Mass, a Fantasy for piano improvised by Beethoven, the first performance of his new Choral Fantasy and, finally, his Piano Concerto in C Major. Seven large works in one sitting!

But programming was not the only bizarre feature of this early nineteenth-century musical marathon. Contemporary accounts reveal that the compositions were not all rehearsed prior to the performance. The concert hall was without heat at the performance mentioned above (it was December 22 and frigid), and Beethoven miscued the performers during the Choral Fantasy, leading to a complete breakdown in that work.

GENERAL CHARACTERISTICS OF SYMPHONY NO. 5

Beethoven made preliminary notes for many of his compositions years before they were actually composed. He jotted down ideas for Symphony

Illustration 8.2 Half the size of the flute, the piccolo's shrill tone tops off the sound of the modern orchestra. It was first used by a symphonic composer in Beethoven's Symphony No. 5. While most flutes and piccolos are made of metal, the instrument played here by Robert Mols is of ebony.

Illustration 8.3 Resonant foundation for the modern brass section, trombones sometimes were used in opera scores before Beethoven added them to the standard symphonic ensemble.

Illustration 8.6 An accomplished performer can convey a remarkable variety of emotions with the clarinet, whose pitch range encompasses everything from low-mellow rustles to piercing screeches. Mozart used the clarinet in his last three symphonies; it rarely was absent in scores after his death (1791). Haydn's Surprise Symphony uses no clarinet; all nine of Beethoven's contain significant parts for two. (Allen Sigel, clarinet)

No. 5 as early as 1800, although the composition was not performed until 1808.

It is one of the nine Beethoven completed, a total that hints at the new image of the symphony, in the wake of the one hundred and more of Haydn and at least half that many by Mozart. With Beethoven the symphony assumes grand proportions and epic style rarely hinted at by earlier symphonists. For him the symphony became a personal testament in sound rather than a richly diverting entertainment.

One feature of the symphonic form retained by Beethoven is its four-movement plan. But even that priority wanes slightly in his Symphony No. 5: there is no pause between the third and fourth movements, and there are direct melodic quotations from the third movement in the last. It was his obvious desire to unify, to bring together things which, though separated in time, are seen to be related. This melodic relatedness in unexpected places is evident within movements also, as we shall see in our more detailed discussions of individual movements.

In spite of the excessive demands made on the first audience to hear the Fifth, the symphony was an immediate success. Its dramatic potency appealed to the nineteenth-century listener much as it does today, and it remains one of the most popular symphonies of all times. It is not unusual, a century and a half after its premiere, to see an audience rise with the sound of its final chords, on the verge of storming the conductor's podium in a fit of musical joy.

Why is the Fifth so different from what an earlier composer might have created? Probably the best single generalization would be that while another composer might show a fondness for a musical pattern, Beethoven became obsessed with his. The product is a frequent devolopment of emotional tension, this tension craftily released in a brilliant climax that shakes the rafters and conveys a euphoria of personal triumph for the listener. The last movement of the Fifth Symphony demonstrates this penchant for driving home a point on a large scale, and its obsessively long final section represents it on a smaller scale. There certainly are other ways of recognizing Beethoven's uniqueness, and yet this is a fundamental way to separate this titanic man from the gentle souls in powdered wigs who came before.

Movement I: Allegro con brio

Drama reigns from the beginning. There is no introductory passage for quieting an audience as in Haydn's *Surprise* Symphony. The first motif, ...⌣ , sets the business at hand, and there is no mistaking that it is weighty business. This is not a melody in the usual sense; it is only a motif that is woven dramatically through the first movement. We even find it interlaced through the later movements in various disguises.

The outline of the movement is sonata form, sectional divisions clearly punctuated by the principal motif itself.

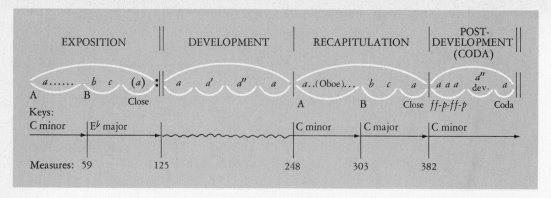

Example 8.1 Mapping of the first movement

The overall result of the long final section is really a grand mutation of the earlier sonata form. Notice that here the total music following the Development section is about equal in length to the Exposition section (if the Exposition is repeated as per Beethoven's directions).

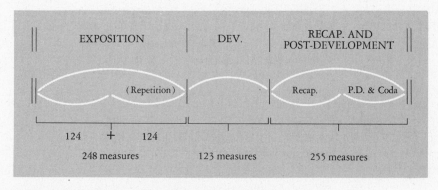

Example 8.2 Relative durations of the large sections, Mvt. I

But there is more here than just an inflated Recapitulation. What indeed has happened is that developmental processes have taken root everywhere; the Development section no longer is the only domain where thematic metamorphosis takes place. Not only has a definite developmental section appeared after the "normal" return of the main themes; here even the Exposition is the site of considerable thematic variation. Both the Exposition and Recapitulation still provide a degree of stability and emotional repose, but they also have sprouted new limbs which reach out to discover the melodic potentialities within their themes. In this way the first fifty-eight measures (*a* in the mapping of Example 8.1) consists of the exposition *and development* of a single melodic pattern.

The principal motif clearly dominates most parts of this movement. What you may not hear at first is its background presence during the exposition of *b*. It remains as a throbbing little bass pattern, even in the midst of these quieter and more lyrical moments.

Example 8.3   The *a* motif within the *B* section, Mvt. I

One of the most dramatic passages in the symphony occurs just before the Recapitulation. At this point a sparse rhythm begins loud, diminishes to a very soft sound, blares out, softens again, then makes a head long rush into the Recapitulation. The passage grows from the principal motif (...—), a good example of the way Beethoven could make a theme grow or even divide into fragments. Example 8.4 illustrates the process that transforms the initial motif into this fragment late in the Development section.

Example 8.4   Thematic growth and fragmentation of the main motif

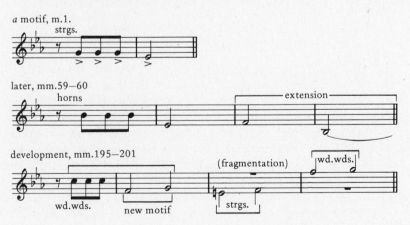

This kind of melodic metamorphosis is a main clue to Beethoven's genius. It adds an element of fascination that some writers call "organic growth." The comparison with a growing amoeba that expands and then divides is not as remote as it first may seem.

Beethoven could have subtitled this movement "Two melodies in search of a form." This is not meant unkindly, for the movement does not lack a keen musical logic. The point is that the listener frequently is led to expect one series of musical events, only to have his anticipations thwarted. Beethoven certainly was capable of pressing any musical conclusion he desired; his musical control was complete. His intention here is to create a series of expectations that are left unfulfilled. And he is successful.

The initial section exposes two distinct melodies in three parts. The second and third parts bear the same actual pattern, but they are made different by distinct changes of key, texture, and timbre. This melody bears in disguise the same *short-short-short-long* pattern of the first movement.

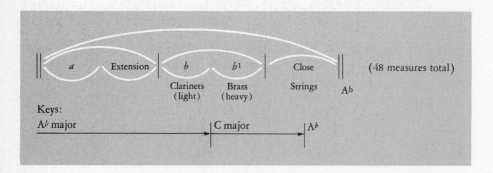

Example 8.5 Theme layout, first section of Mvt. II

It is an interesting passage for several reasons. Its parts are short, the themes themselves announced quickly and then rounded out by quiet little extensions. Nothing seems to get anywhere; as soon as direction appears to be established, momentum slackens and a change occurs.

Once the three parts of the total theme have been sounded, the violas and cellos begin what clearly must be a variation. At least we now know what is happening! Beethoven has tossed off a curiously fetching set of themes and now he proceeds with a set of variations on them. Clarinets and bassoons return with *b*, brass follow suit with the expected *b'*, and the closing passage ensues. All seems to be on schedule.

Variation 2 seems so obvious as to be commonplace. It is merely a slightly decorated version of Variation 1. Violins take over the same flowing figure, cellos and basses add their extension to it. But then, just when everything seems to be in order, the "rules" of variation fly out the window. The clarinet melody we have come to expect turns out to be a quite different dialogue of woodwinds, a passage that lasts twice as long as its counterpart within the theme and Variation 1. But the total ensemble of woodwinds, brass, timpani, and strings finally enters to right the form with *b′*, eventually dissolving into an innocuous little repeated figure. This is passed about among the strings as a bridge to the next section.

Variation 3 begins in minor key, a "pecking" kind of variant accompanied by plucked strings and the repeated figure leftover from the preceding bridge passage. This exotic facsimile of the theme is soon replaced by a full-textured restatement of *a* in its original major key, followed by rather exacting returns of the extensions found in the beginning of the movement. This time, *b* and *b′* are absent; the return of the extensions provides a distinct effect of closure because of its duplication of the beginning sounds of the movement.

Suddenly the tempo picks up, implying perhaps still another rerouting for this capricious movement. Instead, the tempo resumes its original pace, and fragments of the original *a* return once again, closing the movement as it began with a clever succession of melodic fragments. A strange mixture of processive and return form is the outcome. It is a five-section structure in which all parts, with the exception of Variation 2, are of about the same length.

Movement III: Allegro

Only a faint echo of the classical minuet resounds within the third movement. Beethoven replaces this vestige of the polite dance with what amounts to a *scherzo*, although he does not entitle it that. It is a faster-moving gambol that, although still in triple meter, cannot be mistaken for a dance of polite society. The movement's form is still ternary, *A B A* of large sections. The *A* combines a smoothly rising arch with a new version of the . . . — motif of the first movement. The middle section is dominated by textures of melodic imitation built from a fast-moving pattern that seems unable to decide whether to gallop or stand still.

Every section of the movement capitalizes on the driving, dramatic spurts Beethoven punctuates with flashes of silence or sustained sound.

Example 8.6 Mapping of the third movement

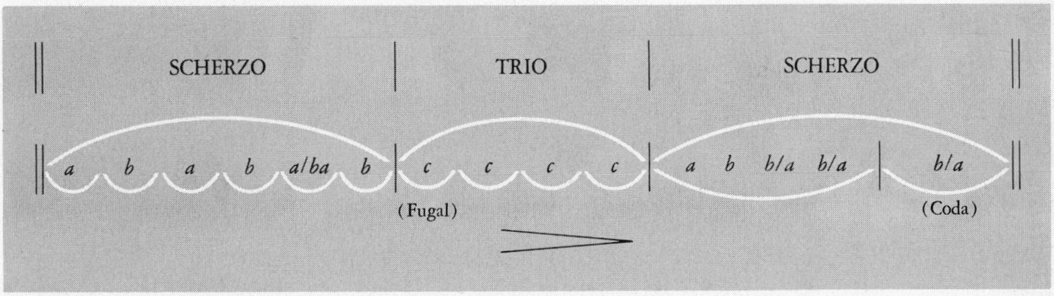

The overall quality is that of decisiveness arrested by wonderment. As in the second movement, these spasms of starting and stopping sometimes create an impression of intentional clumsiness; in the middle of this movement the rapid pattern played by the double basses contributes to that impression. It was this passage the French composer Hector Berlioz was led to characterize as "the gambols of a frolicsome elephant."

The eerie quiet of the final section is an opportune preparation for the finale, which ensues without a pause. It is a rousing breakthrough after the stumbling mystery of the third movement.

Movement IV: Allegro

The disarming final calm of the previous movement grows suddenly into a grand release of all the pent-up energy from Beethoven's orchestra. To boost his power resources, he even adds three trombones, a contra-bassoon, and a piccolo. (This marked the debut of all three instruments into symphonic company.) If the second and third movements seemed at times to dawdle and get sidetracked, this is their triumphal resolution. Except for a brief backward glance to the minor key and theme of the third movement, the tonality is major, and the rhythm is a victorious "grand march" all the way.

In a single gesture Beethoven brings together this and the third movement; he bridges the Development and Recapitulation sections through a quotation of the B theme from that previous movement. And less directly, he neatly unifies all four movements by coming back to still another rhythmic replica of the ...⌒ motif. Now it returns in new melodic garb as the c theme. He even accentuates this reminiscence by devoting most of the Development section to it.

Example 8.7 Mapping of the fourth movement

It is curious that the order of themes in the Recapitulation forms an almost mirror image, for as you can see in the mapping, *a b c d* is followed by the ordering *c b d a*. The *musical process* is by no means that of reversal, however, for the final *d* and *a* have a closing function.

One of the most emphatic terminations in all music occurs next. It is an extended cadence (the *coda*) that is half as long as the whole Development section. Perhaps Beethoven overdid this final gesture. But once we consider that he is here ending the third as well as the fourth movement, the almost endless string of chords seems a bit less comically redundant. Whatever our conclusion about its propriety, it does strengthen our earlier observation about Beethoven's obsession with an idea.

Obsession of a more subtle kind is detectable in the way all four movements incorporate the terse rhythm heard at the very beginning, the motif variously known as Beethoven's "fate knocking at the door" and the allied forces signal for "Victory" during World War II. Example 8.8 shows the transformations this potent little pattern undergoes within the four movements, exclusive of its many developmental appearances.

Example 8.8 Various forms of the • • • ⌐ motif

Overlying the separate movements, then, is this single rhythm. It ties together those parts which in symphonies before Beethoven were related only by key and timbre. This is the grandest form of obsessiveness a symphonic composer might indulge. It represents an attempt to achieve a total unity within a large work, amidst the variety demanded to avoid sheer boredom. Beethoven was not one to bow before such a task.

9
ROMAN CARNIVAL OVERTURE

Hector Berlioz (1803–1869)

The lingering fame of Bach, Handel, Haydn, Mozart, Beethoven, and Brahms fools some people into thinking that all *great* composers were Germanic. The hindsight of history plays tricks of this kind on us, especially when a constellation of geniuses in one geographical area outshines individuals elsewhere. Often overlooked—and almost always slighted—is the chief musical link between Beethoven and modern music. This is the Frenchman Hector Berlioz (*Bahr'lyoze*), who was born in a small country town of southeast France, La Côte-Saint-André.

Reasons for unjustified neglect of Berlioz are not hard to find. Some rest with the composer himself and his artistic monomania; others have to do with the artistic and political unrest of nineteenth-century France; and a final reason is the demonstrable fact that true artistic innovation rarely meets with public approval. Berlioz's innovative streak touched more than just music; his arena was mid-nineteenth-century Europe in all its artistic turmoil.

ROMANTICISM

Berlioz played a leading role in the nineteenth-century drama historians call the *Romantic Era*. The full characteristics of this exciting time are not easy to pin down. But its products in all the arts are important enough to risk a definition of its main features and motivating forces.

Illustration 9.1
Hector Berlioz

Romanticism is perhaps best understood as an attitude. In the nineteenth century it was a reaction against the commonplace, a rejection of "practical" standards for what is exciting or artistically stimulating. The philosopher Bertrand Russell found the polar opposites of the practical and the romantic in two great nineteenth-century figures, the biologist Charles Darwin and the poet William Blake. As he put it, "The earthworm is useful, but not beautiful; the tiger is beautiful, but not useful. Darwin (who was not a romantic) praised the earthworm; Blake praised the tiger."*

The main thread of the Romantic era (roughly 1820–1900) can be traced at least as far back as Jean Jacques Rousseau. Writing in mid-eighteenth century, he rejected the intellectualism, formalism, and worldliness of the classic tradition. Rousseau's ideal was a "return" to what he touted as the simple purity of humanity, the kind of person in whom "the heart should rule the head."

This over-simple view of human nature was unintentionally bolstered (for those patient enough to read his books) by the philosopher Immanuel Kant. Kant found the universe divisible into two distinct realms. One, the realm of what we see, hear, and touch, he called *phenomena*. The other, which is just as "real" but cannot be directly known by our senses, he called *noumena*. This realm of *noumena* was in Kant's view the ultimate reality of existence; it could be known only through faith, through the deep convictions of our intuition: in short, through *feeling*.

A History of Western Philosophy, New York: Simon and Schuster, 1945, p. 678.

These rather high-level conclusions of philosophers had all manner of low-level repercussions among artists and literati who followed in their wake. Kant's notion of the *noumena* side of reality seemed to prove that people's feelings about things are just as respectable as their most careful scientific proofs. Perhaps even more so. This conclusion led many educated people to glorify violent emotion and primitive disorder. And in Rousseau's novels a fondness for the irrational emerges frequently; the reader comes across "fearful precipices," "violent storms at sea," "mysterious pathless forests," and all manner of scenes and events in which nature overwhelms tiny, impotent man.

Rousseau and his advocates were reminding us that we have emotions as well as intellects. For writers, painters, and composers the fashion was a widespread veneration of nature, contempt for formalism, a sentimental view of humble people (who presumably had escaped ruination by "culture"), and a sometimes fiery zeal to remake the world.

This passionate cry to reinstate emotion on a level with intellect was amplified by political, economic, and religious issues that first erupted in the late eighteenth century. Romanticism reached its early zenith around 1830, but its repercussions have not totally subsided today, in politics as well as in music. The French Revolution was its most dramatic early reaction to institutions and assumptions of the past.

The Arts and Romanticism

In the arts the Romantic spirit was first evident as a literary movement. Novelists and poets expressed a longing for the remote past or for a state of natural innocence that had been lost in the industrialization of western Europe and England. In Germany the earliest signs came from contemporaries of Haydn and Mozart: Johann Wolfgang Goethe (1749–1832) and Friedrich Schiller (1759–1805) wrote novels, plays, and poems that became symbols of chronic unrest, a yearning for a fullness of life that still haunts the "generation gaps" of modern times.

England too had deep and early roots in the Romantic movement. William Wordsworth (1770–1850) expressed a mystical adoration of nature, and Samuel Taylor Coleridge (1772–1834) spun out a credible web of the fantistically weird. Lord Byron, Percy Shelley, and John Keats were poets of the same soil and a consonant spirit; they kept Romanticism alive after the enthusiasms of its earlier adherents had waned.

All of this cultivation of the uncommon and adoration of the emotions had a telling effect on some of the most talented composers of the nineteenth century. The sense of longing for a blissful state of "feelingfulness" was admirably suited to musical expression. Kant had himself noted that "music is the language of feeling." So music and Romanticism formed a hand-in-glove compatibility, and other artists aspired to its power to move the emotions. Poets fancied that their poems were in fact "verbal music"; the philosopher Schelling observed that "Architecture is frozen music"; and painters painted "symphonies" of color. Composers returned the compliment by writing "Songs without Words," by composing "Tone Poems," or by fashioning solo songs in which binding marriages were made of music and words.

Illustration 9.2
Some instruments seem ideally suited to suggest special emotions or ideas. The English horn often is used to play simple melodies that evoke the countryside and simple rustic life. Berlioz may have been the first to begin our association of this instrument with the rural troubador. (Nora Post, English horn)

Illustration 9.3
The tuba supplies the very bottom of the brass sound. Although used singly in the orchestra, its projective power is legendary; a gifted player can eclipse an entire ensemble of ninety.

Illustration 9.4
The quest during the 19th century for expanded colors led to rich new sound resources in the orchestra. The bass clarinet provides one of the most resonant tones available, leading one observer to rename it "the velvet foghorn." In the orchestra it often is played by one of the regular clarinetists, who "doubles" on both instruments. (Allen Sigel, bass clarinet)

Program Music

In symphonic music this trend naturally led to a loosened grip by the established forms of the eighteenth-century masters. Thoughtful composers now wished to expand music beyond its mere sonic message. No longer are titles so barren as "Symphony No. 40" or "Symphony No. 5 in C Minor." The wish to merge music with the non-musical had spawned a new genre called *program music*, and with it emerged more provocative titles: *Fantastic Symphony, Harold in Italy* (actually a viola concerto!), *Hebrides Overture, Don Juan, Pictures at an Exhibition, 1812 Overture, Romeo and Juliet, Symphony to Dante's Divine Comedy* and *A Hero's Life* are but a sprinkling of the symphonic highlights between 1830 and 1900.

And with this fusion of the musical and non-musical came a quickened respect for personal individuality and origins. Composers began to think of themselves as German or French or Norwegian rather than as neutral craftsmen unbound by geography. As one champion of the prevailing mood stated, "Romantic art must be 'original'; it must be modern, national, popular, grown from the soil, from the religion and the prevailing social institutions."*

Hector Berlioz could only have seconded the motion.

BERLIOZ'S CAREER

He dedicated his life to the task of making music the serious business Beethoven had proved it could be. As with all great innovators, his creativity was rooted in the past; as with all real creators, his innovations fell on largely unreceptive ears. Despite this drawback, Berlioz worked harder than any composer before him to further the cause of *music as an art*. And that is quite different from just making a living as a musician.

The man was well prepared by his childhood to be a Romantic "original." His early musical experiences were broad and thorough, but for a future composer they were slightly eccentric. He is one of the few composers of the past three hundred years who did not grow up a pianist. Educated by his father, he played guitar and flute and sang rather well. But piano lessons were not part of his early education.

The unforeseen result on the composer of this "deprived childhood" was a superior understanding of how various instruments can be mixed together into exacting ensemble sounds. Composers who are pianists tend to work out their ideas first at the keyboard, only then translating the product to whatever instruments are intended for performance. Now it should be obvious that eighty-eight piano strings are not adequate substitutes for magical mixtures of flutes or violins, trumpets or snare drums.

---

*The lines are from Mme. de Stael's *De Allemagne*, Part II, Chapter 11. Born Anne Louise Germaine Necker, Mme. de Stael was an early defender of women's liberation as well as an apologist for Romanticism in the arts. She lived from 1766 to 1817.

And this is precisely the false assumption Berlioz was spared: he didn't learn to write for the orchestra as though it were a piano by another name. His musical imagery developed in such a way that he could capture orchestral sounds directly, without any kind of sonic translation taking place.

This ability to think directly in terms of orchestral sounds formed a major aspect of his "revolutionary" impact on music. Before his time composers were less conscious of timbre as a primary part of the musical message; rhythm, melody, and harmony were their paramount building materials. A prevailing view held that cirtical *musical* value was not lost when a symphony was played by a piano or a string quartet was played by an organ. After all, a melody is the same whether it is played by a flute or a piano.

Or is it?

For Berlioz (and for other composers who divined what he was up to) the difference *was* critical. A melody played by a piano is an altogether different thing when played by a flute. The flute's breathy resonance provides something the piano cannot reproduce (and vice versa). Berlioz's reputation as a genius of the orchestra stems from just this realization of a simple yet obvious fact: one musical sound cannot replace another.

His professional and personal lives were two intertwined struggles. His personal bent toward dramatic grandeur and his dogged championing of the late works of Beethoven, still considered barbaric by many during the nineteenth century, jeopardized his own acceptance as a composer. And furthermore, some of his music sounded a bit unorthodox on first hearing.

Though his melodies possess their own unique charm, they lack the lyrical lightness of Italian opera, which was the rage of mid-century Paris. His harmonies are simple, but sometimes they are made from "irregular" chord connections that were banned by conservatory professors. He favored conflicting rhythms, asymmetrical phrases, and other kinds of rhythmic irregularities. Sometimes they confused nineteenth-century listeners who had been reared on the unchallenging rhythms of Meyerbeer and Rossini operas.

Even Berlioz's personal life suffered an excess of complications. Despite early evidence of extraordinary musical talent, his life was beset by continuing family objections to a musical career. His father, Louis, sent Hector to Paris only to learn medicine, with the hope that he would return to his small hometown and take over the father's practice. His last intention was for the son to make a lasting connection with the Paris conservatory and harbor any hope for a life as a professional musician.

As if family resistance were not enough, Berlioz's relationship with the women of his life added still another upsetting dimension. He seems to have lived with that strong sense of destiny that propels many a great man. Throughout his life he would set his mind on a love object, holding to it with superhuman tenacity, even when the love was not returned. He fell madly in love with his first wife, the Anglo-Irish actress Harriet Smithson, five years before he met her face to face.

Another touching manifestation of the same character trait is revealed by an exploit Berlioz undertook when he was sixty. It was at that age—now twice widowed and rapidly failing in health—that he attempted to rekindle the flame of an infatuation that had developed when he was only twelve. The object of his affection (an "older woman" of nineteen!) had barely noticed him when Hector's passion had been ignited. When he made overtures of "reconciliation" some fifty years later she was predictably overwhelmed with confused disbelief.

Fate added an ironic twist to the life of this incomparable romantic: Berlioz endured the tragedy of younger loved ones dying before him. Both of his wives and his two younger sisters preceded him in death. Even his lone child, son Louis, died two years before his father. These family misfortunes, combined with the periodic expiration of beloved professional friends, made of Berlioz's final years a prolonged depression. No wonder that at one point he lamented: "I desire only sleep while awaiting something more permanent."

And yet, these personal trials seem not to have checked his supreme energies as composer, concert producer, journalist, and conductor. He was tireless. By the end of his life he had conducted concerts in England, Russia, Germany, Italy, Prussia, and Austria, in addition to enduring a hectic life of composing, concertizing, and journalistic writing at home in France. He even considered offers from the United States (at the time *dis*-united by the Civil War) to transport some of his musical menage there.

By his sixty-fifth year he had completed three monumental operas, four large symphonic works, eight short orchestral works (mostly overtures), and a host of choral compositions, songs, and arrangements of other composers' music. Add to this musical monument a textbook on orchestration, his lengthy *Mémoires*, and essays about almost every musical topic of the era, and one becomes aware of the gargantuan output of the man.

THE FANTASTIC SYMPHONY AND PROGRAM MUSIC

Early notoriety came in 1830 with his *Fantastic Symphony*. This huge five-movement work (about fifty minutes playing time) established its twenty-seven-year-old composer as one very much atuned to his Romantic times, and one who furthermore offered an alternative to the conventional symphonic forms of the eighteenth century.

Berlioz's alternative, as revealed in his symphony, can be expressed most simply by noting its two most conspicuous ingredients: (1) the work is accompanied by a literary guide—a *program*— and (2) a single melodic pattern recurs in different movements as a means for achieving continuity. This technique of tying a large work together through a recurrent pattern (called *idée fixe* with Berlioz) was probably borrowed from Beethoven. There is little doubt that later composers of the nineteenth century who used the same formal principle came upon it through Berlioz. And that includes such notables as Franz Liszt, Richard Wagner, and Richard Strauss.

More has been made of Berlioz's literary guide for the *Fantastic Symphony* than it deserves. Since the story line clearly bore a trace of auto-biography, its conjunction with the five-movement work made an instant public hit, and it has stuck as a celebrated cause to the present day. We need not reproduce the lengthy program here, but its five parts (corresponding to the five movements) bear the following titles: Part I: *Reveries, Passions;* Part II: *A Ball*; Part III: *Scene in the Country*; Part IV: *March to the Scaffold*; Part V: *Dream of a Witches' Sabbath*.

In an attempt to correct misinterpretations of what he intended, Berlioz soon made the following explanation of what he, the composer, viewed as the limitations and goals of any program music.

> He knows very well that music can take the place of neither word nor picture; he has never had the absurd intention of expressing *abstractions* or *moral qualities*, but rather passions and feelings. Nor has he had the even stranger idea of painting *mountains*: he has only wished to reproduce the *melodic style and forms* that characterize the singing of some of the people who live among them or *the emotion* that the sight of these imposing masses arouses, under certain circumstances, in the soul.

Expressing passions and feelings is well within the capability of music. The total output of composer Berlioz was aimed at doing just that. Claims made by writers that he attempted more (or less) must be viewed as loose speculation.

Many of his compositions include sung or spoken texts that control the flow of "passions and feelings." His operas and choral works obviously come under this requirement, but even two of his later symphonies—*Romeo and Juliet* of 1839 and the *Funeral and Triumphal Symphony* of 1840—call for voices, and thus words. In these works he again was following the lead of his idol, Beethoven, who in his Ninth Symphony joined voices with orchestra into a grand symphonic synthesis.

THE ROMAN CARNIVAL OVERTURE

Since their origin in the early seventeenth century, overtures have been relatively brief instrumental introductions for dramatic works like operas and oratorios or, later, ballets. But early in the form's evolution the title became detached from its theatrical parent, and one finds collections of dance pieces, called *suites*, for which an overture is the initial movement.

As befitted their love for literary allusions, nineteenth-century composers developed a distinct one-movement work that can best be called *concert overture*. These compositions most often bore titles borrowed from a literary work by a revered author, from a national event, or from a grand public figure like Napoleon or Byron. Sometimes an overture would be written for an opera, and though the opera would fail, its overture would persist as an independent concert piece.

Berlioz composed six concert overtures. Among these are *Waverley* (a novel by Sir Walter Scott), *King Lear* (a play by Shakespeare), and *Rob Roy* (another novel by Scott). The literary link of *Roman Carnival* is to his opera *Benvenuto Cellini* (whose hero's autobiography furnishes the opera's plot). The opera was composed in 1833.

Roman Carnival was composed in 1843 under the usual conditions of stress the composer seemed to thrive on. He was exhausted from a four-month conducting tour of the musical centers of Germany, he was spending a great deal of time on essays and concert reviews (which provided precious income!), and he was in the final stages of his great orchestration textbook that would be published the following year.

The overture is a brilliant orchestral essay that belies none of the professional or personal worries the composer lived with at the time. (Separated from wife Harriet in 1842, he had set up a separate household with his mistress, Marie Recio.) Though originally intended as an introduction to the second act of *Benvenuto Cellini*, it soon established a separate life to become a veritable "war horse" of the concert hall. And this is fortunate, for the opera, though an acknowledged masterpiece, rarely has been mounted.

The overture's two themes—and there are only two—are extracted from two scenes of the opera. One is the kind of drawn-out plaint that is typical Berlioz. It is a love "song" of faintly peasant simplicity.

Example 9.1   Slow theme, *Roman Carnival* overture

The other theme could not be of stronger contrast. It is a rushing torrent of motion, a rhythmic feast in the spirit of an old Italian dance, the *saltarello*. The melody occurs in several slightly different guises, but its most frequent form is shown next.

Example 9.2   Allegro vivace theme (*B*), *Roman Carnival* overture

It would be easy to conclude that the overture is a simple two-part additive form, an extended *A B* structure. But this would ignore one of the most inventive features of this vibrant work, whose surface shape conceals simple but ingenious processes at work. We can best observe these qualities by referring to the bare mapping shown next.

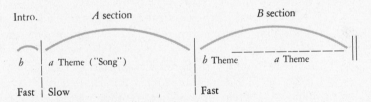

Example 9.3   Overall form of the overture

As our outline shows, the bustling introduction provides a fragmentary preview of the melody that will later shape the second half of the work, section *B*. Within that second half, after the vigorous dance has been well-established, Berlioz craftily injects his love song between repeated flourishes of the *saltarello* theme. The product is a stroke of musical logic, but it is also a characteristic display of the essence of program music. The programmatic gesture is clear: the sweet and pensive emotion of a lover's plaint is incongruously plopped into the middle of a boisterous dance. What before was a pensive song is transformed into a strange reminiscence. It is a memorable mixture of metaphors, and it is brought off by purely musical means.

Aside from this facile programmatic feature, Berlioz's overture provides a succession of engaging musical images. Its patent unity is fleshed out with the kinds of stark contrasts that must have bewildered less able listeners of 1844. The fiery introductory gesture lasts no more than fifteen seconds, yet it contains no less than three quite different textures. And all three are wholly removed from the English horn's slow song that follows.

The "song" theme is itself sounded three times within Section *A*, but its enveloping textures, and the timbres that sing it, are different each time. First the English horn, then violas, and then a mixture of strings and woodwinds sound its deceptively simple contours. This last sounding is especially noteworthy because it incorporates two parts sounding the same melody but slightly out of synchrony. This kind of texture, called *canon*, is usually associated with the most erudite kinds of music, but here it enhances the lyrical mood, entwining the separate but equal lines in a union of sweet harmony.

Example 9.4   The melodic canon in Section *A*, third sounding of the theme

One way Berlioz extends passages and paints an everchanging scene is through abrupt changes of key. A melody will sound in one key and then begin an immediate repetition in another key that obliterates the memory of the old. Sudden rhythmic shifts occur at times within the *saltarello* (*B*). There a constant triple rhythm is interrupted on two occasions by a wrenching change to duple patterns. Clapping a steady pulse, "count off" the rhythm shown in Example 9.5 and you will catch some of the flavor of these rhythmic jolts.

Example 9.5   Rhythmic shifts in the *saltarello*

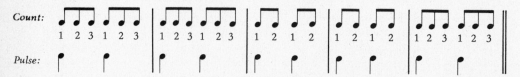

Comment cannot end without brief homage to the way Berlioz has fused instruments of the orchestra with their musical task. Perhaps most

noteworthy to musicians is the way every part rings out with intended clarity. Even when complicated figures accompany a light melody, the composer's sense of balance ensures that the melody will not be lost in a fog of details.

Instruments are mixed to create perfect blends, or sections of the orchestra are pitted one against another (like woodwinds against strings, strings against brass and percussion) in brief imitative snatches that propel the texture forward and provide a kaleidoscope of revolving timbres. There are deft touches everywhere to prove Berlioz's absolute control of this complex machine of sound, the orchestra. Few composers since have not served an apprenticeship with his scores.

IO

VARIATIONS ON A THEME
OF JOSEF HAYDN, OPUS 56A

Johannes Brahms (1833–1897)

BACKGROUND

Our concern next turns to a composer who straddles the fence of the Viennese classic tradition and the Romanticism of the nineteenth century. The picture of a split personality would be complete if Johannes Brahms had managed to be born under the Zodiac sign of Gemini, but he arrived two weeks too early, May 7, 1833. And a truly bullish Taurus he turned out to be!

He shared three personal similarities with his forerunner and idol Beethoven: a high degree of musical talent, a family who lived in semipoverty, and a musician-father of tragic incompetency. It is difficult not to associate the Germanic heaviness of some of his music with the dreary life he endured as a child in the north German city of Hamburg. But it would be more accurate to describe Brahms's unique style as the product of two basic drives: he was a romantic by nature, yet his creative instincts were guided by the forms and processes inherited from his classic predecessors.

By the time he was eight, his father found a local piano teacher for his instruction. Within a year Johannes had proved his talent, even to the extent of jobbing as pianist in local houses of prostitution and dance halls. (The image of a ten-year-old boy playing the piano in such unsavory surroundings might shock us today, but child labor laws were not universally enforced during the nineteenth century.)

Illustration 10.1
Johannes Brahms

During 1843 a leading Hamburg musician, Eduard Marxsen, consented to teach the child. The relationship was testy at first. But the boy's talent was exceptional, and lessons in composition soon crept into the piano studies. Before long Brahms was following an exhausting routine of school, piano lessons, and practice, composing, and the night life of a professional pianist. The grind was relieved in 1847 and 1848 by two summers in the country, where he had his first taste of conducting with a local chorus. These breaks were his cure for semi-exhaustion, and he enjoyed vigorous health until the last years of his life.

Broader professional horizons opened in 1853. Now only twenty, Johannes accompanied the colorful Hungarian violinist Eduard Remenyi on a concert tour. In Hanover he met the celebrated violin virtuoso Joachim, who was impressed by the recent compositions Brahms played for his judgment. Most rewarding, however, was his encounter in Dusseldorf with Clara and Robert Schumann, both of whom were among the most esteemed musicians of Germany.

Since Brahms had been recommended to the Schumanns by the famed Joachim, he was welcomed with open arms by the couple. They provided a receptive audience for his three new piano sonatas, and Robert publicly lauded him in a Leipzig music magazine as a new genius. The event launched Brahms's career. It also initiated the most durable human relationship of his life, with Clara Schumann. Within six months after the three had met, the unstable Robert was removed to a madhouse, where he died in 1856.

Brahms conducted both a court orchestra and a women's choir in Detmold during the period 1857–59. This sleepy little town provided valuable experience in working with the sounds of an orchestra. He was never a truly successful conductor. He lacked the ability to coax the full potential from even his own compositions. A painfully unsuccessful performance in 1859 of his D minor Piano Concerto led him to drop any ambitions of becoming a virtuoso pianist, and by 1860 he quit the position in Detmold to establish a home base in Hamburg, where he conducted another women's choir.

Like Beethoven and Berlioz before him, Brahms bore his share of professional disappointments. Yet he was the first composer to achieve economic security through the publication of his music. The widespread popularity of the piano during the late nineteenth century was a key factor in this success. No composer has ever made a living by royalties from symphonies or string quartets; for Brahms the basic bread-winners were four books of *Hungarian Dances* arranged as piano duets. The first two volumes were published in 1869, gaining the composer some degree of financial security. This led in 1880 to the publication of two more volumes. Revenues from these twenty-one pieces, plus smaller sums from other published works, fees as a conductor, and salaries from brief "official" positions provided the basis of his simple yet comfortable life.

His last real "job" was as Director of Vienna's most prestigious choral group, the *Gesellschaft der Musikfreunde* (Society for the Friends of Music). He assumed that responsibility in the fall of 1872, bewildering this collection of Roman Catholics with his performances of music by Protestant composers like Bach and Handel. His tenure was successful but cut into composing time, so he resigned in 1875.

The fame of most composers of concert music probably was formed most persuasively by the symphonies they composed. This certainly is true with the trio of Haydn, Mozart, and Beethoven, so it may seem strange that Brahms did not complete his first symphony until middle age. There must have been powerful rumblings of insecurity in one who professed to be the guardian of the classic tradition and worked in the immediate shadow of Beethoven!

Brahms produced only four symphonies. In one sense, however, he composed six, for his two piano concertos merge the solo instrument with the orchestra in such a way that they become symphonies with piano. (The critic Hanslick even called the Second Concerto a "symphony with piano obbligato.")

During Brahms's life the noisiest musical personality on the German scene was the opera composer Richard Wagner. An egomaniac of extraordinary musical creativity, Wagner claimed a popular following of devotees for his pseudo-religious music dramas and fitful tracts about music and art. Two people could not be less alike than Brahms and Wagner. They represented for thoughtful people of the times the opposing poles of musical life. Consistent with this opposition, Brahms did not compose an opera. He composed vocal works with orchestra such as his *Alto Rhapsody* and *German Requiem,* and he composed a great treasure of solo songs and pieces for chorus. But his whole musical direction was opposed to that of mixing music and theater.

The image of Brahms in his fifties and later is that of a slightly eccentric figure who, though showered with worldly fame, remained simple and earthy. He was a part of the local Viennese color, a paunchy little man draped in an old brown topcoat, the ashen residue of a constant cigar visible on his vest. In spite of his celebrated capacity for the local beer and a wide acquaintance with the city's ladies of easy virtue, he enjoyed a vast circle of friends who regarded him with affectionate esteem. His life settled into a round of summer composing and winter touring, walking tours around his favorite resort areas and professional tours to spread the music he had composed during the previous summer.

Although he did not produce further large-scale works after 1887, the few chamber compositions, songs, choral pieces, and piano works he did finish reveal that his creative powers had not withered. In fact, his final piano works show an ability to produce music of high value for that medium.

Clara Schumann's death in 1896 was a great loss to Brahms. He attended the funeral in Bonn and never fully recovered from the passing of his greatest friend and love. He was suffering from cancer of the liver; at sixty-three his ability to snap back from upsets was limited. By early 1897 the stubby little man had become an enfeebled spectre of his former self. He died in April of that year.

GENERAL CHARACTERISTICS OF THE VARIATIONS

The *Variations on a Theme of Josef Haydn* provides us with two paradoxes. It lacks the heavy seriousness typical of Brahms's symphonies, so for many people it is not wholly representative of the "true Brahms." The second paradox is that the theme on which the composition is based actually was not composed by Haydn but by a minor composer named I. J. Pleyel (1757–1831). As for the latter curiosity, Haydn apparently borrowed the melody from the original composer without bothering to acknowledge its source, or he may not have known its true origins. At any rate, Haydn did refer to the tune as "Chorale St. Antonii," even though its character hardly suggests sacred origins.

The theme and variations was Brahms's most successful formal model. He frequently turned to it for movements within larger works, but he also incorporated it on a grand scale in this work and in two earlier virtuoso piano compositions. One was based on a theme of Bach's contemporary, Handel, the other on a theme by the incredible violin star of the nineteenth century, Paganini.

One of Brahms's supreme virtues as a composer was the ability to evoke a musical mood in a single brief gesture. The conciseness of the individual variation was an appropriate harness to check the longwindedness that mars some of his compositions. Within the confines of the separate variation his lyrical emotionalism could not run unchecked; a lean but moving music is the result.

Brahms does not create the same kinds of variations on a theme one finds in the music of Haydn, Mozart, and Beethoven. In those earlier models the melodic theme serves as a stable scaffold on which the composer hangs melodic ornamentation. Instead, Brahms moves from variation to variation as though each is a *commentary* on the one just before or on the theme itself. In some variations the melodic parent is lost entirely; only phrase layout and harmonic plan act as ties with the original theme. This more subtle approach was used by Beethoven in some of his later compositions, and in this respect Brahms is his direct descendent.

The *Variations on a Theme of Josef Haydn* was completed during a working vacation in the Bavarian Alps in the summer of 1873. Although it does not rise to the grand scale of his four symphonies, it is a rewarding example of the composer at his best. Its success was immediate; even critics who had recoiled from his mammoth Piano Concerto in D Minor praised its first performance as a triumph.

THE MUSIC

Ten parts form the large outlines, each successive part separated by a brief pause that intensifies the integrity of the single variation. A total view is provided by the outline shown next.

THEME   VARIATION I II III IV V VI VII VIII   FINALE

Three elements remain constant throughout the eight variations, tying them to each other and to the theme: (1) the tonic pitch of B♭; (2) an unchanging form-plan; and (3) a basic harmonic progression. The theme is organized in the following way (and duplicated in each variation):

Example 10.1 Mapping of the Theme and its basic harmonic scheme

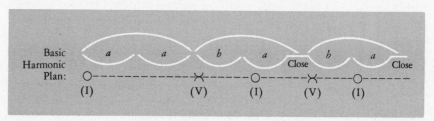

The harmony of the *b* units in the theme (✕) provides one main source of contrast there, and the middle portion of every variation duplicates this fundamental shift. Later variations elaborate the harmonic underpinning of these areas (particularly Variation 6), but the basic plan remains intact.

Variation 1:
Poco piu animato
("a little more animated")

The throbbing accompaniment of the theme is transferred as a stately motif for this variation. It is a dogged rhythm of five articulations; in the beginning it shifts between low and high pitch levels. Strings add smoothly arched windings as a foil to this firm basis. Only a vague kinship relates these patterns to the original theme. Their texture continues into the *b* portion of the variation, but now the motif of five notes has changed to another pitch level, emphasizing the harmonic shift mentioned earlier. When the *a* phrase of the form returns, the motif also returns to its former pitch level. But now it is articulated by high and low instruments at the same time.

Variation 2:
Piu vivace
("still faster")

The momentum quickens still more and the key changes to minor. The five-note motif of Variation 1 is reduced to a shorter jabbing pattern of only two notes. It still articulates the sectional boundaries of the form. The melodic weight of this variation is carried by woodwinds playing a skipping rhythm that can be traced directly back to the first two notes of the theme. Strings accompany these foreground patterns with a rich web of figures. Throughout the variation a provocative quiet is interrupted by spasmodic bursts of the two-note motif. The recurrence of this pronounced loud-soft contrast provides a main element of unity for the variation, along with the skipping rhythms of the woodwinds.

Variation 3:
Con moto
("with motion")

This variation brings a return to a major key and to the more pastoral quality of the theme. Here smooth lines are fashioned into a chorale-like exchange between woodwinds and strings. The motif that was prominent as a binder in Variations 1 and 2 has vanished; a resigned calm prevails. A tighter melodic correspondence can be heard between this variation and the theme, although the rhythm does not resemble the skipping pattern of Variation 2. A gentle undulating contour in the melodies ensures the quiet composure Brahms clearly wished to transmit to his listener.

Variation 4:
Andante con moto
("medium walking tempo, with motion")

The calm of Variation 3 deepens to a pervasive nervous mystery. Aside from a return to a minor key, the nervous quality is partially a result of an interesting rhythmic counterpoint that dominates the texture. The principal melodic character is projected by a slow line that is first played by oboe and horn. This is accompanied by a serpentine figure in the strings that moves twice as fast. Since the slower melody establishes the melancholic tempo, the more active but subdued accompaniment suggests underlying tension. The combination of these two contrasting moods reminds us of the remark, "He's cool on the outside but boiling on the inside."

Aside from its interesting emotional suggestions, the variation reveals Brahms as a master composer, particularly in the way he creates subtle shifts of texture. The technical name for what he does here is *invertible counterpoint*. We can illustrate it easily by showing the way the texture of the initial *a* is turned upside down when it is repeated.

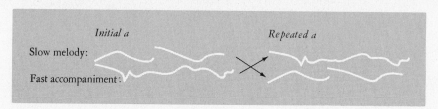

Example 10.2   Inverted texture in Variation I

Similar rearrangements of melodic layers occur in every section of this variation, imparting one of its main elements of continuity.

Variation 5:
Vivace ("very fast")

Things are brightening. The nervous melancholy of Variation 4 yields to a sprightly dance. This happier rhythm, still in the triple meter of the preceding variation, is combined with a change back to the major key of the theme and Variations 1 and 3. The background perpetual motion of Variation 4 shifts to the fore; only rarely does the constant triple rhythm of the opening disappear. Over these unflagging pecks Brahms weaves a falling staccato melody. Although it is based on the same steady rhythm, it sometimes delays just long enough to throw a wrenching syncopation into the flow. The diagram of Example 10.3 shows how this displacement of rhythm comes about.

Example 10.3   Syncopation in the melody of Variation 5

Loud chords interrupt the nimble running motion of this variation in a way reminiscent of the stark contrasts of Variation 4. These disappear from later stages, and a gradual decay sets in that leads to a final delicate peck of sound.

Variation 6 : Vivace

To this point each variation has relied mainly on dialogues between woodwinds and strings for its basic character. Suddenly Brahms seems to remember that his orchestra has four eloquent horns. He turns to them as the leaders of a blustery march, to sing out the slightly camouflaged melody of the original theme. This marks quite a departure from the previous variations, in which melodic relationships with the theme were not easy to hear. Note how the principal pitches of the horn melody correspond to the original theme. (These are doubled by the accompaniment in the violins.)

Example 10.4   Pitch duplications of the Theme and Variation 6

The orchestra sparkles in this variation. Although the trumpets still function as little more than bugles, the piccolo adds its flashy brilliance at the top of the texture, and the contrabassoon adds its gruff resonance at the bottom. The enriched orchestra of Beethoven's Symphony No. 5 has now become the status quo for the nineteenth-century composer.

Variation 7 : Grazioso ("gracefully")

The succession of six variations to this point has cut an ebb and flow of fast and slow, calm and tension. Variation 7 marks a decided decline. It is a gentle wisp whose soothing atmosphere is especially provocative after the bluster of Variation 6. Woodwinds and strings resume their dual leading roles, the blustery horns of Variation 6 all but forgotten in the supporting parts. The melodic kinship to the theme evident in the previous variation vanishes in the dancing lyricism of the melodies here, but the basic harmonic scheme and formal layout remain, true to their parentage.

The rhythm of this variation is reminiscent of an old Italian dance, the *Siciliano*. But true to Brahms's flair for rhythmic upsets, there is occasionally a gentle intrusion. Called *hemiola*, this kind of rhythmic jolt occurs within the latter two-thirds of the variation. Having established the triple rhythm consisting of *long–short, long–short* (♩ ♪♩ ♩), the music suddenly will switch to a duple pattern that consumes the same amount of time, a pattern of *long–long–long* (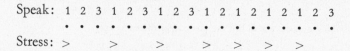). The effect is that of a rhythmic sliding, where solid footholds have been expected.

We can produce the same effect as Brahms's hemiola by setting up a series of accents and then contradicting them by a different pattern of stresses. Speak out the following series of "pulses" with a steady rhythm and you will see what is meant by hemiola when you get into the middle of the series.

Speak: 1 2 3 1 2 3 1 2 3 1 2 1 2 1 2 1 2 1 2 3

Stress: >   >   >   >   >   >   >

Variation 8:
Presto non troppo ("not too fast")

Although it is the final variation, this wispy rustle of sound does not conclude the whole work. In fact, its role at this point is to baffle the listener. It is a tentative, even ambiguous gush of sounds that leads the listener to expect more clear-cut musical images to follow. And they do, in the finale.

The clouded atmosphere has simple causes. The definite meters of previous variations are not present; a constant flow of tones of equal duration is broken by only occasional pauses. These pauses are the only rhythmic accents. The prevailing minor key is not stamped in clearly by the winding melodies; the unbroken hush yields no strong sense of what the end goal might be. The variation is an enigmatic breeze that seems unable to grow into a real wind.

Within this muted enigma Brahms hides a technical feat that deserves comment. The principal melodic phrase seems to bear no detectable kinship to the original theme. But in fact it does, albeit that of a "second cousin." The variation is dominated by a call-and-response ordering between strings and woodwinds that incorporates two versions of the same melodic pattern. One is the inversion of the other.

Example 10.5 Inversional relationship between patterns

This dialogue of reversed contours persists through the variation until the two are sounded together during the last sections.

Example 10.6 Final measures, Variation 8, piccolo and cello only

Listening carefully, you can detect an ingenious correspondence between the melodies seen in Example 10.6 and the original theme. The matching pitches are circled in both parts of Example 10.7 to make clear where duplications occur.

Example 10.7 Piccolo part, Variation 8, compared to theme

Finale: Andante ("medium, or walking tempo")

The foregoing theme and eight variations demands a fitting conclusion. Brahms provides it in a grandiose "coda" that is twice as long as the theme and any one variation. This finale's broad conception and massive texture provide a general summing-up as well as a sense of return for the whole work. Its melodies suggest, then directly restate, parts of the beginning theme. Most interesting of all, however, is the internal structure of this concluding part. It is a series of continuous short variations over a repeated theme.

This variation process in the finale reveals another link between Brahms and his past. It is called *passacaglia* ("Passacah'leea"), and its origins lie in the seventeenth and early eighteenth centuries. Beginning as a short statement in the bass, the same melody is repeated again and again as an unwavering anchor for the patterns that unfold above it.

Brahms's passacaglia works through seventeen statements of its short theme, or *cantus firmus*, before it erupts into the eighteenth. There it turns out to be a stately version of the original theme, a climactic rounding off of the entire composition.

11

PRELUDE TO
"THE AFTERNOON OF A FAUN"

Claude Debussy (1862–1918)

BACKGROUND*

In assessing the value of music of the past, historians often favor composers who can claim one of two distinctions: (1) providing the final synthesis of what has gone before them, or (2) initiating something quite new that influences the future. Claude Debussy lays claim to the latter distinction. Even composers of today acknowledge a debt to the fresh musical path he cut in history. In fact, if one can establish a border between the "old" and the "modern" in music, Debussy's works play a leading role in setting the line.

Like his predecessor Berlioz, Debussy was a Frenchman with pride. For him, the essence of nineteenth-century musical revolution was a reaction against the heaviness and the formalism of German music. His was an extension of the Romantic ideal, but it was a turn to refinement, subtlety, and understatement.

Like most revolutions, Debussy's was not a war waged alone. It is curious, however, that his main compatriots were writers and painters rather than musicians. Through this artistic interaction of late nineteenth-century Paris the word "impressionism" entered history's vocabulary. It is not an easy word to understand. It, like the music and painting it represents, is suggestive rather than definitive. Perhaps it is best understood as it relates to painting.

---

*Additional discussion of Debussy and his music can be found in Chapter 36.

Illustration 11.1
Claude Debussy

Look at the reproduction of Claude Monet's painting in Illustration 11.2. What do you think the painter wished to communicate through it? Was his intention to provide an architectural record, to show us what a railway station was like in France around 1860? Was it to cause us to marvel at the power of locomotives, or to arouse our excitement for a trip on a train?

Illustration 11.2
Claude Monet, *La Gare de St. Lazare*, 1877 (Louvre)

None of these motives seems likely. Monet's scene is too engulfed in smoky haze even to give these intentions a chance of realization. Rather, the scene is an *impression* of a unique split-second in time. It is an attempt to capture on canvas the very atmosphere that resides there for the viewer. Outlines are vague. Objects are barely separated in a diaphanous moment of history. The light, the atmosphere, and the objects will never appear *just that way* again. And this is the essence of Impressionism. It is a fragile art.

In 1867 Monet (Mōnay') exhibited a painting called *Impression: Sun Rising.* Art critics immediately turned the first word of his title against him. Perhaps he was incapable, they suggested, of creating an art of more substance than mere impressions. But Monet's very substance *was* the impression, and his fresh insight was absorbed by a host of contemporaries who cultivated the luminously hazy viewpoint. Pissarro, Manet, Degas, and Renoir were all, in their individual ways, persuaded by this passion for the momentary glimpse, the fleeting shifts of reality as nature's light reveals it to the eye.

A parallel interest was shared by leading French poets of the day. Called Symbolists, they were inspired by the haunting poetry of the American Edgar Allan Poe (1809–49). Their fundamental goal was a direct poetic expression untainted by intellectual complications. They wanted to create a suggestion of mood rather than a description of details. They labored to provide "images" rather than definitions, "symbols" rather than the hard-core thing. One of these poets, Paul Verlaine, stated their manifesto when he remarked that "There is nothing more dear than the gray song, where the indefinite meets the precise."

Verlaine and his literary brethren, Baudelaire, Rimbaud, and Mallarmé, were obsessed with the romantic's desire to "make music through poetry." It was only natural that a talented young pianist-composer, such as Debussy, would be taken in by their heady talk.

DEBUSSY'S LIFE

He was born in suburban Paris in the town of St. Germain-en-Laye. His parents were storekeepers, of modest means and without a trace of musical lineage. His conscious personal attachment to Paris and his affectation of a "dandy"'s role during later years reflect the reaction of a boy born to a humble home on the outskirts of a great city.

Debussy's musical flair erupted early. A woman of considerable musical sophistication, Mme. Maute de Fleurville, took him as a piano student when he was eight. She was not an ordinary teacher; she had been the pupil of the great Polish composer-pianist Frédéric Chopin, she was a friend of the German opera composer Richard Wagner, and perhaps more relevant to our story, she was the mother-in-law of the poet Paul Verlaine. Her careful work with Debussy enabled him to enter the Paris Conservatory in 1873 at the age of eleven.

Debussy's years at the Conservatory were not altogether blissful. He repeatedly proved he had an instinctive musical fluency, yet his independent ways and mocking sense of humor did not win friends among his teachers. When he was fifteen he managed a second prize in piano playing, but the Conservatory's supreme award in composition, the *Prix de Rome*, eluded him until 1884. He finally won this coveted badge of promise with a composition for voices and orchestra, *The Prodigal Son*. (His now deceased compatriot Berlioz had met success only with his fourth try for the prize.)

As is true of many great creative artists, Debussy's most valuable educational moments happened out of school. In 1880 he met the widow of a rich industrialist, a Mme. von Meck. Hired as a kind of musical nanny for the widow's children, he was a member of the household's string trio and played four-hand piano music with his wealthy employer. Most important, Mme. von Meck was a veritable nineteenth-century jet-setter, and the job's main attraction for the youthful Claude-Achille was its reward of travel. In his first year he accompanied the family through Italy and Switzerland. During a later term with the family, in 1884, he was in Russia, where he met the renowned composer Tchaikovsky, a close friend of Mme. von Meck. These travels gave Debussy an early look at the world outside France and a chance to taste a broader musical diet than Paris could offer.

In 1885 his long-sought prize in composition took him to Rome, where he could have spent four years composing and absorbing the atmosphere of the Holy City. But he disliked almost everything there. He cut his prize stay short, returning to Paris for good early in 1887. Except for sporadic tours as a conductor and pianist after fame had come his way, he remained there for the rest of his life.

The artistic and literary influences that led to Debussy's identification as an impressionist—a term he resented—began after his return from the aborted *Prix de Rome*. He joined the artistic circles of the city, acquired a mistress, and became a man consciously in search of his destiny as a composer.

The musical influences on his works were varied. They included the music of the Russian Mussorgsky and the German Wagner, as well as models closer to home like Saint-Saëns, Massenet, and Fauré. His admiration for Wagner waned in 1889. While on a pilgrimage to hear the German's operas in Bayreuth he concluded that the man was a musical genius who lacked dramatic and philosophical horse sense. This turn was the great fork in Debussy's professional path. It symbolizes his open break with Germanic tradition, a conscious effort to find his own French way.

The composition that best reveals his early individuality is a setting of Gabriel Rosetti's *The Blessed Damozel,* for soprano, women's chorus, and orchestra. This he completed in 1888 as proof to his teachers at the Conservatory that his brief stay in Rome had not been wasted. Although the work reveals Debussy's acquaintance with the music of some established composers, the Conservatory's evaluation committee remarked upon its "systematic vagueness" and "lacking of form."

Debussy clearly was not deterred by the committee's judgment. By this time he knew what Hector Berlioz had learned much earlier: the Conservatory upheld a reactionary (Germanic) point of view. Except for a period of creative lapse at the outset of World War I in 1914, he composed works for solo piano, orchestra, string quartet, solo voice, a variety of chamber groups, and an opera. All of these were in a style that his earlier critics would have found systematically vague and "lacking of form."

As a whole, his music is not the stream of vague sounds one might expect from an overdose of impressionism. What most of his early critics found wanting in his music were the clear expository statements and formal outlines of composers of the classic tradition. But this is not formlessness. Debussy associated the *Exposition–Development–Recapitulation* process with a non-French tradition. He wished to break with that tradition, but his critics simply lacked the foresight to acknowledge that the break was even possible, much less desirable. They probably found only an egotist's ravings in Debussy's declaration that the four-movement plan bequeathed by the Viennese masters was an obsolete formula, "a legacy of clumsy, falsely imposed traditions."

Debussy's music is exquisitely shaped. At times it is even marked by the form types of the past. But his passion for a new sound naturally led to a musical organization that demanded a new set of priorities from its listeners. His themes are fragments rather than melodies. His harmonies are ends in themselves rather than a succession of pegs upon which to hang a key. His rhythms sometimes defy meter. His desire was to tread within an atmosphere rather than to hurtle toward a preordained musical goal.

Debussy was an enigmatic personality, a man whose true nature seems more elusive the more one learns about him. This may be true because he appears never to have outgrown the feeling that he was living beyond the intellectual and cultural inheritance of his birth and education. His letters, essays he wrote for newspapers, and reports about him from contemporaries lead the reader to conclude that he was forever in quest of "improving himself."

The personal enigma may have been deepened by his long battle with the cancer that finally killed him. Discovered in 1909, the growth kept him in pain for his remaining nine years and curtailed his professional activity. In spite of the discomfort, he managed to concertize until the beginning of the Great War, when royalties from published works provided the income for a modest life. A second operation in 1917 left him all but immobile, and he did not leave his house from then until the time of his death, which came during a siege by German guns on Paris, March 1918.

Compared with the heralded German composers of the eighteenth and nineteenth centuries, Debussy's musical output was small. Few of his individual works are on the grandiose scale we often associate with "great art." His strength lay in the miniature, where sensuous, refined delicacy carries the weight of the musical message. It is said that Debussy was an excellent pianist but that his concerts were maddening because he played so softly the audience beyond the first few rows of seats could not hear him. This intimacy prevails in his compositions too. Even his largest orchestral works enthrall by their quiet shadings of timbre, rarely utilizing the full sound available from the combined instruments. In this way he taught the world to hear sounds in a new way, just as his painter-contemporaries unfolded a fresh universe of color.

Illustration 11.3
The modern harp joined the symphonic orchestra toward the end of the 19th century. Debussy's *Prelude to "The Afternoon of a Faun"* capitalizes on this instrument's rich variety of sounds. (Suzanne Thomas, harp)

THE PRELUDE

This is program music in a very general and loose way; it evokes an atmosphere rather than describes an event. Its title links it directly to Stéphane Mallarmé's *L'Après-midi d'un faune*, a poem finished in 1876. Debussy had envisioned a more ambitious composition that would have encompassed more scenes of the poem, but the Prelude, finished in 1894, ended aspirations of this more extensive treatment.

According to Debussy, the Prelude represents a general musical impression of the poem. Consistent with the point of view of Impressionist painters and Symbolist poets, he was not one to attempt story-telling in music. He wished only to create a series of moods that fit the emotional overtones of the poem. In writing of the Prelude Debussy once said that "...if [the] music were to follow [the poem] more closely it would run out of breath, like a dray horse competing for the Grand Prize with a thoroughbred."

Mallarmé's poem is the sensuous evocation of a primitive scene. A faun—half man, half goat—awakes in the woods at dawn from a provocative dream inhabited by three lovely nymphs.

Or was it a dream?

He cannot be sure. But he would like to make the nymphs permanent fixtures in his forest home! He launches into a soliloquy that rambles, mainly around the pleasures of chasing pretty girls. He eventually succumbs to a noonday nap and, he hopes, the return of the nymphs.*

From the beginning of Debussy's Prelude the sounds are soft, the pace hesitant. There is a hushed feeling of intimacy that avoids forward thrust. Throughout the work there is an aura of enchantment produced by shimmering sounds that are beautiful in themselves, without reference to how they might function within the total musical structure. The listener is led from one gorgeous mixture of sound to another, each calculated to create its own atmospheric little world.

A part of the music's charm is harmonic as well as timbral. Debussy's chords are of slightly higher density† than those of the Haydn–Mozart palette. They usually consist of four pitch classes, but they still are relatively consonant. Perhaps even more telling in effect is the way these chords only dimly suggest a tonality. This tonal vagueness was a principal point in Debussy's declaration of musical independence. He claimed, as he once reported in a letter, no "reverence for the key." The Prelude frequently glides from one hinted tonic center, or key, to another, like a

---

*A complete translation of the poem can be found in *Claude Debussy,* William W. Austin, ed., *Prelude to "The Afternoon of a Faun,"* (New York: W. W. Norton and Company, Inc., 1970), p. 23.

†Harmonic density is discussed in Chapter 5.

breeze passing through a stand of trees. In some passages the very notion of tonality is beside the point, for the current sound is its own organizational rationale rather than a mere link within a larger chain.

The chords of Debussy's music are sometimes interesting in themselves. The fourth sounding of the principle theme occurs over a chord whose density is much higher than we hear in music of earlier times. It is a sound that became typical of Debussy's harmonies. Example 11.1 shows a simplified version of this passage to illustrate its chords of relatively high density.

Example 11.1   The fourth sounding, principal theme

(6 pitch classes)

Rhythm is equally free. Many passages transmit only a ripple of motion without creating periodic accents that might be mistaken as meter. This is "floating music" rather than "goal-directed," and its lack of rigid rhythmic flow and decisive key is the primary cause of its dreamlike state.

The Prelude is not formless (which would be the same as saying that it doesn't make musical sense!), as some of Debussy's critics reported. What led them astray was the succession of sections that adhered to no traditional formal plan and which lacked the variational or developmental processes of the past. The assumed need of these processes and forms was just the point of view Debussy had damned when he made the remark mentioned earlier about "clumsy, falsely imposed traditions." One artist's nourishment, he knew, could be another man's poison.

If sheer size is a criterion of greatness, the Prelude is not great music. It runs only about nine minutes and can be called "big in sound" during only short periods of that time. The dynamic marking *f* (meaning *forte*, or loud) is rarely used within the score. The orchestra is geared to this more intimate style, dispensing with all brass except for the soft resonance of four horns. A pair of harps is used, and the delicacy of the final measures is spiced by tiny "antique cymbals," whose high-pitched articulations— if they are heard at all—confirm the slow resolution into a final wispy chord.

There are many small sections within the single movement, but there are few strong contrasts. Two main considerations must be made in achieving a conception of the movement's overall form. First, toward the end there is an obvious return to the beginning theme; and second, there are only four emphatic cadences within the full nine minutes (and one of these is at the end). They are marked by asterisks in the mapping shown next.

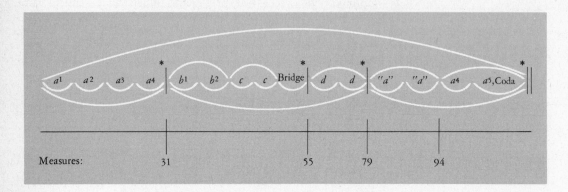

Example 11.2   Mapping of the *Prelude*

The many parts linked by arches in our mapping may seem confusing at first, but these many relationships merely reflect the occasional indecisiveness of the music. One such occurrence lies toward the end, where Example 11.2 shows two short sections, "*a*" followed by *a*⁴. These sections contain the same melodic and timbral characteristics, but "*a*" is a very staid and stable version of that opening flute theme; only *a*⁴ projects a fully convincing sense of return to the beginning. Because of this, the two "*a*" parts function as a kind of *premature return*, lacking the harmonic vagueness that dominates the Prelude's opening.

In view of the various ways sections are interconnected, it is not enough to describe this work as a simple *A B A* form. That conception—without ample qualifications—destroys the obvious fluidity of events that Debussy created within the middle parts. A more accurate conception takes account of the general procession of themes as they occur, but within a series of large musical gestures or "states."

A: Opening Gesture
   Flute melody sounded four times, each varied in harmony and texture. Ends with decisive cadence.

B: Interlude #1 (b, m. 31)

More active rhythms, new timbres and harmonies; improvisatory effect through development of short motifs. Ends with decisive cadence.

C: Arrival Section (d, m. 55)

Implied "goal" of the work. Short lyric melody with stable tonality. Static, thick texture; relatively clear pulse and meter.

D: Interlude #2, or Premature Return ("a", m. 79)

Altered version of opening melody with stable harmony, static texture; a kind of "declamation" that previews the more convincing return of *a* that follows.

E: Closing Gesture (a⁴, m. 94)

Return to harmonic, melodic, and textural make-up of beginning theme; strong sense of recapitulation.

One pertinent question remains for those who wonder how impressionism in music can be related in any meaningful way to the Impressionism of painting. Music is sound in time. How can a composer duplicate the split-second uniqueness painters achieved with their blurred impressions of single moments?

Indeed, the opening section of the Prelude provides one interesting clue about how musical sounds might suggest the "play of light" that typifies the paintings of the Impressionists. Each time the flute's opening melody returns it is bathed in a fresh new tonal environment. Each new sounding is a unique manifestation of the one "object," the flute's sensuous theme. The whimsical play of light on a real-world object is thus imitated in the play of harmonic colors that surround the single melodic pattern.

12

THE UNANSWERED QUESTION

Charles Ives (1874–1954)

BACKGROUND

Claude Debussy's break of the Germanic hold on nineteenth-century art music was not made easily, in spite of Berlioz's preparation of the ground. His challenge came when the Germans Liszt and Wagner were established as spokesmen for "Music of the Future," and was paralleled in other major countries of that period, in Russia, Norway, England, and even in the United States. A birdseye view of the late nineteenth century bares a landscape of continuing nationalism, a scene dominated by composers who wished to produce music that could induce a sense of a land and a people.

Charles Ives accomplished an American musical independence without many of his contemporaries' knowing about it. He was a curiously interesting figure who popped on the scene a bit "before his time." But he left a fascinating heritage that remains vigorously influential today. He was the first composer of art music in this country who displayed an individuality comparable to that of a Debussy or a Beethoven; he was the first composer of symphonic music that is peculiarly American.

THE AMERICAN SCENE

The State of Art   Nineteenth-century America was even less ripe than France for a musical revolution. If today we lament the importation of European musicians and artists, we at least can be comforted to realize that matters have improved.

Illustration 12.1
Charles Ives

In America of 1890 the very word "art" suggested an exotic commodity manufactured only at points east of our Atlantic coast.

There were many concert societies in the large cities of this country, but they were dedicated to the rechewing of music composed by Italians, Poles, Germans, and English. The vitality of the American pioneer had not yet seeped into the veins of those who could compose extended musical works for the concert hall. And yet there was a rich folk-lode everywhere. The embryonic shapes of a native art music were incubated in the hymn singing of rural church meetings, the rhythmic improvisations of minstrels, the plaint of Negro spirituals, and even the sentimental ballads of Stephen Foster. But these buddings of an American family tree were beneath the dignity of those who looked wistfully to Europe for all that was "cultural" and "artistic."

Curiously, there was no shortage of great writers in America at this time. After Poe, whom we mentioned earlier as a model for the Symbolist poets, there came a string of giants in literature. Walt Whitman, Herman Melville, Emily Dickinson, and Mark Twain prepared the way for a later crop headed by Theodore Dreiser, Stephen Crane, and Henry James.

Painting in America was similarly blessed with native individualists —men like Winslow Homer, Thomas Eakins, Sanford Gifford, George Inness, and Albert Ryder. Perhaps most symptomatic of a native awakening in the arts was the birth, in Buffalo, Chicago, and New York, of a modern urban architecture. That beginning was made by men such as Louis Sullivan, H. H. Richardson, Richard Hunt, and Frank Lloyd Wright.

**Social and
Political Reforms**

In a way, the United States came of age as a nation during this period. The Civil War of 1861–65 was its bloody puberty rite. Despite a vast racial diversity, the individual American citizen gradually was growing more urbane, more like his fellows in dress, manners, and thought. A single movement that can be seen as both an effect and a cause of this growing uniformity was the mushrooming of social clubs throughout the country between 1868 and 1888. From a struggling lower and middle class came fraternal organizations such as the Elks, Woodmen, and Moose. Patriotic souls, intent on preserving a sense of their heritage, were solidified into the Sons and Daughters of the American Revolution, Colonial Dames, Mayflower Descendents, and Daughters of the Confederacy. A newborn political and social identity among southern blacks, legally freed by the Emancipation Proclamation, was reflected in new organizations like the United Order of African Ladies and Gentlemen and the Brothers and Sisters of Pleasure and Prosperity. As a means of preserving a religious identity amidst all of this secular clubbing, American Catholics founded the Knights of Columbus.

Whatever their individual aims and methods, all of these groups were powerful forces in welding together a society that, for the first time, showed signs of a public unity. A feeling of national solidarity and thrust was evident in the nation's response to one of its least excusable wars, the war with Spain. That brief conflict erupted over the sinking of the battleship Maine in Havana, Cuba, in February of 1898. More than any other event, this was the cue for the United States' entry as a power into world politics.

President McKinley personally enunciated a national attitude during the same year. He told a Methodist congregation that this country's new responsibility must be to "take them all and educate them and uplift them and civilize them and Christianize them." He was referring to the people of the Philippines, but his words foreshadowed a general foreign policy that would persist for several decades.

And this was the immediate world of Charles Ives.

THE COMPOSER

Ives was the epitome of the crusty New Englander. His character is a clue to how he was able to launch an American music before America was ready for it. Born in Danbury, Connecticut, he was immersed in the writings of Henry David Thoreau, who taught and practiced a total kind of self-realization.

His philosophical guide was Ralph Waldo Emerson, who wrote the rules for American self-reliance and intellectual honesty. His personal application of what he learned from these two men led him to forego the full life of a composer. As Ives saw it, a man who composes music for a living is too much influenced by what will sell, so that he ends up writing music to please others rather than himself. And thus his music, as Ives so quaintly put it, "goes 'ta-ta' for money."

Instead, Ives entered the New York world of business after finishing at Yale. By 1916 he was head of one of the largest insurance companies in the country, but he still composed music on weekends, at night, and during vacations.

His musical success was inversely proportional to his business success. With few exceptions, performers, conductors, and other composers condemned his scores as "unplayable," clearly products of "ignorance rather than talent." Frequent rebuffs led him to adopt a hands-off attitude toward the professional world of music and musicians. His works were rarely played, and then without adequate rehearsal and understanding. At times he even hired musicians to perform his compositions just to check the accuracy of what his imagination had led him to write.

The double life of composer-executive was not easy. In 1918 Ives suffered a permanently damaged heart after an exhausting effort on behalf of fund drives to finance America's role in World War I. From that time until his death in 1954, he composed no further major compositions.

Ives's genius stemmed from two primary virtues: (1) an insatiable curiosity about sounds, and (2) an ability to hear the music of his surroundings with an honest ear. For these reasons he was able to infuse his works with an authentic flavor unmatched by other composers of his time. His American contemporaries, like Edward MacDowell, were trained in European conservatories. They filtered the sounds of their own culture through tainted ears.

Ives could savor the unique beauty of a hymn sung out of tune by untrained voices; he could relish the piquancy of ragged rhythms and wrong pitches played by itinerant musicians. These were the reality of rugged America that was overlooked by less honest minds. Like Walt Whitman before him, Ives took America for what it *was* rather than for what Europeans thought it *ought to be*. Ives fondly quoted Emerson's conclusion that "We have listened too long to the courtly muses of Europe."

And so between 1896 and 1918 Ives wrote his personal testaments to an American music without hope of public acclaim, without any expectation of financial return. His uncanny musical imagery and his passion for native authenticity led him to incorporate new techniques in his music ahead of his European counterparts. Some of the "modern" elements attributed for years to Arnold Schoenberg (music without a sense of key) and Igor Stravinsky (two keys sounding together) had been tried by Ives while those gentlemen were still composing old-fashioned music. But in spite of these technical advances, his music was rooted in the tunes of country fairs, Protestant hymns, Saturday-night fiddlers, and patriotic songs. He even blended these earthy treasures into some of his compositions.

Between 1896 and 1916 he composed four symphonies. Today these are not performed as frequently as some of his more openly programmatic works for orchestra. His *A Symphony: Holidays* is based on "recollections of a boy's holidays in a Connecticut country town." Completed in 1913, its four movements are titled *Washington's Birthday*, *Decoration Day*, *Fourth of July* and *Thanksgiving Day*. It joins the *Three Places in New England* and *Three Outdoor Scenes* in establishing Ives as the spokesman for musical Americana.

Between 1884 and 1921 Ives composed more than 114 songs. He used texts written by himself and his wife as well as selections he combed from Keats, Stevenson, Browning, and Landor and some less renowned poets.

America discovered Ives through his Sonata No. 2 for Piano, the the *Concord* Sonata. This came about only through the dedicated efforts of the pianist John Kirkpatrick. Kirkpatrick performed this monumental evocation of New England in New York's Town Hall in January of 1939. Ives was sixty-five that year, rather too weathered to be hailed as a newly-discovered prodigy. But the *Concord* turned the tide. Apparently a pre-World War II America was able to catch the unique drum tap of its first real composer, where earlier times had turned only deaf ears.

In 1947 his Third Symphony was awarded the Pulitzer Prize for music, and by 1951 the New York Philharmonic was able to muster a performance of the Second Symphony—exactly half a century after it was composed! We cannot doubt that Ives was touched by these belated recognitions, but there is no reason to believe that the pomp and circumstance of overdue fame turned sweet his long-felt bitterness.

His own statements reveal a man who had chosen a path, kept to it, and repented not a whit because others ignored his message. He was merely paraphrasing Henry Thoreau when he once remarked that "Forty thousand souls at a ball game does not, necessarily, make baseball the highest expression of spiritual emotion." That forty thousand did not applaud his music could not turn his stubborn head from its goal.

Ives's character shines through clearly in a series of essays he wrote as a gloss for the *Concord* Sonata. Called *Essays Before a* Sonata,* (though the sonata was composed first), this baring of the soul and mind tells a lot about his motivations as a composer. In justifying his penchant for quoting from "lowbrow" sources, he says:

---

*These essays can be found in *Essays Before a Sonata*, ed. Howard Boatwright (New York: W. W. Norton and Company, Inc., 1970).

The man . . . may find a deep appeal in the simple but acute Gospel hymns of the New England "camp meetin" of a generation or so ago. He finds in them—some of them—a vigor, a depth of feeling, a natural-soil rhythm, a sincerity—emphatic but inartistic—which, in spite of a vociferous sentimentality, carries him nearer the "Christ of the people" than does the *Te Deum* of the greatest cathedral.*

A similar salty tang flavors some of his references to the famous composers of his day. He was particularly wary of conscious mannerisms in all things, particularly in music, and he was convinced that Debussy's music was more manner than substance. He once suggested that it could have had more substance if Debussy had "hoed corn or sold newspapers for a living."

His condemnations of the grandiose works of his German contemporaries were equally emphatic and tart. For them, he allowed that "magnifying the dull into the colossal produces a kind of 'comfort'—the comfort of a woman who takes more pleasure in the fit of fashionable clothes than in a healthy body."†

THE UNANSWERED QUESTION

The Unanswered Question was composed between 1906 and 1908. It makes no attempt to depict American images as such. He at first planned it as a pair of musical "contemplations." It would be called *A Contemplation of a Serious Matter*, or *The Unanswered Perennial Question*. In typical good humor, Ives planned that its sequel would be called *A Contemplation of Nothing Serious*, or *Central Park in the Dark, In the Good Old Summertime*.

This work is more direct as program music than Debussy's *Afternoon of a Faun*. Its simple intertwining of form and "program" make it a most successful evocation of extra-musical associations. We discussed this program briefly in Chapter 5. There our concern was limited to harmony. Since our interest now is the work as a whole, we shall review and amplify what was said there (page 58).

Ives clearly establishes three bodies of sound. Strings represent "the silences of the Druids—Who Know See and Hear Nothing." In performance, they are to be spatially separated from the two other sound bodies, the trumpet and the four flutes. The strings play their dirge-like patterns very softly throughout. They evoke the hymn-like sound of a distant church organ, their timbre subdued by the use of mutes. The solo trumpet's haunting pattern represents "The Perennial Question of Existence." Its motif is repeated almost unchanged over and over again. The four

*Epilogue of *Essays Before a Sonata*, p. 80.
†p. 83

flutes enact the search for "The Invisible Answer," their scurrying for "truth" growing more animated and frustrated each time they supply an "answer" to the trumpet's query. As Ives tells it in the Preface to his score,

> "The Fighting Answerers," as time goes on, and after a "secret" conference, seem to realize a futility, and begin to mock "The Question"— the strife is over for the moment. After they disappear, "The Question" is asked for the last time, and "The Silences" are heard beyond in "Undisturbed Solitude."*

Ives did not share some of his fellow composers' faith in the powers of program music. To him, Richard Strauss's notion that a composer might be able to "portray the breaking of a teacup" through the sounds of an orchestra was pure bunkum. Ives frequently vented his own worries about just what should or could be the relationship between a musical sound and a non-musical idea. In his *Essays Before a Sonata* he provides the following observation about how much and to what extent music can portray the intricacies of an extramusical world.†

> The outside characteristics . . . are obvious to mostly anyone. A child knows a strain of joy from one of sorrow. Those a little older know the diginified from the frivolous . . . But where is the definite expression of late spring against early summer—of happiness against optimism?

The extra-musical idea of the *Unanswered Question* is too simple to demand such subtle shadings of meaning. And thus its success as program music. We could not deduce the poetic ideas of all-knowing Druids, Questions of Existence, and Unsuitable Answers just from hearing the music. But once those ideas are known, the music makes sense to us as a carrier of their meaning.

There are many fascinating things about this beautiful work. We shall discuss only a few. Perhaps most evident from the beginning is the unique form produced by the relatively static, "unchanging" strings, the unyielding "question" of the trumpet, and the progressively more frantic "answers" of the flutes. The result is a strange mixture of strophic and processive form, as we defined those types in Chapter 2. The obsessiveness of repetition is tempered by the variations of the flutes' patterns and by their growth in loudness and tempo that subsides only after the last hopeless stab at an answer.

Also interesting is the harmony, which we touched upon in Chapter 5. Compare the harmonic style of this piece with music written by any other composer around 1908 and the force of Ives's creative genius can be

---

*From the first page of the score.
†From the Epilogue, *Essays Before a Sonata*, pp. 70–71.

appreciated. Before Schoenberg had composed music that was without key (*atonal*) and before Stravinsky had combined two keys at once (*polytonality*), Ives had demonstrated both in this short work. In *The Unanswered Question* the flutes play patterns that are in themselves atonal and which defy the stony anchorage of the string chords in the background.

Even the trumpet's questioning is conducted with a motif that contradicts the simple hymn chords of the strings. Ives's attitude toward tonality was far less emotional than that of most of his contemporaries. With typical Yankee simplicity he remarks: "Why tonality as such should be thrown out for good, I can't see. Why it should always be present, I can't see."

In this composition he uses tonality as one means for separating the three "roles" that are vital to his sketchy program. With refreshing directness, he molds his musical materials to achieve an end, to express an idea that is not in itself musical. And this is the crucial goal of program music.

13

CONCERTO FOR ORCHESTRA

Béla Bartók (1881–1945)

BACKGROUND

Though born in Hungary, Bartók spent his adolescence and teenage years in Bratislavia, which is now within Czechoslovakia. A product of the nineteenth century, he is one of the generation of Western composers who produced the "modern music" of the first half of this century. His remote ties were with the music of Beethoven and Brahms, but his style bears links with a circle of nationalists of the century's end, the "Russian Five." These latter composers (Balakirev, Cui, Borodin, Mussorgsky and Rimsky-Korsakov) had transferred Hector Berlioz's orchestral innovations onto an imposing body of works that, with the impressionism of Debussy, paved the way for twentieth-century music.

Bartók was a brilliant pianist and teacher as well as a composer. Perhaps most notable of all, he was an avid collector of authentic folk music, particularly the traditional songs and dances of his native Hungary. Early in the century, teamed with compatriot Zoltán Kodály, he scoured villages of central Europe in search of genuine Slovak music. (He later even made brief forays into Turkey and North Africa.) The spirit of the folk repertory he found in Hungary and Rumania permeates many of his compositions. In some works he uses actual folk tunes as themes.

For nearly thirty years Bartók served on the faculty of the Music Academy in Budapest, his official post being teacher of piano. This posi-

tion provided a respectable professional base, but his major energies were consumed by composing, concertizing, and assembling the five books in which he preserved the melodies found in his folk music research.

His output as a composer was phenomenal. Best known to concert audiences today are his concertos for piano (3), for violin (2), and for viola, large symphonic works like the Concerto for Orchestra, and compositions for smaller ensembles such as the Divertimento for String Orchestra, Music for Two Pianos and Percussion, and Music for String Instruments, Percussion, and Celeste. Of equal quality and popularity are numerous compositions for solo piano; most imposing of all are the six magnificent string quartets that he composed between 1908 and 1939.

One remarkable set of compositions reveals the man as the dedicated composer, pianist, and teacher he was. Called *Mikrokosmos* ("small world"), this is a graded series of small pieces for solo piano collected into six volumes. These compositions extend from works playable by the rank beginner to some of real concert quality. They were composed between 1926 and 1937.

Dramatic forms shared his attention, too, the result being two early ballets (*The Wooden Prince* and *The Miraculous Mandarin*), a one-act opera (*Bluebeard's Castle*), and a large composition of 1930 for double chorus, male soloists, and large orchestra, *Profane Cantata*. The cantata is based on a Hungarian folk legend, and Bartók provided his own text for this compelling work that argues for freedom of the human spirit.

The composer's most famous contemporaries during his fertile life were the Germans Arnold Schoenberg and Paul Hindemith, and the Russian Igor Stravinsky. Like all three, he became a refugee from a warring Europe, settling in the United States in 1940. Here he earned a bare subsistence in New York City, concertizing with his youthful second wife, pianist Ditla Pastztory, and composing music for occasional commissions. His death in 1945 came from an advanced case of leukemia aggravated by bouts with pneumonia. The story of his final months of poverty, illness, and public indifference is tragic, offering further proof that the talented are not always nourished in a way that befits their contributions to the world.

The Concerto for Orchestra was one of his last orchestral compositions. He would later complete his third Piano Concerto, but the Concerto for Viola and Orchestra was left in sketch form by his death, later to be finished by his student Tibor Serly. The orchestral concerto was motivated by a commission from Serge Koussevitzsky, then conductor of the great Boston Symphony Orchestra. The conductor was a champion of new music, and he made the offer in 1943 while visiting Bartók in a New York hospital. The work was completed during the fall of the same year in Asheville, North Carolina, where the composer had gone to convalesce from his most recent hospitalization. It proved to be the catalyst that drew attention to all of his music. But as irony would have it, recognition came at the very end of his life.

GENERAL CHARACTERISTICS OF THE CONCERTO

The Concerto for Orchestra is just that. There is neither single solo instrument nor separate collection of soloists as in the concertos we shall discuss in later chapters. Bartók's composition harks back to the kind of Baroque concerto (early eighteenth century) in which different instruments of the total ensemble are treated soloistically at various times. It is a virtuoso display of the orchestral force, both as a whole and as separate bodies of timbre. Within its five movements every instrumental section has an opportunity individually and collectively to run a gamut of moods, from what Bartók called "the sternness of the first movement . . . to the life-assertion of the last."

Bartók's orchestra is the modern orchestra itemized on page 82, except that it does not incorporate the piano. The treatment of the instruments of the orchestra and the music itself are by no means self-consciously modern. The style is rather nostalgic, at times lushly reminiscent of the nineteenth century. Its sounds are particularly striking for a work composed in 1943, when many serious composers were confident that tonality, melody, and harmony were to be banished from music forever. It is far more conservative in style than any of Bartók's six string quartets, or the Music for String Instruments, Percussion, and Celeste that he had completed seven years earlier. It hints at little of the "barbaric" quality celebrated in some of his music of the twenties and early thirties.

Movement I, Introduzione: Andante non troppo; Allegro vivace

This is not an introduction whose only function is to quiet an audience, as one finds in some classical symphonies. Its tentative opening serves several functions related to the whole five-movement work. It (1) provides a spacious beginning that suggests the breadth of what is to come; (2) introduces a melodic motif that dominates the first movement; and (3) exposes full themes that return later (in the third movement).

This haunting beginning sets a repeated pattern in the bass that slowly grows in tempo, loudness, and depth. It is a cautious windup for the thrust of the first theme that will follow in the *Allegro vivace*, which marks the beginning of the movement's main body. Our mapping of the *Introduzione* alone reveals five small sections.

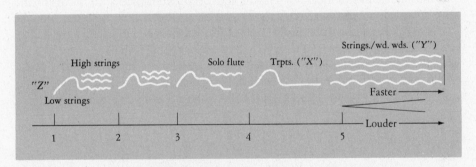

Example 13.1 Layout of the *Introduzione*, Movement I

The beginning pattern, z, sets a melodic motif that pervades the whole movement. Parts x, x', and y are important because they will return in the third movement. It is worth our time to examine these patterns in some detail to understand their melodic primacy. Note that the z pattern is dominated by a melodic skip of a particular size, the interval of the *fourth*.

Example 13.2 Opening bass line, Introduzione

Even more revealing is the pattern of the last four notes in motif z. Reversing the order of its pitches, we see a synopsis of the themes that dominate the first movement.

Example 13.3   Reversal (*retrograde*) of the bass pitches

This opening pattern is the nucleus of the melody that opens the *Allegro vivace* section. If we name the rapid figure that precedes it A^1, call the motif of fourths A^2, and the rather static second theme (essentially a melody of only two pitches!) B, then we have accounted for the principal themes of the whole movement.

Note in Example 13.4 the basic similarities to the sonata form we discussed in the music of Haydn and Beethoven. (Measure numbers and approximate timings are shown in the example for those who might make make use of them.)

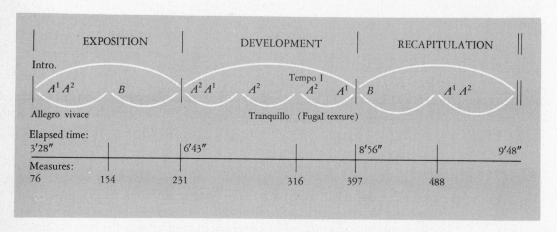

Example 13.4   Mapping of the first movement, Concerto for Orchestra

As our mapping shows, the Development section is dominated by theme A^2. The imitative texture within the latter parts of this section is based on an interesting adaptation of this theme, whose origins might at first elude identification. Note how the theme is derived from a stretched version of motif z.

Example 13.5   Themes of the first movement showing intervals

a. Original theme, Exposition

Allegro vivace

b. Fugue subject, Development (transposed)

The same basic pattern is heard in an upside down version within this highly polyphonic part of the movement.

Example 13.6   Inversion of the fugue subject, Development section

Our last point about this movement has to do with its Recapitulation. It is revealing to speculate why Bartók avoids a more typical return. Why doesn't the *A* theme lead the *B* theme here as in the Exposition? Considering that the entire Development section has been devoted to the *A*¹ theme and various derivations of *A*², it is only fitting that he bypass this "normal" procedure. He opts instead for a return to a less dramatic feeling, with the *B* theme first, as shown in Example 13.6. When the *A* theme does return, its function is really that of finishing off the movement.

**Movement II:
Giuoco delle
coppie ("Game of
Couples")**

We discussed this movement briefly in Chapter 2. There our focus was on its overall form, a large-scale *A B A* design. Here we shall add only a few details that may stimulate your interest in this charming piece of concerted instrumental pairings.

Particularly notable where couples of instruments mark off parts of the *A* section is the way each couple is further differentiated by playing its own special kind of harmony. Bassoons, for example, play their bouncy march tune in a stream of sixths; oboes play their passages in thirds, clarinets in sevenths; flutes intone theirs in fifths; and the muted trumpets are only seconds apart. Example 13.7 illustrates these unique ways of pairing each of the instrument types.

Example 13.7 Harmonic pairings of the instrumental couples

And finally, we must note the clever way Bartók ties the contrasting brass chorale of the movement's middle to the beginning and ending with the sound of the side drum. This instrument provides the beginning sounds, an accompanying rhythm within the chorale, and then, as if returning full circle, the taps of conclusion.

Movement III: Elegia : Andante, non troppo ("not too slow")

This is a mysterious succession of fleeting musical images. At first it can make an impression of unrelated parts. although several sounds and patterns tie it together. It also relates back to the Introduzione of the first movement, for it is here that two themes suddenly reappear. Even the opening string patterns bear kinship with the Introduzione, but now fluttering lines from clarinet, flute, and harp set a more tempestuous tone. The following mapping depicts the main formal divisions and relationships of the movement.

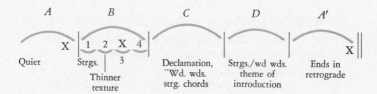

Example 13.8 Mapping of the *Elegia*

Three parts deserve special attention. First is the *x* that occurs in *A*, *B*³, and *A'* sections. It is a curiously static little piccolo melody, essentially a single-pitch line that soars like an unyielding bird above the lower texture. This little pattern acts like a returning thread that helps to hold the separate pieces of loose fabric together.

And second, the theme of B^1 and B^2 is actually the returning melody of the Introduzione. It was sounded earlier, in the first movement, by the trumpets. Here it is played first by the high violins and clarinets.

And third, the main theme of section D is the melody played in the Introduzione by high strings and woodwinds. It returns here in the same kinds of instrumental timbres. After these reminiscences and thematic contrasts, the movement ends in a surprisingly circular return to its opening murmurs, which in their own way are gentle reminders of the opening of the first movement.

Movement IV: Intermezzo interrotto: Allegretto (interrupted intermezzo: fast)

This "interrupted intermezzo" is one of the most charmingly buoyant pieces in the modern orchestral repertory. It is by turns coy, melodramatically romantic, vulgar, and raucous. Yet all of its moods fit together into a convincing succession of images.

Its initial charm lies in its main theme, first played by oboe over a thin string texture of immobile harmonies. Little more than a three-pitch motif of rising contour, it is repeated until it achieves the status of a full-blown melody. It dominates the movement. Its meter is a saucy alternation of duple and triple, which yields a slightly eccentric skipping motion.

Example 13.9   First theme of Intermezzo interrotto and its later inversion

The thin string accompaniment for this first theme gives way to a quite different texture and melodic spirit. Now violas sound a lyrical—almost tear-jerking—new melody accompanied by resonant harp chords. Violins (reinforced by the English horn) take over this romantic line, establishing it as a "heavy" accomplice to the light melody that preceded and, in reduced form, follows. Though brief, the shortened return of the A theme is nonetheless obvious. It returns again as an oboe solo, in the same register and with the same kind of string accompaniment as before.

The *interruption* suggested in the movement's title comes next. In one of the cleverest passages of orchestral music, Bartók leads us from the jumpy three-plus-two rhythm that has prevailed into an "oom-pah-pah" triple, only to transform this comfortable pulsing into a solid "four." And thus enters one of the bawdiest musical images to be heard anywhere, replete with brash trills, skittering runs, vulgar trombone slides, and one of the corniest dance-hall tunes of the century (actually "borrowed" from the Russian composer Dmitri Shostakovitch). All is intentionally satirical. An interruption indeed!

This ribald middle section is further enhanced by the way the movement then affects a full recurrence of the lyrical *B* theme, bypassing for the moment the skittish *A* of the oboe. Theme *A* returns next, but now the upward lilt is reversed to become a falling sigh (as illustrated in Example 13.9). The result is a form of almost mirror symmetry, this gesture bringing the movement to its close.

$$\text{\emph{A} \quad \emph{B} \quad \emph{A'} \quad \emph{C} \quad \emph{B} \quad \emph{A''}}$$

Intro.   ("interruption")

Example 13.10   Mapping of the *Intermezzo Interrotto*

Still another way of viewing the form of this fourth movement would be to conceive of the *B* section as a mere contrast within a larger *A*. Thus the return after the "interruption" is abbreviated, the anticipated *A* returning only after its contrasting foil (*B*) has sounded.

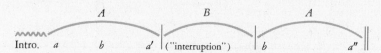

Intro.   *a*   *b*   *a'* ("interruption")   *b*   *a''*

Example 13.11   Alternate conception of form, *Intermezzo*

Either conception makes sense. Only the rather drastic textural, timbral, and melodic contrasts of the lyrical theme (*B* in Example 13.10) lend support to the rondo-like scheme we discussed first.

Movement V: Finale: Pesante; Presto

Like most final movements of large orchestral works, this last movement is a rousing, crashing succession of musical vitality. For the aware listener it also is filled with subtle surprises. Like Beethoven, Bartók sometimes leads his listener astray. A simplified mapping of the overall form is shown next, exposing a sonata form that is only partially appropriate for grasping the complex set of parts found within.

Perhaps the most interesting feature of this movement as a whole is the way it incorporates the developmental and return features of sonata form. Its developmental sections are devoted entirely to pyrotechnics drawn from the closing theme of the Exposition.

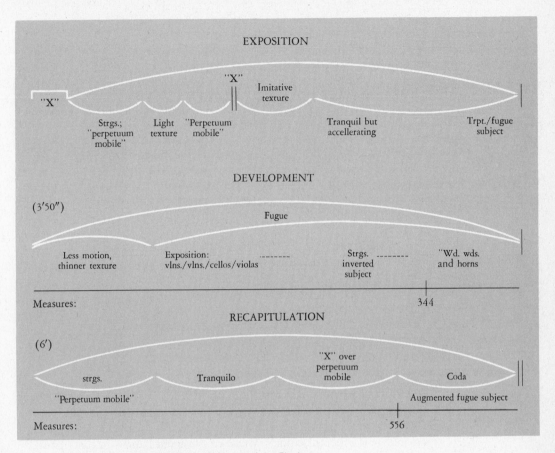

Example 13.12 Mapping of the *Finale*

In the Development section Bartók plies the tricks of the composer's trade with consummate skill and ease. He inverts the theme (see the mapping, middle of the Development), he stretches out its rhythm (*augmentation*) and he even compacts it (*diminution*). Note that an extensively augmented version of the same theme provides the substance of the triumphal brass fanfare that ushers in the movement's long coda.

14

DIVERTIMENTO FOR BAND
OPUS 42

Vincent Persichetti (1915———)

BACKGROUND

Convention frequently plays havoc with people's appreciation of things. We often ignore the potentially moving and beautiful qualities of objects (or people!) surrounding us, simply because we take them for granted and overlook their inherent values. Music of the wind band—or just "band," as it is most commonly called—is a case in point.

Ensembles consisting of only wind or wind and percussion instruments can be traced at least as far back as the marching bands of Roman legions. Most people still associate music-making groups of this kind with military or pseudo-military ceremony. The parade, the football half-time show, and affairs of state that we witness nourish the association. And yet no musical instrument holds a franchise on artistic merit; violins are no more capable of "aesthetic production" than clarinets, and bass tubas are not of themselves incapable of producing beautiful music.

Wind bands have been relegated to secondary artistic roles in Western cultures ever since instrumental music rose to equal and then to supplant vocal music as the highest form of concert music. This happened when the church's domination of music began to wane in the late Renaissance period. (Just to pinpoint a date, let us say 1500.) Brass and woodwind instruments were used for town bands, which in some European communities provided their services for everything from local dances to announcing the time of day, in concert, from atop the local watch-

tower. Sometimes these ensembles played along with choirs, doubling the parts sung; at times they even performed the same works without voices. The name *canzona da sonare* appeared as the title of many instrumental works of the 1600s. It referred to a "song for instruments," denoting a non-vocal work whose other characteristics might be indistinguishable from a work composed for choir.

During the eighteenth century composers often provided music for outdoor gatherings where the superior carrying power of winds was desirable. Mozart on occasion composed "divertimenti" and "serenades" of light, diverting music for wind groups. (The function of such pieces was not altogether different from Muzak of today, the "wall-paper" music that surrounds us but is never really heard.)

English and French composers of the nineteenth and twentieth centuries developed a repertory of concert pieces in addition to marches and "occasional pieces" for ceremonial pomp. The *Funeral and Triumphal Symphony* composed by Berlioz in 1840 used the large military band as its basic force. These sporadic forays by talented composers led to a flowering of the wind band as a medium of considerable artistic quality.

The United States has developed the wind band to a higher level of technical and artistic skill than any other country. Town bands were esteemed by many villagers of early twentieth-century America. Charming gazebos of white-washed gingerbread, still found in the squares of small-town America, were originally built for Sunday afternoon concerts as much as for shading the sweating brows of political orators. Most town

Illustration 14.2 These forty-eight uniformed players joined with the great American "March King" to make the Sousa Band of the 1890s. The modern wind ensemble is not larger, nor is its instrumentation significantly richer.

bands have vanished, along with Model T Fords and nickel beer.* But those bands of yesterday passed on their legacy (and some of their music!) to every high school and college band in the country. There are still many people in America who have not heard a live symphony orchestra, but rare is the citizen who has not heard a band concert.†

The wind band's artistic integrity has mushroomed within the past twenty years, chiefly through the high level of excellence demonstrated by the band of the late Edwin Franko Goldman in New York City and by the Wind Ensemble of the Eastman School of Music. Inaugurated and for many years conducted by Frederic Fennell, this latter group's precise brilliance proved to many composers—as well as to thousands of listeners —that the band could provide music of great finesse and beauty. Since the Eastman Ensemble came into being, few composers of stature have not composed works for that medium. From the work of John Philip Sousa, whose career spanned parts of two centuries, through pieces by the foremost composers of today, a wealth of superb music has been composed for the band.

Goldman's untiring efforts and Fennell's spark at the Eastman School ignited a blaze of imitators, some of whom dropped the name "band" in favor of the less encumbering "wind ensemble." In distinguishing between the two, Fennell once said of the wind ensemble, ". . . we do not believe that it is a band. To qualify for that distinguished classification a group should be uniformed in the tradition of the band, should be able

---

*Some civic bands remain. Most notable today is the Royal Hawaiian Band, which can be heard almost any Sunday afternoon at Kapiolani Park in Honolulu.

†In 1961 Richard F. Goldman estimated that around 30,000 bands of various types existed in the United States.

to march and perform the traditional musical literature of the band, and maintain those time-honored traditions to which the public and its institutions have become so rightfully accustomed."*

More was involved, of course, than a mere name. Of particular significance was the growing conviction that an ensemble of winds and percussion, minus the string body of the west European symphonic tradition, could be viewed as a truly artistic aggregation. The name "wind ensemble" was intended to convey something other than light entertainment or background music for military or civic functions. Along with concert bands, it provides an excellent musical diet for the modern listener.

THE COMPOSER

Although its title indicates "band," Persichetti's work is of the quality cultivated by wind ensembles. It was the composer's first composition for this medium, and it probably is the most widely performed. Following it, in the decade of the fifties, were his *Psalm for Band* (1951), *Pageant* (1953), and *Symphony for Band* (1952). That this latter work is regarded as a major part of his output is attested by Persichetti's listing it as his sixth symphony. Few bands (or wind ensembles!) in America have not played at least one of his works, which by now are revered as late "classics" of the repertory.

Persichetti was born in Philadelphia in 1915. Unlike the composers of the generation that preceded him, his musical training did not include the European sojourn deemed routine for American talents. He is a pianist of considerable prowess, a gifted conductor, and a venerated teacher.

---

*Reported by Richard F. Goldman in *The Wind Band*, Boston: Allyn and Bacon, 1962, p. 138.

Illustration 14.3
Saxophones play principal roles in the instrumentation of concert bands and jazz bands. The alto, tenor, and baritone members of this reed family are shown here. Soprano and bass saxes complete the family, but they are less widely used in ensembles.

For the past three decades he has been associated with both the Philadelphia Conservatory and New York's Juilliard School of Music. His compositions number in the hundreds, covering practically every large and small medium for musical performance. He is one of America's outstanding composers.

DIVERTIMENTO FOR BAND

The title *Divertimento* suggests the lighter tradition of the serenades and divertimenti of Mozart. In its unassuming way, Persichetti's work projects the extroverted vigor one associates with the outdoors and with the stereotyped joviality of American music. It is not music of the avant-garde, even the avant-garde of 1950. In fact its rhythms, melodies, and harmonies are not far removed from Paul Hindemith's *Kleine Kammermusik* of 1925, which we shall discuss in Chapter 38. And yet the music possesses the brash charm and sprightliness that is unmistakably Persichetti.

Even the titles of the six short movements suggest an artistic version of the unabashed band concert in the park: *Prologue, Song, Dance, Burlesque, Soliloquy,* and *March*.

Movement I: Prologue

This opening sets a boisterous tone with its rhythmic drive, biting harmonies, and bare melodies. It approaches the character of a highly developed fanfare, whose mission is to attract attention rather than weave a lasting spell. Its vitality is enormous, its pretensions modest.

A texture of staccato brass chords and woodwind melodic fragments

Example 14.1 Two principal themes of the Prologue

is the basis for almost every gesture within the movement, with percussion underlining the spirit of indomitable force that prevails. The melodic fragments are just that: collections of a few pitches that never quite achieve the full-blown status of a melody. Two prototype fragments alternate with each other. Changing very little themselves, they appear in ever-new garb and rhythmic formations. The first begins the piece, the second is announced soon afterward. They succeed and mix with each other at random.

There is thematic development in this movement, but of a kind quite different from that of a Haydn or Beethoven. Or perhaps *development* is not the most appropriate description. *Thematic variation* is more apt. Each of the two fragments occurs time and again, but always in a reduced or elaborated form, and usually amidst a different texture and harmony. Example 14.2 shows just four different versions of pattern #2. These occur following the version shown above in Example 14.1.

Example 14.2 Four subsequent versions of theme #2

And then at two points in the Prologue the two thematic fragments are joined into one.

Example 14.3 Ultimate merging of the two thematic fragments

The overall result is fetching but curious. Melodically the effect is of "much ado about nothing," for in spite of almost constant changes, one of these two brief patterns seems to be sounding at any moment. Momentum results from the stabbing chords which never settle into a periodic rhythm.

The pungent harmonies of this work are largely the product of mixing simple ingredients to make complex relationships. Individual chords and the relationships of melodies to those chords are typical of what the listener hears in works composed by American composers at mid-century. The passage illustrated in Example 14.4 provides a clear example of the kinds of multi-note blocks that abound in the Prologue and in later movements too. Viewed as a tri-level chord (cornets and trumpets/horns/trombones), it is easy to see that three simple chords are fused into a single complex sonority. The term *polychord* is commonly used to describe this kind of union.

Example 14.4 Polychords in the first movement

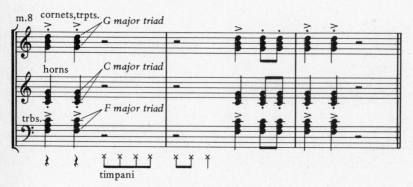

Aside from these brassy chords themselves, harmonic piquancy arises from interesting "conflicts" produced between them and the melodies set against them. The opening phrase of the Prologue, a pattern that returns at two locations, provides a simple example of the kind of *bitonality* that prevails. Look back to the first measure shown in Example 14.1. Note that while the brasses sound their high density chord (six pitch classes),* the high woodwinds sound the first motif in what appears to be a different key. Persichetti's deliberate tonal conflicts between melody and accompaniment are merely simpler examples of the same technique we observed earlier in Charles Ives's *The Unanswered Question*.

Movement II: Song   The soft sameness of this flowing music yields an enigmatic flavor, a stark contrast with the brashness of the Prologue. Its calculated unity

---

*We defined harmonic density in Chapter 5.

comes from a constantly thick and resonant texture in which an undulating pattern weaves its unceasing spell.

A return shape is formed for the whole movement by two properties. In the opening passage horn and clarinets provide the undulating quality by playing separate ostinatos.† These patterns, illustrated in Example 14.5, disappear in the middle section, then return for the final passage. During their absence the cornet intones a new melody, whose contour rises gently to a high point, then descends to its originating pitch.

Example 14.5 Ostinatos of horn and clarinets, beginning of Song

| Movement III: Dance | The form of this movement duplicates the *A B A* outline of the Song, but its mood reverts to the extroverted spirit of the Prologue. Most American composers of Persichetti's generation have on occasion composed deliberately "corny" music. This tripping dance is what might be called "camp," for it is a conscious effort to fuse commonplace ideas with a sophisticated setting. Its principal theme, played first by piccolo, is sufficient evidence that the melodic element is indeed simple and "commonplace." |

The carefree lightness of this first section is interrupted by the full band, *fortissimo*, to begin the middle portion of the form. These heavy chords return as punctuation for very light textures in which stray bits and pieces provide melodic continuity. This brief textural contrast is supplanted by a return of the piccolo with its "hick" tune for the final sounds.

Movement IV: Burlesque

Persichetti's Burlesque is not the burlesque of off-color comedians and strip-tease acts. His title refers, on the contrary, to an atmosphere of mocking comedy, perhaps even caricature. While the Dance was a relatively light satire of "hick" music, this movement is of rougher quality, a broader joke.

As we observed in Chapter 8, Hector Berlioz commented that the scherzo of Beethoven's Symphony No. 5 sounded like the gamboling of elephants. The simile is apt for Persichetti's Burlesque, although here we might replace elephants with the less agile water buffalo. Low bass tubas

---

†An ostinato is any short pattern that is repeated continuously for a period of time.

croon out the first theme to the crisp afterbeats of low woodwinds. This repetitious theme is sounded twice to form the first section, *A*.

Low, gruff sounds give way to a broad texture dominated by flute and piccolo on an incessant little figure. This eerie passage is interesting for its harmonic content. It is another good example of bi-tonality, Persichetti mixing an ultra-simple upper part of the texture in *C* major with the lower parts in *D♭* major. Only three parts are shown in Example 14.6 to illustrate how the two strata in different keys are joined. The flute/piccolo and clarinet lines project the key of *C*. The bass outlines the key of *D♭*. Because of the domination here by the higher parts, what we hear is more of a corrupted *C* major than two clear keys at once.

Example 14.6   Mixture of two keys in the Burlesque, *B* section

Although a return to the tuba's theme occurs following the contrasting texture and bi-tonality of *B*, the form is somewhat more involved than would be indicated by a ternary plan of *A B A*. The closing *A* is considerably elaborated. In fact, halfway through the course of the tuba's returning phrase, trumpets intrude with an imitation. Imitations in other parts continue until lines bearing the theme are piled six deep, three "leaders" and three "followers." This engaging jumble is untangled by a brief coda that recalls the texture and melody of the *B* section.

Movement V: Soliloquy

The pace slackens considerably with this solemn hymn. Its character is largely determined by its slow rhythms, yet harmonies and textures are important in this respect too: they are of simpler structure in this movement than in any other. Most of the chords, for example, are simple triads (three pitch classes), and as in the Song, the texture is full and homogeneous throughout. Each of these factors undergirds the choral atmosphere befitting a hymn.

As befits a Soliloquy, the form of this movement is strophic, although each strophe is varied slightly.* The final strophe effects a sense of return, the melody and harmonies of the first phrase repeated intact.

---

*We discussed strophic form in Chapter 2.

But even here the flute winds a high filigree around this melodic remembrance, causing even it to be a slightly new event.

Movement VI: March

Just as Movement V is most like Movement II, so Movement VI is most like I. And thus an intriguing symmetry of large parts is established for the whole Divertimento. We shall observe a similar arch-like pattern in Bach's cantata, *Christ Lay in Death's Prison* (Chapter 19).

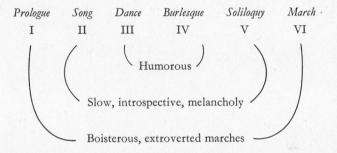

Like the Prologue, this movement features a textural duet in which brass chords exchange and mix with high woodwind melodies. But most engaging of all is the way the opening woodblock rhythm sets a vigorous marching spirit. The whole piece can be viewed, in fact, as a trio of timbres: percussion, brass, and woodwinds. The three join together as a unified ensemble only at the very end.

As in previous movements, a single melody dominates the entire March, while rapidly changing textures and timbres propel the movement to its snappy end. The total scheme is of two large parts, the second an almost exact repetition of the first.

Illustration 14.4 Most communities boast of a high school, college, or civic band as a source of musical pleasure. The Concert Band of the State University of New York at Buffalo, directed by Frank Cipolla, represents the full concert band, whose instrumentation is greater than the usual wind ensemble.

15

TO THE VICTIMS OF HIROSHIMA: THRENODY

Krzystof Penderecki (1933–––)

BACKGROUND

The most shattering world event of the twentieth century was the American bombing on August 6, 1945, of the Japanese city of Hiroshima. This gruesome act of war was also the public unveiling of the atomic age; the bomb dropped that day was the first thermonuclear weapon used against mankind. The city of almost 400,000 inhabitants was largely destroyed.

The *Threnody* by Penderecki (*Penderet'ski*) was composed to memorialize the unspeakable grief associated with the human carnage that was the bomb's aftermath. It is a gripping work or it is sheer noise, depending on the individual listener's ability to respond to its bitter sounds.

Like many works composed since the end of World War II, this piece represents a turn to the most primitive kinds of musical gestures and properties. There is no melody. Harmony is an irrelevant word. Rhythm exists only in the sense that sounds are articulated in patches of time. The composer has deliberately reverted to a kind of musical fundamentalism, wherein events are characterized by thick or thin textures, shrill or mellow timbres, high or low pitches, loud or soft intensities, sharp or soft articulations.

Penderecki's choice of these most elemental properties and processes enables him to create music of elemental power. A threnody—or song of lamentation—for the event memorialized would be trite if it could not move its audience to feelings commensurate with the images invoked by its title. And thus Penderecki's *Threnody* is a shattering piece of music.

172

THE COMPOSER

Born in Debica, Poland, in 1933, Penderecki was first widely recognized as a talented composer in 1959. In that year he won all three of the prizes in composition awarded by the Polish Union of Composers. Since the sixties he has enjoyed widespread fame in the world of music and his vocal and instrumental works have been performed and acclaimed throughout the cultural centers of the East and West.

Since 1972 he has been a Professor of Music at the Yale School of Music, with performances and public appearances throughout this country augmenting his already firm reputation as a composer of merit. With his elder compatriot Witold Lutoslawski, he is one of the few contemporary composers from an Iron Curtain country whose music is of greater musical than sociological interest.

NEW LOOK FOR MUSICAL SCORES

Since his first public successes, Penderecki's music has been noted for its exploitation of new sounds and new ways for making sounds. Like the music of many of his contemporaries, his scores sometimes look more like chartings of sales trends than directions for a musical performance. This strange new appearance of musical notation sometimes is discouraging even to professional musicians. It is nonetheless a necessary by-product of composers' shift of interest from the kinds of detailed musical patterns espoused by earlier composers to patterns mixed from a palette of intense raw sound.

The performer frequently is granted greater freedom of choice in this new music than in that of Beethoven or Debussy. Today a composer may direct the performer (through words or symbols) only to "Play the highest note on your instrument for eight seconds." Exactly *what* pitch results is not crucial; the goal is an especially strident timbre of extremely high pitch. And so the notation for this new music need not look like the score of a Mozart aria.

Performing scores of this kind demands special care from singers and players. They must digest a new set of "directions" for every new composition, arrays of symbols that indicate unconventional ways of playing an instrument. The Frontispiece of Penderecki's *Threnody* provides the following catalogue of special techniques to be used by the fifty-two string players who make up the entire orchestra in this work.

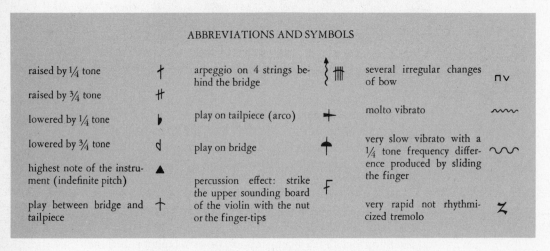

Example 15.1   Performance directions, *Threnody*

Some of these figures require rather strange behaviors, at least from the traditional view of how to play a fiddle. Some call for players to sound pitches that are "out-of-tune" according to conventional Western scales. Others are meant to elicit not the dulcet sounds normally expected from a violin or cello, but rather tones from "on the bridge," where noise components create a scratchiness of indescribable astringency. Still other symbols ask the player to become percussionist, striking the instrument with bow or fingertips. These eccentric sounds account for much of the harsh ring of *Threnody*. One page of its score is shown in the next illustration. The only "notes" of traditional music writing will be found within parentheses toward the top of the page. These notes show twelve violinists what pitches should fill the band of sound depicted by the thick black line.

Example 15.2   Page 18 of Penderecki's score (beginning of Section #6)

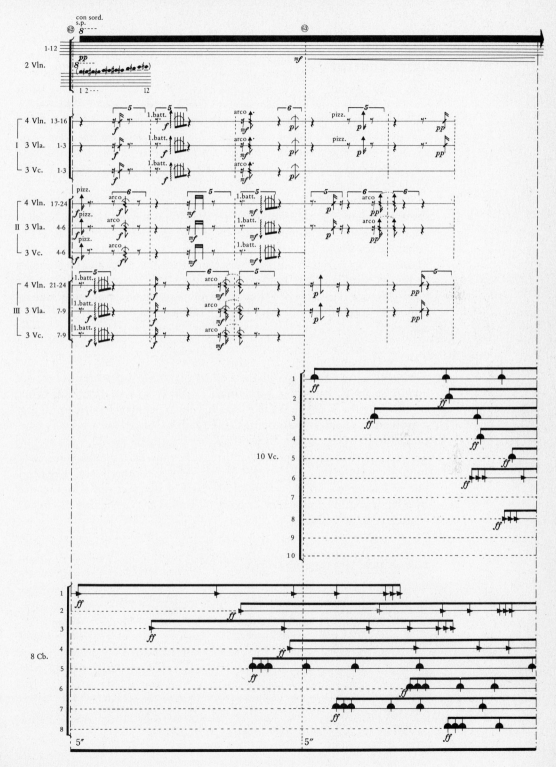

PROGRAMMATIC CONTENT

One word of caution. It is difficult at first to listen to a work such as this without flooding the imagination with associations of real-world events. Lacking traditional melodies, conventional rhythms and harmonies, the sounds of this work tempt one to press on to it a detailed program. And we thus tend only to "hear" diving bombers, screaming ambulances, and weeping victims. The wise listener judiciously curbs the range of these kinds of associations.

One listener's "listening style" would for another listener produce sheer boredom, for still another listener preposterous hokum. So it is impossible (not to mention undesirable!) to draw up a set of "Rules of Behavior for Music Lovers." But it is possible to state unequivocally that *Threnody* is not program music, at least not the kind that actually attempts to mimic sounds of the nonmusical world. And anyone who hears this piece *only* as a reminder of the actual sounds of the event it memorializes stands a good chance of "not hearing" its music.

THRENODY

The work grows from a collection of simple musical gestures. There are formal sections, but these sometimes dovetail, so that one ends while another begins. We shall try to make this elusiveness of formal joints less a problem through our mappings. Like Erb's Concerto for Solo Percussionist and Orchestra, which we shall discuss in Chapter 32, each section derives a part of its uniqueness and unity from a *basic* sound. This basic sound acts as the thematic mortar for a variety of sound blocks. The time-line of Example 15.3 shows only how each of five sections is dominated by a basic sound or sequence of basic events. A more detailed discussion of each section will follow.

Example 15.3   Time-line of the five sections, *Threnody*

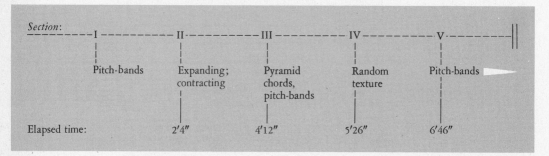

Section I

Four of the five sections consist of two distinct parts, these held together by shared elements or by a first element continuing into the second. This first section begins with separated attacks of high, wheezing pitch-bands from ten groupings of violins, violas, cellos, and basses. These are intensely provocative sounds. Consisting of clusters of pitch separated by only quarter tones,* these tight bands of sound might have been produced by a white noise generator used to make electronic music.† Some of the bands begin to oscillate slightly, separate layers of tone growing suddenly soft while others remain loud. This creates a sense of shifting tone color within the continuing blob of sound.

While the pitch-bands persist, separate bodies (led by cellos) begin a series of random plucked and bowed sounds, each performer executing a series of articulations chosen from four supplied by the composer in the score.** The atmosphere of the music within this passage is strangely

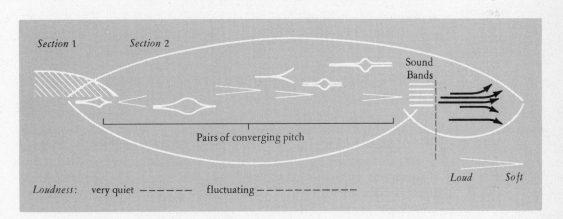

Example 15.4   Mapping of Section II

awesome. We seem to hear a gigantic structure ripped apart by tiny bits, as though a slow-motion earthquake were in progress. By the time the last pane has splintered, the last timber fallen, the texture has reduced to a single pitch, which acts as the closing pivot of the first section.

---

*Pitches of adjacent keys on the piano are a half step apart, so a quarter tone is half the interval one hears from adjacent piano keys.

†The term *white noise* refers to sounds consisting of a collection of many pitches of equal (or approximately equal) intensity. Make the sound of an extended *Sh* and you will have created white noise.

**Musical events like this, in which performers have some choice of what to play, are called *aleatoric.*

Section II

The randomized sound-bits of Section I overlap briefly with the first event of Section II. Now, for the first time, distinct pitch plays a shaping role; paired layers of sound expand and contract, converging at times on a single pitch-point like ghostly distant sirens. At first these bending layers of sound succeed by pairs; sometimes they overlap. A following passage returns to the pitch-bands of Section I, the total bands rising or falling in one grand act of separation. The section thins to a single set of violins, rising finally to an inaudible, enigmatic wisp as its end.

Section III

The ghostly slidings of the foregoing are interrupted by an accented pitch. This is the beginning of a "chord" of fifty-two different pitches, each instrument of the orchestra entering with its own special contribution to a colossal pyramid of sound. By twenty seconds into this third section the low strings attack a new pitch-band with one of the most furious sounds in the work. The band separates, expands slowly, converges to a single vibrant pitch level, then gradually fades away until a single inert tone remains to expire alone.

In its obscure way, this ending gesture of Section III is the most unsettling of the *Threnody*. Following the devastating tone clusters that have preceded, the dying cello tone projects an anxious tension that will be imitated (though not surpassed) by the whole orchestra at the end of the work.

Section IV

This fourth section overlaps with the final, its apparently fortuitous plucks and scrapes merging with the re-introduction of pitch-bands similar to those of Section I. Rhythmic density is greater in Section IV than in any other section of the work. One tiny event follows on the heels of another, with many events—widely separated pitches, scratched chords—overlapping.

Here texture is a disarming splattering of sounds. The pitch spectrum of the full orchestra is covered with blips and grunts that skitter from low to high in rapid succession. The unity of these passages derives from their common lack of apparent order, plucked and bowed sounds emitted with wrenching fury from all over the intruments' strings.

Ordered chaos is joined by knocking sounds made by players striking their instruments' bodies. Forming the transition to Section V, this series of rhythmic blows continues while muted violins begin a high pitch-band to initiate the final section. It is not easy to detect the exact beginning of this fifth section, nor is it important to do so. The joining seam is neatly hidden by the merging of characteristic sounds from each unit.

By the time a second pitch-band has joined the first, it is apparent that a new texture is emerging. Within twenty seconds the five orchestral groups have solidified into an opaque web of as many strands. A final dense chord (fifty-two pitches again!) begins as a roar, gradually subsiding to a pitiful knotted murmur at the end.

Whatever one's estimation of the musical impact of *Threnody*, it is difficult to conclude that the work at any moment strikes a maudlin pose. What the composer expresses he expresses without the sentimentality that could mock the human anguish the world knows as a result of Hiroshima. Just as the victims of the bombing were sacrificed in a holocaust un-imagined before 1945, Penderecki's lament calls upon expressive resources heretofore unknown in music.

We have discussed this work in terms of five sections, as our map-ping in Example 15.3 made explicit. After you have heard it several times and are able to follow the five divisions of our map, it should be simple to further compress the music's shape into a three-part form of larger units. This larger conception corresponds admirably with the two most evident seams in the work. Our last mapping shows how the five shorter sections lie within the three parts of the simpler form. This more unified representation accounts for the most basic sound events that occur in *Threnody*, reminding us once more that the work is a return to simpler rather than more complex musical gestures.

Example 15.5 Mapping of *Threnody*, in three large sections, five parts

VOCAL MUSIC

INTRODUCTION

Singing has always been the primary source of music for any culture. It is the ultimate expression of religious feeling and it is the basis for all folk music. Even the dances of most cultures originated with an accompaniment of singing and clapping. It is difficult to imagine people who have not sung, no matter how modest their vocal capabilities. Our happiest and gloomiest moments seem to demand an outlet in song.

This part of our study covers a period of about fourteen hundred years, from early Christian song to a recent dramatic work by an American composer. An important element in these compositions is missing from all purely instrumental music: a text. The sounds of a symphony orchestra may suggest the erotic daydreams of a faun (as in Debussy's *Prelude*) or humanity's cosmic uncertainty (as in Ives', *Unanswered Question*); but only the human voice can fill in the concrete details of a story line. For this reason, be sure that you know the fundamental ideas of each composition's text before you attempt to understand its music. Vocal composers begin with the meanings expressed by the words they set; the listener can profit by beginning there too.

One critical factor in any song is the way its words are united with its music. The composer takes great care to match the natural accents of the poet's text with the rhythms of his music. And thus a translated text rarely works as well with the composer's music as the text of the original language. The fusion of word and tone he labored to achieve is difficult to recapture in any other tongue. Because of this tight union, all of the vocal works discussed here, with the exception of the two songs by the English composers Dowland and Pilkington, will be heard in foreign languages. You will find this bothersome only if you do not study the English translations provided in our discussions. You may even find that, once familiar with the composition in its original language, any performance sung in a translation sounds strangely inappropriate.

16

GREGORIAN CHANT:
EARLY MUSIC
OF THE CHRISTIAN CHURCH

BACKGROUND: EARLY CHRISTIAN SONG

Music seems to be a necessary ingredient in religious ritual. Find a religion of any era or any culture and you will have found a musical repertory of some kind as well. The worshipful state is conductive to the kind of special message and feeling that is best conveyed by the sung, as opposed to the spoken, word. No wonder that the oldest and most populous religions of all times possess an established body of song that is held in the same high esteem as its artifacts and theological tracts.

The songs of these repertories usually have come from a variety of sources. For the most part they have been gleaned from the traditional music of the culture, their prime virtue being a suitability for the function they are to perform and the particular spirit they are meant to convey. The early music of the Christian Church came about in just this way. It was a body of melodies absorbed from widespread cultural sources, Western and Oriental, Christian and non-Christian.

The early Church movement was not the centralized phenomenon it became during the medieval period, and thus there were, prior to the domination of Christendom by Rome, as many repertories of chant as there were splinters of the Church. Some of these repertories exist today, some do not. Even that of the Roman Catholic Church has been jeopardized by recent attempts to reform the music of its liturgy, a reform that would inject into the service current folk idioms (folk and jazz masses, semi-rock songs, and pop songs of religious overtones).

Illustration 16.1 Pope Gregory the Great sends Missionaries to England

All chants of the early Christian Church had certain musical traits in common.* They were monophonic, and they moved in free rhythms, lacking the metric organization that could suggest dancing (and thus heathen ways) to worshipers. Their semideclamatory style seemed the best to fit the needs of religious expression. Their plainness made them suitable for the generic name eventually adopted for them: *plainsong*.

The most durable of these song repertories is that of the Roman Catholic Church. It is most important to our discussion because, aside from its inherent beauty, its melodies became thoroughly imbedded within the church music of subsequent centuries. Since most chant melodies of the Roman Church were collected during the reign of Pope Gregory I (590–604), it is widely known as "Gregorian Chant."

Today the Gregorian Chant consists of a collection of approximately three thousand monophonic songs that are to be performed by choir and soloist (or cantor). Most of the chant texts are from the Christian Bible. Each chant is designated to fulfill a specific function within the Church season; many of them are parts of the central Catholic rite of the Mass, or Holy Communion.

Gregorian Chant has not always flourished since its inception. We'll discuss some of the music that displaced it when we discuss polyphonic choral music in the next chapter. Let us note for the present that its supremacy began to wane in the eleventh century. It remained as the archaic stepchild of the service, second in favor to the more impressive part-music that eclipsed it in the urban cathedrals of the world.

With centuries of disuse, the authentic traditions of chant performance were lost. The notation used to preserve it was less precise than our modern musical notation, and the oral transmission required to preserve its authentic rhythms did not take place. Later scholars and musicians who have wished to revive its original flavor have been frustrated because they could not be certain their rhythmic interpretations were correct.

The most admired restorations of chant melodies began in the nineteenth century, when monks at the Benedictine Abbey of Solesmes, France, assumed the enormous task of piecing together authentic performances from the sketchy data available. It is to monks of that order, particularly Dom Prosper Guéranger and Dom Andre Mocquereau, that we owe thanks for reviving this ancient art in the face of its probable extinction.

---

*The branches were Byzantine and Russian in the East, Ambrosian, Gallican, Mozarabic, and Roman in the West.

THE CATHOLIC MASS

A detailed discussion of the Roman Catholic Mass would carry us astray. For our purposes it will suffice to note that the service consists of two broad categories: (1) the *Proper*, whose parts are performed only in conjunction with particular times of the Church year; and (2) the *Ordinary*, which is unchanging in its parts, always forming the spine of the ceremony.* Since we shall refer to parts of the Ordinary in our ensuing discussions, the following listing of its five parts will be of some interest. This order of ritual is the basis for the High Mass of the Roman Catholic Church today, just as it was in the sixteenth or eighth centuries.

Kyrie:	Lord, have mercy on us.
Gloria:	Glory be to God.
Credo:	The "creed:" I believe in one God.
Sanctus:	He is holy.
Agnus Dei:	Lamb of God (Christ), give us peace.

(A brief section, the *Ite missa est*, ends the mass, announcing the dismissal of the congregation.)

The ideal setting for listening to Gregorian Chant is within the walls of a cathedral, whose cavernous resonance adds to the quality of its sounds. Outside that context the music does not serve its intended function, and thus a part of its power to evoke a mood of reverence is lost.

KYRIE AND SANCTUS FROM THE MASS

The two movements we have chosen for discussion come from different masses. The *Kyrie* is taken from a mass performed only for feasts of the Blessed Virgin Mary, the *Sanctus* from a mass assigned to the Sundays of the Church year. You will find them of the same style, in spite of their separate origins. Their simple gliding contours are typical of all Gregorian Chant.

Kyrie

The text of this *Kyrie* is that of all *Kyries*. It consists of two lines arranged in the following pattern:

Kyrie eleison (repeated twice)
Christe eleison (repeated twice)
Kyrie eleison (again repeated twice)

---

*For a more detailed discussion of the mass see the *Harvard Dictionary of Music* by Willi Apel (Cambridge, Mass.: The Belknap Press of Harvard University, 2nd Ed., 1966) or *A History of Western Music* by Donald Grout. New York: W. W. Norton, 1964. Most chant

Although the musical forms of chant are not as standardized as their texts, many of the melodies possess return characteristics similar to those we have observed in later music. The phrases of this *Kyrie* are especially interesting in the way they are joined with the nine lines of text. If we assign K to represent "Kyrie" lines, C for "Christe" lines, the following music/text form emerges:

TEXT		MUSIC
	K^1..............a	
A	K^2..............b	A
	K^3..............a	
	C^1..............c	
B	C^2..............d	B
	C^3..............c	
	K^4..............e	
C	K^5..............d	C
	K^6..............e, e, d	

The overall result is a three-part additive form, yet with frequent internal repetitions that provide elements of return.

An even greater unity is achieved by still another return feature that is not shown in our outline. With careful listening you can hear that the final portions of all a, b, c, and d phrases end with the same melodic pattern. This means that only the e phrases lack a connection with all others.

One notable feature of this music can be heard in later polyphonic music. This the way a single syllable of text is appended to a long string of notes. Called *melismatic*, this kind of word setting occurs only rarely in popular music or in the art songs we discuss in Chapter 22.† An extended melismatic passage occurs in this chant in the final *Kyrie*. At this point "Kyrie eleison" is stretched out over the notes of three full phrases (e, e, d in Example 16.1).

For some listeners chant has an exotic sound. Since they are accustomed to tonalities based on the major and minor scales that have prevailed in music since the eighteenth century, the pitches of these melodies sometimes form unfamiliar patterns. This *Kyrie* is not so strange as most in this respect. Its pitches correspond to those of the natural minor scale,**

---

melodies can be found in their original notation in the *Liber Usualis*, which is the official repository of the Catholic liturgy.

†Text settings are called *syllabic* when notes and syllables are matched on a one-to-one basis. This is the most common style in music of today.

**Historically, the correct explanation of the pitch structure of this chant is that it is "in the First Mode," or *Authentic Dorian*.

which can be heard infrequently in the music of composers of the eighteenth, nineteenth, and twentieth centuries.

More important for the listener is the way the total pitches of the melody are organized to project two of their number as pillars of structure. Amidst all of the melody's gliding motion, one or the other of these two pitch classes* begins and ends every phrase; they also form the high/low limits of the total chant's contour. The mapping in Example 16.1 shows their dominating roles in the melodic sheme.

Example 16.1   Mapping by phrases of terminal pitches in the *Kyrie*

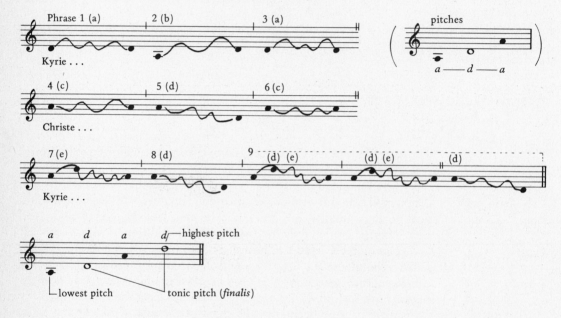

Sanctus

The *Sanctus* of the Mass has a slightly more involved text than the *Kyrie*.

Sanctus, Sanctus, Sanctus	Holy, Holy, Holy
Dominus Deus Sabaoth.	Lord, God of hosts.
Pleni sunt caeli et terra gloria tua.	Heaven and earth are filled with Thy glory.
Hosanna in excelsis!	Hosanna in the highest!
Benedictus qui venit in nomine Domini.	Blessed is he who comes in the name of the Lord.
Hosanna in excelsis!	Hosanna in the highest!

---

*See Chapter 5 for an explanation of pitch class as opposed to *pitch*.

The melody of this *Sanctus* has the same scale basis as the *Kyrie*, although its range is slightly narrower. Like the *Kyrie* its floating contours establish a clear tonal outline that makes two pitches (*A* and *E*) its pillars. They are analogous to *D* and *A* in the *Kyrie*. Only the *Benedictus* phrase begins and ends with pitches that are not *A* or *E*.

Example 16.2 Mapping by phrases of terminal pitches in the *Sanctus**

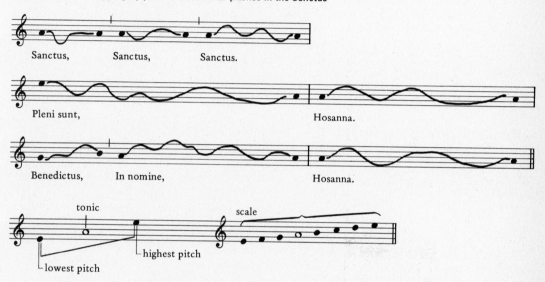

The *Sanctus* has an element of return in its form, though by no means to the degree found in the *Kyrie*. Here the two *Hosannas* are set to the same melodic pattern. If we chart the overall form, the following is the chant's ordering of sections.

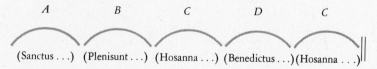

Example 16.3 Form of the *Sanctus*

In spite of these clear sectionings, the simplicity of pitch and timbre used in this music denies strong formal definition. For the listener the

---

*Actually, the highest pitch in the melody is one step above the E that is shown here. Its fleeting appearance (once, in the phrase of *in nomine*) as an upper embellishment of E renders it trivial.

effect is that of soaring human voices, which almost defies a boxing into neat sections that could dilute the sanctity of its message in the ritual of the Mass.

17

SANCTUS AND BENEDICTUS
FROM THE MASS
AETERNA CHRISTI MUNERA

Giovanni Pierluigi da Palestrina (1525–1594)

BACKGROUND

The official purity of Gregorian Chant did not remain unaltered for very long. Like many ideas of man, the decree of its untouchable sanctity was weak insurance against its eventual corruption. Within a few years after its adoption under the rule of Pope Gregory I, its melodies became simply the melodic scaffolding for, rather than the whole substance of, liturgical music.

Composers whose names are mostly forgotten injected textual additions as well as melodic fragments, extending and elaborating the chants beyond their original state. Even other melodies were joined with a chant, creating multi-voice compositions that were the first true part-music.

The Motet

By the middle of the thirteenth century a distinct new musical form had developed from these bendings and inflations of the original chants. Called *motet,* this new polyphonic music originated from the addition of a voice part above the chant itself, its text a paraphrase of the original chant's text. Because of the added words (*mots* in French), this new part, and the resulting composition as well, was called *motetus.* This basic musical compound was the model for Catholic music from around 1250 until well into the eighteenth century.

As a general type, the motet is an unaccompanied choral composition. It is based on a sacred Latin text, often a psalm or a psalm-inspired poem, and it is conceived as a part of the Catholic rite.

191

Illustration 17.1
Giovanni Pierluigi da Palestrina

Naturally, the motet's surface details were altered over the centuries. During a part of its development it consisted of curious joinings of voices singing irreligious texts in French or Italian, along with the Latin plainchant. To us the result seems unspeakable. Imagine the confusion created by a work in which the lowest part (the tenor) sounds a devotional chant in Latin while an upper part sings in French of erotic love!

For some composers of the fourteenth and fifteenth centuries the motet became a kind of musical tour de force; it was a mixture of compositional processes that far exceeded its function as a statement of religious piety.

The foremost early composers of masses and motets were French.* As it evolved, however, the form became synonomous with Flemish composers, men born and trained in the general area of today's Belgium. During the period of 1450–1600 these composers created the very models of religious music in their polyphonic settings of the mass and its single-movement relative, the motet. (A mass is essentially a series of five motets whose texts follow the order mentioned earlier on page 186.)

By the fifteenth century the motet had become a relatively standardized musical process. A single Latin text was used in all voices by this time, and the Gregorian melodic basis was discarded in many works, yielding to compositions free of any pre-composed elements. Usually consisting

---

*The first complete mass composed by a single composer was that of the Frenchman Guillaume de Machaut, who died in 1377.

of from four to six voice parts, its texture was imitative polyphony among all voices, but sections of block chords occasionally broke into this polyphony, for the sake of contrast or to achieve special clarity for special words.

The master of this motet style is conceded to have been the Flemish composer Josquin des Prez (1450–1521). His motets treat successive portions of the Latin text to expositions of each voice in imitative entries, thereby creating a layered texture that became known as the "motet-style." You will encounter the same kind of imitation process in a fugue of J.S. Bach later, when we discuss chamber music. The simple diagram in Example 17.1 illustrates what is meant by layers of imitative entries.

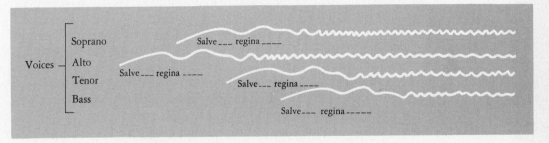

Example 17.1 Imitative entries of voices in "motet-style"*

Palestrina knew the works of Josquin and other influential Flemish composers who preceded him. They were the stylistic ground his compositions took root in, a style to which he added little except for his own flawless technique. By the early years of his life, the motet had spread through Europe to become more than a Flemish monopoly. Italian composers like Palestrina and his Venetian contemporaries Andrea and Giovanni Gabrielli, as well as Spanish, English, French, and German composers, turned to it as the base plan for their religious choral compositions.

Religious Reforms   Of utmost importance for Palestrina was the religious break Martin Luther had begun with his Protestant Reformation in 1519. By the 1560s (when Palestrina was in his mid-thirties) the Roman Church was engulfed in a reform of its own, the so-called Counter Reformation. This attempt to purge elements of Catholic practice that could not stand the onslaught of the Protestant tide was centered in councils of reform. They convened, off and on, from 1545 to 1563 in the north Italian town of Trent.

These prolonged meetings of the Council of Trent were aimed at improving the world stance of the Roman Church. Among its considera-

---

*This is also called "fugal texture."

tions were musical reforms, which were felt to be an integral part of any liturgical changes. The church music of the early sixteenth century, it was felt by the cardinals at these councils, was not without blemish. They had witnessed the encroachment of secular melodies into services. They had suffered the addition of "noisy instruments" (like the organ) to the spiritual quiet of human voices. They had heard the complex "modern" textures that garbled the meanings of scriptural texts. They even knew of sloppy pronunciation and "irreverent behavior" by singers in chapel choirs. These, they felt, would not do for a Church beset with the doctrinal and political appeal of the Protestant movement in particular, and a growing secularism in general.

As with any committee charged with the task of reform, the Trent Council had its share of overzealous souls. Some would have banned all part-music from the liturgy, returning the musical portions of the service to Gregorian Chant alone. Fortunately, less extreme members of the group recognized a danger in excessive reaction; they saved the day for the multi-voiced music that would dominate religious music for several centuries. The Council adjourned for the last time in 1563 without formulating specific measures of musical reform. But a spirit of conservatism was suggested by its lengthy deliberations: the scene was set for a retrenchment in musical style.

THE COMPOSER

Many of the composers discussed in this book are remembered for their creative audacity as well as for their large output. This is not the case with the revered Roman Church composer Palestrina; his music was old-fashioned for his own times. His motets and masses are remembered mainly because they became models for a kind of sacred music that offered a distinct contrast to secular opera and to the Protestant hymns and cantatas of coming decades. Palestrina's talent lay in perfecting old methods rather than in creating new ones.

His life centered around Rome. Born just outside the Holy City in the small town of Palestrina, he had played the organ and sung in and directed the choirs of the principal Roman cathedrals from an early age. He had published his first collection of masses in 1554, while still choirmaster of St. Peter's. His musical style, which we can assume was conservative by disposition, meshed well with the implied reforms of the Council of Trent.

Musical Style   Within his life he composed over 100 polyphonic masses, about 450 motets and assorted other sacred pieces, 56 Italian madrigals on sacred texts, and over 80 on secular texts. In his liturgical works he caught the spirit of sober religiosity appropriate for the Counter Reformation. His music was the exquisitely fashioned but conservative model of the status quo for mid-sixteenth-century Italy.

His musical style in the masses and motets is recognizable by the following characteristics:

1 Unaccompanied chorus of four to six voices (male voices in performances of the sixteenth century);
2 Imitative polyphony in which each of the voices is melodically independent;
3 Melodies (in all voices) which flow smoothly in archlike contours;
4 Unobtrusive harmony in which simple chords (major and minor triads) are the basis;
5 Rhythms which, as the product of combined voices, create a constant flow without projecting a powerful pulse or meter;
6 Occasional sections of block chords as textural conrast to the prevailing polyphony.

Most of Palestrina's motets and masses do not utilize the chant-based techniques of earlier sacred works, but the chant lives on in many of his works in a more subtle way. Serving as the source of motifs, chants are imbedded in the melodies of successive sections of these compositions. (We shall see concrete evidence of this melodic "paraphrasing" in the music discussed subsequently.) Of his 102 masses, the melodic stuff of 79 are partially or wholly derived from a chant of the Gregorian liturgy.

From our discussion thus far, one may have the impression that Palestrina's music is terribly expressionless, cool, and disembodied. By comparision with some of the vocal music we shall discuss later, this is a reasonable estimate. But given the need for the sober expression of religious devotion, a music in which the force of theological dogma is more prized than individual human feeling, his music is unexcelled, the paragon of an otherworldly expression.

He was not immune to the use of the representational tricks of his day; he sets some words of his texts with the stock patterns of musical association used by fellow composers. With the mention of Christ's crucifixion he will combine somber chords; he aligns a rising vocal line with the words "He arose"; and at times he will combine short falling motifs (similar to restrained gasps) with the text "He suffered." All of these are in the tradition of pictorialism used before his time and popular with vocal composers of the whole Renaissance. But Palestrina's word-paintings are less pronounced, more deftly camouflaged in the unfolding texture than those of some of his contemporaries. And thus they should have been, if the propriety of a holy ritual was to be served.

In spite of Palestrina's conservatism, his music holds a special place in history. He is regarded as the Catholic counterpart of J. S. Bach, who would provide the model for Protestant music of two centuries later.

Palestrina's style is the earliest of our past that has been purposely preserved, to be pored over and imitated by later composers as a means for
learning some of the intricacies of composing. Even today, most trained
musicians undergo at some time in their careers the study of "sixteenth-
century counterpoint," which usually means learning how to write the
kind of flowing vocal music we associate with Palestrina.

SANCTUS AND BENEDICTUS FROM THE MASS
AETERNA CHRISTI MUNERA

These two movements (from a single mass) show one of the ways Palestrina incorporated chant melodies in his works. Both are dominated by
the first phrase of the Gregorian Chant *Aeterna Christi munera,* which is
shown next in modern clef notation.

Example 17.2   First phrase of the plainsong *Aeterna Christi munera*

The gentle arch of this melody is symptomatic of the whole of
Palestrina's musical output; its contour of rise-fall can be found in hundreds of different guises in his masses and motets. Example 17.3 shows
three separate appearances of the pattern he derived from the original
chant. Two of the excerpts (*a* and *c*) also show how successive voice entries
accumulate to form the rich imitative texture and the polyphony of words
that make this music so memorable.

Example 17.3   Melodic phrases of the mass derived from the chant

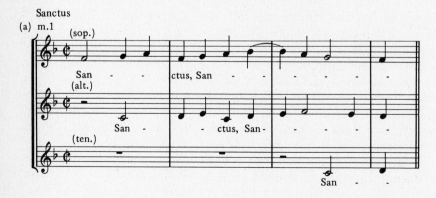

(b) m.32 (sop.)

Ho - sán - na   in   Ex - cél - - - - - sis.

(c) Benedictus (ten.)

Ho - sán - na   in   ex - cél - - - - - - -

Ho - sán - na   in   ex - cél - - - sis.

The "polyphony of words" we just mentioned tells us something about the function of a text in the liturgical music of Palestrina's times. Clearly the words must be known by a listener for them to bear meaning as a part of the music. The word-setting does little to project verbal meaning; its staggered delivery of each word by the separate voices creates a teeming mixture of syllables, which act more as catalysts for melodic motion than for the transmission of a verbal message. The simplicity of the message, known by a congregation as an established part of the mass, makes this possible, of course. (The text of the *Sanctus* can be found on page 188.)

The text provides the formal outline for each movement, and each new line is used by Palestrina as the point at which a new melodic pattern emerges. Formal divisions are not as distinct, however, as they usually are in the music of later times. The section based on *"Pleni sunt"* and the *Hosanna* at the end of the *Benedictus,* for example, overlap with the sections that precede them. This creates a blending that is appropriate to the flowing style.

The following mapping shows how text and texture combine to mark off four musical sections of about the same length. Each new section, or "point of imitation," is identified by the voice (or voices) that begins it.

Example 17.4 Mapping of the *Sanctus*

"Sanctus..."   "Dominus..."   "Plenisunt..."   "Hosanna ..."

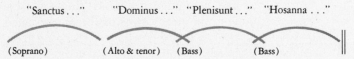

(Soprano)   (Alto & tenor)   (Bass)   (Bass)

It is interesting that the *Benedictus* begins with a reduced texture of only three voices (soprano, alto, tenor), contrasting with the four voices used in the *Sanctus* and the final *Hosanna*.

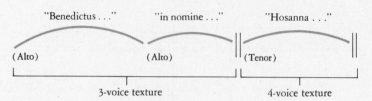

"Benedictus..."   "in nomine..."   "Hosanna..."

(Alto)   (Alto)   (Tenor)

3-voice texture   4-voice texture

Example 17.5 Mapping of the *Benedictus* and final *Hosanna*

We can understand why this music has been revered for four centuries as the ultimate expression of Roman Catholic piety. Although its melodies and textures are rich, it is not the kind of music that calls undue attention to itself or to its performers; it is wholly lacking in the dramatic flourishes that might detract the listener from the religious setting it is intended to enhance. Let us note several things that contribute to its lofty effect.

The separate voice parts are themselves organized within narrow pitch ranges, ensuring that each will melt into the whole texture without seeming soloistic or excessively emotional. Like the soprano part, they each hover for extended periods within a narrow band of about five notes. (Our *National Anthem* covers the same span in just its first three notes!)

Example 17.6 Typical pitch-band of the voice parts

If one is moved to muscular action while hearing this music, it is not the tapping of a toe that is stimulated. It is more likely a slow undulation of the whole upper body, reacting to the steady rolling of musical flow. In fact, the single lines doggedly avoid "sing-song" patterns, their accents grouped to avoid the steady twos or threes associated with dance music. A single excerpt can reveal this flow of changing accents that is a product of durations, pitch contours, and word accents.

Example 17.7 Irregular accent patterns in a single voice passage

And yet, the accent patterns of a single voice part cannot tell the full story of Palestrina's marvelous rhythmic web. We must see how the accents of one voice relate to another's. This will reveal the ingenious way rhythms mix, creating the special quality that makes this music so appropriate for a religious setting. Observe in the next example how the accents of just one other voice relate to the excerpt shown earlier. The two are illustrated as they relate in time. Their accents do not coincide at any point.

Example 17.8 Accent relationships between two voices in the *Sanctus*

The product of as many as four voices moving in just this way—each voice moving in its own unique accent pattern—is an incomparable mixture of rhythms. In spite of their complex relations to each other, they blend together to project a sense of great variety within an overall frame of agreement. Palestrina's brilliance in achieving just this kind of rhythmic counter-pointing of lines is one of the main reasons his music is esteemed as the pinnacle of sixteenth-century choral music. It is the reason his music is revered by composers of today, as a treasure of melodic and rhythmic ingenuity from which to learn the fundamental skills of composition.

18

TWO SONGS OF THE
LATE RENAISSANCE

"Come Again! Sweet Love Doth Now Invite"
by John Dowland (1563–1626) and
"Amyntas with his Phyllis Fair"
by Francis Pilkington (?–1638)

BACKGROUND

Music historians refer to the long span of 500–1450 as the "Medieval Period." An equally appropriate name would be the "Catholic Period." Worthy music unrelated to any form of religious service certainly was composed and performed within that remote millennium; and yet the dominant motivation for its creation was the service of the Roman Catholic faith. The Church continued as a primary source and site of musical creation well past 1500, but the seeds of a rich secular music were well-sown by that time. The predominance today of secular art music is just one other outcome of the four-century split of art and religion. It had begun by the sixteenth century.

A definite change of attitude and products can be witnessed even from the middle of the fifteenth century. In fact, the so-called "Renaissance Period" in music is usually identified as a span of 150 years, roughly 1450–1600. Evidence of this shift of musical production, begun in Italy and transplanted to England, is the kind of music composed by John Dowland and Francis Pilkington.

Dowland was a devoted Catholic, Pilkington a minister in the Church of England. Unlike the music of many earlier composers who were devout, most of their songs are about love. In fact, their tiny musical world reflects the cares of the larger intellectual world of their times: it is man-centered rather than God-centered. They sing of people and their immediate cares rather than of theology and the glories of eternal salvation.

Illustration 18.1
Lute Player by Hans Brossamer, 1537.
Used by permission of the New York
Public Library.

A useful parallel can be drawn between Dowland and some of the popular composer-singers of today. He created straightforward solo songs whose texts deal with some aspect of the human condition. Like Bob Dylan, Cat Stevens, Joni Mitchell, or Paul McCartney, Dowland's music is the artful combination of word and melody. Its uncluttered accompaniments are meant to enhance rather than to intrude. Unlike the polyphonic church music composed by Palestrina, the central ingredient of Dowland's music is a message whose words are reinforced by a single accompanying instrument, usually the lute.

The songs of Dowland and his contemporaries were enormously popular among the sophisticates of Elizabethan England. They project the sense of worldly delight and emotional involvement that were paramount for the aristocracy of that country in the late sixteenth and early seventeenth centuries. For the educated man of those times some proficiency in dancing, poetry, music, art, and the "classics" of Roman and Greek literature was the telltale mark of accomplishment. Since music played a crucial role in the development of refined ladies and gentlemen, composers could publish their works for use by amateurs, who considered it proper and appropriate to sing songs of love for the entertainment of a close circle of friends.

Just as music lovers of today buy recorded albums of a favored artist to listen to in the privacy of their home, accomplished amateur performers of the late sixteenth century bought printed collections of *ayres* for home performance. The writer Robert Puttenham suggests the popularity of such entertainment when, in his *Art of Poesie* of 1589, he speaks of the performance of "Songs for secret recreation and pastime in chambers and company or alone. . ."

Illustration 18.2   Map of England showing Chester, London, Oxford.

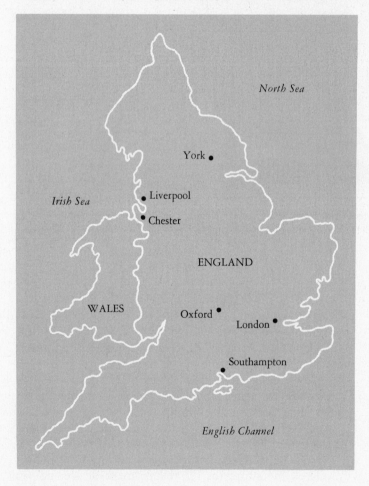

JOHN DOWLAND

Life and Works

This foremost composer of lute songs probably was born in England, although it was long held that he was of Irish parentage.* He came into a time that was beginning to accept the composer as a true professional. As the historian Will Durant explains, the Renaissance artist "was no longer an artisan working anonymously with others on a collective enterprise, as in the Middle Ages; he was a 'single and separate person' who stamped his character upon his works."†

Dowland's professional life began at eighteen, when he took a position in the service of the English ambassador to France. A year in this capacity furthered his competence as a lutenist; it also brought about his conversion to Catholicism, which became a critical factor in his later professional life. Because of antagonism toward Catholics in the English government—we might even use the term "paranoia" to describe the attitude held by some segments of society at that time—Dowland did not get the position he sought: musician in Elizabeth's court.

In 1588 the young composer was awarded the degree Bachelor of Music by Oxford University, along with another famous Elizabethan musician, Thomas Morley. But then as now, an academic degree was no assurance of a job. His continuing failure to find a court post led him to tours of France, Italy, Germany, and the Lowlands (now called the Netherlands). In those countries he was received as an accomplished artist. Returning to England in 1595, he began publishing his songs and lute works, the first collection appearing in 1597. This first book of Dowland's compositions was so popular that five editions were printed during his life.

From 1598 until 1606 Dowland was away again, now as lutenist in the court of King Christian in Denmark. (Christian's home base was Elsinore, the setting of Shakespeare's *Hamlet*). Leaving there in 1606, he made his way back to England, still without an official post to boost his earnings and morale. Absence from home had partially erased his earlier fame. Other composers of popular songs had filled the void during his foreign travels.

It must have been a dismal period for Dowland. Now fifty, he had faded in popularity and his religious affiliation remained a barrier to a court appointment. Although second and third collections of new songs

---

*His Irish origins are proved unfounded by Diana Poulton in *John Dowland his life and works*, Berkeley: U. of California Press, 1972.

†*The Renaissance*, New York, Simon and Schuster, 1953, p. 580.

appeared in 1600 and 1603, his former popularity was not wholly restored. Perhaps exaggerated a bit, Dowland's bleak situation is reflected in the following lines by fellow poet Henry Peacham (Philomel clearly referring to the composer):

> Heere Philomel, in silence sits alone,
> In depth of winter, on a bared bier,
> Whereas the Rose, her beauties once had showen;
> Which Lordes and Ladies, did so much desire;
>   But fruitless now, in winter's frost, and snow,
>   It doth despis'd, and unregarded grow, . . .

The parallel with his later musical counterpart, Wolfgang Mozart, also curiously without appointments equal to his talents, is too poignant to ignore. But it is ironic—and we can hope also factual—that Dowland was, as Thomas Fuller described him over thirty years after his death, a "cheerful person . . . passing his days in lawful merriment."

At last he got the official position he sought in the English court. Ascension to the throne by James I in 1603 had brought a more relaxed and tolerant atmosphere. Dowland was appointed lutenist in the court in 1612, a position he held until his death.

In all, Dowland published three collections of lute songs, leaving eighty-eight separate compositions of that type. He also left more than twenty compositions for solo lute, a small number of hymns, and one book of pieces for lute and viols, the sixteenth-century forerunners of our modern string instruments. Our concern is with his songs, or *ayres*, which clearly represent his main interest as a composer.

The Lute Song as a Type

This is a solo composition with accompaniment, the lute part frequently played by the singer himself. It is a strophic song, usually running to several stanzas. (Some lines are frequently repeated within stanzas.) Its subject matter is almost always the state of love or the anguish caused by strained feelings between lover and beloved. It sees the love relationship as a super-exalted state no human being could really hope to maintain in equilibrium. (And thus the need to write poems and sing about it!)

The lute was thoroughly embedded in the musical lives of Renaissance England. Established in that country as a popular instrument by the fourteenth century, in the sixteenth century it was the favored courtly sound, with the voice or alone. Its most gifted players were entertained in court as local heroes. A complete text for instruction in lute playing appeared in England for the first time in 1565. Its popularity was much the same as that of the guitar in contemporary America. Lines written by Thomas Mace in 1676 testify to the slightly snobbish appeal it still had among the upper strata of English society.

Her Matter's of such High Concern
No Common Folks can It discern;
'Twas ne'er intended for the Rude
and Boistrous-Churlish-Multitude;
But for Those Choice-Regined Spirits
Which Heav'nly-Raptures of Inherits.

This composition was published in Dowland's *First Book of Songes or Ayres* of 1597. The original version contains six stanzas, each set to the same music (and thus strophic), and beginning with a short line such as "Come again!" or "Gentle love."

Dowland came at the end of a long development in England of this kind of accompanied song. His technique is impeccable; his melodies are flowing and clear; his harmonies logically and tastefully underline the meaning of his words. Every musical gesture is calculated to enhance the text, with its message of refined yet strong emotion.

Like many Renaissance love songs, "Come Again!" was composed for very high male voice. This pitch-range, called *counter-tenor*, is what you would expect from a female voice, but the quality is uniquely male. It is an exotic sound for modern ears and attainable by few singers today. One period of music history (in Italy from the sixteenth to the eighteenth century) condoned the use of male voices made high by surgical castration. But the true counter-tenor voice is something else; it can be achieved only through the careful training of a mature voice whose genetic inclination is toward high pitch. The result is the strange effect of male power and timbre at an extraordinarily high range. Once a listener recovers from the first shock of this unusual sound it has a captivating beauty.

Some recordings of the song "Come Again!" leave out stanzas of the original version. The recording by Alfred Deller, who is probably the most famous interpreter of lute songs today, contains only half (1, 2 and 6) of the original six. The text of Mr. Deller's abbreviated version follows.

Come Again!
Sweet love doth now invite
Thy graces that refrain
To do me due delight
To see, to hear, to touch, to kiss, to die
With thee again in sweetest sympathy.

Come Again!
That I may cease to mourn
Through thy unkind disdain
For now, left and forlorn
I sit, I sigh, I weep, I faint, I die
In deadly pain and endless misery.

Gentle love,
Draw forth thy wounding dart.
Thou canst not pierce her heart;
For I that do approve,
By sighs and tears more hot than are thy shafts,
Did tempt, while she for triumph laughs.

Typical of its kind, the text of this ayre is an expression in very refined language of passionate but restrained feelings of love. It is interesting that within each stanza of six lines a considerable musical climax occurs with the end of the next to last line. Dowland creates this sense of thrust toward a point of highest intensity by setting the words to a rising pitch line. The highest point coincides with the last word of the line. Example 18.1 represents this notable bond of word and melody.

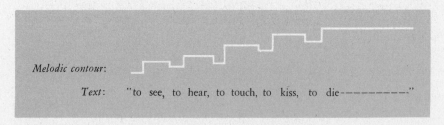

Example 18.1   Association of words and melody in "Come again!"

The same sequence of pitches recurs in stanzas two and three with the following lines of text:

Stanza 2:   "I sit, I sigh, I weep, I faint, I die."
Stanza 3:   "By sighs and tears more hot than are thy shafts."

It is important that you understand completely the musical skill incorporated in this brief passage, where increasing musical tension is allied with a series of words that progress from relatively passive to highly emotional. Observe in Stanza 2 how the word-series begins with "I sit," then progresses to "I die"; the last condition is of greater emotional import than any that precedes. This is a simple example of how one intelligent composer has welded music to words.

As in most late Renaissance songs of this type, "Come Again!" repeats lines within each stanza. Here the last two lines are repeated. This produces an interesting phrase-plan, as shown in our next example.

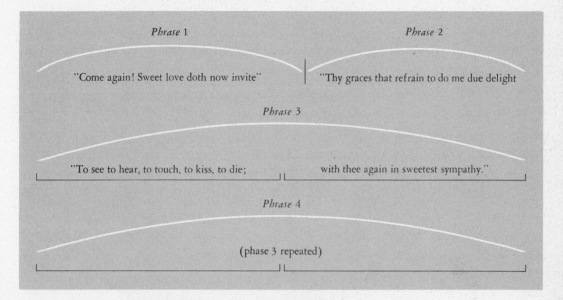

Example 18.2   Phrase form of "Come again!"

To modern ears this song may at first seem too self-consciously tender, too delicately refined. To some it may convey excessive sentimentality rather than the intended exquisite charm. And yet we must remember the social attitudes of its time. Accepting the sense of sophistication attached to just this sort of carefully wrought outpouring of the heart, we can recognize an artfulness. It is quite as capable of moving the twentieth-century listener as it was of moving the small circle who heard it amidst the rustle of velvet and silk in Shakespeare's day.

FRANCIS PILKINGTON

Life and Works   While Dowland was a celebrated man-of-the-world, Pilkington's sphere of activity was tiny and provincial, almost exclusively the town of Chester, which is next to Wales in west-central England.

Like Dowland, he took a degree in music at Oxford. He returned to Chester sometime before 1602, where he was a singer (or "chaunter" as he called himself) in the cathedral. His career as clergyman began around 1602, and he occupied a number of ministerial posts in and around Chester until 1631.

His first published compositions were songs (or ayres) for four voices. These were intended to be sung by four unaccompanied voices or, like Dowland's ayres, by solo voices with lute. In 1613 his first collection of madrigals and pastorals appeared, from which "Amyntas With His Phyllis Fair" is extracted. His final published music was a second collection of madrigals and pastorals which, as Pilkington notes in his Preface, are "apt for Violls and Voyces." This means, of course, that they could be played or sung, as available forces or inclinations might decide.

The Pastoral, "Amyntas With His Phyllis Fair"

On the title page of his first collection of songs Pilkington designates his works as *Madrigals* or as *Pastorals*. but the individual pieces are not so identified by these titles. The differentiation is an intrinsic one, determined by the text and musical style. In general, madrigals are more grave in tone. The pastorals are more vigorous, light-hearted songs with texts about rustic scenes (often suggestively erotic), as was fashionable in Elizabethan England.

The full text of Pilkington's pastoral about Amyntas and Phyllis is typical:

> Amyntas with his fair Phyllis in height of Summer's sun
> Grazed arm in arm their snowy flock; and scorching heat of sun
> Under a spreading elm sat down, where love's delightments done,
> Down dillie down, thus did they sing; there is no life like ours,
> No heaven on earth to shepherds' cells, no hell to princely bowers.

This music's textures are successively homophonic and polyphonic. Its rhythms are sprightly and light-hearted. As in the opening, some sections intertwine parts that are imitative, while in other sections all parts move together in a simple chord-by-chord rhythm.

There are two points we should make about the way Pilkington sets music to his text. First is his play with words, sometimes in a way that shows no concern for whether the listener understands the message. In these sections a phrase of a few words is tossed back and forth so rapidly from one voice to another that individual words are lost in the tumble. In other sections—particularly where voices move together as blocks of sound—the text is as clear as it might be in a solo song.

Pilkington indulges in "word painting" with the line "Down, down dillie-down." At this point the melodic contour obeys its text by stepping down to create a falling melodic line. Perhaps a naive gesture, yet too tempting for a composer of this period to resist. This word/music association is shown in notation in Example 18.3.

The composer appears to have enjoyed this bit of musical onomatopoeia, for he repeats the whole section based on the "Down" text.

Example 18.3 Word-painting in "Amyntas and Phyllis"*

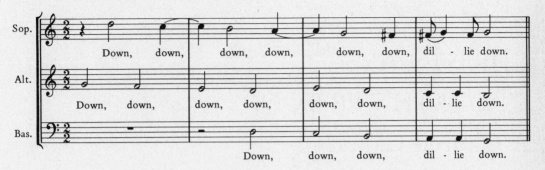

---

*This work can be found (with the other madrigals and pastorals of Pilkington's first collection) in Vol. 25 of *The English Madrigalists*, edited by Edmund H. Fellowes, London: Stainer and Bell, Ltd., 1922.

19

CHRIST LAY
IN DEATH'S PRISON,
A Church Cantata

J. S. Bach (1685–1750)

BACKGROUND

As we suggested in the previous chapter, the pinnacle for music of the Catholic Church was reached during the sixteenth century. Ironically, the religious reforms inaugurated early in that same century by Martin Luther (1483–1546) launched a competing sacred liturgy. This Protestant liturgy reached its own musical zenith about two hundred years later, especially in the rich body of church music composed by Johann Sebastian Bach.

The Protestant Chorale

While the common denominator of most Catholic music had been the melodies of the Gregorian Chant, a similar basis for Protestant music was provided by German chorales. These were collected and composed for that purpose by Luther and his collaborators. The modern hymnals of many American churches still contain some of these songs that were cultivated by the early Lutheran church for its reform movement.

Martin Luther did not envision a total break with the Catholic Church when he introduced his ninety-five points of disagreement with Rome in 1517. Even after his theological debate had led to an irreparable crack in the wall of Christendom, his reforms maintained parallels with Catholic ritual. Lutheran churches, for example, did not throw out wholesale the traditional Catholic liturgy; the music of that liturgy remained as an acceptable part of the service in many of the Reform churches in Germany.

Illustration 19.1
J.S. Bach

Illustration 19.2
Martin Luther's key role in
the reforms of the Christian
church ensured his powerful
influence on the subsequent
history of west European
religious and art music.

The crucial change for Reformation music resulted from Luther's belief that the Christian congregation should participate more actively in the religious ritual itself. For Luther this meant using songs whose texts were in the language of the people (rather than in Latin), and whose melodies were simple enough to be sung by the average parishioner. And thus ensued the collecting, composing, and reworking of a rich new body of melody for the church service: the Lutheran chorale came into being.

Like Gregorian Chant, these chorale melodies came from a variety of sources. Most were German folk songs to which Luther and other composers fitted sacred texts, frequently even translating the words of Catholic hymns into German. Some of the chorale melodies were actual Gregorian Chants, and still others were composed outright by Luther or one of his musical friends. Some chorale melodies were newly composed even as late as the seventeenth century, but those assembled during the fervent early days of the movement were more powerful carriers of the Christian message than their later imitations.

One of the chorales that has survived in some modern Protestant churches is *A Mighty Fortress Is Our God* (*Ein' feste Burg*). It was composed by Luther from earlier sources and first published in 1529. It can be found in most church hymnals today, sometimes bearing a different title, but in other respects the same song. (Its title is "Majesty and Power" in the official hymnal of the Methodist Church.) The straightforward melody, with its text of solid faith, is a symptom of what the chorale was all about for the sixteenth-century Lutheran.

At first the chorales were sung in unison by the congregation without harmony or any form of accompaniment. It was Luther's conviction that music could be a powerful means for instilling lofty thoughts and religious assurance in people's minds. Although he admired the artful music of the Catholic tradition, he cultivated the tunefully simple chorale as the musical bond that could provide believers with a sense of togetherness.

Calvinist Hymns

A similar collection of new religious songs developed in the Reformation movements of France, the Netherlands, and Switzerland. Led mainly by John Calvin (1509–1564), these non-German reformers were less liberal in their acceptance of acts or artifacts carried over from the Roman Catholic ritual. Calvin and his followers were wary of any kind of art as a part of the religious service. They opposed the performance of music associated with Rome or even the singing of hymns whose texts were not taken directly from the Christian bible.

And so the Calvinist churches developed their own counterparts for the chorales used in the German Lutheran movement. Translations of the biblical psalms were set to new melodies or to popular tunes. In 1562 a collection called the *French Psalter* was published for their dissemination.

The psalms sung by the Pilgrims when they arrived at Plymouth Rock in 1620 were of similar origins. They were from a psalter published in 1612 for use by the English Protestants (called *Separatists*) who had fled to Holland. These Massachusetts Pilgrims enriched the repertory even further by publishing their own collection of hymns in 1640. This hymnal was called the *Bay Psalm Book*.

The Calvinists' prohibition of artistic display discouraged the appropriation of their psalm tunes by serious composers. So these melodies were not used as the German chorales had been. The chorale is therefore a more interesting historical phenomenon, since it became the melodic backbone of hundreds of compositions for the church and the concert hall.

Use of Chorales in Art Music

Harmonized versions of the chorales were published for the religious service early in the sixteenth century. Works similar to the imitative motets of Josquin des Prez and Palestrina were composed as early as 1524, a chorale melody replacing Gregorian Chant as a precomposed melodic basis. This was the beginning of a tradition that would persist for over four hundred years, flourishing particularly during the middle and late Baroque period, when Bach lived. Chorales were used as the melodic basis for all manner of art compositions. Instrumental fantasias, variations and fugues, organ preludes, motets, and whole cantatas carried these sturdy reminders of the Lutheran cause. In this way the Lutheran chorale was adapted to artistic uses comparable to the uses of Gregorian Chant that had dominated art music for the previous nine centuries.

The Cantata

The mere title of this kind of composition comes from the Italian word *cantare*, which means "to sing." In earlier use the title provided a simple way of distinguishing sung music from music played on a keyboard instrument (*toccata*, or "touch piece") and music played by blown or bowed instruments (*sonata*, or "sound piece").

The cantata appears to have been a close relative of *monody*, an innovation of the early seventeenth century that developed into opera. (We shall discuss monody presently in Chapter 20.) From its beginnings, the cantata was a vocal composition. It was sung in the vernacular rather than in Latin, and it was commonly accompanied by an instrumental combination of modest size. In its early development it was more often a secular than a sacred composition. In this respect it seems to have replaced the Italian madrigal, which was the favored type of vocal music through the sixteenth century. One of the main characteristics of the early cantatas was their use of vocal solos and duets as short "movements" within a longer piece that maintained some degree of dramatic continuity.

During the two centuries that separate Luther's disengagement from Rome and the compositions of Bach, the church music of most

German and Austrian cities retained strong ties with Italian music. Even composers allied with the Lutheran cause continued for a while to compose in the style of the Catholic motet. Gradually, however, another form developed that was more uniquely flavored by the Protestant zeal for new religious imagery. This was the sacred cantata.

By the time Bach was a mature composer, the cantata was an accepted part of the Lutheran service. In fact, it was assumed that the musical director of any large Lutheran church should compose a new cantata for each week of the Church year, as well as new music for other special events like festivals, funerals, and weddings. Bach composed about 300 sacred cantatas during his tenure as musician in the several Lutheran churches he served.

BACH'S CANTATAS

For Bach the cantata was a composition for mixed chorus accompanied by a small instrumental ensemble. His works usually open with combined chorus and instruments, continue with a succession of movements featuring a soloist, duet, or trio, then close with the full chorus singing a harmonized chorale. Most of the cantatas utilize a chorale (sometimes even several chorales) as the melodic basis for their interior movements as well. As we shall see, all of the movements of his Cantata No. 4 are based on a single chorale melody. This is unique.

In 1723 Bach moved from his post in Cöthen to become musical director of the most prestigious Lutheran church in Leipzig, Germany, the St. Thomas Kirche. Most of his sacred cantatas were composed for the services of that congregation. For many musicians today the term *cantata* is almost synonymous with *Bach Cantata,* although the Western repertory contains examples by many other composers. Even after Bach, masters like Haydn, Mozart, Beethoven, Schubert, Schumann, Mendelssohn, Liszt, and Brahms composed pieces of similar nature. But these usually were for festive concert occasions rather than for church performance.

Bach wrote cantatas for non-church performance too. His secular cantatas were similar to miniature operas, although they were meant to be produced without scenery, costuming, and actual stage action. One of the most delightful "music comedies" of our history is his *Coffee Cantata* (No. 211). Most likely composed for performance in a Leipzig coffee house, it tells the story of a young lady whose father pleads that she forego the pleasures of coffee, the exotic new drink that had delighted the tastebuds of eighteenth-century Germans. (There were as many as eight coffee houses in Leipzig in 1725, which was considerable for a city of only thirty thousand.)

Illustration 19.3
St. Thomas Church in Leipzig, Germany where Bach served last as music master.

The *Coffee Cantata* is worth hearing for its musical value alone, but it is even more valuable in proving that the old cantor of St. Thomas Church had a sense of humor as well as musical genius to spare.

CHRIST LAG IN TODESBANDEN
(Christ Lay in Death's Bonds) Cantata No. 4

Like his Roman predecessor of the sixteenth century, Palestrina, Bach was a relatively conservative composer. His music was not created with an ear to the trends of his time, particularly to the encroachments of opera that were being made into church music of the eighteenth century. His excellence lay in perfecting old rather than creating new models. Several aspects of the Cantata No. 4 confirm this reactionary spirit.

The Chorale Basis   The seven-movement work is based on the seven-verse chorale Luther composed for Easter and published in 1524. He had assembled the text from older religious poetry, and for the melody he reworked an Easter hymn that dates from the twelfth century. So Bach could not have chosen a chorale more embedded in religious tradition. The melody of the original chorale (*a*) and Bach's slightly revised version (*b*) are shown next.

Example 19.1 Sixteenth- and eighteenth-century versions of the chorale melody *Christ Lay in Death's Bonds*

You should note one thing about Bach's version: he changes two pitches (marked by asterisks on the score of *b*). One of these, as we shall note presently, plays an important part in his cantata. The older version by Luther contains the notes of the archaic *Dorian* scale, while Bach's "modernization" is more in line with the minor scales that were common in music of the eighteenth century.*

The text of Luther's chorale, used in its entirety by Bach, is rich in the imagery of Christian belief. It celebrates a fundamental tenet of Christianity: the symbolic sacrifice of Christ's life for the salvation of humanity. Each eight-line verse suggests some parallel between the Christian notion of immortality and Christ's miraculous resurrection from death. (Each verse of the text will appear at the beginning of our discussion of the corresponding verse of the cantata.)

Bach composed this cantata for an Easter Sunday sometime between 1708 and 1714. He revived it for several performances after he had moved

*See the Glossary, "*Church Modes*".

to Leipzig, and for many years historians wrongly assumed that it was composed during that period, perhaps in 1724. The version we have today is probably a reworking of the original score. In 1725 he even added instrumental doublings to voice parts of some verses, most likely because the singers in his choir were not strong enough to produce a satisfactory performance unaided.

In spite of revisions he may have made, the cantata still does not bear the kinds of operatic touches considered fashionable by composers in Germany during the first quarter of the eighteenth century. It is in an old-fashioned style, containing elements that relate it to composers Bach admired, such as Kuhnau, Pachelbel, and Buxtehude. Old-fashioned or not, it is a masterpiece of devout religious feeling, a work that can touch the listener's deepest emotions as well as engage his highest sense of musical awe.

The Sinfonia

The cantata opens with a brief introduction, called *Sinfonia*. Played by the small orchestra of two violins, two violas, and a continuo part,* this somber beginning establishes the work's initial mood and skillfully exposes a simple motif Bach extracted from the first two notes of Luther's chorale melody. If you will look back to Example 19.1 you will see that melody (*b*) has a sharped note as its second pitch. In conjunction with the first note, it forms a falling half step. This simple pattern becomes an obsessive motif within the first half of the cantata. The next example shows how this same interval occurs as a dominating element, sounding four times within as many measures of the *Sinfonia*.

Example 19.2   Principal motif of the *Sinfonia*

Listen carefully and you will hear a fleeting reference to the complete first phrase of the chorale tune just after the opening four measures. Bach's object seems to be to formally identify that which will be the basis for what follows.

We have heard movements already (Haydn's *Surprise Symphony*, for example) in which theme and variations serve as a composition's formal procedure. Bach's cantata is in its own right a theme and variations,

---

*In the Baroque period the continuo part consisted of a bass line. This was played by organ in sacred compositions, by harpsichord in secular works. To this bass the keyboard player added appropriate chords, much as a jazz pianist does. A cello and double bass usually played the continuo part along with the keyboard instrument.

although it appears to reverse the usual order into variations and theme. Seven verses, or "movements," follow the introductory *Sinfonia*. Six of these movements are glorious variations entwined about the successive phrases of the chorale tune.* Only in the seventh movement does the actual theme (meaning the unembellished chorale) finally appear.

But this is not so strange nor so inconsistent with the theme and variation plan as it first may seem: Bach's Lutheran congregation knew the chorale *Christ lag in Todesbanden* long before hearing Bach's cantata. Its appearance at the end comes only as the final realization of a predetermined goal, a return to an "understood" beginning. The whole cantata is a grand extension and elaboration of the hymn parishioners had sung on many an Easter Sunday.

Other aspects of the cantata's form are equally interesting. Its seven verses use voices and textures in a way that forms a symmetrical plan. Note how Verse IV assumes the function of keystone for a simple arch-plan.

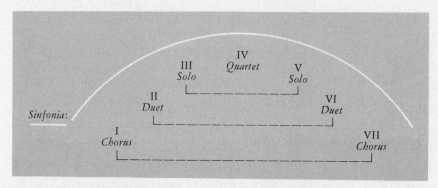

Example 19.3 Symmetrical arrangement of choruses, duets, solos, and quartets in the Cantata

This is the simple yet ingenious way Bach ensures an overall textural unity *and* variety for his composition. It is a plan that makes the cantata more than a mere stringing together of variations on a single tune.

Verse I: Chorus, orchestra and continuo	*Christ lag in Todesbanden* *Für unser Sünd gegegen,* *Er ist wieder erstanden* *Und hat uns bracht das Leben;*	Christ lay in death's bonds, sacrificed for our sins. He is risen again and has brought life to us.

---

*Retaining basically the same melody in several sections like this is called *cantus firmus technique*. A part or voice that carries the dominating melody is called the *cantus firmus*.

Des wir sollen fröhlich sein,	Thus we shall be joyful,
Gott loben und ihm dankbar sein	praise God and give Him thanks,
Und singen Hallelujah.	and sing Alleluia
Hallelujah!	Alleluia!*

This first verse establishes a model of procedure for each of the following movements except the final: its texture is polyphonic and its thematic basis is derived from the chorale tune. Again, there is special emphasis on the two-note motif whose significance we observed in the *Sinfonia*.

The *cantus firmus* process Bach uses most of the time is interesting from a psychological point of view. The chorale melody accompanies itself, moving along in different voices at two, sometimes three different rates of speed at the same time. Each phrase of the tune is sung in slow articulations by the sopranos, separated by long spans of silence. Around and between these spasmodic phrases a rich web of lines weaves a rapid accompaniment, the melodies drawn largely from the chorale tune. The result is similar to witnessing the same movie film projected at different speeds, for one layer of the texture (here the soprano) appears to be the slow-motion replica of its accompanying parts.

In most phrases of this first verse the alto, tenor, or bass voices sings a rapid preview of the chorale phrase that will be sung next by the slower-moving soprano. For instance, at one point the following relationships occur between alto, tenor, and soprano. (The lengths of dashes represent relative durations in each melody.)

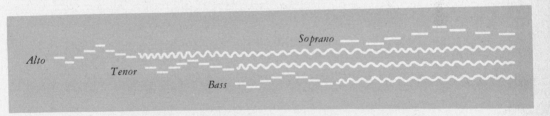

Example 19.4   Pre-imitations of chorale phrases between voices

For those who read musical notation, the following simplified score shows how this series of "imitations-before-the-fact" occur.

This dramatic succession of melodic imitations at two different rates of speed continues until the last phrase; there the soprano's articulation is accelerated to be at the same rate as its accompanying lines. This leads to a bursting *Alleluia*. Moving at twice the tempo of the preceding texture,

---

*In English versions I have tried to preserve basic meaning, sometimes at the expense of literal translation.

Example 19.5 Previous example in notation (simplified)

it completes the movement with a sense of victory of Christ over death.
A complete mapping of the movement, phrase-by-phrase, is shown next.

Example 19.6 Phrase layout, Verse I

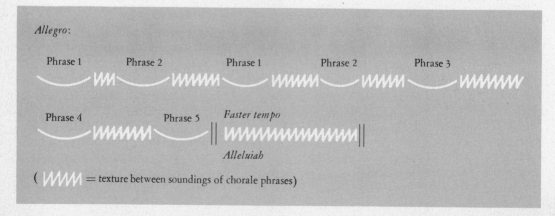

Verse II:
Soprano and Alto
duet with continuo

Dem Tod niemand zwingen kunnt	No one can conquer Death
Bei allen Menschenkindern,	for all of man's children.
Das macht' alles unser Sund	This is the cause of our sins;
Kein Unschuld war zu finden.	purity was not to be found.
Davon kam der Tod so bald	Hence came Death so suddenly
Und nahm über uns Gewalt,	and made us his slaves,
Hielt uns in seinem Reich gefangen.	held us imprisoned in his kingdom.
Hallelujah!	Alleluia!

If we distill this text to its simplest terms, its message is the inevitability of death. Bach's music is appropriately unrelenting. It is a duet between soprano and alto voices, accompanied by a continuo line (organ and bass instruments) that suggests an inexorable plodding toward death as man's fate.

The chorale tune appears in slightly varied make-up in the soprano voice, with a grinding emphasis on the falling motif that dominated the *Sinfonia.* This simple musical gesture is further emphasized by the echo relation Bach fixes between the two voices. Through the first six lines of the text the soprano is the leader in the relationship, the alto its echo But in line seven (*hielt uns,* or "held us") they reverse roles, soprano now echoing the tiny motifs of the alto. (This role changing is much easier to hear in public than in recorded performances.)

In view of its text, the *Alleluia* of this movement is most interesting. People have little to celebrate, after all, in the notion that they are trapped in the grip of inescapable death. Bach's *Alleluia* reflects that sentiment. It is one of the gloomiest *Alleluias* in the history of church music. It projects no mood of rejoicing, eventually ending on a relatively low pitch in the voices, then sinking to a final low tone played by the continuo parts.

In this movement the actual chorale tune, the *cantus firmus,* is varied slightly, particularly during its first phrase, where Bach hammers away with the two-note falling motif.* The motif occurs twice each time as a preview of the chorale tune's complete phrase, as Example 19.7 illustrates.

Example 19.7   Motivic "previews" of the first phrase in the chorale tune

---

*Many writers have equated this falling inflection with the idea of death and grief.

Verse III:
Tenor voice, violins
and continuo

Jesus Christus, Gottes Sohn   Jesus Christ, God's Son,
An unser Statt ist kommen   has come on our behalf,
Und hat die Sünde weggetan,   and has atoned for our sin;
Damit dem Tod genommen   thereby from Death has taken
All sein Recht und sein Gewalt,   all its rights and power.
Da bleibet nichts denn Tods Gestalt, Hence nothing remains but the notion
                                           of death:
Den stachl hat er verloren.   it has lost its sting.
Hallelujah!   Alleluia!

A sense of optimism enters. Christ's life and sacrificial death show humanity a way to salvation. There is hope after all! A lovely trio texture neatly sets forth this aura of quiet but joyful hope. The movement's "neatness" is most evident in the way the rhythms of the three parts are combined. While the tenor sings the *cantus firmus* phrases in relatively unadorned fashion, the bass line moves twice as fast and the violin's rhythms are four times as fast. The result is an uncluttered texture, each part rhythmically separated in a 1:2:4 relationship.

Bach retains his falling motif as a chief ingredient in the accompaniment. Now it has grown to include the third note of the chorale tune's first phrase, forming the main substance of the rapid figures of the violin line. Its predominance is pinpointed by the brackets in Example 19.8.

Example 19.8   Motif of "Death", violin line Verse III

Like earlier composers of vocal music, Bach engages in some rather obvious tonal-painting, or "pictorialism." This is most evident in Verse III when the tempo abruptly slows on the word *Tod* ("death") of line six. Once the text line has been completed, this sudden dramatic attention to death resolves into the former rapid tempo.

Less obvious, but quite as interesting, are some of the instrumental pyrotechnics that precede this halting allusion to the "death of Death." The text tells us that Christ's resurrection has taken from Death its "rights and powers." At this moment the violins—for the first and only time in the entire cantata—play a fitful series of thick chords, as if they are administering the fatal blows to Death personified. To complete this curious scenepainting, the bass line begins a rapid drop, as if to convey the impression of Death falling from His former glory. These events occur with the text line *all Recht und sein Gewalt.*

Verse IV:
Choral quartet
and continuo

Es war ein wunderlicher Krieg,
Da Tod und Leben rungen,
Das Leben da behielt den Sieg,
Es hat den Tod verschlungen.
Die Schrift hat verkündiget das,
Wie ein Tod den andern frass,

Ein Spott aus dem Tod ist worden.
Hallelujah!

It was an incredible war,
that Death and Life fought.
Life gained the advantage;
It has overcome Death.
The Bible predicted this,
how one's death could overcome
    Death itself,
making it a mockery.
Alleluia!

As we noted earlier, the fourth verse occupies a central position, utilizing the forces of soprano, alto, tenor, and bass as do Verses I and VII. This heavier vocal texture is appropriate as musical underpinning for the text, which tells of an all-out war between the forces of Life and Death. The chorale tune persists as a slow-moving line sung by the altos, amidst a winding knot of accompanying voices. The image is that of brusque and powerful motion, a marching that relaxes only with the final chord.

The accompanying textures of each section are molded from successive entrances by basses, tenors and sopranos before each new phrase of the *cantus firmus* is sounded. This maze of intertwining patterns unravels just before the closing *Alleluia*. There the texture melts to a series of imitative fragments, the mockery of Death (*ein Spott*) becoming a brief topic of emphasis among the four voices.

Verse V:
Bass voice, strings
and continuo

Hier ist das recht Osterlamm,
Davon Gott hat geboten,
Das ist hoch an des Kreuzes Stamm
In heisser Lieb gebroten,

Das blut zeichnet unser Tur,
Das hält der Glaub dem Tod für,
Der Würger kann uns nicht mehr
    schaden.
Hallelujah!

Here is the real Easter lamb
that God has given us,
Who high on the trunk of the cross
is roasted in ardent love.

His blood marks our door.
Faith holds this up to Death;
The Murderer can hurt us no more.

Alleluia!

The struggle between Life and Death was decided in Verse IV. Now Bach underlines the notion of Christian redemption, Christ serving as symbol for the "Easter Lamb" of sacrifice. The more tender quality of this verse is in part suggested by the smoothly gliding line of the bass voice;* it is further suggested by a change to triple meter, whose *long-short* rhythms contrast with the duple meters of the preceding movements. Both of these elements of contrast account for the less driving mobility of this Verse, a relaxation of the tension that has dominated the drama up to this time.

---

*Some performances use a solo bass on this part, others the full bass section of the choir.

Bach also provides a change in variation procedure. While accompanying voices "previewed" chorale phrases in earlier verses, now the bass voice is the leader and the orchestral lines the followers. The bass introduces each successive phrase of the chorale tune, violins answering this phrase immediately at the top of the orchestral sound.

Verse V also bears its share of musical pictorialisms. Perhaps the most obvious occurs with the word *Tod* ("Death") in line six of the text (*Das hält der Glaub dem Tod für*). At this point the bass voice plummets to its bottom register, there sustaining a relatively long tone. This is still another way Bach dramatizes death as a despicable state, quite as effective yet quite different from the touch used in Verse III, when the tenor voice arrived at the same word.

Verse VI:
Soprano and tenor
duet with continuo

So feiern wir das hohe Fest	So we observe the highest feast
Mit herzenfreud und Wonne,	With joyous heart and rapture.
Das uns der Herre scheinen lasst,	The Lord reveals for us,
Er ist selber die Sonne,	He is himself the sun,
Der durch seiner Gnaden Glanz	Who through his glowing mercy
Erleuchtet unser Herzen ganz,	wholly illuminates our hearts;
Der Sünden Nacht is verschwunden.	The sinful night has disappeared.
Hallelujah!	Alleluia!

Christ's symbolic victory over Death has dispelled the gloom and terror of Verses I through IV. Verse V has provided the calm aftermath of battle. Now a celebration of God's supremacy is in order. Verse VI returns to the duet texture of Verse II, but its mood is as joyful as Verse II was doleful. Its skipping rhythm in the bass and its rhapsodic duets between soprano and tenor (the "brightest" vocal timbres of the choir) create an unmistakeably festive spirit.

The chorale phrases are clearly imbedded in this movement. They are so extended by vocal embellishments, however, that they serve more as a point of departure than as an unyielding nucleus for the whole movement. Each phrase statement begins as imitation between the two voices, only to dissolve each time into a florid duet in which one word of the text is stretched over many notes.

As we should expect by now, Bach places these jubilant duet lines with care: they occur in the beginning of the verse with the word *Wonne* ("rapture") and next on its text rhyme *Sonne* ("sun"). The same duet patterns come later as the setting for the closing *Alleluia*. An even more direct kind of tonal painting is evident in the very first phrase of the verse. There the soprano's line ("So we observe the high feast") begins in a low register. As it arrives at the word *hohe* ("high"), a sudden wide skip to the high register supplies a simple musical analogy for the text's meaning.

In spite of its similar duet texture with Verse II, this movement's character advances the unfolding Christian drama of redemption to its logical conclusion. Its joyful, dancing tone is good preparation for the cosmic assurance declared by the full chorale that is Verse VII.

Verse VII:
Chorus, orchestra,
and continuo

Wir essen und leben wohl	We eat and live well
In rechten Osterfladen,	on the true bread of Easter.
Der alte Sauerteig nicht soll	The old bread shall not exist
Sein bei dem Wort der Gnaden,	along with the doctrine of mercy.
Christus will die Koste sein	Christ will be the food
Und speisen die seel allein,	and alone nourish the soul.
Der Glaub will keins andern leben.	Our faith will survive on no other.
Hallelujah!	Alleluia!

Little need be said about the final chorale. Its unembellished simplicity is a fitting musical gesture for the end of the cantata. Its brevity provides a balance with the opening *Sinfonia,* both much shorter than the intervening six verses.

In actual church performances for the Easter service, however, the final chorale acts as far more than mere close for the whole cantata. We must remember that Luther's most pressing demand was the congregation's active participation in the church ritual. Coming at the end of the Easter drama, the chorale expresses in words and music the collective faith of the congregation, individuals who have come together in this reenactment of the central belief of the Christian doctrine.

20

THE MARRIAGE OF MUSIC
AND DRAMA: OPERA

BACKGROUND: WHAT IS OPERA?

Opera is a compound art form, its essential ingredients consisting of music and dramatic action. Within the mix there is an orchestra, scenery, stage action, dialogue and soliloquy, costumes, choruses, and, above all, solo singing.

Some operas contain bits of spoken dialogue, some do not. Some are cast in three acts, others in two, still others in four. Some are in only one act. Many of the processes and forms of opera are flexible, and its outer trappings have changed during its three and one-half centuries of development in the Western world. But to be opera, there *must* be staged drama with singing.

Opera demands a willing audience. It is not as easily digested as a pop song or a television movie, for its aim is toward bigger and deeper human experiences than can be commanded by those more modest forms. Furthermore, its full impact—comic or tragic—is felt only if the listener is part of an audience. Crowd psychology manifests some power in sophisticated drama as surely as it does in primitive ritual. The raw excitement of a Hopi snake dance may seem remote from the restrained decorum of an opera house, yet both share the power of merging the individual with a group. This facet of group response is just one of the reasons that live opera is more moving than its canned shadow via radio, phonograph, or television.

OPERATIC CONVENTIONS

Some people are bothered by the conventions of opera, those "understood" elements that brand it as somewhat less than real life. True, it is set to music, characters singing rather than speaking their lines. As everybody knows, real people do not go around singing to each other all of the time!

Even the way singers sing in opera is another convention of the genre. The relaxed voice of pop or folk music is wholly inappropriate; only the elaborately disciplined voice is acceptable, and this "unnatural" quality of the sound upsets some listeners whose tastes favor the Frank Sinatra or Bob Dylan tradition of casual ease.

And since the drama of opera depends upon sung rather than spoken lines, its action takes longer to unfold than does that of a play. A composer's music must consume blocks of time to control moods and build to believable climaxes. Dramatic action sometimes slows or even stops while this occurs. This time-demand of music places a new perspective on acting for the singers, who must prolong stage gestures that would seem fumbling and inept in a play or in the real world.

Because music can provide a background and suggest simple emotions, the text of an opera (called the *libretto*) must be shaved to a minimum of words. So reading an opera's text can be disappointing; it is like reading the mere outline of a novel, for the other two-thirds of its meaning resides in its music and staging.

However, these conventions should be no more damaging for opera than those of other arts, in which human experience is projected in formalized ways, are to them. The aside to an audience, which characters on stage pretend not to hear, occurs in acceptable plays, yet our knowledge of the laws of sound transmission do not lead us to dismiss them as silly. And further, only the most gullible oaf would jump up to strike the villain's flat image on a movie screen, or seriously object that the figures seen on a television screen are no more than one-tenth of life size. These too are conventions. If an audience wishes to receive the impact of the artist's message, they must be accepted—in fact, forgotten.

THE OPERA LIBRETTO

Opera depends for much of its success on a clear and workable libretto. The writer, or *librettist*, is therefore a key figure in the creation of an opera. Successful opera composers are those who are blessed with the collaboration of an experienced librettist, a writer who can turn a phrase to the particular demands of the musical stage. (Some composers write their own libretti.) The history of opera can be viewed with accuracy as

Illustration 20.1 Many operas offer the viewer scenes of splendor and pageantry that might seem inappropriate in more realistic forms of drama. In Benjamin Britten's *The Burning Fiery Furnace* the characters of King Nebu-chadnezzar and his Court Astrologer dictate the rightly ornate costumes shown in this scene. Photo by Jim Tuttle (Opera Studio, State University of New York, Buffalo)

Illustration 20.2
(Left) Verdi's lifelong enthusiasm for the plays of Shakespeare had lasting repercussions for the operatic world. His *Otello* was produced first in 1887 when the composer was 73. Here the title character and his doomed wife, Desdemona, are shown in one of the opera's gripping scenes. Photograph by Louis Ouzer (Eastman School of Music)

Illustration 20.3
(Below) Some of the pageantry of opera is shown in this scene from Darius Milhaud's opera *The Abduction of Europa*, where the chorus reacts to the unfolding action. Photo by Osterreicher (Opera Studio, SUNY at Buffalo)

Illustration 20.4
(Left) The success of an opera performance depends largely on how well it is staged. This set by Robert Winkler heightens the dramatic impact of Ariadne's plight in Richard Strauss' opera *Ariadne auf Naxos*. Photograph by Robert Willoughby (Opera Studio, SUNY at Buffalo)

Illustration 20.5
(Below) Puccini's *La Boheme* has not ebbed in its appeal since it was first performed in 1896. Its sentimental love story of ill-fated love in a Bohemian setting (Paris in the 1830s) revolves about a poet, Rodolfo, and his lover Mimi. Photo by Robert Willoughby (Opera Studio, SUNY at Buffalo)

Illustration 20.6 A part of opera's fascination is found in its staging and costumes, its portrayal of the pomp and glitter of long past ages and customs. Here the principal characters of Mozart's *Cosi fan tutte* deliver the final chorus. Photograph by Louis Ouzer (Eastman School of Music)

Illustration 20.7 Few operas lack at least one scene that is dominated by group or solo dancing. This formal court dance occurs in Tchaikovsky's opera *Eugene Onegin* (1878), which is the best known of the ten produced by the great Russian composer. Photo courtesy Indiana University School of Music

a long succession of tugs to keep musical and dramatic elements in some kind of balance. A decade when plots and stage logic are lost in a lust for exciting vocal display (or local in-jokes) is followed by a decade of equally zealous reform, when dramatic integrity is once more prized above all other considerations.

HISTORICAL BACKGROUND

Forerunners

Formal presentations of drama through music can be traced into the shadowy recesses of man's history. Rarely does the ritual of primitive man not involve music, and ritual is drama. Probably the closest relative of our Western opera was the ancient music drama of China. As one scholar reminds us,* even the invading Mongols of Jenghis Khan and Kublai Khan in the thirteenth century could not dampen the glories of Chinese opera. In fact, that particular cultural collision was enriching: the Mongols merely added to the existing Chinese form the lutes and percussion instruments they brought with them.

West European opera developed first in Italy. The madrigal composers of that country, forerunners of English composers like Dowland and Pilkington, infused dramatic continuity into some collections (or *cycles*) of their songs during the late sixteenth century. Called *madrigal comedies*, these were not staged presentations like opera today, but they did project a simple dramatic plot through music. They usually presented an idyllic scene in an atmosphere peopled by fairy-tale characters or mythological figures. They were the dying gasp of the madrigal and the birth cry of what was to be called *opera*.

Early Development

What came next, around 1600, was viewed by contemporaries as a truly "new music." A talented group of singers and poets in Florence, Italy, hoped to revive what they thought was a form of ancient Greek music. Their revolution was motivated by a refreshing reverence for the importance of their texts, music taking a secondary position in the total scheme. Called *monody* (or, literally, *singing alone*), the highly formalized speech-song they cultivated was accompanied by bare musical resources, often only a solo lute. It was different from the other accompanied songs of the period; it was more declamatory than melodic, more recited than sung. This early characteristic established an operatic convention that persists even today: contrasts between a solo song type that is purely melodic, called *aria*, and another type that is delivered in a semi-recited manner, called *recitative*. The bulk of Florentine monody would for us fit the recitative category.

---

*William P. Malm, *MUSIC CULTURES OF THE PACIFIC, THE NEAR EAST, AND ASIA*, 2nd Edition, Englewood Cliffs, N.J.: Prentice-Hall, Inc., 1977. p. 158.

The essential kernel of this new style caught on with the creative composers of the day—which its originators were not—and thus led to true opera. In fact, this new passion for the word and its dramatic message, and reliance on recitative as its musical vehicle, swept the sacred and secular musical establishments of seventeenth-century Europe. In religious presentations the pious counterpart of opera was called *oratorio*. This sacred form of vocal drama actually developed first.

By 1650 opera was the rage of upper-class Rome and Venice as well as Florence. It even supplied an artistic transfusion for the courtly ballet of Louis XIV in France, providing that country's aristocracy with a healthy new musical dimension. By 1637 opera's broad commercial potential was first tapped with the opening of a public opera house in Venice.

RESUMÉ OF KEY COMPOSERS

It is not difficult to single out the first great opera composer: he was Claudio Monteverdi (1567–1643). It was he who first fused musical richness and dramatic skill with the rather barren monody developed by his Florentine neighbors. His twelve operas, only three of which survive today, were the beginning of a chain of thousands that have been composed for audiences of the West since 1600.*

Of those thousands, few are revived today. Of that few, even fewer are produced very often by modern opera companies. The heartless weeding-out process of time takes its toll, and thus we remember only those composers who survive it.

HANDEL Monteverdi's most notable immediate successor was George F. Handel (1685–1759). Although best known today for his oratorio the *Messiah*, Handel's reputation in the first half of the eighteenth century was forged by the thirty-six operas he composed for the London stage between 1710 and 1741. Born in Germany, he studied in Italy, the country that would remain the mecca for opera composers well into the twentieth century. He transplanted the craft he learned there to his adopted England, with some of the dramatic improprieties it had accumulated since its glorious beginnings with Monteverdi. (These included jokes that were irrelevant to the plot and songs repeated for no reason except to boost the singer's applause.)

GLUCK One composer who fought the battle of drama versus music was Christoph Willibald Gluck (1714–1787). With his librettist, Raniero Calzabiggi, he fashioned, during his mature years, operas that skirted artifici-

---

*In *The Magic of Opera* (Harper & Row, 1972) J. Merrill Knapp estimates that up to 40,000 operas have been composed up to this time.

ality. He avoided the subplots, excessively long solo songs, and irrelevant gags that made some early eighteenth-century operas a kind of lavish variety show.

MOZART Gluck's reforms cleared a path for Wolfgang Mozart (1756–1791), whose opera *Don Giovanni* we shall discuss in Chapter 21. Mozart's operas are major bits of evidence for his unsurpassed musical genius. If he favored any musical form, in fact, it was opera. True to his precocious talent, he composed his first in 1768 at the age of twelve. No first-rate opera theater of today, in this country or in Europe, goes long without producing one of his mature works.

ROSSINI The Italian Gioacchino Rossini (1792–1868) was born one year after Mozart's death, but he lived past the mid-nineteenth century. He composed some thirty-eight operas before he mysteriously abdicated his position as leader of Italian opera—and thus *world opera*—in 1825 at the age of thirty-seven.

Rossini's innate musical talent, which was enhanced by self-teaching, provided opera with the kind of peasant vigor it needed to survive its bouts with stilted formality and theatrical chicanery. His comic opera *The Barber of Seville* (1816) remains an unfaded perennial on opera bills today. His best-known serious opera, *William Tell* (1829), became a model from which the tradition of modern "Grand Opera" stems. (It also bequeathed, unwittingly, the passage most Americans recognize as the theme for the Lone Ranger and his trusty aide Tonto.)

MEYERBEER In the hands of Rossini's French contemporary, Giacomo Meyerbeer (1791–1864), opera inched toward that state of artificiality that spells decline. The complicated and lavish productions his works entail cannot survive the economic realities of our own age, in spite of their high musical quality. One occasionally learns that Meyerbeer's *The Huquenots* (1836) (based on a story of that religious movement of French Protestants) is to be produced. It is grand opera in all of its nineteenth-century splendor and worth the price of admission for the spectacle alone.

BERLIOZ The most durable French composer of instrumental music in the early nineteenth century was also a composer of memorable opera. Hector Berlioz (1803–1869) was more adventurous than Meyerbeer in reacting to the operatic excesses passed to him by his predecessors. He reduced the hard contrast that had existed between recitative and aria (which occurred in just that paired order in operas). In this he anticipated trends more thoroughly realized by later composers, particularly by Richard Wagner. Berlioz injected into his operas the process of thematic recurrence he had used in his symphonic works. This consisted of using particular melodic motifs in association with particular characters, each of these "mottos" interwoven in the musical fabric to create an audible personification of the character, an *idée fixe*.

Like Meyerbeer's, Berlioz's operas are of the spectacle type cultivated in the opulence of nineteenth-century France. His opera based on the exploits of the notorious silversmith (and egomaniac!) *Benvenuto Cellini* (1838), his *The Trojans* (1859), and his *Beatrice and Benedict* (1862) are adequate to ensure that he will be remembered as one of the great composers, although opportunities for seeing these works performed are rare.

BELLINI AND DONIZETTI Vincenzo Bellini (1801–1834) and Gaetano Donizetti (1797–1848) filled the gap in Italy's operatic fare between Rossini and the master of all nineteenth-century Italian opera, Giuseppe Verdi. Both Bellini and Donizetti wrote romantic opera, tragedy with plots of rather heavy melodrama.

Both composers wrote vocal lines that fit the description *bel canto*. This term literally means "beautiful chant," or "song," but it has different meanings for different opera enthusiasts. In its more laudable meaning, *bel canto* suggests clarity and grace of singing style, a smooth delivery by a voice of beautiful tone quality. At its worst, the term has a disparaging tone, referring to an operatic style laden with highly ornamented melodies: in essence, an ostentatious kind of singing. Neither Bellini nor Donizetti was wholly innocent of the latter, although their operas contain enough of the former to rank them high in operatic history.

Bellini composed some of the most graceful melodies ever written for the voice. Some of these are also quite difficult to sing. His best known work, *Norma* (1831), requires singers whose voices can soar with relative ease through the most treacherous passages. If the performers lack this capability of bravura* singing, a production of the opera loses its main point, and the remaining skeleton is revealed as somewhat banal. In this respect, Bellini's operas represent a reversion to the improprieties confronted by Gluck in the eighteenth century, a time when singers, rather than composer and librettist, controlled operatic practice.

Compared with Bellini, Donizetti is somewhat more to the modern listener's taste. He composed around seventy operas, not all of which are in the heavy romantic vein championed by his contemporary. His *Don Pasquale* (1843) is a comic opera that wears well with age. One of the several operas he wrote in French, *The Daughter of the Regiment* (1840), is frequently produced today.

---

*The technically correct term is *coloratura*.

VERDI Giuseppe Verdi (1813–1901) was, and is, an Italian national hero as well as a revered composer of opera. His early works were championed as triggers for political and social change during times of Italian unrest. Plagued by governmental censorship and (an entrenched bias among opera patrons for *bel canto* showmanship,) he nonetheless managed to produce twenty-six operas. Some of these compare favorably with Mozart's in making stage characters come alive, and their music is supremely effective.

Verdi's penchant for naturalism helped to change the prevailing *bel canto* tradition into a hardier kind of musical theater. In this accomplishment he cleared the air of artificiality, leading directly to the realism of later composers like Puccini. His *Rigoletto, Il Trovatore, Aida,* or *Otello* can be heard somewhere in America during any opera season. They are staples of the repertory over half a century after their creation.

WAGNER The Italian Verdi, the German Richard Wagner (1813–1883), and the Frenchman Georges Bizet (1838–1875) mark the grand finale of romantic opera as it existed in the nineteenth century. The German of this trio was in his unique way one of the musical geniuses of all times. His operatic goal was nothing less than a grand synthesis of all the arts into a fantastic blend of *music drama* (a term he preferred to *opera* for his later works). His success in achieving that ambitious goal is still debated, but his success in composing operas of profoundly gripping music is unchallenged. In the process he also developed operatic techniques and a musical language that provided new paths for opera and for music in general. From his *The Flying Dutchman* (1843) to his *Parsifal* (1882), Wagner's works for the stage remain astonishing monuments of music history.

One of his most important technical accomplishments, tried earlier by Berlioz, was that of *leitmotif,* wherein a musical motif is used to suggest a particular dramatic idea or is associated with an individual character. Wagner's use was more adventurous than Berlioz's. In combination, all the motifs of a single opera form a musical counterpart to the dramatic action. As the opera continues, each motif may be transformed to be consistent with changes of the idea or character it represents.

Complementary to the *leitmotif,* Wagner abolished in his later dramas the recitative-aria succession, replacing this set structure with a seemingly endless melody. With it, musical action seems to float without the disruptive stop-and-go of earlier operas.

BIZET The French member of the triumvirate of late nineteenth-century opera, Georges Bizet (1838–1875), was a prolific talent, yet he is remembered today chiefly for his opera *Carmen,* one of the four of five operatic "hits" of all times. *Carmen* is such a moving theater piece, such a string of brash and catchy tunes, that one easily suspects its glamour to be only skin deep. It is a solid work, though, justifying rehearing over the years and the most careful musical analysis. It is not the kind of grandiose path-breaker Wagner relished; it is instead a straightforward piece, one of those lucky strikes when composer and librettist (in this case two: Meilhac and Halévy) cut the near-perfect gem.

DEBUSSY   Reacting to the pretentious grandeur of Wagner's music dramas, Claude Debussy (1862–1918) strained the essence of opera through the fine mesh of his French sensibility and composed his lone contribution, *Pelléas and Mélisande*, in 1902.

This opera is truly revolutionary, for in some ways it returns to operatic origins. Although enveloped in a sheen of beautiful orchestral sounds quite remote from the monody of 1600, its vocal lines are faintly recitative in style, a curious harking back to the clarity of text coveted by the Florentine composers. In defending his strange "new" way of preserving the integrity of his libretto, Debussy said ". . . A character's sentiments cannot be expressed continually in a melodic way, since dramatic melody should be different from melody in general."

Debussy's delicate masterpiece remains singular in the repertory of modern opera: its uniqueness deters imitation, combining as it does a modern orchestral enclosure with an archaic kind of minimal-melody. It is not a popular opera, for it contains none of the ingredients well calculated to raise a cheering audience to its feet. Its charm is subtle, exquisite and, for that, daring.

And so Debussy's super-refined *Pelléas* and Wagner's mythological pageants were more dead ends than beckoning paths for future operatic development. The hindsight of the twentieth century enables us to detect more lasting potency in Bizet's *Carmen*, with its slice of life of common people possessed by primitive emotions. For the most part, operas of the past seventy years have used librettos that are close relatives of movie and television scripts.

PUCCINI AND *VERISMO*   A direct line of descent can be traced from *Carmen's* realism of 1875 to a style of Italian opera at the turn of the century called *verismo*. The word refers to the *verity*, or "truth to life," of the librettos used by such composers as Pietro Mascagni (*Cavalleria Rusticana* of 1890), Ruggiero Leoncavallo (*Pagliacci* of 1892), and the most durable of them all, Giacomo Puccini (1858–1924).

For some opera buffs the word *opera* means about the same things as the name Puccini; his *La Boheme* (1896), *Tosca* (1900), and *Madame Butterfly* (1904) are as close as any to being the most popular operas in the world. True to the *verismo* pattern, they goad our blood pressure with scenes of premature death, torture, adultery, execution, attempted rape, cultural clash, suicide, and practically every other voyeuristic thrill we take for granted in modern cinema. What they possess that Hollywood lacks is some of the most compelling music ever composed.

Puccini was blessed with an intuitive sense for what works on the stage. His ability to create music that depicts his characters and their every mood makes his operas the enduring successes they have remained since their premieres.

BERG Perhaps Puccini's equal in musico-dramatic talent, but in a more sordid vein, the Austrian Alban Berg (1885–1935) composed only two operas, one of which he left uncompleted at his death. His *Wozzeck* (1925) is one of the few operas produced since 1900 to be widely heralded as a masterpiece. Its plot unravels the dingy but gripping lives of tragic people, real "losers" of the world. Its music is a sound-world of frightening dramatic force, its drama perhaps the grimmest of all times, yet quite as moving as any. His unfinished opera, *Lulu* (1937), is of basically the same mold and utilizes in a more thorough-going way the serial method of composition Berg learned from his teacher, Arnold Schoenberg.

GERSHWIN The popular culture of the United States has never supported grand opera with the devotion one finds in Italy and Germany and, to a lesser extent, France. Despite well-meaning attempts to transplant European tastes to this soil (beginning as early as the eighteenth century), few healthy roots have taken hold—those of opera least of all. There are, no doubt, tangible reasons for what approaches a national rejection syndrome for opera. These reasons would make quite an interesting story in themselves. More germane to our discussion is the hybrid strain an American developed: *Porgy and Bess*, by George Gershwin (1898–1937). This earthy drama was finished in 1936. It is a cross between the *verismo* of Puccini and the *musical* of Manhattan, a vigorous cross-breeding of American pop song and Italian operatic processes.

Gershwin's fame was established on Broadway, which was *the* musical street of America during the era of the twenties and thirties. In his Broadway shows Gershwin composed engaging songs for post-World War I America, the musical grist that would be ground and reground in every nightclub and dance hall of this nation and Europe. Just as these songs* have survived the ravages of uncountable performances by great and not so great entertainers, his *Porgy and Bess* has sustained not infrequent jabs from noble critics. Many have found it just another example of Gershwin's overstepping his native talent, a New York sophisticate aping the culture of a Negro ghetto.

---

*Just a few titles are "But Not For Me," "Lady Be Good," "I Got Rhythm," and "Fascinatin' Rhythm."

Composed during the jazz age, the opera is fittingly based on the lives of southern blacks. Its music, its theme, its humanity, and its actions are timeless. Songs culled from the opera—like "Summertime," "It Ain't Necessarily So!" and "Bess, You Is My Woman Now"—can sustain our intellects and emotions quite as admirably as the most polished aria by Rossini and Puccini.

BRITTEN AND MENOTTI   Since Gershwin, few other opera composers have managed to arouse a general enthusiasm of any breadth and longevity. Two who have are Gian Carlo Menotti (1911–) and Benjamin Britten (1913–1976).

The Italian-American Menotti is in some ways the operatic kin of Gershwin. His works mingle a Puccini-like operatic form with the slightly less heady aroma of the Broadway musical. His chamber opera *The Medium* (1946) is one of the most haunting dramas ever set to music, as piquantly tuneful as a Mozart aria, as theatrically sound as a Bergman film.

The Englishman Britten, on the other hand, favored the more conservative operatic tradition of Bizet, Verdi, and undiluted Puccini, still managing to inject an originality of his own into that well-tested mold. His *Peter Grimes* (1946), *Billy Budd* (1951) and, with some exotic twists of his own, *Curlew River* (1972) are within this line of descent. Even his smaller productions, or "chamber operas" like *Albert Herring* (1947) and *The Turn of the Screw* (1954) are more like small-scale grand opera than any other dramatic type.

Few twentieth-century composers of high reputation have not composed at least one opera; many have composed considerably more. For a composer opera is a "high-risk investment." Its blending of drama, music, and stagecraft makes it more complex than any other musical form; its composition is proportionately more time-consuming; its economic rewards are, unfortunately, inversely proportional to its headaches. The wonder is that so many have devoted years of their creative lives to it. When they have, and have done it well, the legacy for the musical world has been supremely rewarding.

21

DON GIOVANNI

Wolfgang A. Mozart (1756–1791)

BACKGROUND

Within the history of Western music there is no figure quite so extraordinary as Wolfgang Amadeus Mozart. He was one of those rare creatures who, endowed with a prodigious musical gift, was blessed with a family and a culture that could nourish his genius.

His father, Leopold, was a violinist, composer, and teacher of considerable reputation in Salzburg, Austria, where he was assistant director of the local archbishop's chapel. Music was a daily professional and social activity for him, and his young son entered this scene with an enormous power of absorption. By the time Wolfgang was six, Leopold was aware that his son possessed a rare talent and that his future merited constant attention. In fact, Wolfgang was on the concert trail from the age of six, displaying his phenomenal gifts as a virtuoso performer.

The product of Leopold's careful teaching (as well as the sophistication developed by travels as a prodigy) was an overwhelming musical facility. Wolfgang played organ and violin as well as harpsichord and piano. He composed his first symphony at eight, his first opera at twelve. It was the good fortune of posterity that he matured into one who could surpass the glories of childhood conquests, rather than rest with the remarkable yet immature feats of a wonderchild.

Mozart's accomplishments were not matched by his worldly lot. His mature years were marred by a luckless inability to secure an official

Illustration 21.1
Wolfgang A. Mozart

post that would ensure a steady income. It is ironic today to realize that far lesser men occupied positions in the courts of Austria during his day, while he was driven to seek funds from wealthy friends. His only official post was that of Chamber Music Composer to the Emperor, and that was more a badge of honor than a source of income. Even that was granted to him just four years before his death in 1791. He earned large sums of money during some of his years in Vienna, yet he lost heavily in gambling debts. When he died, there were not sufficient funds to bury him in a private grave.

His home was Salzburg (far western Austria), but he left a minor position in the archbishop's chapel there in 1781 to settle in Vienna. The move brought immediate performances of his works and an abundant collection of students. But his flash of prosperity and fame in the musical capital was brief. His financial condition dipped just as his musical genius began its most spectacular rise. In Vienna he was in contact with the older Haydn, whose influence became even more pronounced than before. His most prized symphonies, concertos, sonatas, string quartets, and operas were composed during this ten-year period of financial hardship.

Although he admired Haydn and revered his friendship, he was quite a different kind of person. His senior by twenty-four years, Haydn was more the peasant, more the hard-working musical laborer who accepted the semi-servile status of a court musician. He worked hard at composing.

Mozart tossed off sonatas and symphonies the way the normal literate person would write a letter to a friend. He possessed a musical facility, in playing or in composing, that was born of a life of music-making. His life was, indeed, making music, and those early years of flowering talent, carefully tended by his incomparable father, contributed to this extraordinary skill at putting sounds together.

MOZART AND OPERA

As we mentioned, Mozart's early years were spent in Salzburg, Austria, where his father worked as a musician in the archbishop's service. Salzburg at that time was bound to Italy by strong political and religious ties. Italian was the accepted language of the court. Italian music had been the favored style there and in Vienna since the previous century. Mozart's affinity for opera thus came as naturally as playing the piano, for Italian music meant *opera,* and, generally speaking, opera meant *Italian.*

His first trip to Italy came in 1769 at the age of thirteen; it was like the religious pilgrim's first trip to the Holy Land. The influences on his musical idiom, however, were not solely Italian. He had soaked up the operatic music of France and Germany during his travels as a child prodigy.

Italian opera had long been essentially of one type. Its libretti had revolved around characters of antiquity (frequently mythological), and its music had maintained a clear distinction between *recitative* and *aria*. Called *opera seria,* its dramatic character was for the most part serious and somewhat artificially formal. These conditions had been challenged by some earlier composers like Gluck, and several Italian composers had even challenged the seria type itself. They had turned to librettos of lighter tone that provided comic scenes, a general atmosphere of buffoonery (and thus the term *buffa*). Around 1750 a German parallel to buffa developed that was in the same light style, yet different in that it replaced recitative with spoken dialogue. Naturally, this Teutonic version was sung in German, and it came to be known as *Singspiel.*

Mozart composed operas of all three types, but he forced the conventions of each to serve the needs of his own musical and dramatic wishes. *Don Giovanni,* for instance, is in many respects like opera buffa, but its mixture of comic with tragic events prevents its fitting any of those three categories. His *The Magic Flute* of 1791 is fundamentally German Singspiel, but its profoundly moving music, its symbolism of Freemasonry (which Mozart took quite seriously), and its specific elements more akin to seria and buffa, make of it, for the times, a new kind of German opera.

With these reminders that Mozart was far too creative to depend on stereotypes, we can characterize his seven mature works according to the following scheme:

Opera seria: *Idomeneo, King of Crete* (1780) and *The Clemency of Titus* (1791);

Opera buffa: *The Marriage of Figaro* (1786), *Don Giovanni* (1787), and *Thus Do They All* (*Cosi fan tutte*, 1790);

Singspiel: *Abduction from the Seraglio* (1782) and *The Magic Flute* (1791).

His acknowledged masterpieces are the buffa operas and one of the Singspiel type, *The Marriage of Figaro*. He abandoned the Italian seria type when he moved to Vienna in 1781. It was in that year, while still living in Salzburg, that he composed *Idomeneo*. The later opera of the same basic style, *The Clemency of Titus,* was a hurried job, composed in the incredible span of eighteen days for the coronation of Leopold II of Czechoslovakia. (Mozart was almost penniless at the time, so he rushed to complete this most welcome commission.)

Appeal of Mozart's Operas

An appropriate question would be "What makes a Mozart opera so great?" The answer is best provided by the individual listener who takes the time to learn some of the music and understand what stage action accompanies it (most appropriately by seeing a live production!). There are some generalizations to be made, nonetheless, which indicate the source of his appeal that has persisted for over two hundred years.

First, he worked with excellent librettists, men who were true collaborators and who could reduce a libretto to the bare bones demanded by a musical production. For his best operas he was allied with Lorenzo da Ponte (1749–1838), a cooperative artist as well as a genuine professional of the theatre.

Second, Mozart composed music that could express human character as effectively as could a spoken line or stage gesture. The melodies his characters sing, combined with their orchestral accompaniment, magnificently personify the individual character. This genius for character delineation in music, wedded with a libretto that projects a sense of real people feeling real emotions, produces fully credible drama.

Mozart's other operatic assets can be stated more briefly, although they are no less important. He seems to have had a special insight into what would work on a stage, what an audience would accept as "reality" within the unreality of operatic conventions. He also knew what a singer could sing. He molded his characters' melodic lines to fit precisely their vocal capabilities as well as the stage characters they assumed with the role.

Accepting the "set forms" of eighteenth-century opera—the recitative, the aria, the ensemble (two or more characters singing together), and the cliché of choral finales for all acts—Mozart nonetheless made them serve his own dramatic and musical needs. When they occur, they occur in a way that reinforces the drama of the whole opera rather than just satisfying a convention.

And last, he was capable of reflecting the tragic and the comic in his music, those two opposed conditions of human existence that in real life do come close together but are not easily set side by side in a dramatic work. *Don Giovanni* brilliantly displays this gift to make people laugh and cry within a single scene.

DON GIOVANNI

If we could choose a single main dramatic theme for this opera it would have to be "the wages of sin for a Don Juan." There are a multitude of subordinate themes within the plot, but revenge—both human and cosmic—for the lechery of the main character looms largest throughout the opera. Surrounding this basic theme, one finds much ado about love (base and pure!), the darker side of human compulsion, and the sheer comedy of being human (and thus fallible).

Knowing the entire opera is a rewarding dramatic and musical experience. A man can at one time identify with Giovanni's compulsive lust for women and later with the "clean" image of his main rival Ottavio, and still at other times feel compassion for the jealous young peasant Masetto. Even the Commendatore, who begins the opera as a protective father and ends it as a statue, represents the noble and selfless father figure.

Women can find their identity-matches too. The aristocratic and uncompromising Anna will appeal to some; the ditched but hopeful Elvira offers solace to others; and the susceptible but loyal Zerlina projects an archetype of reluctant but desirable femininity. It is the identifiable humanity of its main characters—aristocrat or peasant—that makes da Ponte's libretto the credible tale Mozart could fashion into a masterpiece.

The libretto is cast in two large acts, each divided into five scenes. A scene-by-scene synopsis should give you a perspective of the complete opera.

Act 1 : Scene 1 : Entrance to the Palace of Anna's father, the Commendatore

Giovanni's man-servant, Leporello, broods while acting as lookout for his master's latest amorous escapade. Suddenly, Giovanni's attempted seduction of Anna is aborted. Struggling to free herself, she leads him outside, where the commotion is overheard by her father, the Commendatore. He enters the scene, duels with Giovanni, and is killed. Giovanni escapes without revealing his identity. Anna's fiancé, Ottavio, appears.

Rather than chase the culprit, he consoles Anna and joins her in swearing vengeance on her assailant and her father's murderer.

Note that the opera's course has been established with this first scene:

1   Giovanni is a heartless philanderer;
2   Anna is a staunch and pure aristocrat;
3   The Commendatore put honor above life;
4   Ottavio is honorable but perhaps less than effectual;
5   Leporello is a schemer in his own right, but he is stuck with the secondary role of servant, which he detests;
5   A motive of revenge has been established for the ensuing action.

Scene 2:
A Street Outside the City

The roaming Giovanni and Leporello come upon Donna Elvira, a former lover of Giovanni's whom he recently jilted. She is crying, but Giovanni seems caught in a confrontation. He cleverly slips away, leaving Leporello to console her. This now leaves Elvira, as well as Anna and Ottavio, in pursuit of Giovanni for revenge.

A group of young villagers enters the scene. They are celebrating the forthcoming marriage of their friends Zerlina and Masetto. Giovanni and Leporello join as welcomed guests. The master immediately spies the pretty bride-to-be. The party moves to Giovanni's castle, where Giovanni showers her with flattery and attempts to seduce her.

Giovanni's newest escapade is interrupted by the entrance of the pursuing Elvira. Her accusations of infidelity impress the young Zerlina. The heated confrontation is overheard by Anna and Ottavio, who begin to suspect Giovanni as the culprit they seek. The guileful Giovanni escapes again.

Scene 3:
Giovanni's Castle

A gala party in honor of Zerlina ensues. It is really an elaborate ruse for Giovanni's continuing pursuit of the pretty peasant girl.

Scene 4:
The Garden of Giovanni's Castle

The now-jealous Masetto fusses with Zerlina for her intolerable acceptance of the older man's attention. She begs forgiveness. Giovanni appears, inviting them inside. The three vengeful pursuers of Giovanni (Elvira, Anna, and Ottavio) appear in party masks and are invited by Leporello to join the group. The web tightens around the still remorseless Giovanni.

Scene 5:
The Ballroom of Giovanni's Castle

Amidst the festivities, Giovanni entices Zerlina to another room. Her ensuing screams interrupt the dance in progress, whereupon the dauntless Giovanni drags Leporello before the crowd, suggesting that it was he, not the master, who was the cause of the maiden's fright. Nobody is fooled. Anna, Ottavio, and Elvira now reveal their identities and confront him. Still cool, Giovanni draws his sword and escapes his accusers.

Illustration 21.2
(Left) Don Giovanni's incredible transition to the flames of hell provides one of opera's most gripping scenes. In the Eastman School of Music production shown here he melts away in an ingenious cloud of "smoke." Photo by Louis Ouzer

Illustration 21.3
(Below) The ball in Giovanni's castle is really an elaborate cover for the old lecher's advances on youthful Zerlino. Mozart's music for this scene combines the on-stage musicians in a fascinating mix with the off-stage orchestra. Photo courtesy Indiana University School of Music

Illustration 21.4 Don Giovanni's sorry character is refreshingly contrasted with the simple peasant nature of Zerlina and Masetto, whose engagement is celebrated in this scene from a production by the Eastman School of Music. Zerlina is surrounded by her peasant friends as Masetto looks on approvingly from the rear of her wagon perch. Photo by Louis Ouzer

Illustration 21.5 Don Giovanni (left) and servant Leporello are the center of attraction in this scene at the ball within Giovanni's castle. The object of their discussion is the youthful peasant girl Zerlina, who is at the far left of the stage. Photo by Louis Ouzer (Eastman School of Music)

Illustration 21.6 This scene from an Eastman School of Music production of the opera shows Don Giovanni's last supper as a true bacchanal, complete with beautiful women, a live band and a hearty feast—as well as poor Leoporello in service. Photo by Louis Ouzer

Act II: Scene 1:
In Front of
Elvira's House

Giovanni placates Leporello, who complains about unfair treatment. Elvira has taken Zerlina into her care, and thus Giovanni, the imperturbable girl-chaser, has come to seek her out. Master and servant exchange clothes to confuse their identities. Leporello draws away Elvira, who rejoices over the presumed return to her arms of her beloved Giovanni.

Disguised as Leporello, Giovanni sings a soulful aria to Zerlina. Masetto enters, looking for a chance to give the older man a good drubbing. Giovanni takes advantage of his mistaken identity as Leporello and unmercifully beats Masetto.

Scene 2:
A Darkened,
Mysterious Ruin

Leporello's impersonation of his master is too convincing; he cannot shake the ardent Elvira. Anna and Ottavio enter, out to find Giovanni and kill him. This forces the issue for Leporello, who reveals his true identity. He eventually escapes from Zerlina, who has attempted to hold him in check as one less nuisance.

Scene 3:
A Cemetery

Leporello and Giovanni meet after midnight in this eerie spot. In the darkness they come upon a monument erected to the memory of Anna's murdered father, the Commendatore. It is a larger than life replica of the old man. In typical irreverent jesting, Giovanni invites the statue to dinner. In an unearthly scene, the stone figure nods acceptance. Giovanni takes the gesture in his stride; Leporello is left trembling.

Scene 4:
A Room in Anna's
Castle

This is the calm before the storm. Ottavio consoles Anna, urging her that Giovanni's punishment will inevitably come, and soon. She rejects his plea that they marry now, insisting that her emotional wounds must heal first.

Scene 5:
(Finale) Giovanni's
Dining Room

Leporello serves the master's dinner in splendor. Elvira enters, making one final plea for reconciliation. Giovanni rejects her with characteristic mockery. Hopeless, she leaves, only to scream at the sight of the Commendatore's statue entering the house. Its ponderous steps approach Giovanni's room, which it enters to announce, "You invited me: I have come!"

Giovanni remains cool. Leporello cowers under the dining table. The stone guest asks that Giovanni return the compliment of his visit. Carefully avoiding any suggestion of cowardice, Giovanni replies "Yes!" and accepts the cold hand of death to shake and thereby seal the bargain. Still fearless, Giovanni spurns a final chance at repentance for his ill-spent life. A fiery blast emerges from the stage and Giovanni is swallowed in flames with cries of terror. Done in at last!

Epilogue*

Elvira, Zerlina, Masetto, Anna, Ottavio, and Leporello gather about the ruins of Giovanni's castle, each singing (separately and as an ensemble) of the appropriate end that has befallen the late scoundrel.*

What is the message of all this? There are several messages, but the paramount one clearly is that of the ultimate fate for those who do not mend, or at least repent of, their evil ways. It is a Christian notion, quite fitting for the Roman Catholic Mozart and his largely Catholic audiences.

But aside from this largest dramatic metaphor, there are others which have to do with the nature of people. Through their characters Mozart and da Ponte show us how men can be honorable and deceitful, humorous and serious, virile and impotent, patient and impulsive. And they demonstrate that women can be indulgent as well as unapproachable, loyal but coquettish, strong but also susceptible. Mozart brings off this broad range of emotions with the deft grace of a master, from the foiled seduction of the first scene to the furies of Hell at the end.

We shall study closely only the final two scenes. The first is a brief set of recitatives and arias between Anna and Ottavio.

Scene 4:
A Room in Anna's
Castle

Only Anna and Ottavio are present. The dialogue begins with a recitative by the two, accompanied by bare sustained chords in the orchestra.† At Ottavio's suggestion that Anna is being cruel (the word *crudele*) the orchestral background assumes a more important role. Since any recorded version you hear will probably be sung in Italian, we show the first part of each new line of the libretto to the left, a brief English synopsis of the text to the right.

OTTAVIO
Calmatevi, idol mio . . .
Be calm. The scoundrel's crimes will be punished.

ANNA
Ma il padre, O Dio! . . .
But my father, Oh God!

OTTAVIO
Convien chinare il ciglio . . .
It's best to accept what fate gives us. Relax. We can be married tomorrow.

ANNA
O Dei! Che dite?
Oh Lord! What are you saying? At this moment! . . .

---

*In some productions of the opera the Epilogue is deleted, the action ending with Don Giovanni's bizarre death.

†Recitative with this kind of minimal background is called *recitativo secco*; recitative with a more active orchestral background is called *recitativo accompagnato*, or "accompanied recitative." In some performances a harpsichord plays the chords for *recitativo secco* passages.

OTTAVIO
E che? ...   What's that? Would you make my lot
                                                 worse with delays? That's cruel!

ANNA
Crudele? ...   Cruel? Hardly. Don't mistake my
                                                 devotion to you.

(The recitative section ends and Anna begins an aria.)

ANNA
Non mi, dir, bell'idol mio ...   Don't say I am cruel to you. You
                                                 know my loyalty. Calm your suf-
                                                 fering so I won't die of grief.
                                                 Maybe Heaven will pity me at
                                                 last.

OTTAVIO (This portion is deleted in some recordings.)
Ah, si segua il suo passo; ...   Ah, I must follow her. I must share
                                                 her suffering. With me her sighs
                                                 will be lighter.

Scene 5:
(Finale) Giovanni's
Dining Room

Our synopsis of this scene will be divided into nine parts to aid you in
following a recorded performance. Each part will be marked by a denoted
change in the music or by some other easy cue.

   Part A: A table is prepared for dinner. A small orchestra is set up
to play at one side of the room. Leporello serves his master.

GIOVANNI
Già la mensa e preparata; ...   The table's ready; play now, for I'm
                                                 paying for it. Set the table,
                                                 Leporello.

LEPORELLO
Son prontissimo a servir.   I'm waiting, ready to serve.

GIOVANNI
Giacchè spendo i miei danari ...   Since I'm paying for this, I want to
                                                 enjoy myself. Play.

   Part B: Giovanni sits, the musicians begin to play an aria from the
opera *Una Cosa Rara* that has competed for popularity with Mozart's
opera of the past year, *The Marriage of Figaro*. Note Leporello's pun.

LEPORELLO
Bravi! "Cosa rara!"   Great! A rare piece!

GIOVANNI
Che ti par del bel concerto?   What do you think of the concert?

LEPORELLO
È conforme al vostro merto.   It fits your needs.

GIOVANNI
Ah, che piatto saporito!   Ah! What a tasty morsel.

LEPORELLO (in an aside)
Ah, che barbaro appetito! . . .   Wow! What an appetite he has! I may
                                                     faint at the sight of his gluttony!

GIOVANNI (also in an aside)
Nel veder i miei bocconi, . . .   Watching me eat so heartily, he
                                                     thinks he might faint.

(The two repeat their individual asides.)

Part C: The orchestra changes to a new tune. Leporello recognizes it. It is from Giuseppe Sarti's opera *I due litiganti*. Again, a pun (for Mozart's day) from Leporello.

LEPORELLO
Evvivano i "Litiganti!" . . .   Hail to the litigants!

GIOVANNI
Versa il vino! . . .   Pour the wine!

LEPORELLO (doing as ordered)
Eccellente marzimino!   Excellent marzimino (the wine)!

LEPORELLO (switching plates in an aside)
Questo pezzo di fagiano . . .   I'll sneak some of this pheasant on
                                                     the sly.

GIOVANNI (aside)
Sta mangiando, cuel marrano! . . .   That oaf is eating! I'll pretend not to
                                                     have noticed.

Part D: The stage musicians now play a well-known tune from Mozart's previous opera *The Marriage of Figaro*. Leporello chews the food he has just snitched.

LEPORELLO (hearing the new tune, his mouth full)
Questa poi la conosco pur troppo!   I can't say much for that tune.

GIOVANNI (without looking up)
Leporello!

LEPORELLO
Padron mio?   Yes master?

GIOVANNI
Parla schietto, . . .   Speak clearer, you rascal!

LEPORELLO
Non mi lascia una flussione . . .   My bad cold keeps me from speaking
                                                     clearly.

GIOVANNI
Mentre io manio, . . .   Whistle for me while I eat.

LEPORELLO
Non so far.   I don't know how.

    GIOVANNI (now looking at him)
Cos'è?   What's that?

    LEPORELLO
Scusate, scusate! . . .   Excuse me! The cook is really excel-
                                       lent; so excellent that I wanted to
                                       try some too.

    (Repetitions of the previous thought come from both characters to the end of this part.)

    Part E: Elvira enters in great excitement.

ELVIRA
L'ultima prova . . .   To prove my love for you, I'll forget
                                       your deceit.

    GIOVANNI AND LEPORELLO: What's this?

    ELVIRA (now on her knees)
Da te non chiede . . .   I won't even ask your thanks for my
                                         loyalty.

    GIOVANNI
Mi maraviglio . . .   I marvel at what you say, but I can't
                                         keep standing if you won't stand
                                         up.

    ELVIRA
Ah, non deridere . . .   Ah! Don't mock me!

    (Dialogue continues between the three characters. Giovanni makes clear his disinterest; Leporello vents his shame at his master's callousness.)

    Part F: Hopeless, Elvira leaves, spies the approaching figure of the Commendatore's statue and screams, running back through the room to exit elsewhere.

ELVIRA
Ah!

    GIOVANNI AND LEPORELLO
Che grido è questo mai?   What's that screaming about?

    GIOVANNI (to Leporello)
Va a veder che . . .   Go see what it is.

    LEPORELLO (going outside)
Ah!!!

    GIOVANNI
Che grido indiavolato! . . .   Everybody's screaming? What's the
                                         matter?

LEPORELLO
Ah, signor! per carità, ...

Ah, Sir! For goodness' sake, don't go out there. The marble man, all white ... Ah, master! I tremble. If you'd seen it or heard how it goes tap! tap! tap! tap!

GIOVANNI
Non capisco niente affatto.

I don't know what you're saying.

LEPORELLO (imitating loud steps)
Ta! Ta! Ta! Ta!

GIOVANNI
Tu sei matto in verità!

You're out of your mind!

LEPORELLO
Ah, sentite!

Ah! Just listen!

GIOVANNI
Qualchun batte! Apri!

Someone's knocking! Open it!

LEPORELLO
Io tremo!

I'm trembling!

(The dialogue continues until Giovanni finally opens the door himself, while Leporello hides under the dining room table. The marble statue of the Commendatore enters; the music slows, assuming a far graver mood.)
Part G:

STATUE
Don Giovanni, a cenar teco ...

Don Giovanni, you gave me an invitation and I've come.

GIOVANNI (still cool)
Non l'avrei giammai creduto; ...

I wouldn't have believed it, but I'll do the best I can. Set another place now, Leporello.

LEPORELLO (from under the table)
Ah padron! ...

Ah, master! I'm as good as dead!

GIOVANNI
Vanne, dico!

Do as I say!

STATUE
Ferma un po'! ...

Stay here! Those of heaven do not eat the food of earth. I didn't come to eat; I have more serious matters.

(A three-way scene ensues, the statue offering one last chance of redemption to Giovanni, who refuses to show a change of heart. Leporello provides background counterpoint with his trembling pleas that he be left out of this matter completely.)

The end of this part comes with:

GIOVANNI (a cry of anguish)
No, No!

STATUE
Ah, tempo più non v'è!   Ah, your time is up!

Part H: The statue exits, the pit of Hell opens, and the music increases in momentum. Giovanni succumbs at last.

GIOVANNI
Da qual tremore insolito, . . .   My body trembles. I feel the spirits
                                            attack me. What are those flames
                                            of horror?

CHORUS OF SPIRITS (unseen)
Tutto a tue colpe . . .   This is nothing compared to your
                                            sins! Come! It gets worse . . .

GIOVANNI
Chi l'anima . . .   Who is torturing me? What is the
                                            poison in my veins? What force is
                                            dragging me to Hell?

The scene ends with Giovanni in a state of terror, Leporello interjecting his cries of horror and astonishment at the proceedings. Giovanni gasps a final "Ah!", followed by a brief cadence in the orchestra.

Part J: Epilogue: This aftermath of Giovanni's spectacular end fulfills the conventions of opera buffa by providing an ensemble reaction to the drama's climax. Its function here is to provide the sense of revenge that is due Anna and Ottavio, Masetto and Zerlina, Elvira and Leporello.

In this final part the group has gathered around the late Giovanni's palace. Leporello relates to them the colossal fate of his master. The group agrees, in song, that "Such is the end of false villains." This final part is frequently omitted from modern productions of the opera.

22

NINETEENTH CENTURY
ART SONG: Four Songs
from *DICHTERLIEBE*

Robert Schumann (1810–1856)

BACKGROUND

If by "song" we mean words put to music, then songs have been around since people began to make music. It is a curious irony of history, however, that this simple and direct outlet for musical expression waited until the nineteenth century to become a popular medium for the most talented composers. Prior to that time the ayres of John Dowland and some of his contemporaries came closer to being carefully wrought compositions than the songs of other centuries. But aside from the music of those Elizabethan songsters, exquisite unions of words and music occurred mainly in religious works for chorus or in dramatic works like opera.

Serious composers sometimes did compose solo songs as separate compositions. But compared with their total output, these were a mere handful. This state of curious neglect changed radically during the first thirty years of the nineteenth century; from that time until now, serious composers have regarded the wedding of music to text for solo voice as a more artistically commanding pastime.

We can find causes for this sudden turn to the intimacy of the solo song. For the most part they are entwined within the larger movement of nineteenth-century Romanticism.*

One product of nineteenth-century Romanticism was a new con-

*Romanticism is discussed more thoroughly in the background sections of Chapter 9.

sciousness of a national soul, which in turn led to widespread sentimentalism about folk song. After all, it was felt, if peasants—the "noble savages" of Rousseau—are to be venerated, then their music also must possess unique value. It must bear qualities that in art music have been washed away by oversophistication. And so composers of art music, like Johannes Brahms, could declare with straight faces that their goal was to match in their own creations the simple beauty of folk song. Of course, only *folk* can create real *folk song*, so honest efforts, while frequently producing beautiful music, rarely achieved stated goals.

The immediate forebears of actual art song were English and Scotch Romantic ballads. These were attempts by learned poets to recreate the atmosphere of ancient folk ballads. Imitations sprouted in Germany, but some of the imitations soon surpassed their models in quality. In the hands of geniuses like Franz Schubert (1797–1828), Robert Schumann (1810–1856), and Johannes Brahms (1833–1897) these songs became the German art song, or *Lied*.

The Art Song

What makes a song an *art song*? The difference is not intrinsic value. Comparing a folk song with the song of a polished composer is like comparing a cactus bloom with a cultured rose: each has its own beauty.

Perhaps the simplest explanation lies in the different ways the two combine music with words. In folk song there is rarely a *necessary* connection between music and text, except for the obvious demand for corresponding rhythmic accents. There are even many folk texts (like *Streets of Laredo*) set to quite different melodies. The nature of a true folk song, its evolution sometimes spread over generations of singers, leads to music that, although fitting and appropriate, does not provide a tight reinforcement for the text's imagery.

With art songs it is different. The composer takes over the poet's images and creates a new expression in sound; if it is a successful song the poem is only one part of a new creation. This means that an art song is a *musical* expression of the poem's imagery, just as the original poem was a *verbal* expression of that imagery. Music and words must mesh precisely to create a clear and unified image for the listener. And thus Schubert creates a piano accompaniment in one song that whirs to suggest underlying agitation, for its text deals with a girl who sings of her lover as she works at her spinning wheel. We find the same kind of fused imagery when Schumann has the piano part of "I wept in my dream" (Song 13, *Dichterliebe*) intone a funereal chant while the poetic image is that of the dead lover in her grave. These kinds of music/text associations are the stuff of art songs.

Franz Schubert was Robert Schumann's immediate predecessor as a composer of solo songs. The older man composed over six hundred songs in his brief life, setting texts by Goethe and Wilhelm Müller as well as Heinrich Heine, who wrote the poems of Schumann's *Dichterliebe*. Like Schumann, Schubert was a master of musical imagery. His melodies and piano accompaniments evoke a poem's implied meanings as faithfully as music can. Yet compared with Schumann's, his songs bear closer kinship with folk origins in at least one respect: they more often are set in the strophic form so characteristic of folk song, each of the poem's verses accompanied by the same or only slightly varied music.

Composers' Support   By the time of Schubert and Schumann the patron subsidies enjoyed by composers of earlier times were as good as dead. Composers of the Romantic period composed for a different set of conditions than did their eighteenth-century counterparts. Very few held church positions as did Bach, nor were there court appointments to be served like that of Haydn.

Now the composer generally composed for posterity, true to the Romantic ideal of longing for another time. He composed more for the "perfect" audience, which might have been a small circle of friends or an idealized body known only to his imagination. It is during this era that the notion of the yet unappreciated genius first takes hold. It would have been sheer folly during an earlier period of history to suggest that a composer was "before his time." But the idea had great currency during the nineteenth century, as it still does today.

SCHUMANN'S TURN TO ART SONGS AND THE *DICHTERLIEBE*

Schumann had published only solo piano works before the year 1840. Aside from being a composer for the piano, he fancied himself a potential piano virtuoso. With some encouragement from Friedrich Wieck, who later would become his unwilling father-in-law, he had steered his ambitions in that direction. It is a matter of record that on occasion he had demeaned the solo song as a "lesser" art. His mind must have changed dramatically around 1840: he composed nearly one hundred and fifty songs during that year alone.

The previous year had been one of testy gloom for one of such weak psychological fiber. He had inwardly faced the reality of his limited promise as a concert pianist, and his projected marriage to Wieck's daughter Clara (who was already an acclaimed concert pianist) had been blocked by her spiteful father. Fearing that he would lose his celebrated charge and that she would be diverted from her career, Friedrich Wieck found Robert's talent less rich, his professional prospects less favorable than formerly.

In 1839 the desperate young couple filed suit to win the legal right to marry. One result of Robert's anxiety over the pending court ruling was his feverish immersion in song composition. *Dichterliebe*, a cycle of sixteen songs on poems of Heinrich Heine, was a major part of this activity. Since the poems of *Dichterliebe* are saturated with images of unfulfilled love, it is easy to link Schumann's anxious state with his sudden burst of enthusiasm for songs. A favorable ruling in Clara and Robert's suit was handed down in August, 1840. They were married the following month.

Heine's Poetry

Schumann found the texts of *Dichterliebe* in a collection of Heine's poems that had been published thirteen years earlier as *Lyrical Intermezzo*. He merely followed fashion when he chose to set them to music, for the thirty-six poems had been instantly popular in Germany. Schubert, Mendelssohn, Franz, Silcher, and, later, Brahms, also selected from these texts for their songs.

Each of Heine's poems is a brief outpouring of the unsure lover, usually associating images of nature with the absent loved one, or relating dreams as previews of brutal truths yet to come. In his songs Schumann treats each poem as a separate basis for a complete musical composition. Each sets its own appropriate mood, rises to its own timely climax, then finishes with a musical gesture befitting its emotional connotations. This means that every musical property—rhythm, melody, texture, harmony, and timbre—is carefully composed to form a tight relationship with poetic meaning.

The Music

Schumann's music does not overshadow the voice and its all-important words. In fact, poetic rhythms are preserved intact, word accents are reinforced by musical accents, and the full meaning of each line and every word is allowed clear projection by the composer's melodies.

Of the sixteen songs of the cycle, we have chosen four that represent a cross-section of moods and yet offer some perspective of the whole cycle.

Song 2:
"From my tears spring forth"

Aus meinen Tränen spriessen
Viel blühende Blumen hervor,
Und meine Seufzer werden
Ein Nachtigallenchor.

Und wenn du mich lieb hast, Kindchen,
Schenk' ich dir die Blumen all,
Und vor deinem Fenster soll klingen
Das Lied der Nachtigall.

From my tears spring forth
many blossoming flowers;
And my sighs are becoming
a choir of nightingales.

And if you love me, dear,
I'll give you all the blossoms,
and before your window shall sing
the song of the nightingale.

This delicate whisper of song links the three images most touched upon in the whole group: tears, flowers and, most of all, the lover who longs for a shared love. The quiet restraint of the text is reflected by its music. The chant-like voice barely exceeds a range of three notes, hovering within the singer's mid-range. The piano texture is appropriately thin and light, and it never rises above *piano* (or "soft"). The total effect is that of an audible reverie, the lover sharing aloud his hopeful but unsure state of mind.

Unlike many songs of the cycle, the piano provides no interludes between vocal phrases or a postlude to resolve the drama of upturned poetic images. It is curious that the voice ends each of its phrases on an inconclusive note, the piano providing termination as a brief afterthought. This effect of suspended tension in the voice completes the overall impression of an inconclusive reverie of an unsure lover.

Note also the form of this brief song. The first two lines of text consume one complete musical phrase that is repeated for the third and fourth lines. The shift of perspective in line five ("And if you love me, dear") brings a slightly contrasting musical setting. Then lines 7 and 8 bring a faintly varied return of the beginning phrase. In only seventeen measures the composer has wrought a full musical form containing a departure and a return that fit the succession of images in his text.

Song 3:
"The rose, the lily, the dove, the sun"

Die Rose, die Lilie, die Taube, die Sonne,
Die lieb' ich einst alle in Liebeswonne.

Ich lieb' sie nicht mehr, ich liebe alleine
Die Kleine, die Feine, die Reine, die Eine;
Sie selber, alle Liebe Wonne,
Ist Rose und Lilie und Taube und Sonne.

The rose, the lily, the dove, the sun,
I once loved them all ecstatically.

I love them no more; I love only
the tiny, the refined, the pure, *the one*;
She herself, the fount of all love,
is rose and lily and dove and sun.

The hovering tenderness of Song 2 is dispelled by the first few sounds of this light-hearted frolic that celebrates the poet's world of love. The rhythmic hestitancy of the earlier reverie is replaced by galloping lines of pure abandon. The sense of private testimonial projected by the previous song gives way to youthful exuberance; now the singer seems to be telling the whole world how his "One Love" consumes his total love.

The musical characteristics of this song are worth special attention because of the way they project an atmosphere of buoyancy. The tripping lightness of the melody is confirmed by the rhythm of the piano part, which divides hands in a rapid oscillation, like the nimble steps of perpetually moving feet. Schumann strengthens the punch line of Heine's poem by repeating, as the last phrase of the voice part, "I love only the tiny, the refined, the pure, the one." The piano's postlude returns to the beginning of the song, suggesting that the exuberant lover will probably continue forever this baring of his soul to the world.

The song's form clearly avoids the strophic organization we associate with folk song. Although a middle line of the text is repeated at the end, the musical phrase-form is *a a b c*. The piano postlude provides a final sense of return, rounding off the contrast of the voice's final two phrases.

Song 13:
"I wept in my dreams"

Ich hab' im Traum geweinet.	I wept in my dream.
Mir träumte, du lägest im Grab.	I dreamed that you lay in your grave.
Ich wachte auf, und die Träne	I awakened, yet the tears
Floss noch von der Wange herab.	still flowed down my cheeks.
Ich hab' im Traum geweinet.	I wept in my dream.
Mir traumt', du verliessest mich.	I dreamed that you had left me.
Ich wachte auf, und Ich weinte	I awakened, yet I wept,
Noch lange bitterlich.	still long and bitterly.
Ich hab' im Traum geweinet.	I wept in my dream.
Mire traumte, du warst mir noch gut.	I dreamed that you were still mine.
Ich wachte auf un noch immer	I awakened, yet as before
Stromt meine Tranenflut.	my flood of tears continued.

This song introduces the spectre of envisioned death that, with tears and flowers and love, occupied a good part of every Romantic's consciousness. Heine's text suggests a funereal dirge, with its monotonous repetitions and near-repetitions of lines. Schumann takes the poet's cue. The keening solo voice is answered by low, brooding piano chords. Voice and piano do not sound together until a suggestion of hope arrives with the third verse of the poem. The lonely statements by the solo voice within the first two verses reinforce the image of the dreamer's solitude within this fitful reminiscence.

The anxiousness of the situation is ingeniously underlined by the short phrases of the first two verses. A sustained melodic phrase doesn't occur until the climactic third verse, which tells that the tears continue, in spite of a more hopeful outlook.

Schumann uses silence brilliantly in this song to drive home a picture of the dreamer's solitude and lack of assurance. Even the piano's postlude of continuing gloom is dramatically separated by a penetrating quiet from the voice's final phrase.

And finally, one aspect of the song—too easily ignored—has to do with the rate at which events unfold, the kind of rhythmic density we discussed earlier in Chapter 3. If we graph the rate at which voice and piano articulate their statement-answer phrases in the first verse, we can see how the composer has not just created a funereal state: he has also suggested the dawning hope of the dreamer as he wakens from his troubled dream, only to sink again at his realization that the tears haven't stopped. In Example 22.1 the voice and piano statements are linked as a single event; each event's relative duration is depicted by the length of its encompassing bracket at the top.

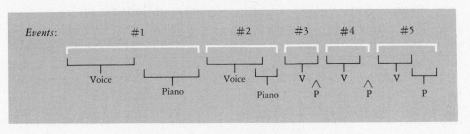

Example 22.1   Relative density of events, Verse I

Text: #1 = "I cried in my dream."
          #2 = "I dreamed that you lay in your grave."
          #3 = "I awakened,
          #4 = and the tears
          #5 = still flowed down my cheeks."

The point here is the way momentum increases on "I awakened," as though musical events quicken to correspond with waking from the dream (events 3 and 4). But events again subside with the realization that the tears do continue to flow, even if it was only a dream (event 6). In fact, Schumann has divided the poet's four lines of text into five unequal musical phrases. In this way he creates a musical parallel for the meaning of the poem.

**Song 15:
"From ancient
fairytales"**

Aus alten Märchen winkt es	From ancient fairy tales
Hervor mit weisser Hand,	a white hand beckons;
Da singt es und da Klingt es	there are songs and sounds
Von einem Zauberland.	from a magic land.
Wo bunte Blumen blühen	Where bright flowers blossom
Im goldnen Abendnicht	in the golden light of evening,
Und lieblich duf end gluhen	and innocent, sweet faces glow
Mit brautlichem Gesicht,	like the face of a bride,
Und grüne Bäume singen	And green trees sing
Uralte Melodien,	ancient melodies,
Die lüfte heimlich klingen	the breezes whisper gently
Und Vögel schmettern drein,	and birds warble there,
Und Nebelbilder steigen	And dim images rise
Whol aus der Erd' hervor	from the earth
Und tanzen luft' gen Reigen	and dance airy reels
Im wunderlichen Chor,	in an incredible chorus,
Und blaue Funken brennen	And blue sparks fly
An jedem Blatt und Reis,	on every leaf and twig
Und rothe Lichter rennen	and red lights swirl
Im irren, wirren Kreis,	in weird, fantastic circles,
Und bunte Quellen brechen	And murmuring springs break
Aus wildem Marmorstein,	from rough marble boulders,
Und seltsam in den Bächen	their strange reflections in the streams
Strahlt fort der Wiederschein.	radiating forth.
Ach könnt' ich dorthin kommen	Oh, if I could go there,
Und dort mein Herz erfreu'n,	and there my heart delight,
Und aller Qual entnommen	and be released from its cares,
Und frei und selig sein!	and free and blessed again!
Ach, jenes Land der Wonne,	Oh, that land of bliss
Dash seh' ich of im Traum,	I often see in dreams;
Doch kommt die Morgensonne,	but when the morning sun comes,
Zerfliesst's wie eitel Schaum.	It disappears like foam.

This eight-verse evocation of Never-Never-Land is the longest poem of the *Dichterliebe* cycle. It boasts every cliché of the Romantic's fantasy, from magic lands of fairy tales to the lover's heart burdened by the remorse of lost love. It is a veritable catalogue of nineteenth-century escapism. Schumann's music brilliantly underpins the emotion of the poem's successive ideas, from the vision of magical nature to the eventual realization that all's a dream: it vanishes under the harsh light of reality.

The voice's eight verses are framed by the piano's prelude and postlude; the former sets the idyllic mood and the latter reminds us of the dream just vanished. In addition to its framing function, the piano plays a major role in maintaining the robust character of the song, ensuring that it does not deteriorate into the silly fairy tale it easily could become. These punctuations come as interludes between verses 2-3 and 3-4, helping to relieve the constancy of the voice part in the first six verses.

Strictly speaking, the form of this song is additive: no verses exactly repeat a previous verse. But Schumann accomplishes a stroke of genius in the way he separates the music of verses 7 and 8 from the earlier verses. In those last two verses the poem halts its long recitation of the glories of the magic land; in verse 7 reality intrudes with the line "Oh, if I could go there. . .," implying that escape from the everyday world is really out of the question.

The poetic change of perspective brings the first real break in the plunging flow of the song. From there until the singer's final word it is a sinking scene. After the repeated cry "*Ach!*" the piano's momentum relaxes, the texture quiets, and then the voice begins to sing a stretched-out version of the melody of verse 1. That is, the rate of unfolding suddenly subsides to about half as fast. Example 22.2 compares the melody of verses 1 and 7 to make clear this musical feat, the composer suggesting a fading dream by quoting an earlier melody at a slower rate.

The remainder of the song uses the same technique; verse 8 is an augmented variation of the melody of verse 4. With the final line ("It disappears like foam") the tempo subsides to a dying gait to utter the final gasp, the acceptance of reality. It is fascinating that the piano postlude now echoes the very beginning of the song, only to dissolve into the slowed rhythms of verses 7 and 8, then die with its four ultimate chords.

These skillful strokes of musical imagery go far beyond the simple tone-painting we heard in the songs of John Dowland and Francis Pilkington. Schumann's technique is more subtle. He uses ingenious music/ text associations to get across the emotional content of a whole poem rather than just the literal meanings of individual words. His evocation of a reverie in this song, when the inaccessibility of a dream-world is faced head-on, is far removed from Pilkington's use of a descending melody on the word "down." It is even an advancement over the simple association Bach draws between death and the descending melodic motif of *Christ lag in Todesbanden* that we discussed in Chapter 19.

Example 22.2 Comparison of rhythms in verses 1 and 7

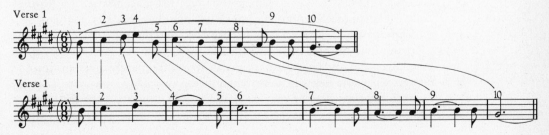

23

ANCIENT VOICES OF CHILDREN

George Crumb (1929———)

BACKGROUND

If any generalization can be made with authority about music composed since 1950, it would be that composers have become fascinated with sound for its own sake. Regardless of what rhythmic, melodic, or harmonic function they might serve, recent composers saturate their works with unique and compelling timbres. The listener is confronted with this quest for the unusual in vocal music as much as in pieces for instruments, like Penderecki's *Threnody* (Chapter 15) or Erb's *Percussion Concerto* (Chapter 32).

There was a day when the concert singer could expect some artistic success when he or she had developed the "pear-shaped tone" demanded in the traditional art song and operatic repertories. But that day of comfortable simplicity is slowly fading. Composers of today are finding new ways of treating the voice, new ways of incorporating a poetic text in their works, and new ways of relating the voice to its accompanying textures.

The sincere composer's intent has not changed. His goal is still to communicate feeling to his listener through the medium of language organized in musical patterns. The sounds he uses, the patterns they form, and even the way he utilizes the poet's words frequently differ enormously from what one hears in a Schumann song or a Dowland ayre. Through electronic processes he may filter the voice's tones to alter their timbre, chop apart syllables, reverse a sound so that its decay precedes its attack,

Illustration 23.1 George Crumb. Photo by Scott Braucher, *The Arizona Daily Star*, Tucson

or even drop a soprano's pitches into the range of a foghorn. But whatever the composer does is done in an effort to project a unique but meaningful world of sound imagery to the listener.

George Crumb uses the human voice in quite unconventional ways to sing equally unconventional kinds of patterns. He clothes these high-impact patterns in a fantastic array of instrumental sounds. He is not a composer of "electronic music" in the sense that he uses electronically generated sounds. He does frequently call for the electronic amplification of conventional instruments like piano and voice, however, as well as new ways of altering the timbres of traditional instruments.

THE COMPOSER

Crumb was born in Charleston, West Virginia, in 1929. Aside from a year spent in Germany studying composition with Boris Blacher, his training took place at Mason College and at the University of Michigan. (His teacher at Michigan, Ross Lee Finney, has trained an imposing crop of composers of Crumb's generation.) Like most modern composers, Crumb's professional life is a mixture of writing and teaching music. Since 1965 he has been a Professor at the University of Pennsylvania in Philadelphia.

In addition to grants and prizes for his work awarded by numerous foundations and governmental agencies, he received for *Ancient Voices of Children* both an award from UNESCO and a recording prize from the Koussevitsky Foundation in 1971.

We shall discuss the unusual instrumentation of this work presently. Some of Crumb's earlier compositions show a comparable daring in choices of timbres. His *Songs, Drone and Refrains* (1968) calls for baritone voice, electric guitar, electric bass,* piano, and percussion. *Night of Four Moons* (1969) includes banjo and electric cello, along with alto voice, alto flute, and percussion. Parts of a work for electric string quartet called *Black Angels* were borrowed to create some of the cosmic atmosphere in the Hollywood movie *The Exorcist* in 1974. Three of his most recent compositions, *Makrokosmos* I and II for electric piano solo, and *Makrokosmos* III for two pianos and percussion, call for groans, shouts, whistling, and other vocal contributions from the pianist.

Some listeners are at first repulsed by the sounds they hear in Professor Crumb's music, assuming that the composer's message is too extreme to be meaningful, if not a downright put-on. A more indulgent attitude can be more rewarding. If it is a part of the composer's "duty" to transmit through his music something of a personal world view, then it is only reasonable to expect frightfully evocative images coming from music created during our thermonuclear age.

ANCIENT VOICES OF CHILDREN

Composers frequently come upon poetry that expresses their own feelings in a special way. For George Crumb, this is the case with the poems of the late Spanish poet Federico García Lorca. *Ancient Voices* is only one work of a cycle of works based on Lorca's texts, a cycle beginning with *Night Music* I (1963) and including *Madrigals* (1965–69), *Songs, Drone and Refrains* (1968), and *Night of the Four Moons* (1969).

As we shall learn, Crumb's use of Lorca's words is sometimes eccentric; his manner of setting them to music is not always the direct kind of syllable-to-note fusion we hear in traditional song. That he even uses Lorca's original Spanish texts for compositions to be heard mainly by English-speaking audiences is one hint that his intentions are not simple.

---

*By "electric" here we mean electrically amplified, usually by means of sound pickups attached to a conventional instrument.

In describing his motivations in composing *Ancient Voices* he explains: "I have sought musical images that enhance and reinforce the powerful yet strangely haunting imagery of Lorca's poetry."*

In creating the musical images he seeks, Crumb adds passages of nonsense syllables to Lorca's texts, using the singer's voice as if it were an instrument to be "played upon" with special tone qualities. And to dramatize the sense of childlike innocence projected in Lorca's words, he augments the solo soprano voice with a secondary role for boy soprano.

---

*From the composer's notes in the Peters score.

Illustration 23.2
The brilliant singing of Jan DeGaetani has helped bring success to a number of George Crumb's vocal works. Some were even composed with her voice in mind. Photo by Louis Ouzer

The accompanying ensemble sounds he uses in this work are compatibly exotic. The basic instrumentation consists of percussion (three players), mandolin, oboe, harp, and electric piano. But Crumb's ensemble is flexible and hardworking: the mandolin player doubles on musical saw; the pianist switches at two points in the work to toy piano; the oboist also plays chromatic harmonica; the percussionists even sing as a choir in Song IV.

Perhaps most striking are the unconventional sounds the composer elicits from his small band. The soprano part ranges from highly virtuosic vocal gymnastics—including sounds like sneezes, whispers, coughs, and flutters—to a simple lyricism suggestive of folk song. The mandolin is played at times with a glass rod rather than with fingers, some of its strings intentionally mistuned to produce a special intense expression. The mandolin player is asked to "bend" pitches, making them sound strangely out of tune. The pianist mutes strings with hands and with a chisel, creating weird slides, thumps, and echoes heretofore foreign to the favored instrument of Mozart and Chopin. And the harp plays on occasion with paper threaded among its strings to produce an ethereal rattling.

All of these sounds are tepid, however, when compared with the strange beauty of the solo voices singing directly into the resonating strings of the amplified piano. The work is a virtual Esperanto of captivating new sounds.

As we suggested earlier, the "meaning" of *Ancient Voices* is not obvious. It casts haunting images more than it tells a tale. As George Crumb has said, Lorca's poetry suggests "primary things: life, death, love, the smell of the earth, the sounds of the wind and the sea." Certainly one concern of the composer and poet is the adult's loss of innocence, the loss of the "voice of the child." In this, Lorca's words and Crumb's music tell us that achieving maturity means renouncing the simple joys of childhood.

The work contains five songs and two dance interludes, which the composer urges be staged with solo dancers. Like many recent compositions by composers of Crumb's generation, *Ancient Voices* is a mini-drama whose theatricality can be expanded as the site and resources of a production allow. The score itself directs some minimal stage happenings. The boy soprano sings offstage until the end of the final song, when he joins the soprano onstage. The oboist removes to the wings for offstage passages at the end; the soprano at times sings facing into the strings of the grand piano as well as facing the audience. And thus, aside from the potentiality of the two staged dances, a rudimentary ritual is built into the work's performance.

Song I: "The Little Boy Was Looking For His Voice"	*El niño busca su voz.* (*La tenía el rey de los grillos.*)	The little boy was looking for his voice. (The king of the crickets had it.)

En una gota de agua
buscaba su voz el niño.

No la quiero para hablar;
me haré con ellá un anillo
que llevará me silencio
en su dedo pequeñito . . .

In a drop of water
the little boy was looking for his voice.

I do not want it for speaking with;
I will make a ring of it
so that he may wear my silence
on his little finger . . .

The soprano begins with a fantastic vocalise of nonsense syllables. It is a rhapsodic paean of waxing and waning rhythms, its tones reverberated with shimmering unearthliness from the amplified strings of the piano. Harp and piano punctuate these cascading spasms of sound with dry drumming patterns. Singer and instruments alternate their sounds, the final resolution of this antiphony coming from backstage in the tuneful "after-song" of the boy soprano. The lines of Lorca's text are divided between the two singers, as shown in the mapping of our first example.

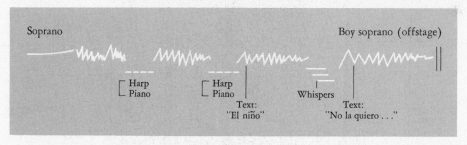

Example 23.1   Alternations of forces in the first song

The song progresses from dense rhythms to a relaxed pace at the end, where the boy's song has the faint air of Spanish folk music. His last words fade away without a final punctuation from the instrumental accompaniment. The evocation of dark feelings has ended with the innocent song of a child.

Dance Interlude I: "Dances of the Ancient Earth"

The atmosphere of primitive ritual set in the first song is preserved by this rhythmic incantation. Oriental and flamenco sounds are fused from its timbres and rhythms. Melody is no more than obsessive serpentine windings around a single pitch.

A collection of pitches—a scale—channels the patterns in a way that occurs frequently in Crumb's music. We can illustrate this exotic tonality, so prominent here and in other of these movements, by quoting from the opening oboe solo. Stripped of its decorative gasps, this hypnotic melody bares as its raw material the scale shown in Example 23.2. Sound these pitches at a piano and you will hear the tonal matrix of the dance. The same pitch relationships can be heard later in the movement.

Example 23.2 Scale basis for "Dances of the Ancient Earth"

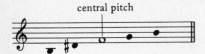

There are shouts of "Kai!" (meaning nothing, except pure excitement) and loud whispers of encouragement from the players as this dance runs its course. At three locations the rise-fall theme of the principal instruments is echoed by clapped stones, whose pitches are shaped by the player to imitate a melodic contour.

The form of the dance is articulated mainly by timbres and textures, with brief silences forming solid partitions between sections. These hesitations of silence are symbolized by circles (3 = three seconds) in the mapping of the next example.

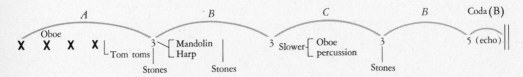

Example 23.3 Mapping of large sections, "Dances of the Ancient Earth"

A part of the Oriental flavor of this movement comes from the mandolin, some of whose strings are deliberately mistuned, and whose percussive bursts sound like a Japanese koto. There are hints of Oriental textures too. The harp and mandolin engage in a heterophonic duet, in which both play about the same series of pitches, but slightly out of synchrony.* The coda passage also contains this same-but-different kind of union. In our example we have connected notes of the same pitch to show how they do or do not occur together.

Example 23.4 Heterophonic texture in "Dance Interlude I," Coda

---

*See Chapter 6 for a discussion of heterophonic texture.

Song II:
"I have lost myself in the sea many times"

Me he perdido muchas veces por el mar	I have lost myself in the sea many times
con el oído lleno de floras recien cortadas,	with my ear full of freshly cut flowers,
con la lengua llena de amor y de agonía.	with my tongue full of love and agony.
como me pierdo en el corazón de algunos niños . . .	I have lost myself in the sea many times
Muchas veces me he perdido por el mar.	as I lose myself in the heart of certain children.

In each of the preceding movements we have noted how instruments punctuate vocal statements. The free outpourings of the soprano in Song I were bridged by percussive strikes from harp and piano, and the long oboe phrases in "Dances of the Ancient Earth" were separated by shouts and plucked tones of mandolin and harp. The same process appears in a curious way in Song II. Curious, because now it is the voice that marks off phrase endings with whispered fragments from the text. And thus a unique turnabout is accomplished: the sung text enacts a background role to the slithering lead of piano, vibraphone, musical saw, electric piano, and harp. The succession of events is simple in form, if tantalizing in sound. Our outline portrays only the foreground events as they are punctuated by the whispering voice.

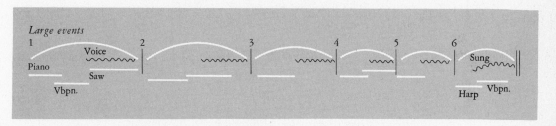

Example 23.5 Form of Song II

Only with event #6 does the soprano revert to an ordinary singing style, dropping the speaking tube through which she has been whispering to close the song with a graceful hummed line.

Within the song a ghostly atmosphere has been maintained by all manner of unusual sound production. The piano is plucked, its sliding patterns produced by moving a chisel along the metal strings. The harpist has scraped strings to make whistling sounds, and the musical saw's eerie tone is sufficiently extraordinary without further manipulation. It is an unprecedented song in the whole history of song.

Song III:
"From where do
you come, my love,
my child?"

¿De dónde vienes, amor, mi niño?	From where do you come, my love, my child?
De la cresta del duro frio.	From the ridge of hard frost.
¿Que necesitas, amor, mi niño?	What do you need, my love, my child?
La tibia tela de tu vestido.	The warm cloth of your dress.
¡Que so agiten las ramas al sol y salten las fuentes alrededor!	**Let the branches ruffle in the sun and the fountains leap all around!**
En el patio ladra el perro, en los árboles canta el viento. Los bueyes mugen al boyero y la luna me riza los cabellos.	In the courtyard a dog barks, in the trees the wind sings. The oxen low to the oxherd and the moon curls my hair.
¿Que pides, niño, desde tan lejos?	What do you ask for, my child, from so far away?
Los blancos montes que hay en tu pecho.	The white mountains of your breast.
¡Que se agiten las ramas al sol y salten las fuentes alrededor!	**Let the branches ruffle in the sun and the fountains leap all around!**
Te dire, niño mio, que si, tronchada y rota soy para ti. ¡Cómo me duele esta cintura donde tendrás primera cuna! ¿Cuando, mi niño, vas a venir? Cuándo tu carne huela a jazmin.	I'll tell you, my child, yes, I am torn and broken for you. How painful is this waist where you will have your first cradle! When, my child, will you come? When your flesh smells of jasmine flowers.
¡Que se agiten las ramas al sol Y salten las fuentes alrededor!	**Let the branches ruffle in the sun and the fountains leap all around!**

The ghostly hush of Song II gives way to what at first appears to be a return to the soprano's opening vocalise. But this virtuoso recital—again with nonsense syllables—turns out to be an introduction to a driving rondo in bolero rhythm, called "Dance of the Sacred Life Cycle." It is the middle of the composition and its longest movement.

The poem's text is split between soprano and child, who remains offstage. Since many lines, like the first two, suggest a dialogue of mother and unborn child, the two voices sing these as an exchange.

Soprano: "From where do you come, my love, my child?"
Boy Soprano: "From the ridge of hard frost."

Other lines are spoken in high dramatic style, the dialogue continuing between the two singers in longer exchanges. In the song the poem's lines are at times reordered, so that later lines occur before earlier lines. Crumb clearly cares less that listeners hear each word than that they be carried along by the obsessive exuberance of rhythms and joyous shouts.

The momentum is unflagging. The soprano's final statement of the text's last line is the cue for the resounding crash that breaks the spell and ends the movement.

Song IV:
"Every Afternoon
in Granada"

Todas las tardes en Granada,   Every afternoon in Granada,
todas las tardes se muere un niño . . . every afternoon a child dies . . .

The soprano's two lines of text are used up during the first half of this movement. The second half is dominated by a quotation, played on a toy piano, from a simple harpsichord piece J.S. Bach composed for his second wife, Anna Magdalena. The total effect is surrealistic.

Why would a composer graft a Bach piece, played on a child's toy, onto a mournful song about children who die in Granada? Perhaps the very need to ask the question provides a partial answer. It is indeed an awesome mixture of images, a compelling reincarnation of the musical past.

The song's dream-like suspension is in part provided by its harmonies. The first half unfolds over a simple chord (C♯ major triad) sustained by the voices of the three percussionists, the marimba, and the harmonica. The second half switches to a different chord (G minor triad) played by marimba and later joined by the singers.

While the toy piano plays its excerpt from Bach's *Bist du bei mir* ("If Thou abide with me"), background harmony forms the same kind of bitonal relationships we observed earlier in parts of Persichetti's Divertimento for Band (Chapter 14). While the melody is played in D♭ major, the oscillating marimba chord projects the key of G minor.

Example 23.6 Bitonal relationships between melody and chord in Song IV

The emotional residue of Crumb's strange combinations is more that of dreams than of the ordinary world. Like Salvador Dali's watches that melt before the eyes, or stampeding giraffes whose necks trail crimson

flames, the listener is confronted with musical images that do not go together. Those who know Spain's sunny capital of Granada can particularly appreciate the contradiction between its southern gaiety and children dying in the afternoon sun.

Dance Interlude II:
"Ghost Dance"

This strophic dance is played by mandolin, its sinuous melody produced by sliding a glass rod along the string that has been plucked.* Its phantom accompaniment is a trio of maracas, whose players punctuate their spectral rattlings with whispers.

The maracas lie silent during the second half of the dance, leaving the mandolin to wind its way alone through melodies formed from the scale we illustrated from Dance Interlude I. The total form of the movement is thus a strophic *A A'*.

Song V:
"My heart of silk
is filled with lights"

. . . *Se ha llenado de luces mi corazón de seda*	. . . My heart of silk is filled with lights
de campanas perdidas, de lirios y de abejas	with lost bells, with lilies, and with bees
y yo me ire muy lejos,	and I will go very far,
más allá de esas sierras, más allá de los mares,	farther than those hills, farther than the seas,
cerca de las estrellas, para perdirle a Cristo	close to the stars, to ask Christ the Lord
Señor que me devuelva me alma antiqua de niño . . .	to give me back my ancient soul of a child . . .

This final song brings together elements of earlier moments in the song cycle. After a crashing series of chords, cymbals and sleighbells form a backdrop for the rhythms of harp, mandolin, and toy piano. The jangling bells and cymbals end with ominous low chords, which are later to be repeated several times as framing joints for events within the song.

The first dark chord introduces an oboe passage, a faint return to that instrument's theme in Dance Interlude I. At the end of the solo, the oboist walks offstage, from whence echoes of the same pattern will come later.

The soprano begins while the third dark chord fades to inaudibility. Her phrases arch rapidly from low to high, dotted with dense chords from the percussion. This passage ends with the fourth line of text, another ominous chord from harp and piano, and the offstage oboe renews its plaintive theme, growing fainter with each new statement.

---

*This is called "bottleneck technique" by guitar and banjo players.

With quiet, slow resolve, the soprano begins a new section that grows until she is singing at the top of her range, supported by chords like those of the movement's beginning. This intense moment is the beginning of the end.

The solo voice is left unaccompanied. Her last two lines of text shape passages that dissolve slowly, while the boy soprano joins her at the piano for a final exchange, a fantastic set of echoing imitations. The little boy has recovered his voice from the crickets, but its plaintive final cries seem doomed to vanish into the unrecoverable past.

The outline shown next is a guide to the events we have just reviewed. As in Example 23.3, circles enclosing numbers represent boundary silences.

Example 23.7   Mapping of Song V. "My heart of silk . . ."

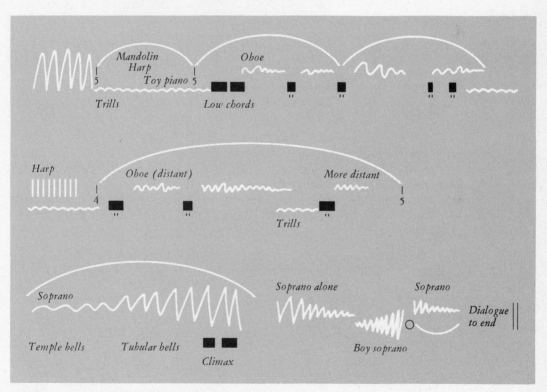

IV

THE
CONCERTO

INTRODUCTION

The word *concerto* refers to the combining of separate musical forces in a "concerted action." Compositions bearing the title do just that, in one way or another. The most familiar to modern listeners joins a solo performer with a large ensemble. This combination provides a relatively dramatic situation for music-making, for it suggests the unbalanced struggle of one against many.

Two simple conditions have made the concerto an especially successful modus operandi during the past three hundred years. One is the condition of contrast afforded between the solo instrument and the sound of the large group. The other is the inherent excitement suggested by the need of the solo performer to play extraordinarily well. To match the numerical superiority of the large body of instruments, the soloist must be a virtuoso who overwhelms through sheer technical display. This latter condition can engage a listener who is not particularly moved by purely musical factors alone.*

Not all concertos pit just one solo against an ensemble. Bartok's Concerto for Orchestra (Chapter 14) uses many instruments from the symphony orchestra in solo roles at various times within its five movements. Bach's Brandenburg Concerto No. 2, discussed in the next chapter, is a special type called *concerto grosso*. In this kind of concerto a small group of soloists is combined with a larger accompanying orchestra. Bach's work uses a soloistic group of recorder (or flute), oboe, violin, and trumpet. A number of modern composers have turned to similar kinds of combined soloists in their concertos. The Swiss composer Rolf Liebermann composed a Concerto for Jazz Band and Orchestra in 1954. More recently, Donald Erb, whose work for percussion soloist closes this part of our study, composed a Concerto for Rock Band and Orchestra that was premiered by the Detroit Symphony in 1970.

Whatever the solo instrument or instruments featured in a particular concerto, that work's most immediate appeal for the listener usually centers around what the soloist plays and how well he or she plays it. In this respect, the concerto is the culminating form for the virtuoso performer. It provides the setting within which the superb player can reveal the control, the manual dexterity, and the musical sensitivity which make a true artist. Without these the concerto is an exercise in empty sounds; without the concerto, modern artists would lack an adequate outlet for their artistry.

---

*It is worth noting that the concerto first developed as a popular form during the late seventeenth century, a time when virtuoso performers began to appear and human individuality became a flourishing ideal in Western society.

24

BRANDENBURG CONCERTO NO. 2 IN F MAJOR

Johann Sebastian Bach (1685–1750)

BACKGROUND*

Both the solo concerto and concerto grosso were cultivated during the late seventeenth and early eighteenth centuries. The solo concerto developed most vigorously in Italy, a violin usually playing the leading role. Composers such as Albinoni, Vivaldi, Torelli, and Tartini composed works for solo violin and small orchestra. These men were violinists, so they wished to create vehicles for their own brilliant performances.

Italy during this time was the seat of opera as well as instrumental music, and the dramatic flair of this vocal form naturally rubbed off on the solo concerto. In fact, the slow movement of many an early Italian violin concerto is like an aria without words.

The solo concerto was as popular in Germany as in Italy. One of J.S. Bach's contemporaries, Georg Philip Telemann, composed over one hundred and seventy. In addition to the Brandenburg Concertos, Bach himself composed solo concertos for harpsichord and orchestra and also for solo violin. Even his Suite in B Minor for Flute and Strings is in essence a flute concerto cast as a collection of short dance movements. Yet Bach's musical conception did not favor the solo concerto, with soloist as protagonist and coequal with a larger group. His solo concertos are not *solo* in the same way as Mozart's, which were composed about half a century later.

---

* Discussions of Bach and his times can be found in Chapters 19 and 29.

Illustration 24.1
Johann Sebastian Bach

Bach's most famous contemporary, George F. Handel, was of a different orientation. His life was dominated by the concert hall rather than the church. The twenty-four solo concertos he composed "for harpsichord or organ" reveal his more natural flair for this kind of virtuoso piece. With Bach, he furthered a shift from solo violin to solo keyboard within the concerto. It was a deflection of preference that would hold for composers even into the nineteenth century.

THE *BRANDENBURG* CONCERTOS

Bach did not name his six orchestral concertos "Brandenburg." This is the title history has bestowed in identifying the cause for their composition. The son of the ruling Elector of Brandenburg (Germany) was impressed by a performance by Bach that he heard in a neighboring town in 1719. He requested that the great composer provide some new works for his own local orchestra. Bach sent the six concertos to Christian Ludwig two years later. And thus all six works are now known as "The Brandenburg Concertos."

Although all six were composed in the same year (1721), there are some differences among them. Two of the six (Nos. 3 and 6) do not make a clear separation between a solo group, called *concertino,* and a large ensemble, called *ripieno*. Concertos 1, 2, 4, and 5 are of the true *concerto grosso* type, however, for they use a small solo ensemble along with a larger orchestral body of strings and harpsichord.

The *ripieno*—the large group—normally consists of first and second violins, violas, cellos, and basses, with wind instruments added in some works. The bass part of the *ripieno* is performed by double basses and cellos, but some works have a second bass part that is played by a cello and the harpsichord. This second bass persists constantly throughout the texture, which gave rise to its name, *basso continuo* (or "continuous bass"). In performances of a concerto the harpsichord player must improvise chords to fit the harmonies of the composition, much as a guitar or piano player provides chords that are not written out for a popular song. This "constant bass" of Baroque instrumental and vocal music is one of its most readily identifiable features. Sometimes called *thorough bass*, it persisted in orchestral music until the time of Haydn and Mozart, who helped establish the basic orchestral style of the late eighteenth century.

This second of the Brandenburg Concertos piques the interest of modern listeners because of its solo trumpet part. Written for a small valveless horn, it soars far higher than the modern trumpet usually ventures, except in some of the screaming playing of jazz performers.

Since the players of these eighteenth-century trumpets had to perform complicated melodies without the aid of valves to change pitch, they cultivated a technique of playing called *Klarinblässen*. This consisted of playing high in the instrument's range of natural harmonics.* The technique was discontinued in the late eighteenth century, when trumpets became the more docile members of the orchestral family that we hear in the symphonies of Mozart and Haydn. With the advent of valves in the nineteenth century, the need for this playing technique disappeared completely. Today the parts of Baroque music usually are played on horns smaller than the modern trumpet but which have the added blessing of valves.

---

*See the Glossary, *Harmonics*

Example 24.1   First page of Bach's score for the Concerto No. 2

CONCERTO NO. 2

This work calls for a concertino group of trumpet, recorder (often replaced by flute), oboe, and solo violin. It is accompanied by an orchestra (ripieno) of violins, violas, cellos, basses, and harpsichord. There are times in recorded performances when, lacking visual clues, the contrasts of texture that help mark off the form of a concerto grosso are not wholly clear.

Following the lead of the Italian Antonio Vivaldi (1678–1741), a composer Bach greatly admired, the concerto is in three movements, *fast, slow, fast*. Also similar to the Italian master's practice, the second movement provides stark textural contrast with the two outer movements. In it Bach dispenses with the ripieno and the solo trumpet, leaving only the recorder, oboe, violin, and basso continuo parts.

Two aspects of this concerto reflect the general musical practice of Bach's era: (1) a tempo for each movement that is unflagging from start to finish, and (2) loudness levels that are "terraced" rather than "shaded," there being two basic levels, loud and soft. The practice of *crescendo* and *diminuendo* (gradual increases or decreases in loudness) did not become a part of general musical practice until after Bach's time.

Movement I: Allegro

Although there are two main themes in the movement, a listener is misled to expect only these as indicators of overall form. One main determinant of sections is the textural contrast provided by the concertino versus ripieno that is basic to the concerto grosso. Furthermore, the contrasting timbres of the trumpet, recorder, oboe and solo violin are exploited fully by Bach in imparting a sense of progress to the musical flow. A complete charting of the interchanging of forces in the movement reveals the care shown in this aspect of the form. Some of these parts last only two measures; none is longer than eight.

Ripieno	Violin	Ripieno	Oboe	Ripieno	Flute
Ripieno	Trumpet	Ripieno	Trumpet	Ripieno	
Trumpet	Recorder (or flute)	Oboe	Recorder	Ripieno	
Concertino	Ripieno	Concertino	Ripieno	Concertino	
Ripieno	Concertino	Ripieno	Concertino	Ripieno	

Notice the almost constant pattern of return in these twenty-six tiny units, the ripieno group forming enclosures for an individual soloist or the concertino group. This pattern of return was known during the Baroque period as *ritornello form*. It is sometimes applied today to any music in which a returning pattern plays a dominant role (in Italian *ritorno* = return). Viewed from our own perspective, these rapid exchanges in Bach's Concerto produce a rather nervous kind of rondo.

One or more of the solo group can be heard throughout the movement, along with the constant basso continuo. The most striking textural changes occur when the ripieno joins to create a full ensemble, called *tutti* (all together). Thus the composer works with the following basic kinds of combinations:

Soloist (or soloists) with continuo	Total concertino with continuo	Tutti (full complement)

The prevailing melody in this movement has a triumphal quality that may remind you of a fanfare. This is a natural response because of the static nature of the pattern; it consists of a repeated motif and an unchanging harmony, as shown in the next example.

Example 24.2   Main theme of the first movement

(Allegro)

Movement II:
Adagio

While the first movement is in a major key, the change to minor in the second movement reinforces the contrasts of new texture and timbres. Now the concertino (minus trumpet) plays, with only the basso continuo providing its accompanying foil.

This beautifully flowing movement grows from an accumulation of imitating parts. It is the kind of fugal texture we described in Chapter 17, in which several parts successively imitate each other. In the beginning of this movement the solo violin is answered by the oboe, the recorder then topping off the layers of the texture with its own version of the theme, which itself sounds most like a gentle sigh of resignation.

Example 24.3   Principal theme, Movement II

Andante

A secondary melody enters as a counterpart with the oboe's entrance. It assumes a more significant role just before the end of the movement, sharing thematic primacy with the first theme at the very end.

Example 24.4   Secondary theme, Movement II

As a whole, the form of this movement is best described as processive. It grows from the continued development of the single melodic "sigh" and its accompanying theme, devoid of impressive seams that would impede the steady flow. The persistence of the basso continuo is more evident in this movement, because of its lighter texture, than in the first movement.

This is not exciting music in the usual sense. It is exquisitely moving, however. It is a clear example of the kind of earthy pathos Bach was so capable of molding from relatively simple patterns.

Movement III:
Allegro assai

Returning to the driving force of the first movement, the last seems even more frantic. Absent during the second movement, the trumpet now makes a brilliant return, leading with the first piercing statement of a theme that is to dominate the entire movement. This theme is the subject of a fugue.

Example 24.5   Principal theme, Movement III

The exposition of the first section is shaped from follow-the-leader entries of this theme by the oboe, recorder, and violin, in the wake of the trumpet's opening solo. The static contour and repetitious rhythm of this theme are offset by the melodic bits and pieces that accumulate along the way. Trills—typical of Baroque music—throw momentary jolts into the prevailing spirit of perpetual motion. The most significant of the secondary theme fragments is a descending line, a simple sequence,* shown in the next example.

Example 24.6   Secondary theme, Movement III

The overall form of the movement emerges from a series of imitative entries by the solo parts; each series is a grouping of the four soloists in a turn-taking order. As in the first movement, texture plays a crucial role. Three sections are marked by textural, tonal, and thematic separation, as illustrated in Example 24.7.

Of special interest within the second section of this movement is the way the ripieno parts shed their secondary status to participate in the development of the principal theme. It is in this section that the most

*See also Example 7.1, which shows a melodic sequence.

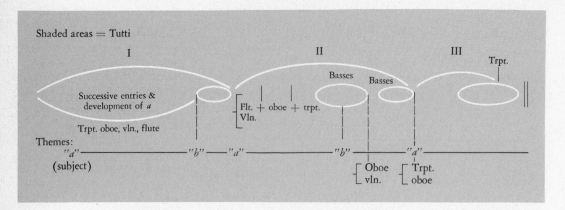

Example 24.7   Mapping of the form, Movement III

frequent changes of key occur. This series of events creates a certain instability that makes this part of the movement similar to the Development section of a classical sonata form. In this respect it is worth noting that the trumpet again sounds the main theme at the end, providing a sure spirit of return to the form. This final flourish closes the elaborate developmental cycle that has just ensued.

The total effect of Bach's Concerto is that of no-nonsense music. It is rich in musical imagery for the careful listener, yet it contains not a hint of excess drama, no suggestion of padding for the sake of extraordinary effect. It is music to delight the performer as well as to engage and reward the listener. Its lack of pretense is perhaps its greatest asset. Its solid musical virtues have managed to woo listeners for two hundred and fifty years.

25

PIANO CONCERTO NO. 20
IN D MINOR, K. 466

Wolfgang A. Mozart (1756–1791)*

BACKGROUND

Bach's Brandenburg Concertos were not *solo* concertos in the sense that single instruments are pitted as coequals against an accompanying ensemble. As such, those works, including the Concerto No. 2 discussed in the previous chapter, were typical of the past rather than pace-setters of the day. With Bach this kind of concerto—the concerto grosso—reached simultaneously its peak and end of development. The solo concerto emerged during its waning years, replacing it as the favored form by the time of Bach's death in 1750.

The "Sensitive Style" (*empfindsamer stil*) Younger composers of the mid-eighteenth century began to shy away from the severity and monumentality of the elder Bach's style of music. They cultivated instead an easier, more gracious kind of music in which elegantly turned melodies and homophonic textures replaced the polyphonic complexities of the old Leipzig cantor. This stylistic shift coincided with a time when the composer's main sphere of activity moved from the church to the salon of aristocrats or to the public concert hall.

Two of Bach's sons were a part of this evolutionary scene. The older, Carl Philip Emmanuel (1714–1788), composed fifty-two solo concertos that reflect the stylish new music but retain many ties with the concerto

*Chapter 21 contains additional information about Mozart.

Illustration 25.1 Mozart with his father and sister. Mother's likeness (on the wall) completes the family group.

grosso. His younger brother, Johann Christian (1735–1782), produced concertos that in spirit and technique are close to the later works of Mozart. (Mozart met Johann Christian in London while touring as a child prodigy.)

Appeal of the Solo Concerto

It was Mozart, and to a lesser degree Haydn, who forged the formal and stylistic traits we recognize today as the necessary ingredients of the classical solo concerto.

The appeal of the solo concerto is not difficult to explain. It provides a dramatic framework for musical display that is unmatched except in opera. The solitary performer is cast as the primary figure on a field of many performers, the accompanying ensemble. The two forces are not physically equal, but the composer's music makes them so. The soloist can detach from the larger body to comment on its events; he can defy the larger body as protagonist; or he can join with it as equal partner. The potentialities are simple and basic, yet they are powerful when utilized by a skilled composer. All of the possibilities of a one-against-many relationship are there.

Mozart and the Concerto

Mozart worked with the concerto form from childhood to the last months of his life. He was a brilliant pianist whose livelihood came largely from public concerts, so he naturally produced works that could display his skills to their best advantage. But this was not his sole motivation: he composed concertos for other solo instruments too. Aside from his twenty-three concertos for solo piano, there is one for two pianos. And then there are works in which the solo role is assigned to violin, flute, clarinet, bassoon, or horn, and even one concerto for flute and harp combined. An excellent violinist, Wolfgang played the violin concertos himself until, in 1777, he tired of that instrument.

Since the piano concertos were written for his own performances, they are richly endowed with the virtuoso qualities that can make a good piece of music sound like a personal triumph. They abound with passages of rapid scale patterns, rushing chordal figurations, and gorgeous melodies. When executed with apparent ease, they can endear a pianist to an audience.

THE CONCERTO IN D MINOR

This work was composed for a public concert Mozart played in Vienna early in 1785. It has been one of his most popular concertos in the intervening two centuries. Its strong hold on listeners is largely a product of its highly dramatic character. It is music that hints of the future, for many of its passages project the dark, introspective atmosphere that later would be cultivated by composers of the mid-nineteenth century. In the light of this quality, it is interesting to note that the D Minor is one of only two piano concertos Mozart composed in a minor key after his move to Vienna in 1781. The other fifteen of that period in his life are all in major keys.

Like Bach's Brandenburg Concerto No. 2, this work is in three-movement form, a succession of fast, slow, fast that is favored for the solo concerto to the present day. All three movements are storehouses of engaging melody. In fact, the listener can at times feel overwhelmed by the sense of an endless procession of catchy tunes. The first movement is in a modified sonata form, whose details we shall discuss momentarily. The second is a prolonged dramatic song in a return form of A B A C A. The third movement is a dashing rondo, whose bountiful themes seem inexhaustible.

Mozart thoroughly explores the textural possibilities his solo–ensemble combination provides. We hear the orchestra alone, piano alone, the two combined, and the two as adversaries. Whatever the stance, the result is continually dramatic music, music that rises to the level of the symphony in aesthetic weight and impact. While solo concertos of the late eighteenth century tended to be merely brilliant display works of a light character, this concerto is as imposing as any composed in the nineteenth century, and almost every major composer of both centuries wrote at least one.*

---

*The solo instrument of these concertos written by composers from Beethoven through Brahms, Mendelssohn, Grieg, Schumann, Saint Säens, Tchaikovsky, and Rachmaninoff, was usually the piano. The violin was a far-removed second runner.

Concerto First-movement form

Composers of the classical concerto solved the problem of providing an appropriate preparation for the featured instrument's entry by modifying the sonata form of the symphony's first movement. In the concerto first movement the orchestra plays an Exposition of its own; then the solo enters and a second Exposition ensues. Sometimes this second Exposition is essentially a repetition of themes heard in the first; sometimes it differs markedly in content. Since the Exposition of standard sonata form was most often repeated, it is easy to see the concerto modification as its direct descendant. In broad terms, the two compare as six main sections.

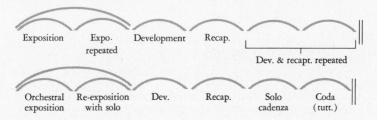

Example 25.1   Comparison of sonata-form and concerto first-movement form

The solo cadenza, which normally provided a final mopping-up operation for the soloist, was in fact an ultimate Development section when played by pianists who, like Mozart, could improvise fluently. With later pianists who could not—and this includes most concert pianists of today—the cadenza could be a vacuous but vigorous key-thumping. When properly treated, it replaces the repeated Development section of the early sonata form.*

Movement I: Allegro

Mozart's first movement adheres to the modified plan of Ex. 25.1 and the piano cadenza written by Beethoven (which almost all modern pianists use) provides an additional developmental flourish before the end. The next illustration and the discussion based on it can provide some perspective for this tightly-packed movement.

---

*The scores of some symphonic first movements indicate that the entire Development and Recapitulation sections were intended to be repeated. Most conductors ignore this practice today.

Example 25.2   Mapping of the large parts, Movement I

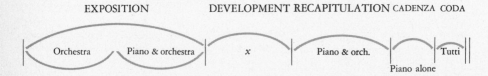

The "double Exposition" demands a closer look. It is a stream of themes and textures and piano-orchestra tactics. While the piano joins with the orchestra in returning to themes exposed earlier, its entrance is made with a theme all its own (theme c), and another new theme is announced later (theme d). In all, the piano's Exposition segment supplies two themes which did not appear in the orchestral preview of the beginning.

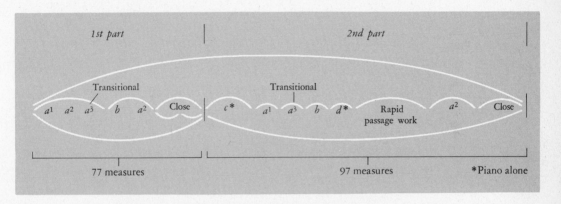

Example 25.3   Thematic outline of the Exposition section

The section in the mapping called "rapid passage work" lacks strong ties with earlier passages; its musical function is to provide sheer bravura for the soloist, who by this time is amply warmed to the task. The orchestra's role during this display of rapid finger work is wholly secondary, providing little more than chordal backgrounds.

DEVELOPMENT   The seam that separates Exposition from Development is neatly hidden in this movement. Since the entrance of the solo piano (playing the c theme in a major key) marks a distinct textural and tonal juncture, we shall regard this as the beginning of the developmental processes.

What follows is a series of paired developments of themes a^1 and c, each pairing moving to a new key area. First the orchestra sounds the syncopations and triplet figures that began the work (a^1); then the piano settles into the more lyrical c theme. At first it is in minor, later in major. These give-and-take sequences end with the orchestra turning full-time to the triplet figures of a^1 and the solo piano racing through rapid patterns, until it is left alone in a cadence that leads directly into the Recapitulation. The mapping shown next provides an overall view of this series of rapidly changing events.

DEVELOPMENT

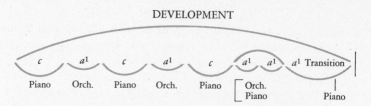

Example 25.4 Outline of themes developed and main instruments

RECAPITULATION The return is like a marriage of the two expository sections at the beginning, but with a crucial difference: the solo cadenza breaks in just prior to the coda. Beethoven's "composed improvisation" is a masterpiece of development in itself.* It begins with trills underlined with fragments of theme a^1, all of this framed by rapid chord passages. In succession, themes d, a^1, and c are given their due in textures of rapidly changing keys.

All of this ends as it began: with flowery trills (which are the direct signals for the conductor that the cadenza has run its course).

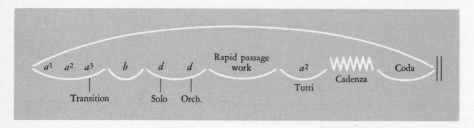

Example 25.5 Mapping of the Recapitulation section

One thematic change occurs in the Recapitulation: theme c is passed over. This is understandable, for c was most prominent in the Development section as material for the solo piano. Aside from this adjustment, the cadenza, and the return of the d theme in minor rather than in major, the Recapitulation bears the usual strong resemblances with the Exposition section.

Movement II: Romanze

Piano and orchestra were relatively equal participants in the first movement. If we may be forgiven such homely metaphors, the orchestra graciously invited the piano in to join in its musical excursion (as welcome guest, but as *guest*, nevertheless).

---

*Mozart improvised the cadenzas when he played his concertos. Although he did write out cadenzas for performances by friends and pupils, none of these survive today.

The guest has taken over in the *Romanze*. Now the piano leads the way at all times, the orchestra following and assisting where needed with its docile background resonances. Every new theme is introduced first by the solo. What began as a joint venture has developed into a spotlighted monologue.

A change from the usual concerto middle movement, the Romanze is a showcase for the piano, which is by turns pensive and determined. Quiet reflection is the dominant mood, but one extended section (*C* in Example 25.7) projects a more willful tone. Everything is laid out in the neat, symmetrical phrases that textbook definitions of "classical music" have immortalized. The first thematic section, for instance, is a thirty-two-bar song form whose melodic bits follow a binary sheme.

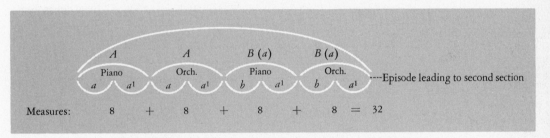

Example 25.6 Thematic outline, first section of the *Romanze*

Although the second thematic section begins in the same key as its predecessor (*B♭ major*), it turns to the key of *F* major within its course. And thus this hint of tonal departure helps to strengthen our sense of resolution when the *A* theme returns. The greatest contrast comes with the *C* section, however, where texture, rhythm, theme, and key provide a stark contrast with the foregoing events.

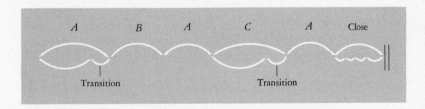

Example 25.7 Mapping of large sections, *Romanze*

Movement III: Rondo—Allegro assai

This massive finale is a fine example of what we called a hybrid form in Chapter 2. Mozart calls it a rondo. Indeed its spirited gait and thematic outlines fit that description. But there is an evident grafting of sonata form on to this extended rondo. The term *sonata-rondo* has been applied to just such instances by most writers.

In terms of largest sections, the following synopsis describes the movement:

1   Exposition of three distinct theme-groups, a^1–a^2–a^3–a^4; b^1–b^2, and c; short solo cadenza.
2   Brief return to theme a^1; extended development of a^4 and a^1.
3   Return, in tonic key, of themes b^1, b^2, and c; extended solo cadenza; brief return of theme a^1.
4   Final section in tonic major key, consisting of themes c, a^2, c and coda.

So what Mozart has put together is a series of alternating themes, one of which returns to an extended Development, then gives way to an abridged Recapitulation of themes left undeveloped. To this a final section is added, a triumphant finish in the tonic major key. It rounds out the movement and provides a suitable ending for the entire work as well.

It would be more confusing than helpful to illustrate all of the seven themes we mentioned in our outline synopsis. We shall limit our discussion and excerpts to the most crucial shaping elements of the movement. These are theme a^1, which provides the return aspect of a rondo form; theme a^4, because of its function in the Development; and theme c, which is prominent at the close of the movement. The beginning measures of each are shown in the series of Examples 25.8.

Theme a^1 leaps off with a broad chord outline, a pattern known as the *Mannheim Rocket.**

Example 25.8a   Theme a^1, first five measures

Theme a^4 consists of a series of short patterns separated by silences. Add the "rocket" upswing of a^1 to its first measure and its kinship with a^1 would be more obvious. Before this theme has gone far, theme a^1 in fact takes its place.

---

*This quaint name derives from the popularity of the rapid leaping pattern with contemporaries of Mozart from Mannheim, Germany.

Example 25.8b   Theme a^4, the piano's halting variant of theme a^1

And then theme c has the character of a closing gesture.

Example 25.8c   The closing theme, c

The mapping shown next is ordered to show the sonata form outline of the whole movement, but asterisks mark the returns of theme a^1 that provide the strong return characteristics of a rondo.

The first solo cadenza in this movement is only a brief respite of running motion in preparation for the first return of the rondo theme, a^1. The second, which prepares for the fragmentary return of a^1 after the Recapitulation, is a true developmental passage. Beethoven's composed cadenza is used here too; its main goal is a final dramatic display of fragments drawn from theme a^1, with attention shown about midway to theme a^4.

This is a buoyant movement; it is a rondo in spirit and in formal outline, and it is packed with tuneful display. But it is not a frivolous movement. Unlike the final movements of the concertos composed by Mozart's contemporaries, it is not a lightweight bit of fluff whose singular virtue is to send an audience away happy but empty-headed.

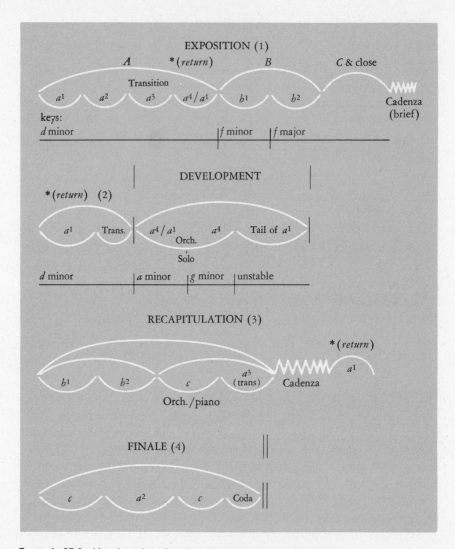

Example 25.9 Mapping of the four large sections of the final movement

26

VIOLIN CONCERTO

Alban Berg (1885–1935)

BACKGROUND

Berg's Concerto is an example of *twelve-tone*, or *serial music*. There was a day when the very mention of those terms was enough to arouse violent reactions from the most benign music lover. Just thirty years ago, in fact, music associated with this method of composition was in many circles maligned as "mathematical" (and thus sterile), "artistically depraved," and even a product of the devil incarnate. Like most prejudices nourished by ignorance, opinions of this kind managed only to cloud the issue of musical meaning and value. That exquisite music might be written while utilizing procedures of serial composition, as well as by using any "method," seemed lost in the heat of emotion.

Arnold Schoenberg developed his "method of composing with twelve notes" sometime prior to 1922. Its basic premise was derived from his wish to organize musical sounds in some way that could replace tonality. By the middle of this century the premise had been proven valid, at least as *one* means among others of achieving this end.

The approach is simple, although the execution can become quite involved. The composer organizes the twelve pitch classes of the chromatic scale* in any succession suitable to his purposes. This succession, or *row*, then remains as an ordered set to be used as a reference for all melodic

---

*See "*Chromatic*" in the Glossary.

Illustration 26.1
Alban Berg

and harmonic events within his composition. The row is a reservoir of pitch relationships that guide the composer in organizing tonal materials.

The usual by-product, of this systematic ordering of notes, is music that is *atonal*, music that does not project a sense of pitch focus (as we discussed the principle in Chapter 4). All pitches are in this respect musical equals, none regarded as intrinsically nor structurally more central to the musical process than another. And thus composing a work "in the key of such-and-such" becomes an obsolete principle.

BERG'S CAREER

Alban Berg was a pupil and close friend of Schoenberg. It was only natural that his revered teacher's principles should be adopted by him. It was Berg's good fortune that he possessed the talent and individuality that enabled him to adapt the twelve-tone serial procedures to his own creative impulse. He, perhaps more than any other composer, disproved for posterity the false prophecy of early critics that Schoenberg was sealing the doom of music with his highly rational methods.

In his operatic masterpieces *Wozzeck* and *Lulu,* in his *Lyric Suite* for string quartet, in numerous songs, and in his Violin Concerto, Berg produced music that is as beautiful, as emotionally stirring as any music written before or after. That some of these were composed using serial procedures is to a great extent beside the point. Once we are aware that the music uses a particular method, we can attend to it *as music,* just as we would the products of Bach and Mozart.

The Violin Concerto was initiated by the American violinist Louis Krasner, who in 1934 asked Berg to write a large-scale work for him to play. Berg procrastinated. Only with the tragically premature death of the daughter of his close friends Alma Mahler and Walter Gropius* was he spurred sufficiently to set to work. The dedication, *"Dem Andenken eines Engels"* ("To the memory of an angel") suggests that the Concerto was conceived by Berg as a kind of Requiem for the youthful Manon Gropius. Ironically, the work became his own memorial; he died from an insect sting in 1935, just before the work's premiere by Krasner in 1936. He lived only six months after completing this, his final composition.

THE VIOLIN CONCERTO

It is risky to read composer's intentions into works which bear no program, but we are on safe ground when we suggest that the Violin Concerto implies two states of being in its two movements. The first movement is a musical analogue to the short and tender life of Manon Gropius. The second movement is a tonal suggestion of the catastrophe of her death and the triumph over consequent grief for those who knew and loved her. This general scheme is undergirded by the two tunes quoted in the two movements. The first is a Carinthian folk song, the other a Lutheran chorale melody as harmonized by J. S. Bach.

The concerto's two large movements are each organized in two parts, producing a total layout of four extended sections. The violin is rarely silent; as one might expect, the soloist is faced with a grueling test of physical endurance, to say nothing of the skill and control demanded of one who is to project the riches found in this score. Aside from the demand made on finger technique, the prevailing lyricism of the solo part calls for a resonant tone that can be coaxed from the very extremes of high and low pitches in rapid succession. It is not uncommon to find the very top and bottom of the instrument's range exploited within a single measure. This is indeed music for the virtuoso performer.

---

*Mrs. Gropius was the former wife of the composer-conductor Gustav Mahler. Gropius was one of the great architects of the early twentieth century, associated with the Bauhaus in Germany.

One general characteristic that is notable in the total concerto is the relatively frequent ebbing of tempo that marks its flow. Unlike most of the music of eighteenth-century composers, Berg's Concerto projects a rhythmic life quite the opposite of perpetual motion. It waxes and wanes by the moment. Its textures thin and thicken momentarily. For the most part it avoids the singular thrust that carries through from beginning to end in the dance-stimulated music of earlier instrumental music. Its overall effect is rhapsodic, mercurially potent as a message of high emotional content.

First Movement: Andante

Before listening to this movement, it might help first to know its overall shape, primarily because the sectional divisions are not as forceful as they are in earlier concertos. Its form is that of a large middle that is framed by two somewhat shorter sections. The symmetry of this scheme is complemented by smaller scale symmetry, in that the middle portion itself is a framed structure, as shown in Example 26.1

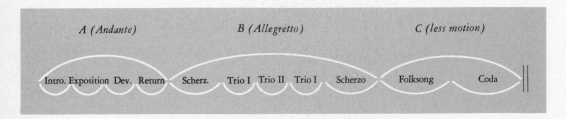

Example 26.1   Mapping of the first movement of the *Violin Concerto*

Since tempo and tonality do not provide sharp distinctions between the sections of this form, the parts are most readily identified by contrasts of texture, changes of theme, and greater and lesser degrees of rhythmic density.

The opening statements by harp and clarinet, imitated by solo violin, establish a tentative, dreamlike atmosphere. These arching lines persist until low strings and bassoons form a thin accompanying web over which the solo violin intones the principal melodic ingredients of the movement. This sharply rising line is countered presently by its mirror form (an inversion) that starts high and descends to the level where the first pattern began.

These introductory and first themes reflect so directly the twelve-note series on which the work is based that we shall dwell a moment on its characteristics. Berg has organized it in such a way that it provides two simple but powerful ingredients: (1) The first eight notes provide an extended series of skips; and (2) the last four notes provide a series of whole-tone steps.

Example 26.2   The twelve-note series of the Concerto

As we mentioned before, the long descending line played by the solo violin is a direct inversion of the earlier rising line, its contour now reversed.

Example 26.3   Inverted version of the first theme

Even the harmonic strands that accompany this early section are molded from the twelve-note row. The next example shows how the composer derives simple chords from his series of notes by using collections of three or more at a time.

Example 26.4   Chords derived from the series

Similar processes of derivation occur throughout the Concerto. Sometimes they are applied with strict conformity to the series of twelve notes, sometimes not. We shall note other clear invocations of the series when they occur later in the work.

The remainder of the first passages of the Concerto are devoted to the continuous development of the profile of this first theme. The section ends with a brief yet clear sense of return to patterns suggestive of the Introduction. The middle section, *Scherzando*, follows.

Rhythmically, Berg's middle section is a spiritual cross of the classical minuet and the earlier *Branle*, a rustic singsong dance. A definite triple meter prevails, yet syncopation adds a turn that could only confuse any dancer who might try to "keep with the step." A succession of singsong melodic figures fills this area of the *Scherzando*, providing a tuneful and relaxed atmosphere of nostalgia for things past. Although the actual melodies vary considerably, the contour illustrated in Example 26.5 recurs over and over again, a delicate cascade of melodic grace, clearly kin to the skips of the first part of the twelve-note series.

Example 26.5   A main melody of the Scherzando

Unlike the typical trio of a classical minuetto, Trio I of this movement shifts toward greater rather than lesser intensity. Violins and violas together sound a new motif; its shape is a series of interrupted arches that descend by steps.

Example 26.6   Principal theme of the first Trio

The strings are answered with this new image by the solo violin, playing chords of commanding force in triple stops.* The first Trio ends with this solo line dropping its last arch into the first sounds of Trio II, a lighter texture dominated by interchanges between woodwinds (especially flutes) and the solo.

---

*A string player performs three different pitches on three different strings in a *triple stop*.

The symmetry of this entire middle portion of the movement is completed when Trio I returns in a wholly different garb; now the arching theme of that section is played by the bass trombone below a series of thick string chords.

The return of the *Scherzando* section is signaled by clarinets, but the seam separating it from the ending Trio I is obscured, the solo violin line dovetailing the two sections. A more definite return is made when the solo violin plays the principal melody at the very end of the section.

As the mapping in Example 26.1 reveals, the end of the first movement is characterized by the surprising intrusion—like a naive child's voice into arguments of philosophers—of a folk song melody. The fragile, haunting quality of this strange quotation is reminiscent of the toy piano quotation in George Crumb's *Ancient Voices of Children.**

To grasp just how Berg achieves the otherworldly quality that pervades this passage, listen to the difference between the two settings of this tune as they appear in the next example. The first version (*a*) is the tune as it might be harmonized in an actual folk song setting, while the second utilizes Berg's accompanying harmonies. His setting pits the melody against a harmonic fabric that makes it seem alien, transcending the worldly elements of earth, air, fire, and water. This is another simple example of bitonality.

Example 26.7a Typical folk song setting of the Carinthian folk song

Example 26.7b Berg's setting of the same tune

---

*Chapter 23.

The folk song vanishes as mysteriously as it appeared, as a more animated texture dissolves into a suddenly transparent but poignant chord that ends the movement.

Second Movement: Allegro; Adagio

The first movement generally moved from a condition of tentativeness and relaxation to one of tension. The second movement reverses that order. It begins as a slashing, powerful recitation, essentially a composed cadenza for the solo violin, accompanied by furious spasms from the orchestra. A suggestion of impending tragedy hovers over this scene, as if a curtain might suddenly rise behind the orchestra to uncover a drama in progress toward some tragic end. This tense orgy of sounds subsides to a delicate texture. Two flutes, accompanied only by low figures from the solo violin, recall the main rhythm of the preceding section.

It is at this point that a series of delicate echoes of the first movement begins. Flutes sound the main motif of Trio II, and solo violin returns to the wide-ranging up-and-down figures that dominated the very opening of the Concerto. The section continues as a texture of two bare parts, solo violin accompanied by a solo viola from within the orchestra. The tempo, themes, and texture of the initial "cadenza" reappear, tension mounts once again, and one of the supreme climaxes of the work dissolves into its incredible Chorale.

Example 26.8 Lutheran chorale *Es ist genug* as harmonized by J. S. Bach (first phrase)

Once you have heard this concerto several times, you probably will agree that the Chorale is its final goal. Its melodic simplicity is so stark, its harmonies so clear and direct, its texture so finely chiseled that it stands as one of the most compelling points of arrival in all music.

The chorale was chosen by Berg for clearly programmatic reasons; its text, *"Es ist genug,"* ("It is enough") enunciates a spirit of worldly resignation.

It is enough! Lord, when it pleases you, release me from harness. My Jesus comes. Goodnight, oh world! I go to a heavenly home.

The harmonic setting of this melody is alone adequate invocation of "another world" to suggest the acceptance of death. In its first statements the harmonization is the one Bach used in his Cantata No. 60, *Ewigkeit, du Donnerwort*.

If you will look back to the twelve-note series shown in Example 26.2 you will see that the whole-tone steps at the end correspond with the first melodic figure of the chorale tune. This link between elements was no accident, of course, but a carefully planned aspect of the concerto's overall design.

And thus a composition conceived within the modern twelve-note method closes with the statement of a melody composed in the seventeenth century and harmonized in the style of an eighteenth-century master. The magical synthesis of three centuries is capped, just before the coda, by the brief return of the delicate Carinthian folk song that closed the more earthly first movement.

27

CONCERTO FOR CLARINET AND STRING ORCHESTRA

Aaron Copland (1900———)

BACKGROUND

The pre-Depression era of the twenties was the adolescence of American arts. A kind of reckoning time for the United States in foreign and domestic affairs, it also ripened a bountiful crop of writers, painters, dancers, architects, and composers who could claim native vintage. It is an irony of history that Paris, France, should have played a crucial role in the incubation of this mass coming-of-age.*

Everybody who was anybody in the arts made his way to Paris at some time or another between 1920 and 1930. Or so it seems in retrospect. Germany's grip on American music was broken by the outset of World War I in 1914; the war itself and the subsequent economic collapse of the German nation wiped away any remaining pockets of dependence. Now Paris provided the mecca of talk and action that has always acted as the catalyst for artistic fermentation.

Aaron Copland was merely one of many American composers who followed the crowd. The musical cricle of this crowd gathered around the studio of Nadia Boulanger, who can claim a greater influence on American composers between 1920 and 1950 than any other person. Copland

---

*See also the discussion of early jazz, which coincides with this vibrant period of American history.

Illustration 27.1
Aaron Copland

joined her classes at the American School in Fontainbleau in 1921, the first of a wave of expatriates that included Virgil Thomson, Roy Harris, Walter Piston, Marc Blitzstein, Quincy Porter, and Douglas Moore.

THE COMPOSER

Early Years

The son of Russian immigrant parents, Copland had grown up in Brooklyn. He attended New York public schools, helped tend his father's department store, and took piano lessons from his older sister. To France he took with him some fluency in composition, an enormous talent, and an abiding love of the music of his native land. These endowments were enough to make his three-year study with Mlle. Boulanger productive, yet not so overpowering that his native streak would be erased.

Many of Copland's early compositions reveal a healthy regard for jazz music without actually being in that idiom. It is an associative atmosphere in most cases rather than a substantive link. It was his conviction that composers who were American could, and would, produce a native music in due time without being overly conscious about it. From the beginning, it was his wish to write music that could "speak of universal things in a vernacular of American speech rhythms and contemporary dance music, such as the Charleston."

His American debut as a composer came in New York in 1925. This was the premiere of his Symphony for Organ and Orchestra. Since then he has established himself as the best known and most widely performed composer of American birth. His direct interest in jazz influences ended with the 1920s, and the following decade brought forth works more akin to the music developing in Europe at that time. His Piano Variations and Short Symphony date from that period.

His "Common Man" Music

By 1936 Copland's musical interests shifted once more. Now he seemed drawn to a less formalized kind of music, even to music that could be performed by non-professionals. A chamber opera, *The Second Hurricane* (1936), and *Outdoor Overture* (1941) were composed for high school students. This concern for an approachable kind of music developed into the mature musical style most people associate with Copland today. It is an earthy music, tuneful, rhythmically virile, and frequently spiced with folk-like melodies or actual quotations from folk songs.

His production in the single decade of 1938–48 includes movie scores and ballets as well as scores for purely concert performance. Copland scored the music for *Of Mice and Men* in 1939, *Our Town* in 1940, *The North Star* in 1943, *The Red Pony* in 1946, and *The Heiress* in 1949. He was awarded an Academy Award for this last movie.

Perhaps most significant during this era were the delightful works he composed for ballets. Involvement with exponents of an exciting new American form of the dance—artists like Agnes DeMille and Martha Graham—spawned music for *Billy the Kid* (1938), *Rodeo* (1942) and *Appalachian Spring* (1943–44).

All of these works echo images of the American soil, a music immediately meaningful for the average concertgoer as well as for the connoisseur. This basic directness of expression did not happen by accident.

Copland was in fact responding to a felt need of the world of art music. He had begun to feel dissatisfied with the wall that seemed to separate the living composer and the music-loving public. He wanted to avoid the fate reserved for composers who work in a vacuum, unsure of just for whom they are composing music. And thus one finds in Copland's music of this period occasional quotations from folk songs, cowboy ballads, Mexican tunes, and the hymns of Protestant America. Even when no direct quotation is made, the melodic and rhythmic substance of his music is suggestive of music of the people.

This affinity for directness of appeal led to the unique style that is immediately recognizable as "Copland." The textures of his music are clean and spare; they are in no way reminiscent of the Germanic heaviness that preceded him. His harmonies are for the most part simple and clear, more akin to church part-songs than to the tangled complexities of other twentieth-century art music. There is a fundamentalist ring to his music, an open conviviality that, like the music of Mozart, overwhelms with its simple logic. Even his most recent music, some of which returns to the more abstract characteristics of European models, bears the unmistakable stamp of his singular voice.

THE CLARINET CONCERTO

This work was composed in the late 1940s for Benny Goodman. It eloquently reflects what Copland meant when he once remarked that he no longer felt the need of seeking out "conscious Americanisms." In the Concerto he does not quote jazz tunes or folk songs. He does not incorporate saxophones or jazz drums. And yet there is no mistaking that this music could have been composed only by one who knows jazz well, who revels in its timbres, rhythms, and processes. It is not jazz. But it comes close to it at times. It occasionally even smacks of an improvisatory quality that reminds us of the "hot licks" of the fluent jazz soloist.

Illustration 27.2 Benny Goodman's versatility extended from wildly improvised jazz to the most highly controlled art music. Joining the clarinetist in this trio are Joseph Szigeti (violin) and Béla Bartok (piano).

Since the clarinet's voice could be lost in the crowd of a full symphony orchestra, the Concerto is scored for a lighter ensemble of only strings, harp, and piano. The solo's integrity is preserved at all times by careful spatial deployments of parts. When the orchestra plays heavy chords, the clarinet is in the upper part of its range where a shrill power ensures that it will be heard. When low orchestral sounds accompany, the solo line is kept free of encumbrances by careful pitch and rhythm separation. These are composer's rules-of-thumb learned only after many years of experience, and Copland knows them well.

The harmonies of the Concerto run the gamut from quite consonant to highly dissonant. The opening section is dominated by relatively simple chords whose density rarely goes beyond three pitch classes. But some passages of the final section achieve a high level of tension through chords embodying up to six and seven different members. Both extremes of harmonic content are nevertheless couched in textures that produce a sense of tonality. Tonic orientation changes often and freely, but at most points within the Concerto pitch focus is evident.

The overall form of the Concerto has its kinship with the traditional three-movement scheme favored since Mozart, but its parts are encompassed within a single-movement span. A simple view is represented in Example 27.1.

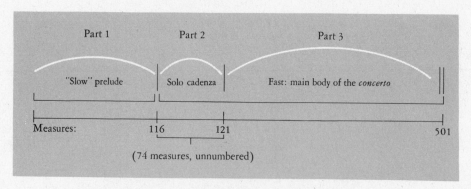

Example 27.1 Mapping of the Concerto

The sections do not form balanced parts unless A and B are regarded together, as contrasting yet functionally "introductory" parts to C, which clearly is the lengthiest part of the work. Considered in this way, a binary outline emerges that shows the first two parts approximately matched in musical "weight." Still another interpretation can view the first part as a separate prelude, the cadenza as a genuine introduction for Part 3. This latter view has merit, for as we shall see, the clarinet's cadenza exposes themes that are basic to Part 3.

Part 1 : Slowly and Expressively

This is lean music of intentional simplicity. Its character hints at a remote musical influence Copland must have felt during his student days in Paris. It possesses the almost static, reverie quality of the music of Eric Satie. Satie was the spiritual leader of a group of French composers, *Les Six*, of that second decade of the twentieth century. Their rallying cry was anti-art, anti-serious music, and especially anti-Wagnerian passion. The first part of this Concerto suggests the lackadaisical atmosphere that marks some of that group's attempts at deflation of artistic pomposity. The opening "oom-pah" accompaniment establishes a lazy character that hovers over this first part. Even the initial clarinet melody is dominated by a falling inflection that suggests a gentle, resigned sigh.

These two musical images dominate Part 1, never repeated exactly, always assuming a slightly varied guise. A relatively brief episode of quiet strings separates these four interpretations of a single texture and melody, as Example 27.2 portrays.

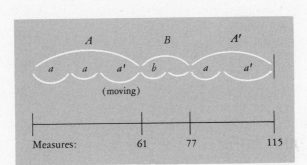

Example 27.2
Mapping of Part 1

Part 2 : Cadenza

The final moments of Part 1 form a dissolving gesture, a resolution of the gentle tension established in the last varied statement of theme *A*. Its end is marked by an even more prominent focus on the clarinet, which introduces the tentative rumblings of one of the longest solo cadenzas in the concerto literature. This cadenza performs four main functions for the piece as a whole: (1) It provides a stark contrast of texture and timbre for its framing parts; (2) it exposes themes that become prominent in Part 3; (3) it exploits the tonal, rhythmic, and registral capabilities of the clarinet; and (4) it even satisfies our expectation that a concerto composed for Benny Goodman should bear some jazz flavor.

Although the cadenza was composed by Copland, it suggests improvisation.* One brief pattern follows on the heels of another, each sounding suspiciously like a fresh perspective of the last. Two different patterns

---

*This section is really a grand "stop-break" of the kind used by the great jazz soloists like Louis Armstrong.

actually appear within this quasi-jazz "ride," and they will return in Part 3. One is a simple arched fragment of slightly swinging style, the other a two-unit motif that rises twice but falls at the end.

Example 27.3 Two main motifs of the *Cadenza,* Part 2

a. Somewhat faster

contour of *a:*

b.

contour of *b:*

Part 3:
Ritmico Vigoroso
(vigorously
rhythmic)

The free-swinging rhythms and high- to low-ranging pitch of the cadenza yield to a completely new texture and timbre. This contrast is indelibly marked by an emphasis on high, brittle sounds, a palette of sharp and rigid accents that suggests mechanical origins. It is metronomically-paced music, dominated by crisp articulations of high strings and the percussive attacks of the piano, which enters the Concerto here for the first time.

The sectional divisions of this final part are complex because they are many. In essence, they form a simple plan: a vacillation between the "mechanistic" new theme and the jazzy pattern exposed in the cadenza (theme *A* in Example 27.3). The alternation of these two ideas, bridged at times by two different patterns, forms the basis for the entire final part. We shall call the bridges *X* and *Y*.

$$
\begin{array}{lcccccc}
1 & & 2 & 3 & 4 & 5 & 6 & 7 \\
A & A/B & B & B/A\ A\ B & B^1 & B^1 & B^1\ B/A & \text{Coda}
\end{array}
$$

1		X	2	3	Y	4	X	5	Y	6	Y	7	
A	A/B		B	B/A A B		B¹		B¹		B¹ B/A		Coda	
						Clarinet; slap bass		Orchestra				(B)	

Example 27.4 Mapping of Part 3

These seven "thematic" and five "bridging" units represent a process of continuous variations on two main themes, one of which was introduced in the cadenza. (And a significant melodic role is played in bridge *X* by motif *B* of the cadenza.) Each main theme represents a slightly antagonistic character. Theme *A* has the tick-tock tinkle of a music box, while *B* is a loosely swinging pattern with jazz overtones. Copland combines them (*A/B, B/A*) and he opposes them in succession. It is interesting that although the opposition begins with *A* (played by the orchestra), freer, jazzier *B* wins out by dominating the coda.

At some points in this final part Copland overtly calls to mind images of the swing music of the late 1930s, the period when Benny Goodman was billed as "The King of Swing." In the section numbered 4, for instance, the clarinet rips off versions of the *B* pattern to the accompaniment of slapped bass pizzicatos. Once a technique of "hot" bass fiddle playing, this unique percussive sound is achieved by slapping the bass strings against the instrument's fingerboard. Even the melody line here has the contour and rhythm of a "walking bass" that harks back to a style once cultivated by the rhythm sections of jazz combos.

Aside from the prevailing syncopation of this third part, harmony plays a featured role in projecting its crisp and lively nature. What we have called the "mechanistic" sound of theme *A* is in part a product of highly dissonant combinations, two or more tones at high pitch level that suggest strikes of metal against metal. These are chords of low density (two–three pitch classes) but high dissonance.

Example 27.5   Chords of high dissonance and low density, Part 3

A different kind of dissonance can be heard at various climactic points, particularly within bridge *Y* just before section #4. There, and at similar locations just prior to section #6, chords of considerable density (six–seven pitch classes) create a less jangling, more ponderous kind of harmonic tension. Note the structure of the harmonies illustrated in Example 27.6 as one instance of these more turgid chords.

Example 27.6   Chords of high dissonance and high density, Part 3

Copland's concerto is pleasant, tuneful music. It is not the kind of heavyweight, emotion-packed music we might associate with the concerto of the nineteenth century, the Romantic era. Compared even with Alban Berg's Violin Concerto, it represents the gentler touch. Its American optimism and good-natured sprightliness are its main sources of charm. It is also what any good concerto must be: a successful vehicle for testing the virtuosity of a solo performer. As this work clearly proves, heaven need not be stormed to achieve that objective.

28

CONCERTO FOR SOLO PERCUSSIONIST AND ORCHESTRA

Donald Erb (1927----)

BACKGROUND

A concerto for the likes of drums and xylophones would have been laughed off any eighteenth- or nineteenth-century stage. Only in the present century, with our more liberal conception of what is acceptable musical tone, could this family of instruments risk the role of featured sound, joining the imbedded tradition of the piano and violin. As the composer Donald Erb has noted, "In our time, a new, and I think, peculiarly American virtuoso, the percussionist, has made an appearance. We live in an age of great percussion players, and it is only fitting that virtuoso pieces should be written for them."*

Some cultures have always favored percussion for making music. West African drumming is widely recognized as an unmatched art, and the gamelan orchestra of Indonesia—"Javanese music"—is a remarkable collection of gongs, xylophones, drums, and various other mallet instruments that produce incomparable music. But out own musical tradition has been slow in recognizing the value of these kinds of sounds, except in secondary musical roles.

Erb's concerto is not the first whole work to feature percussion in a virtuoso role. The French composer Darius Milhaud (1892–1974) composed a successful Concerto for Percussion and Small Orchestra in 1930,

---

*Program notes of the Cleveland Symphony Orchestra (Klaus Roy)

Illustration 28.1
Donald Erb

and the Mexican composer Carlos Chavez (1899–––) finished his stirring Toccata for Percussion in 1942. (The Chavez work does not utilize orchestral accompaniment.) At last then, the gradual acceptance of beaten skins, wooden and metal bars, brass cylinders and plates as legitimate members of the orchestra has culminated in the full liberation of this exotic resource.

The belated achievement of status for percussion is the end of a long development. It began with the admission of kettle drums into the eighteenth-century orchestras of Mozart and Haydn—then purely as secondary or background sounds, of course. It is surprising only that equality was so long in coming: by the middle of the nineteenth century a single percussionist commanded the power to drown out all other combined forces of the orchestra. In addition to his control of the balance of sound power, the modern percussionist also possesses the broadest set of timbres available from a single orchestral section. It is a range of colors equaled only by the most sophisticated electronic synthesizer. As Donald Erb suggests, "Nothing in the symphony orchestra has as much appeal from the standpoint of pure sound as does the percussion section with its enormous variety of instruments." In his Concerto the single percussionist divides his energies between the following seventeen sound-makers:

Snare drum	Marimba	Woodblocks	Piano (beat with mallets)
Temple blocks	Vibraphone	Xylophone	Glockenspiel
Chimes	Bongo drums	Timbales	Cymbals	Tom tom drums
Bass drum	Castanets	Maraca	Whip (snapped)

Illustration 28.2 Modern percussionists must play every manner of instrument that is beaten. This soloist is shown operating amidst xylophone, marimba, two triangles, two gongs, a tam tam (large gong), two sets of wind chimes, eight separate drums, five temple blocks, and a single suspended cymbal. (Donald Knaack, percussionist)

THE COMPOSER

It would be strange to find a composer of Erb's generation untouched by jazz. The influence of jazz drumming is evident in many parts of the Concerto, particularly in the third movement's extended cadenza, where the jazz "trap set" dominates. This influence stems naturally from the composer's early participation in jazz groups as a trumpet player and arranger. Born in Youngstown, Ohio, Erb, like most precocious musicians of his time, found his most gratifying musical outlet in the freedom and creativity of jazz improvisation. His youthful experiences led to formal study in composition in three different American schools, Kent State University, The Cleveland Institute of Music, and Indiana University. The result is a highly trained composer, who carries within his marrow the musical image of Charlie Parker as well as Wolfgang Mozart.

THE CONCERTO

Characteristics

Erb's Concerto vividly embodies characteristics typical of music composed for orchestra since around 1950. Like the music of Penderecki and Crumb, his works are rich successions of engaging sounds, sounds we normally associate with the orchestra as well as sounds unimagined before 1950. No instrument is limited to its conventional playing techniques. Wind players buzz through their mouthpieces; string players scratch strings with fingernails; the pianist strokes that instrument's strings with a pop bottle, or reaches inside to pluck them like a harp; wind players even rattle their instrument's keys instead of blowing through mouthpieces. And in addition to these strange manipulations, performers on occasion are invited to improvise their own parts, within guidelines laid down by the composer.

The product is something quite remote from the controlled elegance of a Brahms symphony or a Chopin nocturne. And yet, the Concerto is audible proof of Erb's own claim that "Sound is endlessly fascinating in its own right."

Lest we be led astray, however, we must hasten to note that this work is not merely an extended series of fascinating sounds. On the contrary, a musical logic prevails; a large musical pattern emerges. We shall discuss the nature of its shapes presently.

The Concerto bears other characteristics that separate it from the music of earlier times. It is not melodic in the traditional sense; it does not sing to us with the extended phrases of Mozart or Schumann. It consists, rather, of a complex mixture of fragments which, together, form a textural identity, a sense of unity. There are discernible motifs, particularly in the second movement; rhythms recur and pitch contours are passed from low to high. Such "tunes" as exist are mere brief "noodles," snatches of melody that derive meaning only by being associated closely with others of their own kind.

The most elementary structural feature of this work is a set of what we shall call *basic articulations*. These permeate each of the three movements, each announced in the beginning of its respective movement. The roll of the snare drum initiates the first movement, for example, and this sound is to play the role of that movement's basic articulation. Harp and string tremolos and then woodwind trills ensue. They are but individualized variants of this basic articulation—what we might loosely call *theme*.

In the second movement a sliding sound, or *glissando*, performs the same thematic function. From its beginning, the piano, harp, and trombone establish this simple gliding gesture as a motif for subsequent development.

The third movement is dominated by clicking sounds. The initial clicks from the rim of the snare drum, later fluttering tones from the brass, and rapid slaps from strings all serve to develop and enrich within the movement the character of its archetypal clicking sound. In this way each movement is the exposition and development of at least one fundamental sound event, its basic articulation.

Harmonic Style

Another striking thing about the Concerto is its harmony. The word in fact ceases to be wholly appropriate for describing simultaneous sounds as they occur in this composition. Tightly clustered pitches form the staple vocabulary, creating massive densities that are better described as *texture* than as *harmony*. These knotty chords sometimes occur as an accumulation of sound layers. A typical instance can be found in the first movement when a total of eight layers gather together within the duration of a single measure, as illustrated in Example 28.1.

Example 28.1 Cumulative "chord" in Movement I

At several points in the Concerto players are partially responsible for creating their own parts. The resultant mixes of sound at those times defy the meaning of "chords." The product is harmonic chaos, in the sense that any one such "chord" is not *harmonically* different from any other.

The point is not that the composer is incapable of writing harmony. The point is that he does not use the property of harmony as a means for shaping his music. Harmony is merely a by-product of texture, and the unvarying ultra-high degree of dissonance and density helps to maintain harmony in this inconsequential role. There are no points within the work, when two or more parts are sounding at the same time, where a high level of dissonance is not present. Thus the polarity of consonance–dissonance, of tension–repose found in earlier music is not present.

New Structural Resources

These characteristics of the Concerto suggest that it is in some respects a primitive kind of music, in spite of its sophisticated resources and techniques. Although such a description may seem to harbor contradiction, it is accurate. The Concerto does not possess the melodic, harmonic, rhythmic, and textural definers we know from traditional music except in very basic (and quite different) ways. Instead, it is music of extraordinarily sophisticated materials shaped by the most rudimentary processes. Textural contrasts—in terms of thicknesses and thinnesses—play a dominant role; the rich reservoir of timbre is a critical agent of contrast; and loudness levels determine to a great extent the partitions of form, silence frequently acting as the main clue that a section has ended. And "themes," as we have explained, are simple, raw gestures, like sliding pitch, recurring rhythm, or a distinctive tone color.

Curiously, *unity* in the Concerto is achieved principally through its constant *variety* of sounds. This may at first seem paradoxical. But if you engage in some different activity every few movements, the sameness of constant change creates its own kind of unity, the act of change itself becoming the event that is repeated to establish a sense of constancy. And thus it is with the sounds of the Concerto, which on first hearing seems to be a bombardment of unremitting diversity.

One additional attribute of this work must be mentioned, even though it cannot be enjoyed in a recorded performance: its visual attraction. The percussion soloist is understandably busy attending his array of sixteen different kinds of instruments, assaulting them with almost as many different kinds of beaters. This in itself provides physical movement that is visually engaging. The composer has furthermore built a kind of "choreography" into his score, using a separate collection of instruments for each movement, each set grouped in a slightly different location in front of the orchestra. In this respect it shares the theatrical bent of George Crumb's *Ancient Voices of Children* (Chapter 23).

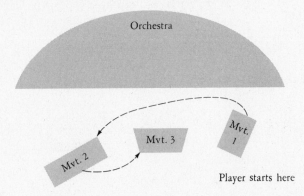

Example 28.2   Distribution of solo percussion in the *Concerto*

Movement I	*Movement II*	*Movement III*
Snare drum, marimba, four woodblocks, piano (played with mallets), and five temple blocks	Vibraphone, xylophone, glockenspiel, chimes	Snare drum, bongos, timbales, suspended cymbals, temple blocks, large and small tomtoms, bass drum, castanets, whip, maracas

This means that the visual focus for each movement is on a slightly different space, while its aural focus rests on an ever-changing kaleidoscope of sound. In movement III the favored setup is a jazz (or "trap") set, consisting of bass drum, snare, tomtoms, bongos and cymbals, this unit acting as the central sphere within which the player operates.

First Movement: Slow–fast–slow

In spite of its several elements of complexity, Erb's first movement cuts a simple *A B A* form. Beginning and ending sections of orchestral passages frame the percussionist's preoccupation with his snare drum, marimba, woodblocks, piano (whose strings he strikes with mallets) and five temple blocks.

The snare drum introduces the first basic articulation of the movement. It is a roll, which for a drum is the only means for sounding a "sustained" tone. The roll begins barely audible; then timbres from the orchestra gradually join with their own versions of sustained sound. First harp, then flute, closely followed by violins, piano, and bassoons enter into a developing conglomeration that will grow to a deafening climax.

This roaring passage ends with the higher woodwinds stating the second basic articulation of the movement, a wedged pattern* that will be echoed immediately by the percussionist on marimba. It can be seen in the second half of Example 28.3, along with the first basic articulation that begins the pattern.

Example 28.3   Solo marimba, beginning of Section *B*, Movement I

Within the mid-section of the movement it is the percussionist's show. Swtching rapidly from marimba to woodblock to inside the piano, where he strikes and rolls mallets on the strings (and metal soundboard!), he creates a constant stream of changing tone color. Rhythms are split into short segments to be divided among temple blocks, snare drum, and marimba, while pecks and isolated layers from the orchestra provide accompanying punctuations.

This fury grows to a peak, which is in fact the beginning of a strange twist of concerto tradition: the full orchestra plays its own eight-second cadenza! Each player is provided with patterns from which to create an improvised part. In the performance directions within the score (page 3), Erb tells players that "the sound should be very loud and frenetic. Improvise on assigned material, mostly very fast and high. The material may be transposed or altered." (Or stated more bluntly, "Do your own thing!")

The orchestra cadences abruptly, leaving the bare snare drum roll that ushers in the mounting return of *A*.

Movement II:
Slow

The basic articulation of this movement is sounded by harp and piano at the outset. It is a sliding sound that returns again and again with an eerie rise or fall, finally to end the movement as it began. Orchestra and soloist engage in a dialogue that is more matched now than in the previous movement. The soloist is mainly occupied with the more brittle sounds of his battery, xylophone accounting for most passages.

Amidst continuing slides from the orchestra, a curious rhythmic

---

*"Wedged" because its pitches form a contour like a toppled triangle, $<$. Note the notation of the pattern in Ex. 28.3.

motif is introduced. It becomes a thematic binder, returning many times, like a dogged rapping that cannot be exorcised. Its appearances are evident in the mapping shown next, where we have denoted its returns simply as *motif X*.

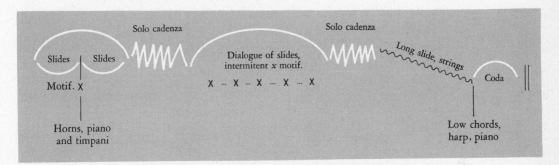

Example 28.4 Outline mapping of passages in the second movement

Some of the strange sounds within this quietly taut movement are as interesting for how they are performed as for their intrinsic merit as sounds. The piano's first slide is created by moving a pop bottle over its strings. At two points in the coda section a rustling sound is produced by the woodwind players rattling the keys of their instruments vigorously. And throughout the movement wind players are directed to "bend" pitches, creating an uncanny effect of sliding about a single pitch.

Movement III:
Fast–slower–fast

The calm before the storm has ceased. Now the storm itself begins. The basic sound, or *articulation*, is the clicking figure heard at the outset. A rapid alternation among solo snare drum, bongos, and timbales establishes a rhythmic pace that is underlined by sporadic pecks from harp, timpani, and piano. The texture grows until a new basic articulation sounds, first in trumpets, then in woodwinds. This second terse pattern is a three-pitch figure of skips that will provide the developmental basis of the coming section. First it appears as a rising articulation, next falling and at a faster rate. The two early versions are shown next.

Example 28.5 Basic articulation #2 of the third movement

This is meager melodic fare, reflecting the clear intention of the composer to bypass any extended patterns in the lyrical tradition of Western music. These two statements lead to a pause that separates the first section from the second.

In section 2 the skip-articulation prevails in a multitude of disguises. It rampages through the solo percussion lineup, cymbals, bongos, timbales, temple blocks and snare drum sharing the full pattern and its assorted fragments in a frantic succession. Around this brilliant display of mallet work, the orchestra inserts its own statements of the main motif as well as bursts of fluttering figures that provide a background. Brass players "sing" the basic articulation through their horns, string players snap fingers against their instruments' fingerboards, and the pianist strikes forearm-length clusters. All form a concerted display of the basic articulation and its ramifications.

Another protracted silence marks a third section. The pace slows, events erupting in separated bursts after an initial figure from castanets and piano. In these passages the percussionist improvises, as the composer notes in the score, "On everything." Late in the section he turns to a more ordered plan, attending to bongos, timbales, and snare drum in preparation for the final grand cadenza that is the climactic passage of the whole Concerto.

The solo cadenza is played with the percussionist seated, like a jazz drummer, amidst the tools of the trade. The scoring of this section is too humorous to miss, so we have reproduced it in our next example. It clearly could provide adequate guidance only for a percussionist who knows exactly what to do for approximately sixty seconds, without fretting much about the composer's preferences in drumming. (The assorted onlookers of the animal kingdom are not a part of the actual notation!) And yet, what Erb shows supplies more information than Mozart wrote out in his scores for soloists' cadenzas!

The movement's coda is but a mad rush, orchestra and percussion together, for the end.

Example 28.6 Notation for the solo cadenza, page 73 of Erb's score

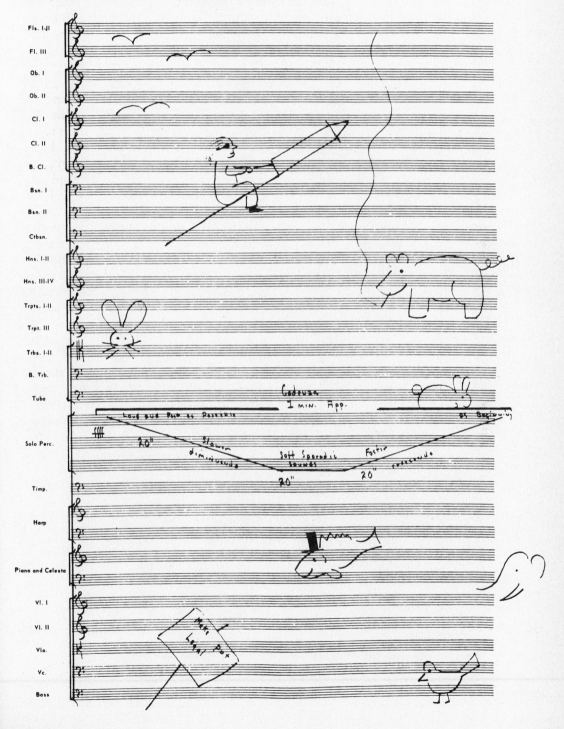

PART V

SOLO
AND
CHAMBER
MUSIC

INTRODUCTION

Most of the world's music is not as grand in scale as an opera, a symphony, or a concerto. In fact, a feeling of intimacy is as much sought after in art music as it is in folk music, where a singer and guitar may provide the total musical resources. Some of the most eloquent music of Western civilization was composed to be heard in quarters no more spacious than a living room, with listeners barely separated from performers.

This is the essential meaning of *chamber music*. It is music whose forces and musical intent are best accommodated by the privacy of a small gathering of friends rather than a public place like a concert hall or cathedral. In this sense, the art songs of Robert Schumann we discussed in Chapter 22, composed for the salons of nineteenth-century Europe, are true chamber music.

It is impossible—and not at all necessary—to draw a hard line that divides *chamber* music from *concert* music. But any ensemble that numbers over a dozen players stretches the chamber dimension rather tightly. The music of a four- or five-piece jazz combo is chamber music, while that of a large dance band of a dozen or more instrumentalists is not. And yet, a four-piece rock group, with its boosted power of electrical amplification, exceeds the bounds of chamber music. Its audience can be as large as any concert hall or even an entire valley can hold. So the distinction is mainly one of numbers, but even then the separation is at times a fuzzy one.

The demands made on the performer of chamber music are often quite different from those made on one who performs within a large ensemble. The singer of an art song faces a separate set of problems from the singer in a large choir. In chamber music each part is performed by a single instrument or voice. This places the total responsibility for that strand of the musical web on a single musician. One violinist in a symphony orchestra can miss a note without destroying the overall musical effect; the violinist in a string quartet can ruin a performance by making a similar error.

The demands on the listener are somewhat different too. A small, intimate chamber group is incapable of achieving the mighty sound and rich variety commanded by a symphony orchestra or wind band. The brute physical power of these larger ensembles provides a potential emotional force that in itself can be compelling for the listener. The chamber ensemble must rely on more ingenious methods to captivate its audience, depending on a narrower range of timbres and less mighty sounds for its effect. It is a more subtle art, and for this very reason it is a more gratifying source of musical enjoyment for some people. Just as a fine engraving can be as enjoyable to the viewer as a giant oil painting, a string quartet can be as rewarding for the listener as a symphony.

The chamber music and the concert music of our culture do not differ radically in the kinds of forms and musical processes they contain. In fact, you will find a wealth of parallels between the chamber works discussed here and some of the works for large ensemble of Part II. The form of a minuetto in a Mozart quintet or a Beethoven quartet is fundamentally the same as that of a minuetto in a Haydn or Beethoven symphony. Even the harmonies, melodies, rhythms, and textures have much in common with those of their more awesome kin. Having heard one, it should be that much easier to go to the other and unravel its musical message.

As in Part IV, we shall begin with the music of J. S. Bach.

29

PRELUDE AND FUGUE NO. 16
IN G MINOR,
THE WELL-TEMPERED CLAVIER,
BOOK I

Johann Sebastian Bach (1685–1750)

BACKGROUND*

Bach's mature years were spent in five different posts, none more than seventy-five miles away from the others. Now in the southwestern edge of East Germany, the towns of Arnstadt, Mülhausen, Weimar, Cöthen, and Leipzig provided him a succession of homes, as well as music workshops of sharply contrasting opportunities. It is usually risky to suggest that a composer wrote a particular work because of a specific social or private stimulus. But in Bach's case most of the music he composed can be tied to the particular job he held at the time and the special function the work would fulfill.

In 1717 he moved to Cöthen from Weimar, where he had served a dual role as church organist on Sundays, violinist and clavier player in the ducal orchestra during the week. The new job provided a boost in prestige and salary, but it posed one serious disadvantage: there was no Lutheran service and thus no need for his masterly organ improvisations, no demand for him to compose sacred cantatas. The court at Cöthen was sternly Calvinist, so only unaccompanied hymns were allowed in the liturgy. And thus Bach, widely acclaimed as Europe's most formidable organ virtuoso, was left with no official outlet for his primary musical interests.

---

*See Chapters 19 and 24 for further discussions of Bach's music and life.

Illustration 29.1
Johann Sebastian Bach

Illustration 29.2
Map of Germany

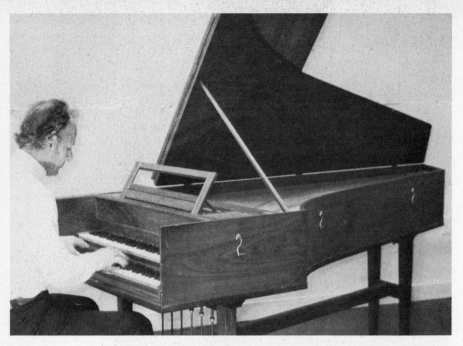

Illustration 29.3 Modern demand for authentic performances of the keyboard music of Bach, Handel, and their predecessors has led to the resurrection of the harpsichord. This instrument's six foot-pedals control the loudness levels and timbres available from its two manuals.

On the other hand, the atmosphere of the court and the attitude of his new employer were far more congenial than he had experienced in Weimar. Now thirty-two, he simply adapted to the new set of opportunities, composing instead for the various instrumental ensembles provided by the court (where the Prince himself played clavier, violin, and viola da gamba). He also shifted his interest to the harpsichord and clavichord, thereby sublimating the loss of the organ forced upon him by his changed responsibilities.

BACH'S MUSIC

The Clavier

Bach's six *Brandenburg* Concertos* were composed during his fourth year in Cöthen; another year and he had finished the first volume of his renowned collection of preludes and fugues, the *Well-tempered Clavier*. This latter work, along with his several keyboard partitas and suites, was a powerful agent in elevating clavier instruments to the preeminence they enjoyed during the eighteenth century. They were to be eclipsed only by the rising popularity of the piano at the close of the century.

The word *clavier* was used in Bach's day to refer to one of two keyboard instruments, the harpsichord and clavichord, and at times even the

---

*The second of these concertos is discussed in Chapter 24.

chamber organ. The former two are very much alike in sound, producing their tones by tangents plucking (harpsichord) or striking (clavichord) strings. While the harpsichord is a larger instrument of comparatively robust sound, the clavichord is limited to very intimate salon performances, its tones readily masked, even by normal conversation.

Today Bach's keyboard works are played by harpsichord or clavichord and frequently on the piano. Since the piano also is a *clavier*, its use seems justified, although certainly not anticipated by the composer. (Some musicians violently oppose this position. They argue that the heavier tone of the "romantic" piano does violence to Bach's intentions, which they presume to know in detail!)

Meaning of Bach's Title: "Well-tempered Clavier"

The complete title Bach gave his collected preludes and fugues is interesting, both for its flowery length and for what it suggests. His manuscript copy was headed with the German equivalent of the following:

> "The Well-tempered Clavier, or preludes and fugues in all tones and semitones, both with the major third, or *Ut, Re, Mi,* and the minor third, or *Re, Mi, Fa.* For the use and practice of young musicians who desire to learn, as well as for those who are already skilled in the study, by way of amusement; made and composed by Johann Sebastian Bach."

What this wordy preface tells us is more startling than may first come to mind. In 1722 instruments of fixed pitch, like organs and harpsichords, did not play with any great euphony in "all tones and semitones" (meaning "in all keys"). Their pipes or strings were tuned to accommodate some keys rather well, but excursions into other keys could produce chords so raucous that the sounds were likened to the "howling of wolves."

Nature of the Preludes and Fugues

Compromise tuning systems had been developed during the late seventeenth century, and these leveled out the most blatant crudities that troubled the old tuning systems. Bach's collection of pieces for "well-tempered" performance was not the first of the kind. Other composers were toying with series of compositions that ran through many different keys. The results sometimes were of indifferent quality, however, and Bach's is probably the only one of these attempts at tonal democracy that you will ever hear.

Das wohltempierte clavier is exactly what Bach's title claims: "preludes and fugues in all tones and semitones," and in major and minor keys (which is what all of the "major and minor thirds" and "*Ut, Re, Mi*" references in his title are about). The following partial listing can provide you with an idea of how the forty-eight pieces are ordered within the collection. (The second volume, composed twenty-two years later, is arranged according to the same plan.)

Prelude and Fugue No. 1 in C Major;

Prelude and Fugue No. 2 in C Minor;

Prelude and Fugue No. 3 in C♯ Major;

Prelude and Fugue No. 4 in C♯ Minor;
    and so on, until the final pair,

Prelude and Fugue No. 24 in B Minor.

Although the pairing of prelude and fugue for each key implies some close connection between the two, there is none. They are just in the same key. There is no thematic kinship, for example, between the *G* minor Prelude and its partner; transposed to *C* minor, that prelude could pair as convincingly with the *C* Minor Fugue. In this respect, the forty-eight are quite separate little masterpieces. The preludes do not function as introductory gestures for their respective fugues.

Both the preludes and fugues vary considerably in length, style, and gravity. Bach seems to have deliberately plumbed the depths and heights of emotion. He foraged widely among musical types—dances, both gay and grave, as well as more somber models—in completing the parts of this wide-ranging composition. But his styles and moods are fitted into a simple succession of pairs as segregated as the ones in Noah's Ark. The first member of the couple, the prelude, is always straight-forwardly "melodic" and usually homophonic. The second is always a fugue, in which a texture of two or more parts weaves out a series of developments of a *subject* that is announced solo at the beginning.

The fugue cannot be defined with precision as a musical form. Like a family, it is more a set of relationships than it is an objective "thing," and, as in families, the relationships between individual parts vary from close to distant. But a fugue is always one thing; it is a polyphonic texture, its two or more parts constantly vying for prominence as the "principal" voice.

This state of concerted individuality in a fugue is proclaimed early on, for it begins with tiered statements of its "subject," each part taking its turn in sounding that subject in an accumulating texture. The *fugal exposition* was an important musical process before compositions were ever called "fugues." A succession of such imitative textures was identified as "motet style" in the polyphonic sacred music of the sixteenth century.*

Most fugues are shaped by several distinct sections of imitative texture, each based on a single subject as the vehicle for continuing development.† And most fugues—particularly Bach's—provide a closing gesture

---

*A discussion of motet style can be found in Chapter 17.
†There are *double* and *triple* fugues which contain two and three subjects respectively. Most fugues, however, are monothematic.

toward the end, several musical events conspiring to affect a sense of return. (This latter condition is not a trait of all fugues, however.)

THEMATIC DEVELOPMENT IN FUGUES What is most interesting about any fugue is the way the composer goes about developing its subject. There are about as many techniques of development as there are fugue composers, but three can be found in most fugues. We can use the subject of Bach's Fugue No. 16 in G Minor to illustrate all three: *fragmentation*, *inversion*, and *stretto*.

In Example 29.1 the complete subject of the fugue is shown first. The three excerpts that follow show how that subject, or some part of it, has been "developed." In music, *development* refers to change that does not wholly obliterate the original.)*

Example 29.1   Fugue subject and three processes of development

In the first excerpt we see how Bach molded a line from only a part (*b*) of his full subject. Using only this fragment, he creates a rising line from its repetitions.

---

*See the discussions of sonata form in Chapters 7 and 8 (Haydn and Beethoven).

The second excerpt shows only one instance of many in the G Minor Fugue where the rhythm of particle *b* is combined with a contour that is the opposite (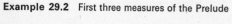) of the original *b'*s contour (⌒). Because of this reversal, this process is called *melodic inversion*.

The third process involves the whole subject. *Stretto* occurs when imitations of the subject begin before the full subject has finished. This kind of compression usually comes at the end of a fugue, although it occurs in some fugues at various locations.

Not all fugues contain these three procedures, but very few do not contain at least two of them. Since any fugue will have an original melodic subject, its composer will apply developmental techniques to it that best fit its unique characteristics.

PRELUDE NO. 16 IN G MINOR

This brief but unhurried piece uses tonality and theme to bind its parts tightly together, tonality and texture to effect sufficient variety to avoid boredom. Its single theme spawns a very slight mutation before it has gone far; theme or its mutant are ever-present in the remainder of the Prelude.

The theme sounds first in the top of the texture, its hypnotic rhythm a repeated figure that is "prepared" by a long trill. This initial appearance can be seen in the first two measures of Example 29.2, which also shows how the opening top line fills in the tonal space between a high and low *G*.

Example 29.2 First three measures of the Prelude

The slightly altered version of the theme merely splits one of the previous articulations in two parts (becoming — •••• — rather than the previous pattern of — — •• —').

As we mentioned before, tonality serves both a unifying and a contrasting function in the Prelude. This may at first sound contradictory, but the mapping in Example 29.3 shows how these opposing characteristics are nonetheless accommodated by the one musical property, how the piece divides into two halves whose extremities are bounded by the key of *G* minor.

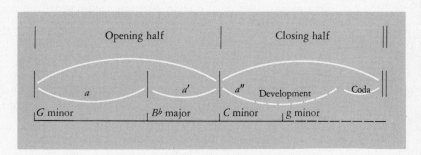

Example 29.3 Mapping of the Prelude's sections and keys

This binary design is most convincingly shaped by texture, the property that probably carries more impact for the listener than tonality. Bach uses one texture as a kind of recurring landmark in the piece. At the beginning we hear a combination of three parts that can best be represented by the following design:

Example 29.4 Distribution of parts in the opening measures

The continuation (called *a'* in Example 29.3) begins with this same texture, except for the very special way it has been turned upside down to assume the following distribution:

Example 29.5 Textural inversion of measure 7

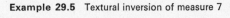

And then, as if to assure us that this special texture is to be interpreted as a kind of formal road sign, the second half of the Prelude begins with it in the form shown in the previous example. Now, however, it is in the new key of *C* minor. Curiously, this textural cue, along with the extended trill, then disappears from the Prelude; the second half of the work lacks the clear sectional divisions of the first half. In this respect the "closing half" projects a more distinctly processive* character, its principal motif bandied about in a three-way conversation between its parts. This array of exchanged "comments" is nowhere more evident than in the final two measures. Brackets pinpoint each of the entries of the theme, which here is the variant version.

Example 29.6 Imitative entries of the final two measures

FUGUE NO. 16 IN G MINOR

While the Prelude makes sense as two halves in which textures provide the main shaping force, the Fugue's form is a bit more involved. It falls into six short sections, although the seams are sometimes neatly camouflaged. Before we discuss how these sections relate one to another, you may find it helpful to refer back to the subject of the fugue illustrated in Example 29.1

Bach reveals in this piece how he can excise the second half of a theme, then develop it until it emerges to a coequal prominence with the

Example 29.7 Combination of subject's halves, measures 2–3

*We introduced the processive form type in Chapter 2. The processive aspect here is that of a theme introduced and then carried through a developmental process.

first. As we saw earlier, he separates this fragment from the second half of the subject, then molds it into an accompanying foil for the first half.

Since in subsequent sections of the Fugue Bach accompanies the whole subject with its fragmented half, this secondary motif assumes considerable significance. When this happens in a fugue the pattern so used is called the *countersubject*. As with the preceding Prelude, there is no measure in the Fugue in which one of these subject particles is not sounding; most often, both can be heard, winding their ways through some new complementary union.

The mapping shown next identifies the thematic foregrounds and keys for each section. Observe the correspondence of key design with that of the Prelude: *G minor, Bb major, C minor,* and *G minor.*

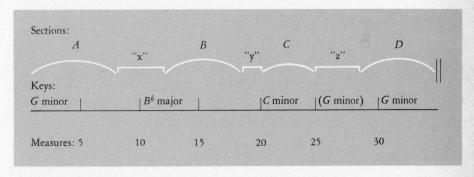

Example 29.8 Mapping of the *Fugue,* showing large sections and keys

If we tie the various textural and developmental events of the Fugue together with this mapping, we can get some idea of the dynamic relationships between its parts.

SECTION A: FORMAL EXPOSITION Each of the four "voices" states the subject theme in successive entries. The texture accumulates in the order of separate ranges, *medium high, high, low,* and *medium low.*

SECTION X: EPISODE The term *episode* does not mean "unimportant." In fact, fugue episodes frequently generate more musical excitement than their neighboring expository sections. The term denotes sections in which the whole fugue subject is not present. This episode is an interesting interweaving of countersubject fragments (the countersubject, remember, is itself a fragment of the subject).

SECTION B: SECOND EXPOSITORY SECTION A decisive cadence precedes this point; the texture suddenly thins to one part; the subject enters once more, now in a major key. A set of imitations ensues, not unlike those of the first section. But now the part-entries are reordered in terms of high/low distribution: *medium-high, low, high, higher.*

SECTION Y: EPISODE This area is a brief climactic point in which the countersubject is again the sole thematic element. It leads almost imperceptibly into a new series of subject statements, section *C.*

SECTION C: THIRD EXPOSITORY SECTION Still another order of imitative entries, lowest voice now leading, answered by *high,* and then *middle-range* voice.

SECTION Z: EPISODE 3 This extended episode plays an important role in the unfolding scenario. Its bass line is hewn from fragments of the now-familiar countersubject, while a fluid dialogue is formed by the two upper parts.

Although this passage begins in *G* minor, it proceeds to flirt with several other keys without settling on any one. There is reason behind this fickle behavior: the passage is a calculated "delaying tactic" that prepares for the dramatic reentry of the subject in the subsequent final section. In this episode the repetitions drone on, so that the eventual return of the subject, in the tonic key, bears an especially awaited message.

SECTION D: STRETTO AND FINALE As if to make the apparent even more obvious, Bach renders this final statement a case of thematic overkill. The subject returns in the compressed ordering, or *stretto,* we illustrated earlier in Example 29.1c. Three statements are crowded into half the normal time span consumed by as many statements of the subject in Sections *A, B,* and *C.* The stretto clearly enacts an ultimate flourish, a gesture to complete the action of the whole fugue.

The two inner parts of the texture then press home an effect of imminent finality, each sounding the complete subject one more time. The subject, which has now undergone a probing series of developmental states, has returned to its original state, none the worse for the workout.

30

QUINTET FOR CLARINET AND STRINGS, K. 581

Wolfgang A. Mozart (1756–1791)

BACKGROUND*

Composers of all historical periods frequently had particular groups or individual performers in mind when composing a work. The history of music is dotted with instances of personal relationship—in some instances genuine collaborations—between composer and performer in the production of outstanding compositions. Mozart's Quintet was composed with a great clarinetist in mind, the virtuoso Anton Stadler. He probably deserves credit for revealing to Mozart the marvelous technical and tonal possibilities of this instrument. Having composed the Quintet in 1789, Mozart followed it in 1791 with the stunning Clarinet Concerto, K. 622, again for performance by Stadler.

Although the clarinet has been improved somewhat since the late eighteenth century (particularly its key mechanism), no composer has surpassed Mozart in writing music precisely tailored for it, music that is truly idiomatic. He puts the instrument's best foot forward at every moment, emphasizing the rich warmth of its low register, the penetrating brilliance of its high notes, and its ability to breeze through veritable cascades of sound. All of these traits are evident at various times in the Quintet, as well as in the later Concerto.

This work is of the mature style of Mozart, written only two years

---

*Additional biographical information about Mozart can be found in Chapters 21 and 25.

before his death in 1791 (and thus two years following the composition of the opera *Don Giovanni*). It is additional proof of what most musicians concede: no other composer composed such superb music with the facility we associate with more menial tasks.

THE QUINTET

Scored for clarinet and strings, the Quintet merges the traditional string quartet (two violins, viola, and cello) with a solo instrument of contrasting timbre. As could be expected, the clarinet frequently is pitted as musical protagonist and conversationalist with the body of strings or with a solo string, usually the first violin.

Solo sonatas of Mozart's day usually contained three movements, but the Quintet, like most string quartets and symphonies, is a four-movement work. As in those forms, the third movement is a minuet (or menuetto), the second movement a slow-paced contrast with the faster motion of the other movements. The last movement is a theme and variations, an uncommon form to find as the final movement of any large work, such as a symphony, concerto, or string quartet.

Movement I:
Allegro ("fast")

A better example of classical melodiousness, grace, and formal symmetry would be hard to find. As in most first movements composed during the middle and late eighteenth century, the Exposition section is a parade of contrasting yet compatible melodies offered up for developmental scrutiny and then, in the Recapitulation, revisited in their "resolved" states.

Although there are two distinct sections in the Exposition, there are no less than five different melodic patterns. First let us establish our perspective by noting the layout of this first section.

342

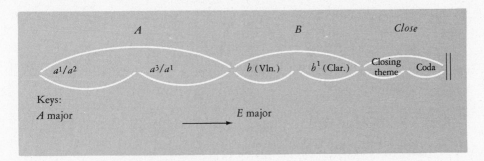

Example 30.1 Mapping of the Exposition, Movement I

Translating these abstract markings into musical events can best be done by referring to the melodic and textural characteristics that shape each one. The first two, a^1 and a^2, appear in a call-response association between strings and clarinet. The string pattern is like a slow-moving hymn, while the clarinet's response is a broad arch that sweeps from quite low to high.

Example 30.2 Themes a^1 and a^2 of the first movement

Having exposed these contrasting ideas, Mozart brings off a simple yet brilliant feat. First the clarinet and then the cello stack still another theme (a^3) above and below the slower articulations of a^1. This latest thematic unit prevails until a climactic thick texture drops off to the quiet thinness that is the beginning of theme b. In true classic style, the boundaries between the two formal sections are clearly drawn. Aside from the thinner and different texture, a silent beat separates them; and now the cello begins a plucked bass line.

Example 30.3 Beginning of Section *B*, first movement

The next decisive break in flow occurs with the closing section. Here strings and clarinet again form a call-response relationship for two phrases, the Exposition ending with a single sounding of the a^1 pattern.

DEVELOPMENT It is the a^2 theme that dominates the Development section, although a single phrase of a^1 is heard close to the beginning. By the time the listener is convinced that development is in full swing, Mozart has combined the second half of the a^2 theme with its first half. This neat compression of the two parts usually finds the clarinet playing the slower articulation, strings moving twice as fast with the other part. Refer back to the clarinet line shown in Example 30.1 to see how the patterns shown in Example 30.4 are derived from that earlier statement.

Example 30.4 Dovetailing of two parts of theme a^2 in the Development

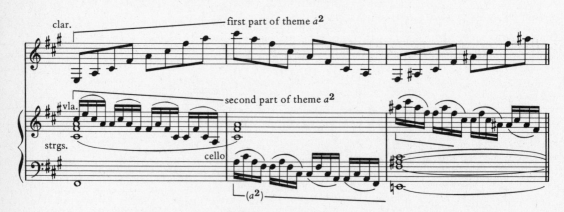

RECAPITULATION A sustained pattern in clarinet and first violin links the Development with the return of theme a^1. At this point you will notice that Mozart now reverses the roles found in the Exposition, for the clarinet plays the hymnlike tune while the first voilin responds with the a^2 pattern.

Aside from minor deviations, this final large section duplicates the thematic succession of the Exposition. Now, of course, the second theme group (*B*) sounds in the tonic key rather than the dominant. The mapping of the whole movement shown next indicates main keys touched during its course as well as themes and textures. While Exposition and Recapitulation are exactly the same length (seventy-nine measures in the score), the Development is almost exactly half their length (thirty-eight measures).

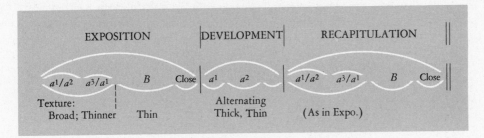

Example 30.5   Mapping of the first movement

Movement II:
Larghetto
("moderately slow")

Melody is the paramount shaping property in the binary form of this movement. Now the clarinet leads the ensemble, sounding its long, slow melody over the simplest of string undulations. A contrasting texture, in which clarinet and solo violin exchange principal and secondary roles, separates the first section from its return. Although the movement appears to divide into equal halves, the second "half" is a slightly abbreviated version of the first.

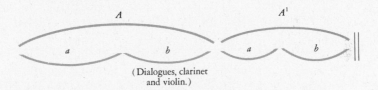

(Dialogues, clarinet and violin.)

Example 30.6   Mapping of the second movement

To provide the sounds most appropriate for this unhurried movement, Mozart directs violins and viola to play with mutes fixed to their bridges, thereby subduing their usually more resonant tones. These muted timbres, combined with the predominating texture of broadly spaced chords, figure prominently in establishing the movement's tone of hushed solitude.

Movement III:
Menuetto

This Menuetto is somewhat extraordinary, though by no means unique: it contains two trios rather than the usual one.* As you may recall from

---

*The first movement of Alban Berg's Violin Concerto (Chapter 26) contains a Scherzo in which two trios form the middle section.

other menuettos we have discussed, the ordinary menuetto follows a ternary scheme of menuetto–trio–menuetto. But if there are *two* trios, as in this *Quintet*, then a form of *A B C A* emerges.

Although this movement is mostly in a major key, the first Trio is in minor, which offers an immediate contrast with its framing sections. But an even more fundamental procedure is used to delineate section from section. This is the way the clarinet's role in the proceedings is planned. The following listing gives a general idea of how form and instrumentation relate.

> *Menuetto:* Clarinet joined with strings as top voice
> *Trio 1:* Clarinet silent
> *Trio 2:* Clarinet solo, string background
> *Menuetto:* As in the beginning

The second Trio is quite lively, the solo clarinet enacting the spirited leading voice in a rousing country-style dance. The peasant quality of this section is reminiscent of the dance that sired the more sedate Viennese waltz, a boisterous Austrian fling in triple meter called the *Ländler*.

Movement IV:
Allegretto con Variazioni ("fast, with variations")

This final movement clearly represents the processive form type, but with a strong hint of return at the end. It begins with a simple theme sounded by strings and laced with brief interpolations by the solo clarinet.

If broken down into its component parts, the design of the total theme is *a a a a b a b a* (assuming that performers repeat sections as indicated by the composer).

Variation 1 retains a pronounced kinship with the theme, but a winding counter-melody is pressed into the texture, like fresh icing on a day-old cake, by the clarinet. In this variation the clarinet's ability to project beautiful lines of flowing tones, some of them widely separated in pitch, is masterfully exploited.

Variation 2 sports a new texture: a string trio of violins and viola is accompanied by occasional pulsings from the cello, this overlaid by the clarinet's counter-melody. The rhythmic character of this variation is imposing; a kind of jerky movement dominates the first and last sections of the first violin part, accompanied by triplet patterns in the remaining violin and viola parts. The jerky quality here is reinforced by Mozart's frequent sudden shifts from loud to soft.

Variation 3 immediately sounds different. Its minor chords oppose the major that has prevailed in previous variations. This variation seems more a distillation than an ornamentation of the original theme. It lacks the melodic thrust of its preceding variations, projecting a kind of fragmentary wistfulness. The viola carries the main melodic burden. Solo clarinet adds only rudimentary background patterns, like afterthoughts to the viola's tentative statements.

The unique virtuoso capabilities of the clarinet are first thoroughly exploited in Variation 4. It lopes through agile figures, forming an embroidery of the rather literal restatement of the theme's melody, whose image has faded in the preceding three variations. Major chords dominate the texture again, and the smooth sheen of this variation provides a fitting background for the nimble clarinet. This is an interesting study in variation, for although the original pitches of the parent theme are still relatively intact, the texture is vastly changed. The middle section grants the first violinist a twin-billing with the clarinetist, a kind of dialogue between equal protagonists in a drama.

A short bridge spans the change of tempo from fast to slow, which provides the main contrast between Variation 4 and Variation 5. Marked *Adagio* ("very slow"), this is the only time in the full set of variations that a fast tempo does not prevail. The variation has a more resonant sound, capitalizing on the prolonged tones made possible by the slower pace. The jerky rhythms of Variation 2 return during the beginning of this variation, but its most striking feature comes at about midpoint. This is the sweeping upward pattern played twice by the solo clarinet.

Once more, a bridge links variations. The relatively plodding tempo of Variation 5 grows into the rapid *Allegro* of No. 6, which closes the movement. This final variation imposes a hint of return form, violins and solo clarinet restating in the beginning the original version of the theme's melody.

It is soon apparent, however, that no simple return of the theme is at hand. Imitation between the low cello and high clarinet ensues, ushering in a far more interesting intertwining of patterns than has occurred before. A sustained pedalpoint in the cello begins about two-thirds of the way through, suggesting the imminency of a close. A repeated cadence pattern accomplishes this close as a kind of tag-end to the variation.

31

STRING QUARTET
OPUS 18, NO. 1

Ludwig van Beethoven (1770–1827)

BACKGROUND*

Perhaps it is worth noting that composers of all ages have composed music for the kinds of music-making apparatus they found around them. Some have exercised considerable power in altering the ensembles their society provided them—adding new instruments, abandoning old ones, or on occasion even creating quite new resources or combinations of sound sources. And yet, the culture to which a composer is born largely determines the way his music will be used, and thus the kind he will create.

The trained composer of 1500 found a career in the Church. Today he usually seeks professional security on a college or university faculty. In Beethoven's time, grants from individuals, members of a prospering industrial class or moneyed royalty, provided financial sustenance for the serious composer. These same patrons provided sites and occasions for private performances of chamber music. Public concerts and sales of printed music had become welcome supplements to the revenues available from aristocratic connoisseurs, who themselves had begun to supplant the Church in this function since around 1600.

We discussed some of these conditions of the composer's livelihood in Chapter 8 in reference to concerts of Beethoven's orchestral music.

---

*Further discussion of Beethoven can be found in Chapter 8.

Illustration 31.1
Ludwig van Beethoven

What we did not mention there were the numerous chamber compositions —quartets, trios, and solo sonatas—that came into being because a wealthy patron could ensure remuneration and perhaps immediate public (or private) performance. The six quartets of Opus 18, for example, were dedicated to Prince von Lobkowitz, whose name was only one of many noble titles in a long list of Beethoven dedications.

Knowing only Beethoven's symphonies and concertos—the "big" works—means knowing only one facet of his creative output, and a severely limited facet at that. He composed at least forty-seven works for chamber groups of various kinds, a number that excludes his many solo sonatas. Most notable of these are the seventeen string quartets.* More than works in any other medium, the quartets reflect not only his musical uniqueness but even the personal metamorphosis he endured during the second half of his life.

BEETHOVEN'S MUSIC

Three Style Periods   Biographers normally divide Beethoven's creative years into three distinct periods. All seem to agree that the first extended to around 1800, a period distinguished by the young composer's awareness of his forebears (especially Haydn and Mozart). A second period began when this still

---

*Only sixteen of the quartets are full works consisting of several movements. One, Opus 133, is actually an extended single movement, called *The Great Fugue*. It was composed originally as the final movement of Opus 130.

Illustration 31.2 Although established as a principal medium during the eighteenth century, the string quartet still reigns as the source of chamber music. The Rowe Quartet concertizes throughout the world.

youthful man became aware that his hearing was impaired, that total deafness might be the result. Naturally, it was a time of inner turmoil. His works from that time begin to suggest a conscious striving to express that which was uniquely himself.

The third and final shift in style appears in works composed after about 1814. These "late" works are laced with powerfully introspective and rebellious tone that colors his most challenging music.

His string quartets embrace each of the three periods. They provide adequate evidence that the divisions represent more than historians' whimsy. Listening to an "early," a "middle," and then a "late" Beethoven quartet is like witnessing the evolution of a brash young genius into a titanic power.

The Quartets

The six quartets of Opus 18 amply bear the genetic traces he inherited from his Viennese predecessors. As we shall note momentarily, however, they possess enough individuality to prove that their creator was his own man. He was thirty years old when he finished composing them, and this suggests that he had awaited the creative maturity that would ensure the indelible stamp of their composer. For him, composing a string quartet was serious business.

The second group of quartets, the three of Opus 59, were composed during his middle life period, as were the quartets Opus 74 and Opus 95. Those of his last style-phase begin with Opus 127, which was first performed in Vienna in 1825 (just two years before the composer's death).

Even the groupings by opus numbers* of the quartets suggest one of

---

*The word *opus* is Latin for *work*. Composers' compositions are often numbered by the order of publication.

the ways this brooding man reshaped the course of music history. Each of the later works is a total musical testament in itself. Opus 18 includes six separate quartets; the next group, Opus 59, contains three; and then each subsequent opus number refers to a single work. By then Beethoven had discarded the very idea of a *collection*, emphasizing the singularity of each quartet by setting it apart. This isolation of the later works is further reinforced in the way each subsequent quartet grows in formal complexity, each carrying still further the developmental techniques inherited from Haydn and Mozart.

And thus, by themselves, the quartets trace the development of Beethoven the composer. They also trace the origins of much that transpired in music of the nineteenth century, after his death in 1827. By embodying self-expression in his music in a direct and compelling way, by turning his back on the neat predictability of eighteenth-century forms and gestures, Beethoven laid the foundation for the reigning obsession of nineteenth-century Romanticism: individualism.

After Beethoven, a composer no longer could be content as a mere expert mixer of sounds. From that time hence, the composer was assumed to be a spokesman for his own unique world-view, whose medium of expression happened to be musical sounds rather than words. The phrase "tone poet" is only one hackneyed indication of this drive to express oneself, which dominates the remaining decades of the nineteenth century.

Thematic Development in Beethoven's Music

Attempts to distill into a single phrase or word something so varied and complex as a composer's total output are of course futile. Beethoven's music projects its uniqueness in a multitude of ways. And yet, one trait crowds out all others: *thematic development*. More than any composer before or since, his conception of musical unfolding revolved about the successive transformations of a single melodic idea, in ways that created a new event but retained sufficient symptoms of its parent pattern to be identified.

While the unfolding of a Mozart or Haydn movement depends largely upon a succession of contrasting themes, Beethoven's music seems to grow from one state to another. It is as if his music embodies a sonic cell that expands and contracts, divides and multiplies, each event providing a new insight into the nature of the "cell" in its original state.

Thematic development was one of the crowning features of the Viennese classical style. But while development in a movement composed by Haydn or Mozart normally occurred in sections expressly set aside for that purpose, it becomes the overwhelming motivation for most of Beethoven's music; it may occur at any point within the course of a work. In some of his compositions the phrase "continuous development" is an apt description of this unfolding process.

STRING QUARTET OPUS 18, NO. 1

Beethoven worked over his compositions like an alchemist searching for the magic potion. He improvised at the piano, sketched out ideas in his notebooks, and reworked old ideas until they bloomed into exactly the musical flower he sought. Because of his working habits it is sometimes impossible for us to know when the composition of a work began. Although first published in 1801, the six early quartets were begun sometime in 1798. We do know that the quartet listed as No. 1 was finished (actually after No. 3!) in 1799, but this version was considerably revised before it appeared in print. Each of the six of this group provides an accurate view of the composer in midstream between the melodic, harmonic, and formal gestures of the Viennese classicism of Haydn and Mozart and the more individualistic characteristics of his more mature music.

Although Quartet No. 1 is in the usual four movements of the classical quartet, Beethoven replaces the traditional menuetto of the third movement with a scherzo, a change he would make later in the four-movement symphony as well (first in his Symphony No. 2). This single change implies the composer's determination to increase the power and emotional depth of the tradition he inherited. There is no suggestion of the formal ballroom in Beethoven's scherzo, no faint hint of powdered wigs or the graceful motions of delicate feet. Now the third movement has altogether severed its ties with polite dance, achieving a status quite as "heavy" as its three associated movements. (Beethoven incorporates a menuetto in some of the other quartets of Opus 18, however.)

Movement I:
Allegro con brio
("Fast, with dash")

In basic form this movement offers no surprises. Its shape is governed by the Exposition–Development–Recapitulation design we have seen earlier in works of the classical period. And yet, Beethoven's stamp is evident with the first melodic pattern. A terse motif of the kind that opens his Symphony No. 5, it is just the kind of fundamental "cell" that provides material most suitable for development. Not unlike the • • • —— motif of the later symphony, this simple declarative pattern is not absent for

Example 31.1   Main motif

long during the entire movement. It is continually recast and transformed, yet it retains an obvious correspondence with the original motif.

Don't overlook the inherent drama in this little figure. Its most potent feature is the silence that breaches its repetitions, adding a suggestion of hidden power. It is a straightforward pattern, exposed in a typically Beethovian no-nonsense way.

Example 31.2 First four measures

Beethoven seems reluctant to turn from his gripping first theme in order to expose a second theme. He finally does, only to turn back immediately to further statements of the initial motif. Our next mapping is drawn to reveal only the general way these two themes occur within the Exposition section.

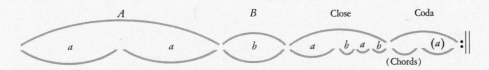

Example 31.3 Mapping of themes in the Exposition

Note in the mapping how fully the single *a* motif dominates this long expository section of 114 measures, consuming almost four-fifths of its span. It would appear that a Development section as such has been preempted by this opening Exposition!

Of course, Beethoven finds a way. In the Development section he bears down even harder, putting his motif through still new paces. About half as long as the Exposition,* the Development teems with compressed imitations, all four instruments answering one another with fragments split away from the main motif.

---

*This is true only when performers do not repeat the Exposition section, as per Beethoven's notation.

Example 31.4   Imitative exchanges of fragments from motif *a*

The latter half of the Development section shifts from these hammering imitations to a homophonic texture, the two violins shaping the motif into a series of phrases in dialogue. The developmental atmosphere is changed but by no means swept away. Each phrase shifts to a different key, and the motif is compressed in a way that causes its final note to act as the beginning of a new statement.

Example 31.5   Phrase drawn from motif *a*, latter part of the Development

The four dialogue statements of this section grow into a thick texture that sweeps on to a powerful Recapitulation. There is no doubt at this juncture of the movement that a return has been effected, yet even here Beethoven is not content with an exact restatement of his theme. In the beginning of the movement motif *a* was announced quietly (*p*) and in a relatively thin texture. (See Example 31.2.) But its return is couched in a texture twice as thick and considerably louder than its earlier version. Return is nonetheless established. The key is *F* major, as in the beginning, and those crucial punctuating silences have been reinstated as the dramatic tail of the theme. (They are absent within the Development.)

The Recapitulation section at first appears to be closely modeled from the Exposition. Actually, its first section is a considerably abbreviated and altered version of its earlier counterpart. But the most evident difference occurs toward the end of the movement, where Beethoven, still unwilling to turn loose of his motif, fashions a coda from its fragments. It is in fact a brief final fling at development.

Movement II:
Adagio affettuoso ed appassionato ("Slow, tenderly and with passion")

This soulful lament provides a dark contrast for the first movement and the skittish movement to follow. Whether Beethoven really intended it to portray the tragic final parting of Romeo and Juliet, as some writers have suggested, can remain for us an unresolved question. It is indeed "tender and impassioned" music, as its subheading prophesies.

A subdued atmosphere is projected immediately by the resonant low string chords (mostly minor) and the solo violin melody that winds slowly upward. Even the steady persistence of the accompanying chords produces a sense of doleful plodding toward a deliberate but melancholy end.

One might reasonably assume that a composer would cast a lament such as this in a relatively simple form. But, in fact, the movement unfolds an Exposition–Development–Recapitulation plan, with typical Beethoven touches added that save it from sterility. Even within this highly stylized design, musical events at times manage to sound passionately rhapsodic, wholly lacking the strong forward thrust we normally associate with sonata form.

The overall plan of the movement is especially interesting. Beethoven separates the two statements of his first theme in the Recapitulation, and the Development section is fleetingly brief (approximately one-tenth of the movement's duration).

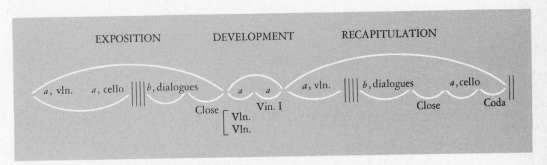

Example 31.6 Mapping of Movement II

Texture plays an important role in this brooding scenario. While the *a* theme is presented as a long, sustained line over a throbbing accompaniment, the *b* section exposes several melodic bits as dialogue between pairs of instruments. Now the texture thins, a more delicate atmosphere settles in, and each instrument takes its turn at the rapid falling runs that dominate this passage.

The Exposition section rarely rises above a whisper, so the opening of the Development, marked *forte* by Beethoven, erupts as a shocking intrusion. And then in the Recapitulation, as if to link it with the brusque drama of the preceding passages, the violin and cello restatements of the *a* theme alternate between soft and loud, adding a calamitous undercurrent to the return of this plaintive melody. These alternations of soft and loud create a curious synthesis of the theme's appearances in the Exposition and Development sections.

Movement III:
Scherzo, Allegro
molto ("very fast")

As we remarked earlier, Beethoven's replacement of the traditional menuetto with what he calls a scherzo adds breadth and dash to the quartet form. Haydn had used the same title on occasion in earlier quartets, but the music so designated still bore the spirit of a menuetto, albeit a somewhat livelier one. With Beethoven the term assumes a more definitive function: his scherzos gallop along at breakneck speed, developing melodic strands in an obvious ploy to raise musical eyebrows rather than dancing feet. The same *A B A* design unfolds, but the spirit is engagingly different.

Themes come and go in rapid order in this movement, yet two are most memorable because they define the formal outlines and provide Beethoven's melodic grist from which to mill his developments. The first consists of two patterns that are combined in the beginning but are later separated. The lower, marked #1 in the cello line of Example 31.7, finally emerges as the dominant pattern of the two.

Example 31.7   The two patterns of theme *A*, the Scherzo

The second prominent theme also bears two distinct parts, but these always are sounded successively rather than together. They occupy the middle section of the work, the Trio. The two ideas are so strikingly different that only Beethoven would have dared team them together. The one is a jerking series of leaps, the other a smoothly curved arch against sustained chords.

Example 31.8 The two patterns of theme *B*, the Trio

Much of the shifty playfulness of this movement comes from its unpredictable changes of key. Beethoven molds sections from sequences of the short motifs, and a change of key coincides with almost every new sounding of the basic pattern. The Scherzo begins unmistakably in *F* major; two measures later it suggests *G* minor; two more measures and *A* minor seems definite; but by the end of the whole phrase *C* major has prevailed. And then the second phrase begins in *A♭* major!

The Trio likewise mounts a parade of briefly touched keys, creating a play of allegiances that, as much as the rhythms and textures and melodies, conveys precisely the skittish character Beethoven intended.

Movement IV:
Allegro ("fast")

This finale offers the listener another glimpse of Beethoven finding it difficult to stop, spinning out melodies until he can be sure that every semblance of life has been drawn from them. As per the classical tradition of fourth movements, it is a sonata form, but its procession of themes at times resembles a rondo run amok.

One obstacle to the listener's grasp of the overall form occurs when the Development section begins with an exact recurrence of the principal theme. But this apparent settling into a simple return shifts abruptly, to follow a course quite opposed to the repose and stability associated with true recapitulation. Example 31.9a depicts the large sections of the movement, while 31.9b fills in the welter of details. Note particularly the comparative durations of the three large sections.

It is a complex structure, but a rewarding flow of musical ideas that no mapping can do full justice. We shall leave it after only one major point.

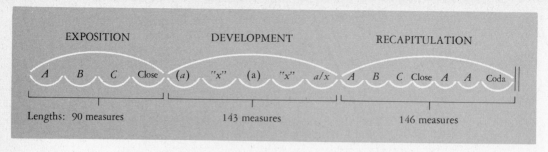

Example 31.9a Simplified mapping of the form, Movement IV

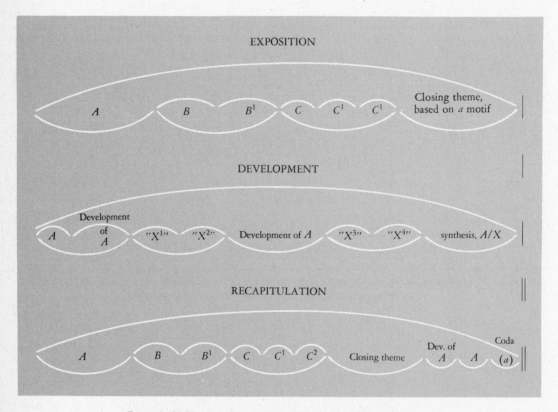

Example 31.9b Detailed mapping of the same movement

Perhaps the most curious aspect of the Development section is the surprising introduction of a new theme (shown as "*x*" in the mapping of Example 31.9b), which Beethoven proceeds to sandwich in two places between developmental gyrations of the principal motif. This new theme's rhythm has already occurred in the closing section of the Exposition, as melodic foil for fragments of *A*. But nothing quite like it has preceded its appearance here in the Development.

This new theme's simple contour and rhythm, as well as its ultra-simple texture, make it contrast markedly with the surrounding contrapuntal developments of the principal motif. It has the effect of an unwelcome melody bursting in on far more staid happenings. It can't quite be ushered out politely, for it keeps returning, always in a new key, three times.

Beethoven apparently relished what he obtained by introducing new themes within a Development section, for he tried it again in subsequent compositions. Not content with deploying "Developments" within Expositions and Recapitulations, he went even so far as to add "expositions" into Developments!

32

PIANO MUSIC OF THE
ROMANTIC PERIOD:

Mazurka in A Minor, Opus 17, No. 4,
Frédéric Chopin;
Prelude No. 2 (Voiles), Preludes Pour Piano,
Book I,
Claude Debussy

BACKGROUND

That first genius who hooked up a key mechanism for plucking strings cleared as big a hurdle as did the inventor of the wheel. His mechanized harp—which is what a harpsichord really amounts to—opened a Pandora's box of musical sounds. It is still disgorging its contents.

In J. S. Bach's day the harpsichord and its smaller relative the clavichord were the staple keyboard instruments of music outside the church. (The organ was favored in the church.) Some tinkering instrument makers of the late seventeenth and early eighteenth centuries substituted striking hammers for their plucking quills. The hammer action overcame the harpsichord's main limitation: its inability to produce tones of controlled loudness. The resultant instrument was named in a way that discloses what its inventors considered to be its prized virtue. It was called *pianoforte*, which literally means "soft-loud."

Around 1709 the Italian Bartolommeo Cristofori had perfected a reliable hammer action whose noise did not compete unduly with the tones of the strings. Within fifty years the pianoforte was well on its way to replacing the long-reigning harpsichord and having its name shortened to *piano*. By the mid-nineteenth century it had become the supreme musical instrument of the day, although it still lacked some of the refinements we know. It was an immensely popular instrument. Ownership was a virtual symbol of gentility for those who claimed the possession of "culture."

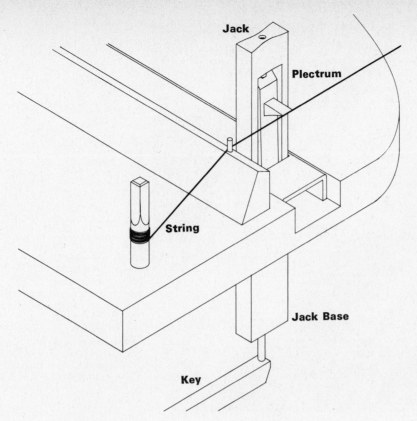

Jack

Plectrum

String

Jack Base

Key

Illustration 32.1
Harpsichord mechanism

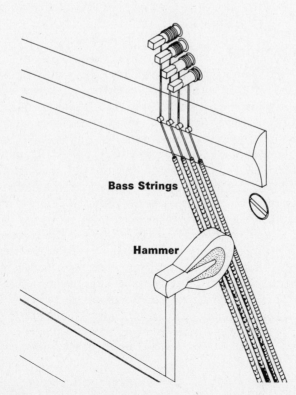

Illustration 32.2
Piano mechanism

Bass Strings

Hammer

Illustration 32.3
This interior view of an upright piano shows a single hammer poised in striking position. The heavily wound strings provide the lowest pitches for the instrument. Note how the slightly higher-pitched strings (to the right) are thinner.

IMPACT OF ROMANTICISM

Music reflected the impact of the nineteenth-century Romantic movement in several ways. Its most evident manifestation was a wealth of intimate music—the art song for voice and piano* and "parlor pieces" for solo piano. These works for piano were not the sonatas, suites, variations, or preludes and fugues of earlier eras. Now it was the "character piece," a single movement composition that often bore a title consistent with the atmosphere evoked by its music. Even works of abstract title, like *Étude* or *Impromptu*, might as well have been tagged with more poetic identities, for they too were character pieces in which a singular mood, or character, pervaded the musical substance.

These relatively brief evocations of romantic sentiment were composed by virtually every major composer of the nineteenth century, all of whom, with rare exceptions, were virtuoso pianists. Since the piano's popularity had installed that instrument as obligatory furniture in middle-class parlors and aristocratic drawing rooms, these modestly proportioned compositions provided a welcome source of income for their creators.

---

*We discuss this other intimate kind of music of Romanticism the art song, in Chapter 22.

There was a bumper crop of "Bagatelles," "Songs Without Words," "Impromptus," "Rhapsodies," "Childhood Scenes," "Preludes" (without fugues!), "Intermezzos," and "Nocturnes," not to mention pieces bearing titles of explicit programmatic intent. Most were rather brief and unpretentious, but a few were long and quite involved with musical development.

As with any particular musical repertory, many of these pieces justly deserved the fate of obscurity they suffered with passing decades. A substantial number will survive, however, as long as pianos are played. Two of the most gifted composers of the period were Frédéric Chopin and Claude Debussy. Both were brilliant pianists and both composed solo works of this type that have outlived the time of their creation.

Illustration 32.4
Frédéric Chopin

FRÉDÉRIC CHOPIN (1810–1849)

Although widely known as Polish, Chopin (*Show'-pâ*) lived almost half his life in France. His Polish mother was of noble birth, yet she and her French husband were employed on the staff of a wealthy Warsaw family when Frédéric was born. In the manner of a true Romantic, this sensitive young genius maintained a national pride, even to the extent of infusing much of his music with allusions to his native country's music. This is especially evident in his mazurkas and polonaises, both of which were modeled after Polish dances.

Most composers create music for a wide range of media. Beethoven is remembered for his symphonies and string quartets as well as for his piano sonatas; Mozart composed operas and masses in addition to symphonies and sonatas. This latitude of performing apparatus appealed to composers of the nineteenth century too. But not to Chopin. His output was almost exclusively for solo piano.

While other composers wrote music for the piano that could have been composed as well for orchestra or string quartet, Chopin created music precisely gauged for the piano alone. Transcribed for another medium, it is robbed of its most vital property, the piano's tone. Many critics have disparaged him because of this curious limitation in his work. But it seems foolish—particularly in an age of specialization such as ours— to ignore the fact that here was a genuine specialist, one who did only what he did best (and better than anyone else). Many had written solo piano works before him, but it was Chopin who created a genuine "piano style" and made the solo piano composition a ranking branch of this musical tree.

Paris, 1830s

Paris was the artistic mecca of Europe when Chopin settled there in 1831. Its population still boasted enough wealthy patrons (some of whom were Polish émigrés like the young composer) to sustain a glittering musical life.

In the larger Parisian scene the operas of Rossini and Meyerbeer were the pacesetters of the day. Their monopoly was threatened by the youthful Bellini, who was Chopin's friend after his arrival in 1833. The literary scene was no less bright, with Honoré de Balzac, Stendhal, Alexandre Dumas and Victor Hugo in residence. Even Heinrich Heine, whose poems would become the text for Robert Schumann's *Dichterliebe* a decade later, was in Paris at this time. In art salons the paintings of Delacroix were scandalizing art lovers who found the raw passion of Romanticism too rich for habits trained on the cold realism of painters like Ingres.

Young Chopin was admirably suited, by physique, temperament, and musical inclination, to become a leading character in the musical act of this heady artistic revolution.

He was not an immediate success with the concert-going public, but he managed to captivate a powerful segment of the aristocrats who frequented the city's private musicales. Despite the tubercular condition that eventually killed him, he lived a vivacious life, composing, teaching piano students, and playing for a circle of friends that included some of the luminous stars of the French sky. One member of his charmed circle was Aurore Dupin, his mistress and emotional stabilizer. She also was nineteenth century France's most liberated woman—though her liberation stopped short of dropping her novelist pen name of George Sand.

Chopin as Pianist

Chopin clearly had limitations as a pianist. His strength lay more in the feeling he projected than in the sort of blazing technique displayed by his contemporary Franz Liszt. (Chopin readily admitted that Liszt could play Chopin better than Chopin could.) But any shortcomings he may have had were offset by the emotional power he could transmit within the intimacy of a Parisian salon, a site he much preferred to concert halls for his playing.

Contemporary accounts suggest that his playing was unique in the way his rhythm would ebb and flow within an established tempo. This holding back and thrusting forward was merely one aspect of his very personal expression, but it led a few honored musicians to suggest (as did the composer Berlioz) that he had trouble "keeping the beat." Today this style of playing is expected in performances of his music. Called *tempo rubato* ("robbed time"), its subtle leanings within measured time are valued as far more interesting than a strict beat-by-beat interpretation.

Chopin composed a wealth of music during his short life. In addition to the many polonaises, waltzes, mazurkas, preludes, and études he wrote, there are works for piano and orchestra (including two concertos); there also are large works for solo piano which overstep the bounds of the character piece. These include three sonatas, four scherzos, four ballades, a *barcarolle* (boat song) and a *berceuse* (lullaby). But his most intimate and characteristic music can be found in the musical miniatures, like the mazurkas and polonaises.

Mazurka in A Minor, Opus 17, No. 4

Despite his immigration to Paris, Chopin retained emotional ties with his native Poland throughout his life. The nostalgia he must have felt surfaces in many of his works, although never as direct quotations of folk songs or patriotic hymns. Especially his mazurkas reflect his origins, transplanting the Polish peasant's words, so to speak, into the sentences and paragraphs of sophisticated French salon music.

The mazurka was a dance in triple meter in which a considerable amount of exchanging and returning of partners took place between couples. It was not a dance of the ONE . . *two* . . *three*, ONE . . *two* . . *three* accents of the waltz and minuet. In it, the dancers' most pronounced movement usually came on the second beat of the 1 . . 2 . . 3 pattern, and the music usually contained skipping rhythms like those illustrated in the first beats of the patterns in Example 32.1

Example 32.1 Typical rhythms and accents of the Polish Mazurka

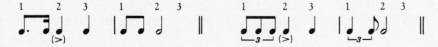

In his piano mazurkas Chopin retained these rhythmic idiosyncrasies of the dances he had witnessed as a child on the outskirts of Warsaw. But while the original dances were of moderate to rapid tempo, his stylized replicas run the gamut from a breakneck gallop to a brooding shuffle. The Mazurka in A Minor is of the more somber cast, suggesting palpitations of the heart more than stampings of the heel.

Within the work's basic *A B A* form, Chopin creates the melancholy sensuousness that separates his music from that of the composers who preceded him. Though a simple work in form, rhythm, and texture, it is overlaid with the melodic and harmonic finesse that gives his music its direct appeal and its one-of-a-kind integrity. The following mapping shows how the mazurka's ternary plan is organized from sixteen small units, each of which is eight measures long.

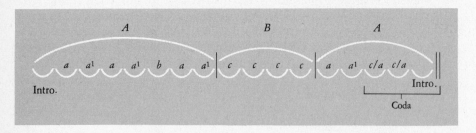

Example 32.2 Sectional mapping of the *Mazurka in A minor*

Along with melody, harmony plays a major role in shaping the largest parts of this scheme, for the framing *A*'s are in minor and the middle *B* is in major.

From its beginning, the music makes clear that it is occupied with more than the mere evocation of mazurka-twitches in the muscles. It has a particular atmosphere to transmit to the listener. There is a tentative air about it, a sense of quiet nervousness that cannot be altogether subdued.

Example 32.3 Introduction and first two phrases of the *Mazurka*

Within this first twenty measures we hear the melodic, harmonic, and textural staples that stamp the piece as genuine Chopin. Using the mazurka's simple rhythmic and textural conventions as a base, he manipulates melody and harmony to transform homely matters into exotic fare. If a second-rate composer had written this Mazurka, he might have produced something like the music shown in Example 32.4. (If you don't play the piano, have a friend play the two versions of Examples 32.3 and 32.4 for you as a basis of comparison.)

Example 32.4   A less masterful version of Chopin's first twenty measures

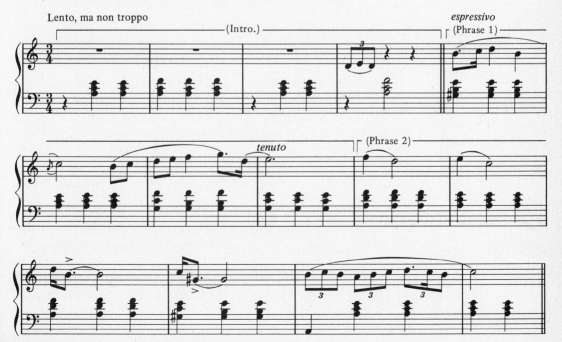

Why is Chopin's version superior? The revision of Example 32.4 contains the same rhythms, the same homophonic texture, and almost the same melody. And yet the several changes produce music that has lost the haunting charm of the Chopin.

The main reason has to do with harmony. Chopin's music has an unsettled quality about it. The sounds float, arriving at points where harmonic repose normally would occur but without actually landing. This ambiguity is not fortuitous. The composer controls it by only hinting at a sense of key, the tonic chord remaining conspicuously absent until two whole phrases have gone by.

The defiled version of Example 32.4 completely misses Chopin's point. It plods along, stepping flat-footed from one to another cadence on the tonic chord. While Chopin's version only *suggests* the key of *A* minor, our revised version leaves the listener in no doubt, wearily alighting on it again and again (measures 3, 6, 10, and 14). And thus one of Chopin's secret ploys—harmonic ambiguity—is missing.

Still another kind of harmonic ambiquity can be heard in the opening section. It occurs in the second phrase (beginning in measure 9), where melody and harmony briefly twist away from the already weak framework of *A* minor, then wind their paths back via a series of gliding chords and melodic drops. Compared with this masterly stroke of tonal liberty, our uninspired version (Example 32.4) retains its steady course without a touch of drama. No ambiguity; no poetry; no Chopin!

The middle section (*B*) of this Mazurka totally dispels the enigmatic harmonies of the opening. The tonality has shifted to major. Now overstatement replaces understatement: members of the tonic chord (*A* major) sound on almost every beat, hinting the drone of a piper (who might very well have played for a peasant dance). Where ambiguity reigned before, utter clarity now holds sway.

The ending of this piece is especially fascinating in that its final sounds suggest that it doesn't really end. By using as a coda the series of chords that formed the introduction, Chopin causes his mazurka-reverie to float back into the Slavic shadows from whence it came.

Before we leave this engaging romantic miniature we should note its improvisatory character. It sounds as if the composer sat down at his piano with the desire to create a wistful bit of nostalgia, using the Polish mazurka only as a fragile guide. The very simplicity of the work's form and the repetitiousness of its phrases (in both the *A* and *B* sections) reinforce this plausible reconstruction of its creation. As you may notice, the formal shaping comes from repetitions of single phrases, one phrase for the *A* section and another for the *B*. Looking back at the mapping of Example 32.2, you will find that both the initial and final *A* sections consist of two kinds of phrases, *a* and *a'*. In fact, the *a'* is merely a melodic decoration of *a*, rapid decorations replacing some of the more stolid patterns of the lead phrase.

Looking back now to Example 32.3, compare the notation of measure 15 with its prototype in measure 7. Then compare measures 18–19 with measures 10–11. The more elaborate rhythms in these embellished measures reveal Chopin's shimmering melodic style. Breathless streams of pitches crowd the beat, as if to revolt against the cramping three beats of their measures.

Illustration 32.5   Claude Debussy at his home

CLAUDE DEBUSSY (1863–1918)*

Although his creative years came more than a half-century later, Debussy was the next major link after Chopin in the growing chain of composers of piano music. Like that of his Polish predecessor, his refined musical imagery was weaned on the piano's sounds, so that instrument was basic to his creative output. The music he produced has been basic to the pianist's repertory since it was created, and it has proved to have been seminal for the whole of modern music.

He knew well the music of Chopin. He was even the editor, in 1913, of the first French edition of Chopin's works. Since he composed his own collection of Études for the piano later in 1915, it is evident that his rekindled interest in that composer's music, which included two dozen études, accomplished more than just the repayment of his considerable financial debts.†

---

*Debussy's life is discussed in some detail, along with the Impressionist movement, in Chapter 11.

†Debussy was paying alimony to his first wife and maintaining his own small family of wife and daughter at the time.

But aside from this evidence of direct influence, Chopin's graceful miniatures were an obvious backdrop for the whole of Debussy's piano music. Naturally, he composed no mazurkas or polonaises; he was much too full of his own Frenchness to stoop to such foreign borrowings. And yet his piano pieces are not in the sonata tradition of German classicism. They are character pieces, and most of them bear the kinds of titles the nineteenth century had evolved for just that kind of music. They are exquisite distillations of the Romantic obsession for mood, a gallery of soundpaintings of moonlight, gardens in the rain, leaves flooded by sunlight, and mist on the sea.

Debussy's Piano Works

Debussy's earliest published work for piano was *Suite Bergamasque*, which though finished in 1890 was not published until three years later. This collection of four short pieces is only symptomatic of the composer's later mastery of piano writing. Its Prelude, Minuet, "Clair de lune" ("Light of the Moon"), and "Passepied" are deft character pieces, but they are not the polished atmospherics of his later impressionism.* The more definitive mood-paintings came later, between 1903 and 1913, with collections called *Estampes* (or literally, "engravings"), two books of *Images*, and especially the two books of Preludes.

It is in the Preludes—twenty four of them in two volumes—that the piano character piece reaches its apex of evolution, and Debussy proves for all the world that he is the rightful heir to Chopin's legacy.

Despite their collective title, each Prelude bears its individual subtitle, each a cue for listeners that what they are about to hear can be associated with an extra-musical image. Prelude No. 10 (Book I) is called "La Cathedrale engloutie," for example. What images, or *impressions*, come to your mind when considering the vision of a *sunken cathedral*? Debussy's original impetus was an ancient Breton legend. It tells of a cathedral rising on occasion from the seafoam, its bells tolling and its priests chanting, only to sink back into its watery abyss as mysteriously as it appeared.

Or what mental states are induced by Prelude No. 6, whose title is the evocative "Des pas sur la neige" ("steps on the snow")? The phrase itself is an impressionistic delight, whose power to catapult our imagination into boundless ice-white wastes is considerable. In conjunction with Debussy's delicately whispering tone poem the title guides our perceptions, nudging them in one particular direction rather than another. Like his Prelude to the *Afternoon of a Faun*, each of his piano Preludes is program music in the most general sense: none attempts to relate a story;

---

*The third of this set, "Clair de lune," is closer to his later music than the others. It is an excellent piece, although so overplayed and misused for "soap opera" backgrounds that its haunting beauty has become a musical cliché.

each proposes only a fundamental "feeling in sound," which can be fleshed out as vividly as the listener's imagination and inclination might allow.

Prelude No. 2, "Voiles"

Debussy's pithy title offers the image of "veils," which probably was his metaphor for the gently undulating riggings on sailing ships. The scene is faintly ominous, as directionless and unpredictable as random breezes sweeping a harbor. The Prelude is a brilliant study in monotony, yet a monotony that is strangely captivating.

It isn't difficult to hear how Debussy presses home this overall impression of monotonous unpredictability. A principal means is harmony. The same six-note scale and chord form the basis for the entire work, with the exception of a fleeting ray of sunlight that peeks through about two-thirds of the way. The scale contains only whole-tone relationships, and the harmony is composed of any combination of just those six (or fewer) pitch classes.

Example 32.5   Whole-tone scale and some of the resultant chords in "Voiles"

Since the successive pitches in a whole-tone scale are equidistant, melodies and chords based on them alone provide no intrinsic sense of differentiation. Without differentiation there is a sameness that defies tonality, and most of "Voiles" is atonal, i.e., lacking a sense of tonic or key center.

The opening thematic strand (which returns near the end) sets a tone of random rustling which, when repeated several times, always projects a quality of sameness. The random effect was carefully planned by Debussy. If we use a spatial representation of the opening theme, we can show that its length and the time intervals separating its entrances vary considerably. These non-periodic repetitions of the theme help to imply the randomness of the scene.

Example 32.6 Principal motif: its changing lengths and separations

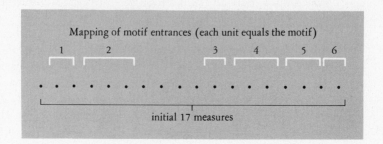

To this gentle thematic spasm two other textural layers are added, forming a rich three-ply of opposed yet strangely compatible parts. The first added layer is a low pedal point. It articulates in a random pattern at first, develops a more even rhythm, then proves to be an obsessive anchorage for the rest of the texture. It drops out only at the final phrases of the piece.

The third textural layer, introduced just after the low pedal, is a gentle line of equal durations. It acts as a simple foil for the less stable undulations of the initial theme. One of these two patterns, always associated with the incessant low pedal tone, dominates the first section of "Voiles." This play of textural layers against one another provides much of the sense of motion, limited as it is, for the entire work.

The singular quality of "Voiles" is reflected in its form, which many of Debussy's contemporaries would have described as "formless." The music is a succession of passages which, although stamped with thematic differences, are all so much alike in texture, tonality, and rhythm that contrast is minimized. The overall effect is that of tiny motions within unchanging boundaries.

There is a brief climactic passage, however, a brief gusting that portends something more spectacular than the enigmatic rufflings of before. This sudden bright passage is the only one of this work that breaks the spell of ambiguity. By comparison, it is a simple passage. Its tonal simplicity results from the use of a pentatonic (five-note) scale, which Debussy frequently turned to when he wished to suggest the simplicity of the outdoors. Note how the scale of this passage differs from the sameness of the whole-tone scale. It contains intervals of different sizes, and it is used in a way that makes E♭ the tonal center for the passage.

Example 32.7 Pentatonic scale of the climactic section, "Voiles"

The abrupt rise to a peak lasts only six of the work's sixty-four measures. The passage is too brief to provide a true contrasting section, a genuine *B* in a ternary design. Rather, it is consistent with the metaphor of sails in the wind, a motion that subsides as suddenly as it arose from gentler breezes.

The whole-tone passages return, now as harp-like brushes of sound. Finally the opening motif returns, a close for the formal circle that by returning implies the end. And remarkably like Chopin's Mazurka in A minor, "Voiles" "finishes without ending." In fact, one is left with the distinct impression that the music did not stop: the breeze merely died away.

33

KLEINE KAMMERMUSIK, OPUS 24, NO. 2

Paul Hindemith (1895–1963)

BACKGROUND

Hindemith was among the displaced German artists and intellectuals of World War II, many of whom escaped Hitler's madness by coming to the United States. Born in Hanau, he studied music in nearby Frankfurt, where he played viola in the municipal opera orchestra and methodically created a staggering list of compositions.

Spreading fame as a composer and viola virtuoso helped him secure a prestigious position at the *Hochschule fur Musik* in Berlin, which he held until 1935. Though he was known by then throughout the world as a composer of imposing stature, Hitler's Ministry of Culture nonetheless recognized him as a "Jew lover," his music as hopelessly "decadent." (Considering their source, these accusations could have been enjoyed as compliments, but there was considerable political discomfort associated with them.)

The premiere performance of Hindemith's opera *Matthias the Painter* was banned in Germany in 1935. Hindemith took this act as the proverbial handwriting on the wall. He left for the United States in 1937, where he made his home until the misery of Hitler's war had eased. Displacement to the U.S. was simplified by the offer of a professorship at the University of Buffalo, New York. From there he moved to Yale University, where many of the young composers of that era flocked to study with him. Within the

Illustration 33.1
Paul Hindemith

decade 1940–50 he was probably the most influential composer in this country.

After the end of the war in 1945 a flood of interest emerged among American composers in the serial methods of composing developed by Arnold Schoenberg.* These were alien to Hindemith's artistic temperament. He moved to Switzerland in 1953, a base from which he could conduct concerts throughout Europe, teach at the University of Zurich, and compose. It is ironic that his life, which had taken him all over the world, ended close to his birthplace: he died in Frankfurt in December of 1963.

Reputation as a Composer

Hindemith's reputation has always been that of the quiet, careful craftsman, a composer who perhaps would have been more comfortable living during an earlier age. As a public figure he lacked the messianic flair of Schoenberg and the calculated flamboyance of Igor Stravinsky, both of whom were more newsworthy figures. He never quite achieved their public recognition, although he created no less music of enduring value than they. He missed the kind of scandalous splash Stravinsky had enjoyed when his ballet *The Rite of Spring* erupted into a riot at its premiere in 1913.

---

*See pages 297–298 for a brief description of Schoenberg's method.

And he boasted of no revolutionary methods like Schoenberg's, which critics could praise or damn. So as a public figure his lot was rather bland by comparison with some of his artistic peers.

Musical Output

Like his esteemed predecessors, Hindemith wrote music for practically every medium of the concert tradition. Concertgoers know him best for his orchestral works or for his numerous solo sonatas. But he in fact composed a dozen operas, none of which has ever become a repertory piece in the world's opera houses. (And this tells us as much about the conservative stance of the world's opera houses as about the value of Hindemith's operas!) He also composed art songs, choral music, sonatas for piano, sonatas for organ, cantatas, a host of string quartets, and a sizable collection of pieces that are useful in teaching young people to perform.

We used the word "craftsman" a few lines earlier in reference to Hindemith's public image. This is an especially apt term for him. One of his significant publications was a book whose title in translation is *The Craft of Musical Composition*. In this two-volume set Hindemith suggests that the composer fits sounds together to make music in much the same spirit that a carpenter fashions wood into cabinets or a cobbler molds leather into shoes.

Consistent with this homespun view of the composer's task was his conception of the function of music in life. To him it was an informal, everyday pastime as much as a ritual for the concert hall. Although he composed lavish operas and grandiose symphonies that require the skills of the world's best performers, he championed music as more than a spectator sport. In his view the average citizens would be better off acting as performers more, reacting as passive spectators less.

To this end, Hindemith wrote a number of works for amateurs. With his composition students he stressed the need to compose for realistic consumption rather than for a dubious posterity. He was a wholesome antidote for the romantisism of "art for art's sake," which, if unbridled, can sweep composers off their idealistic feet and justify creating music that is talked about more than it is heard.

Because of this rather practical side, Hindemith was widely known as the composer of *Gebrauchsmusik* ("useful" or "utilitarian" music). People who had never heard a note of his music spoke glibly of him as a composer of *functional music*. At times the phrase evoked the spectre of a music so scrubbed clean of "prettiness" that it sounded frightfully dull. Like most slogans, the *Gebrauchsmusik* tag misled many to a false conception of what it described. A great deal of Hindemith's music is quite as impractical as Beethoven's or Wagner's, and quite as moving—quite as "uselessly beautiful"—as the music of any composer of history. It so happens that much of it, like the "Little Chamber Music," is composed for "practical" ensembles like a woodwind quintet.

KLEINE KAMMERMUSIK, Opus 24, No. 2 (1922)

For musicians this is "fun music." Although the composer certainly weighed every note he wrote on the balance of "How will it sound?", one of his principal aims was to create music the five performers would delight in playing. In a woodwind quintet no performer is the leader; each assumes this role at one time or another, depending upon the demands of his part. And in any chamber ensemble the final musical product can be no better than the inputs of its individuals.

The *Kleine Kammermusik* is scored for the traditional woodwind quintet of flute, oboe, clarinet, horn, and bassoon. (The flute player uses piccolo in the second movement.) The work is organized in five separate movements of contrasting mood, each a miniature character piece of its own, each a tuneful vehicle for the melodic play of the five instruments as soloists and as collective ensemble.

Movement I:
Lustig ("Playful")

This rollicking opener sets the generally light tone of the whole work, the "diverting" quality suggested by the word *Kleine* in Hindemith's title. Nothing particularly profound is said, but every sentence is exquisitely turned. Although there are clear sectional contrasts in the movement, a single galloping rhythm can be heard from beginning to end. It is a combination of ___ .. , which in musical notation consists of the pattern .

The clarinet leads off with a first theme dominated by this rhythm, as is the accompanying texture. The oboe's turn with the same melody follows, and then the flute's. A thinner and quieter texture ensues, establishing a second formal section. The new melody cuts a flatter contour, but the background holds doggedly to the galloping rhythm that dominated the *A* section. This less jagged theme is joined by still another, one that rapidly sweeps up and down in an acute arch. The two patterns alternate as dual themes of the entire *B* section.

The *A* theme returns, but this time in the oboe's version, which in the initial *A* section came second. The flute's version of the same theme follows immediately. The texture dissolves. There is a brief silence, and then the bassoon breaks into a slow revision of the *B* theme. Any notion that this is a genuine return of the *B* section is soon dispelled; it is apparent that these events are in fact the beginning of an end, the Coda. The plan of the total movement consists, then, of the following major parts:

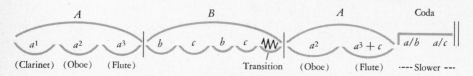

Example 33.1 Mapping of the first movement

Hindemith packs the end of this movement with brief reminders of the middle section. This edges the movement's form beyond a simple *A B A* plan. The surprise combinations of theme-particles within the final *A* and the Coda provide more than just a rounding off for the sake of an ending: they create an ultimate summing-up of all that has gone before. We shall find this same kind of "final synthesis" in subsequent movements of the quintet.

Movement II:
***Walzer* ("Waltz")**

An undercurrent of frivolity surfaces occasionally in the first movement. It breaks through to become slapstick humor in this somewhat-tipsy waltz. The movement's slightly out-of-joint melody, accompanied by a cliché waltz pattern, suggests that this is a musical satire. The movement contains the required parts for a rondo form but not the arrangement.

Example 33.2 Mapping of the *Waltz*

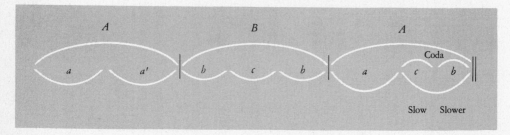

Perhaps the most pertinent question we might ask about this piece is: "What makes it sound satirical, slightly tongue-in-cheek?"

Events in the opening *A* section provide some early clues. The bassoon and horn begin the section with a hackneyed accompaniment that sounds like every corny waltz ever composed. This take-off on the *oom–pah–pah* waltz rhythm is trite to a fault—too trite, in fact, not to be clowning for a composer of Hindemith's sophistication. And then the clarinet's melody is much ado about nothing, an elaborate roller-coaster that barely meshes with its waltz accompaniment. Either the composer is poking fun at waltzes or the band is drunk!

Example 33.3   Opening passage of the *Waltz*

The *B* section is more than just a fresh melody. It also is a new texture made up of terse repeated patterns in each instrument. The bassoon and horn seem to be stuck with their *oom–pah–pah* ostinato; the clarinet repeats its single falling pattern; the oboe theme is about as lyrical as a message in Morse code. The total effect is one of musical treading-of-water—going no place. No wonder the horn's more singing interlude (*c* in Example 33.2) provides welcome relief from this humorous conglomeration.

The ending of the Waltz mimics the first movement's coda by offering a brief synopsis of themes heard in the middle section. Here the code-like tattoo of the oboe shapes the parting strains of this eccentric waltz. It ends with a whimper rather than a bang.

Movement III:
Ruhig und einfach
("Placid and
simple")

This movement lasts no more than five minutes, yet it rises to the nobility of a haunting dirge. It is a jewel cut from utterly modest stone. Its relaxed pace is a change from the steady pulses of the previous two movements, but much of its unique quality comes from the duet textures Hindemith uses for thematic statements. First is the flute/clarinet duet (a^1), then oboe/bassoon (b^2), and later flute/clarinet (a^3) and oboe/clarinet (a^4). These echoed couplings provide a unity for the movement that is not suggested by its thematic content.

Like the previous two movements, this one has a basic return. Also like its predecessors, it joins themes in the coda which earlier have been heard separately. As the mapping of Example 33.4 shows, the *B* section contains a prominent ostinato. Its ghostly vestige returns in the coda, but now in conjunction with the *A* theme rather than the *B*. The unusual mixture of timbres, tonalities, rhythms, and themes in this coda produces one of the most memorable passages in all music.

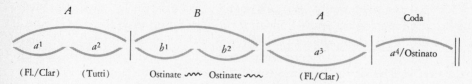

Example 33.4 Mapping of the third movement

Movement IV:
Schnelle viertel
("In fast quarters")

The fourth movement is less a *movement* than a punctuative exclamation. Its function within the whole work is much that of a seventh-inning stretch, when each player clears the lungs for a final go. And its form is best described as "five players in search of a cadenza!" Sandwiched between six soundings of the same mock-ferocious rhythm, each horn takes its turn at the brief glory of a ritualistic ruffle. It all ends without seeming to have accomplished very much—except for that refreshing "clearing of the tubes" before the finale, which follows without pause.

Movement V:
Sehr lebhaft
("very lively")

This is a driving finale in which rhythm is the dominant force. Pounding, even rhythms alternate with wily syncopations whose irregularity wrench the listener's perspective, creating momentary losses of the beat. The movement is shaped by five large sections of contrasting textures, rhythms, and melodies. The strongest contrast occurs when rhythmic density reduces, the texture quiets, and a comparatively lyrical melody enters. This forms the beginning of what we show as section *C* in our mapping.

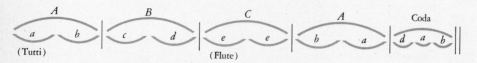

Example 33.5 Overall form of Movement V

The now-familiar synthesis of themes occurs in this movement too. Themes *d*, *a*, and *b* form the coda in that order. It is interesting that in the return of section *A* the order of themes *a b* is reversed to *b a*. This simple change diminishes the predictability of events. In a form consisting of several short themes, predictability can be annoying.

The flowing harmony of Hindemith's music is more a product of melodic than of chordal planning. That is, harmonies frequently result from the way individual parts move in their respective melodic paths. Examples of this kind of *linear harmony* can be found throughout the *Kleine Kammermusik*. A simple instance occurs at the beginning of this fifth movement, where the texture divides into top and bottom layers whose paths move in opposite directions. Notice the smooth rise and fall in harmonic density this passage yields, as depicted by the numbers below each resultant chord.

Example 33.6   Linear harmony in the fifth movement

The rhythmic disjointedness of many passages in this movement gives a frantic nervousness to the proceedings. The second theme (*b*) illustrates the typical way syncopation occurs here, the two layers of its texture projecting contradictory accents within the phrase, then coming together at the end. The segment shown in Example 33.7 is the beginning of theme *b*. Brackets have been added to show how accents in the upper part fall just after those of the lower part.

Example 33.7   Conflicting accents between parts in theme *b*

A large-scale element of unity is suggested in this movement in the way the separate sections do or do not contain prolonged syncopations of this kind. It is worth noting that themes *a*, *d*, and *e* are rhythmically straightforward, while themes *b* and *c* clearly display this rhythmic shiftiness.

34

ENCOUNTERS IV

William Kraft (1923–––)

BACKGROUND

Within this century—and especially during the past fifteen years—chamber music has evolved from a collection of set forms and relatively fixed ensembles into a wide open range of musical types. The main tradition consisted of sonatas, quintets, quartets and trios, solo songs, and the variety of solo works like preludes and fugues composers had produced since the middle of the seventeenth century. Recent chamber music boasts an unprecedented array of forms and instrumental combinations. It even embraces works "composed" directly on magnetic tape (and thus "tape" or "electronic" music) that demands no live players for its reproduction.

The impact of tape music was great during its early years of development, particularly during the decade of the sixties in this country. For listeners its first flush of success was soon tempered by its most awesome shortcoming: the absence of a much desired sense of "human presence." Audiences found loudspeakers less than captivating as the sole sources of musical sounds. In spite of our universal use of and delight in recorded music, we seem to prefer musical emanations from human action rather than from purely mechanical oscillations. Many composers have met this challenge with a healthy compromise: the artful blending of human performers with taped sounds.

Illustration 34.1
William Kraft

Encounters V is just one example of how the two can be mixed effectively. In its second movement, the sounds of a prerecorded tape are coordinated with the playing of two performers. Since the tape's sounds are those of human production—speech and music—this is not an example of "pure" electronic music*. For the performer and listener, however, its function is the same; the two elements, live and prerecorded, are treated as integral elements of the single composition. The tape's sounds become, as it were, a "canned" part of the composition's performance.

THE COMPOSER

We mentioned the high artistic esteem enjoyed today by percussion when we discussed Erb's *Concerto for Solo Percussionist and Orchestra* (Chapter 28). William Kraft is palpable evidence of this high status, for he is a percussionist as well as a composer. Rummaging back through the history of Western music, you will find no other composer of public acclaim whose personal music-making was done on drums. Most composers of the past have played piano. The composer-percussionist combination could have happened only in the twentieth century.

Kraft is principal percussionist and tympanist with the Los Angeles Philharmonic Orchestra. He is also a teacher and a conductor, at one time holding the title of Assistant Conductor with the Los Angeles orchestra.

---

*The sounds of "pure" electronic music are produced wholly by sound generators whose basic operations are like those of an electronic organ. Tapes whose sounds are from nature (animate or inanimate) are usually called *musique concrète*.

That he is a composer of merit is attested by performances and recordings of his music by major symphony orchestras and chamber groups throughout the world.

Born in Chicago in 1923, Kraft is one of several contemporary composer-performers who have elevated drums, gongs, bells, xylophones, and all manner of beaten instruments to the position of eloquence they hold in the art music of today.* He also is one who has infused much of his music with direct commentaries on the world about him. One of his large works for orchestra, *Contextures: Riots—Decade '60*, is an elaborate musical reflection upon the racial strife of that troubled decade. And while the obvious "meaning" of *Encounters IV* is a musical encounter between two performers, at another level it suggests a conflict between the human longing for peace and the world reality of war.

ENCOUNTERS IV

The Three
Movements

The programmatic content of this work—its second level of meaning—is made more apparent than in most program music of the past. This is possible because the taped sounds of the second movement provide for the listener definite associations with nonmusical ideas. As with other program music, however, its more "musical" references to the conflicts of man are less readily detected unless the listener has been primed with some necessary bits of information.

The first movement, entitled "Strategy," begins with the muted trombone playing an awesome rhythm, which in telegraphic code means "Make war to make peace." The meaning of this passage goes undeciphered, of course, for those who do not know Morse code. But the format of the work as a whole capitalizes on the dramatic plot of one sound force (trombone) pitted against another (the percussion). In the first movement, for instance, twelve "attacks" by trombone are met by twelve "counterattacks" from the percussion.

The second movement, which we shall discuss in detail presently, is called "Truce of God." Its title alludes to the peace of the Sabbath, or, more generally, any respite from man's deadly inhumanity to man.

The third movement is called "Tactics." It provides an appropriate musical finale through a virtuoso "all-out war" between the two instrumental protagonists. It is a mounting fury of sounds, a rich lexicon of playing techniques for modern trombone and percussion. The movement's final sounds subside with a return to the kinds of rhythmic code that began its first movement.

------

*Most notable of those composers who have made percussion a leading force in music is another American, Harry Partch.

Encounters IV thus shares with many recent chamber works a distinct element of drama. Like George Crumb's *Ancient Voices of Children*, its musical scenario suggests simple stage actions that correspond with its extra-musical intent. In this respect it departs drastically from the "absolute music" of the traditional chamber concert, in which any suggestion of histrionics would be viewed as irrelevant (if not downright boorish!). Unfortunately, these suggestions of drama are less vivid on recordings than in live performance.

Our discussion will focus on the second of the three movements.

Movement II: "Truce of God"

As we suggested earlier, the listener is confronted with two psychological planes in this haunting movement. We might refer to them as two "historical times," for the live performers represent the immediacy of *now*, while the tape's sounds project an aura of the past, as it hovers about any present time. Even the trombone's erratic melody is derived, almost note-by-note, from a Catholic song of the thirteenth century. And so the attentive listener is enveloped in a curious blending of past and present, borrowed and new.

Since the taped sounds may pique your curiosity most, we shall discuss them first.* They form a hovering presence, a clawing background to remind us, ever so faintly, of the past "glories" of war. This collage of reminiscences in sound begins with the distant strains of patriotic songs from World War I.

The utter silliness of such lyrics as "You're one of Uncle Sammy's boys, you have no use for any noise" conveys an immediate image. Like a faded photograph in an old album, it whisks us into another time-plane that is separate from but runs parallel with the present. The series of images is consistent. Bits of songs, speeches, and military marches float up through the foreground sounds like phantoms of an unconscious past, their power to stir patriotic fervor in our breasts long since withered away. It is a compelling blending of emotions in sound.

The leading melodic role is the trombone's. It plays a grotesque adaptation of the medieval song *Beata viscera* ("Blessed Child"), which was originally composed by the French composer Perotin (1160–1220). The text of this Latin hymn celebrates the birth of Christ as mediator between God and man, one of its lines reminding us that Christ's coming pronounced "the peace of God and man." (*Dictavit federa Dei et hominis.*) Its first melodic phrase is shown in Example 34.1a. The *b* portion of the example reveals how the composer derived the new melody from the notes of the old.

---

*The prerecorded tape for this movement was executed by William Malloch.

Example 34.1

a. First phrase of *Beata viscera*, Perotin

Be - a - ta vi - sce - ra Ma - ri_____ e Vir - gi - - nis,

b. Wm. Kraft's derivation of the trombone part

(+ = tones stopped with a plunger;
o = unstopped)

Note exactly how the composer has molded a drastically new melodic line from his Gothic model. The relatively smooth pattern of the original is overhauled by displacing successive notes far above or below their original locations in pitch space. And utilizing the ultimate techniques of the virtuoso trombone player, Kraft has created a disturbingly angular statement from his ancient model.

Even the listener who knows the tune of *Beata viscera* would find it difficult to recognize the parentage of Kraft's trombone part. Aside from the pitch displacements, the new melody makes uncommon demands on the most agile player, covering excessively low and high pitches in rapid succession, and at times calling for trills, flutterings, tones stopped with a plunger, and machinegun bursts that demand precise control.

Even the forces of the modern percussion battery are enlarged for this evocation of a mock peace. The movement opens with the bell-like sounds of steel mixing bowls. The player uses, in addition to these common kitchen wares, a collection of drums, gongs, vibraphone, and drum-rims to achieve the gamut of events, from tranquil to shattering, that interweave the trombone's gospel of peace.

The wealth of sounds heard here causes one to pause, to wonder why the world of music took so long to rediscover the splendor of percussion as an expressive vehicle. Here its interjections weave a sound-world of foreboding, reminding us, along with the tape's images, of the inherent futility of the trombone's message of hope.

The liberation of percussion, as an independent musical force, awaited the 20th century. The emergence of women as virtuoso performers has developed within the same period. Karen Ervin, for whom William Kraft composed *Encounters IV*, is one of the most capable percussionists of today. Photo by Marcia Lowery

PART VI

JAZZ

INTRODUCTION

The simple word *jazz* covers a lot of time and space. Because it embodies so many features, defining it is less easy than listing some of its more obvious ingredients. The closer one comes to a tight dictionary-style definition, the greater the risk of missing some kinds of music properly identified as "jazz". We might again repeat Louis Armstrong's reply to the lady who asked "What is jazz?" ". . . if you gotta ask, there ain't no" use in me tellin' you!"

Its characteristics are not vague. It is music in which percussive rhythm is especially prominent, usually with a powerful sense of pulse and meter. It is wholly or partially improvised music, and thus music in which performance and composition are fused in a single creative act. And last, it is music of unique timbres, for it has traditionally shunned the string instruments of art music in favor of trumpets, trombones, saxophones, and drums.

The remote African roots of jazz are perhaps most clearly reflected in its fundamental dependence on this latter family of soundmakers. With rare exceptions, jazz does not occur without a thudding bass drum, a jangling cymbal, and the "cha-booms" of small drums, not to mention the myriad of other unique sounds available from the jazz drummer's battery of hardware. Beyond these basic dimensions we'd best not venture; listening to the real thing can fill in the gaps.

ORIGINS AMONG AMERICA'S BLACKS

As a distinguishable musical type, jazz first developed among America's blacks during the late nineteenth and early twentieth centuries. The very denial to them, an oppressed people, of participation in America's mainstream provided the motivation for a unique culture. Jazz was the vibrant musical manifestation of this uniqueness.

Work songs of the Southern cotton fields, individualized improvisations of the white man's tunes, impassioned hymns crying for passage to "the promised land," and soulful laments of frustration in living were the early outcroppings. All were forms of spontaneous cathartic expression through song.

Early jazz was a folk music of singular ethnic stamp and economic class, and therein lay its vigor and considerable staying power. As early as 1903 the Negro leader W.E.B. Dubois recognized the primacy of the black musical gift to the world. As he put it, ". . . the human spirit in this new world has expressed itself in vigor and ingenuity rather than in beauty. And so by fateful chance the Negro folk-song—the rhythmic cry of the slave—stands today not simply as the sole American music, but as the most beautiful expression of human experience, born this side of the seas."*

The very origins of the word *jazz* have been disputed since the music itself became recognized as worthy of consideration. One of the most probable explanations was provided by the enormously talented black conductor James Reese Europe (1881–1919). In the *Literary Digest* of 1919 Mr. Europe explained the word as a corruption of the name of a prominent musician, a Mr. Razz, who led a four-piece band in New Orleans around 1905. According to this theory, word-of-mouth transmission caused Razz's Band to become Jazz's Band, and eventually evolved the general noun, *jazz*.

---

*From *The Souls of Black Folk*, Chicago: A. C. McClure & Co., 1903, page 251.

Joe "King" Oliver was Armstrong's first mentor. This early photo of Oliver's band suggests a more formal scene than prevailed at a typical Southland jazz gathering. The performers "Baby" Dodds (drums), Bill Johnson (trombone), Armstrong (cornet), Oliver (cornet), Honore Dutrey (banjo), and Lil Hardin (piano).

SEPARATION OF JAZZ AND ART MUSIC STYLES

From the time it was first recognized in America as a distinct kind of music, jazz has existed in a two-class world. For those who mold public opinion and taste, it has been a second-class citizen, following the more prestigious lead of transplanted "classical" music. Although social attitudes have contributed to this inglorious state, there also have been quite formidable technical reasons.

The musician trained in the art traditions of Bach, Beethoven, and Chopin has found it difficult—if not downright impossible—to improvise in the manner demanded in jazz. The classical musician makes music by reading musical notation; improvising patterns from sketchy resources is the direct antithesis of anything the "educated musician" learns in his training. "Playing well," to an Isaac Stern or Vladimir Horowitz, means playing somebody else's notes.

Aside from actual notes, even the phrasing of the two kinds of music form an obstacle to easy movement from one style to the other. The performance of art music is formal, exacting, and precise; jazz is informal, spontaneous, and at times refreshingly blasé about a few missed notes. The discipline of the one is based on rigorous adherence to externally imposed standards; the other accepts the changing norms of its most revered practitioners. And thus most symphonic musicians have sounded like ducks out of water, jazz musicians like chickens out to sea, when each tried to play the other's music.

In the public mind a subtler but perhaps more imposing barrier has separated the two styles. The "classical" style has the grandeur of two centuries of west European culture behind it, much of this from the patronage of royalty. Jazz, on the other hand, is well-known as the product of New Orleans bordellos, street parades of rag-tag amateurs, and speak-easies reeking of bootleg gin. Lacking musical judgment by which to appraise quality, many people have adopted the questionable criterion of "social value," dismissing jazz as mere peasant entertainment.

The history of jazz can be divided into about as many separate strands as there are jazz performers. Since it is by definition an outpouring of the individual's very being, there are as many styles as there are individual creators. For our purposes we shall divide its history of some seventy-five years into four main periods, each of which can be represented by musicians who were prominent artists within that time period and general stylistic persuasion.

35

EARLY JAZZ:
THE BLUES OF BESSIE SMITH
AND LOUIS ARMSTRONG

BACKGROUND: THE BLUES

Origins

The root system for the elaborate tree of jazz lies in the blues. We have discussed one aspect of the blues—its harmonic basis—in Chapter 5. But defining a music only by its harmonies is like describing a beautiful woman by the length of her spine. The nature of the blues runs far deeper than a mere succession of chords can describe.

It is a literary form of three verses (*A A B*) and a rhythmic pattern of three phrases of four-beat meter. But most of all it is a poignant expression of human feeling. Each of these characteristics alone is a necessary but by no means sufficient basis for coming to grips with the real thing. Probably Duke Ellington came closest, in his colorfully poetic way, in a line from the blues-based movement of his *Black, Brown and Beige Suite*: "The blues ain't nothin' but a dark cloud markin' time."

As a vocal expression, blues is strongly autobiographical and suggests an unhappy background. The great blues singer of the 1930s, Jimmy Rushing, tied the prevailing sentiment of the blues to poverty. "The blues," Rushing claimed, "came out of the spirituals, the he-and-she songs, the work songs—all of it. Rich people don't know nothin' about the blues, please believe me."

The subject matter of blues texts is as varied as the troubles of mankind—religion, sex, marital strife, superstition, death, disease, guilt, hunger, crime, racial segregation, bad weather, joblessness, gambling and, on occasion, brief respite from a heavily-burdened life.

The geographical seat of early blues was the South—Louisiana, Texas, Mississippi—with a marginal spread into lower regions of the Midwest. Around the turn of the century its specialists developed a spontaneous musical expression from the country song styles of that part of the land. These blues artists went under the colorful names of Lemon Jefferson, Bumble Bee Slim, Memphis Minnie, Leadbelly, and Big Bill Broonzy. All of them were musically illiterate by academic standards.

The blues as song was immediately absorbed by early "hot" performers who played the clarinet, banjo, trombone, saxophone, trumpet, or piano. It is said that the great cornet player Bunk Johnson *played* the blues at Economy Hall in New Orleans as early as 1911. It is a matter of record that the Original Dixieland Jazz Band recorded such works as *Livery Stable Blues, Barnyard Blues,* and *Mournin' Blues* in sessions of 1917–18. Certainly the blues today is known as much as a purely instrumental music as a vocal form.

Early Blues Singers

The earliest blues singers are known only by their reputations. The record industry was not available in 1905 to preserve their earthy efforts for posterity. The great Leadbelly was recorded only after his prime, through the considerable efforts of the musicologist John Lomax. (Some of the Lomax recordings were made in the jail cell where the singer was serving a sentence for murder.) The first blues singer who produced commercial recordings was Mamie Smith, who cut a first disk for Okeh Records on February 14, 1920. Her second effort, called *Crazy Blues*, stirred black America to the beat of this unique American music, creating a market that did not subside for a full decade.

Female singers, like Mamie Smith, first established blues as a popular commodity. Mamie's successes were followed by Ma Rainey, whose fame covered the pre-Depression years of 1923–29. During that era Ma recorded over one hundred disks (which in that day bore only two songs). Her name and her particular brand of the blues were household fare throughout the black ghettos of the United States and the intellectual ghettos of western Europe. It is a sad commentary on racial discrimination and the economics of music that she died in obscurity in Georgia in 1939.

Although a younger woman, Bessie Smith was a third *prima donna* of the blues. Her rich years coincided with those of her mentor and model, Ma Rainey. (She was not related to Mamie Smith.) At the time of Bessie's advent into the world of recordings, her male counterpart, Louis Armstrong, was singing the blues and playing cornet with King Oliver's Creole Jazz Band. From 1923 Oliver's output of such recorded classics as *Riverside Blues, Canal Street Blues,* and *Dipper-mouth Blues* (later called *Sugarfoot Stomp*) set the pace for the public view of jazz music in the world at large.

One man closely associated with early blues—even called "Father of the Blues"—was William Christopher Handy (1873–1958). Handy's name was spread over the world with his two songs *The Memphis Blues* and the *St. Louis Blues*. The sheet music publication of the first in 1909 and the second in 1914 marked the first of several events that led to the popularity of this three-line soul music of the honky-tonk singer. Handy captured in these two songs the subdued longing expressed in songs he had heard from the streets and bawdyhouses and cotton fields of the South, a spirit he described as a "joyousness calculated to drown out underlying apprehension."

Later Development of Blues

The early 1930s witnessed a synthesis that fed new vigor into the mainstream of the blues. The small instrumental combinations, or "combos," typical of the early hot bands began at this time to grow, eventually to become relatively sophisticated collections of fourteen to twenty instrumentalists. The enlarged ensembles of Bennie Moten (Kansas City Orchestra), Count Basie, Fletcher Henderson, Duke Ellington, and Benny Goodman developed a more polished version of jazz called *swing*.

This slightly tamed version of hot music was, according to W. C. Handy, "Just a dressing up of jazz." But its cross-fertilization with the gutsy pathos of blues insured its substantial musical base. The great Jimmy Rushing's recordings with the Count Basie band in the mid-thirties presented the twelve-bar blues in new settings of resonant saxophones, crisp, punching brass, and driving rhythm section. These eclipsed the less fussily orchestrated backdrops of the past. The blues had come a long way from the dance halls and street parades of New Orleans.

As a form and style the blues persists. Since its rise to respectability some forty years ago, we could hear some version of it somewhere in any large city of the world, at least once during any day of the year, even in Tokyo and Bombay.

There have been white singers capable of convincing authenticity in singing and playing the blues, in spite of the subtle shadings derived from its black origins. An old-line jazz trombonist of the swing era, Jack Teagarden, managed a reasonable facsimile with his husky Texas drawl; Woody Herman, who rose to prominence in the "Big Band Era" of the 1940s, worked with his own "band that plays the blues;" and more recently the hoarse holler of the late Janis Joplin frequently achieved the soulful torment of which the blues so eloquently speaks. These exceptions noted, however, its innovators and masters—past and present—are black.

BESSIE SMITH (1897–1937)

Although Gertrude "Ma" Rainey was the pioneer of the female blues singers, it was her protégée Bessie Smith who first reached fame as a

Illustration 35.1
Bessie Smith

recording artist. Bessie was discovered by the older singer in her hometown of Chattanooga, Tennessee around 1909. From that time until
around 1919, when they parted (on less than friendly terms), the young
singer toured with the minstrel troupe that billed Ma as "the Mother of the
Blues." Their breach of friendship was never repaired. In later years
Bessie even ignored the professional and artistic credit due her early tutor
by claiming W.C. Handy as her original inspiration.

Bessie's first recordings were made in New York in the 1920s. One of these, *Down-Hearted Blues*, sold over 780,000 copies, testifying to the near-fanatic response her voice commanded. Although known as "Empress of the Blues," Bessie Smith did not confine her singing to just that form. Her public and recorded performances were laced with the popular tunes of her day as well. Her style was more citified, less the country blues of Ma Rainey. The jazz climate was ripe for this more urbane version of the Southland's music. Her records reinforced her box office appeal and the result was sensational.

According to all reports, a public performance by Bessie Smith was a volcanic ritual. Carl Van Vechten, who saw her sing in 1925, tells us that "She began her strange, rhythmic rites in a voice full of shouting and moaning and praying and suffering, a wild, rough, Ethiopian voice."

But public idolatry gradually turned to apathy, and the "rites" became a hollow sham. Bessie's personal life deteriorated into a wasteland of hard drinking, squandered money, and emotional tantrums. She faced, as all public entertainers eventually must, the decline of her popularity. With the emergence in the early 1930s of the less earthy swing style, even the acceptance of her style of singing waned. She died in Mississippi in 1937, the victim of a flaming automobile crash, bequeathing to a disinterested world her monument of over one hundred and eighty interpretations of the songs of her era.

The Midnight Blues (1923)

Midnight Blues is a relatively straight blues of the twelve-bar plan we discussed in Chapter 5. One discrepancy between it and the model occurs in the last two of the four verses of the song: unlike the first two verses, they do not conform exactly to the text plan of *A A B* that is most common.

Fletcher Henderson is the pianist who accompanies Bessie in this recording. His name will emerge later in our discussion of the early swing era. The contribution he makes in *Midnight Blues* is crucial, especially the mood-setting he provides the singer with the brief introduction. This is a pianistic imitation of tolling bells, an attempt to musically preview the gist of the text that follows, whose principal topic is the hasty departure of an errant lover. As Bessie tells it in the second verse, "You left me at midnight; clock was striking twelve." And thus the *midnight* blues and the "tolling" of Henderson's piano.

Henderson's accompaniment also illustrates the basic "stride" style of practically every jazz pianist of the period 1920–45. Listen carefully to the texture. Its lefthand part (lowest pitches) sets the plodding beat, the right hand sounding block chords and, on occasion, patches of melody. The style is much the same as Frédéric Chopin's, the left hand providing a bass on strong beats of the meter, chords on weak, as an accompaniment to melody. The result is a flow tightly channeled within four clear beats, each pulse articulated, but the first and the third slightly more pronounced. This overall "two-beat" pattern within a "four-beat" meter persisted in jazz well into the swing era. Example 35.1 shows a representative sample of the style.

Example 35.1 Typical texture of early jazz piano style

The Bessie Smith Style

Hearing Bessie Smith for the first time, you might well wonder, "Why all the fuss? What distinguishes her singing from that of any other folk or pop singer?" Anticipating such questions, let us note a few distinct qualities that justify her lingering fame.

First is the almost male resonance of her voice. Only the vibrato, rapid but uniform, suggests its female source. It is a strong voice, and there is nothing tentative in its enunciation of the bitterness felt about a broken trust. From the initial "Daddy, Daddy! Please come back to me!" there is no question that her message carries total conviction. This is not the crooning of a pop singer or the show biz delivery of a Broadway star. It is real. If we could hear Bessie's tones without the words they would sound like a trumpet, and this is one main characteristic of the early jazz singer's sound: the ideal is instrumental rather than the operatic "pear-shaped" tone.

Another facet of Bessie's style is the emotion projected by her slides between pitches, a suggestion of wailing that underscores the plaintive resignation felt about a lost love. Although she hits pitches head-on when she wishes, there are frequent slides* such as occur on the last "Daddy" of each of the first lines of text. These are by no means products of technical imprecision. They are a direct result of the singer's intent to project an emotional state suggested by the words.

After all, the story is a grim one. The subject's lover has fled at midnight without warning, an unconscionable departure. The song implies

---

*The musical term for such slides is *portamento*.

that this is a troubled reminiscence of the actual event, a product of that mental state that occurs only in the solitude of late night, "the meanest" of all blues, the "midnight blues."

And last, the keening quality is advanced by a waxing and waning, a lazy kind of rhythm. There are subtle anticipations of beats—the tone starting *before* the beat warrants it—and the extension of syllables or whole words past where they "should" end. Combined, these anticipations and prolongations suggest the natural speech patterns of an emotional statement. Together with the strategically placed pitch slides, this rhythmic freedom completes a picture of the pining lover who has been unceremoniously rejected. They create that "dark cloud markin' time" Duke Ellington defined as the real blues, the melodic speech that makes the blues more than just another song.

LOUIS ARMSTRONG (1900–1973)

Ask any jazz buff to name one person who can best represent the whole of jazz. The most likely reply will be "Louis Armstrong." The main reason for this one man's power of representation was his endurance as a superb jazz singer and trumpet player, but he also possessed one of the most captivating personalities ever associated with art or entertainment. He was a throbbing dynamo who could express the bitter messages of life in music without the slightest suggestion of insincere melodrama. His growling voice and playful trumpet were merely separate manifestations of the same love of life.

Louis's music does not suggest the pathos of Bessie Smith's. His style removes the blues one step from personal feeling, rendering it a set of emotions for detached comment. His is the blues of Southland reminiscence rather than the direct blues of human misery. The value of his music derives from creative and technical competence as well as from the projection of deep feeling. *Satchmo*, as intimates called him (in honor of his enormous "satchel-mouth"), felt deeply. But his music reflected an inborn joviality, a sieve of optimism through which his every comment was strained. And thus he achieved the beautiful paradox of jazz, which Martin Williams has identified as "a paradox wherein joy and anguish may be momentarily resolved."

Armstrong's Early
Career

Armstrong was born in the black ghetto of New Orleans. Although his scant formal music training did not occur until he was thirteen, musical creativity came with his first pair of shoes. As a street urchin, he picked up change by singing and dancing impromptu "concerts" on the streets of the famed Storyville district. A playful but illegal celebration with a gun on New Year's Eve of 1913 led him to become a ward of the Colored Waifs Home. It turned out to be one of the luckiest bangs in music his-

Illustration 35.2
Louis Armstrong

tory; the Director of the Waifs Home band, Peter Davies, subsequently taught Louis the rudiments of cornet playing.

His first real job as a musician was with a famed hometown group, Kid Ory's Brownskin Band. Even then he could not read music; that bit of technical finesse had to await his joining the band of the legendary Fate Marable, a group that played a more elegant kind of jazz than Ory's band. By 1921 Louis's success was relatively secure when the great King Oliver, then the cornet virtuoso of jazz, called him to play second cornet with his band in Chicago. By 1925 he was testing his powers in New York with the band of Fletcher Henderson and making his first recordings with the Clarence Williams band.

A seasoned performer, Louis returned to Chicago in 1925, now to lead his own band. This would be a precedent for every band formed later during the Big Band Era; most were organized expressly as background for a leader featured as jazz soloist. In spite of his association with larger bands from that year until his death, Louis's original love for jamming with the smaller New Orleans-style groups brought him back to that format repeatedly. In these combos emphasis was on the individual and group improvisation, processes too readily lost in the arranged music of the larger bands.

Armstrong sang and played and clowned from his earliest days of public exposure. In 1926 he switched from the mellow-toned cornet to the brassier sound of the trumpet, an act that was prophetic for the swing era, when the trumpet almost totally replaced its predecessor of New Orleans fame. He even invented—or so it appears—a style of singing, called *scat singing*, that further tied the vocal and instrumental sounds of jazz together. His first recorded example in that style was in a song called *Heebie Jeebies*, which he cut in 1925 along with *Gut Bucket Blues*.

This new way of singing consisted of improvising words as well as music. It led to the singing styles of some of the prominent figures of later times like Cab Calloway, Ella Fitzgerald, and Dizzy Gillespie. The scat song symbolized the acceptance of the human voice as a genuine musical instrument rather than a mere purveyor of words. It became an instrument through which jazz improvisation was as possible as with a trumpet or saxophone.

Louis Armstrong was a musical hero to the black population of America after 1925. It is an interesting peripheral fact that critical acclaim from the larger musical world came first from Europe, before his music was recognized by the white press of the United States as more than indelicate showmanship. His many tours of western Europe and Scandinavia prior to World War II established his name in those parts as a veritable synonym of American music.

Gut Bucket Blues (1925)

Louis doesn't sing in *Gut Bucket Blues*, but he does engage in some of his famous background patter. These introductory monologues provide insight into his jocular style and reveal the raspy sound of his incomparable voice. But his playing (here on cornet) is paramount in the three ensemble sections as well as in his single twelve-bar solo. Aside from the blues form and the basic New Orleans style, his playing is the cement that holds the piece together.

A mapping of the work makes clear its hybrid (strophic and return) basis, solo improvisations forming a center framed by the Dixieland-style tutti sections (where everybody goes at once).

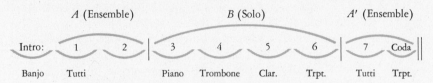

Example 35.2 Mapping of overall form, *Gut Bucket Blues*

The instrumentation of this piece is memorable in several respects. It lacks the usual bass (sometimes tuba in the early years of jazz) and it lacks drums. The rhythm section consists of only banjo and piano. Otherwise, the trio of lead instruments (trombone, clarinet, and trumpet) is typical of New Orleans bands. The personnel is especially noteworthy, harboring a veritable Hall of Fame of early jazz. There are Edward "Kid" Ory (trombone), Johnny Dodds (clarinet), Johnny St. Cyr (banjo), and Lillian "Lil" Hardin (at that time Armstrong's wife) on piano. Armstrong introduces the musicians as they play their respective solos, from "Aw play that thing, Mr. St. Cyr. Lawd!" to "Blow that thing, Mr. Johnny Dodds!"

The texture of ensemble sections is worth special attention. In its orthodox New Orleans way, it is an interesting polyphony. In these sections the trumpet leads while the clarinet provides high-register melodic elaborations. The trombone adds a less active background pattern that is semiaccompanimental. Its lower part emphasizes the first beat of each measure, reinforcing the meter stroked by banjo and piano. This lower and less "melodic" kind of trombone part, occasionally graced with raucous slides, was dubbed "tailgate trombone" in early New Orleans days. When some of the early jazz groups played parades from the beds of wagons, the trombonist usually assumed a position at the rear, or "tailgate," to accommodate the extensions of his horn's long slide when playing its lowest notes.

In the final ensemble section, trumpet and trombone play a "riff duet" behind the clarinet's free improvisations. Unlike the two earlier tutti sections, simultaneous improvisations of all members, typical of New Orleans style, do not occur here. The play of clarinet against the trumpet-trombone coupling maintains a unique kind of counterpoint, nonetheless. At times the clarinet appears to be sounding *almost* the same line as the trumpet, creating a heterophonic texture similar to that heard in the ensembles of Japanese traditional music.*

The final solo Armstrong plays in the short coda is the kind of "stop-break" passage he pioneered. This brief example of an unaccompanied

---

*See the discussion of heterophony in Chapter 6 and the discussion of Japanese traditional music in Chapter 39.

solo, where rhythm instruments stop and the soloist soars away on his own, can be found throughout the repertory of jazz. It occurs frequently in the interior phrases of Armstrong's music, providing a fascinating contrast of texture as well as a chance to reveal Armstrong's superior jazz instincts and playing.

36

ENSEMBLE JAZZ:
THE SWINGING
OF DUKE ELLINGTON
AND BENNY GOODMAN

BACKGROUND

Shifts in musical styles are not legislated, and thus they occur rather haphazardly. There are several ways to distinguish the jazz of 1925 from that of 1935, but the most obvious change to note is a somewhat general one: the latter was more carefully planned and more fastidiously executed, and it usually was played by a larger ensemble.

The causes of greater sophistication and precision of this later jazz are not difficult to find. Jazz had become a marketable commodity in the larger cities of the United States. It therefore drew to its fold musicians of greater skill than the untutored singers and players who originated it. Clubs in Chicago, Cleveland, New York, Pittsburgh, Kansas City, Washington, D.C., and Atlantic City catered to a population who found jazz an exhilarating change from the Strauss waltzes and Victor Herbert medleys that had graced the dance salons of times past.

The prohibition days of 1920–23 seem to have whetted the appetites of the American night club set for hot music as much as for bootleg liquor; certainly jazz and jazz musicians flourished, once the smoke of economic disaster had partially cleared after the opening days of the Great Depression. In fact, for many years afterwards, the serious jazz player had to live down an unfortunate equation many people held between his art and bathtub gin.

Illustration 36.1 The big bands of the 30s and 40s at times projected a gaudy show-biz image as much as they sustained the growth of real jazz. Note the leopard skin stands used by the musicians in the photo of Benny Goodman's orchestra of 1944, just at the twilight of the big band era.

By 1922 New York had felt the impact of blues-inspired music of the Southland, as it was imported via Chicago. From this time on, lower Manhattan and Harlem gathered momentum as jazz centers of the country. The "ricky-tick" music some of the New York bands had cultivated in speakeasies and review clubs began a slow metamorphosis as soon as performers closest to jazz roots infiltrated New York in the mid-twenties.

Louis Armstrong arrived by way of Chicago to inject a dose of Delta-land jazz in recordings made by the Clarence Williams band. Jack Teagarden moved there a few years later from Texas, with his trombone and vocal expertise with the blues. Duke Ellington, playing New York since 1922, hired veterans from New Orleans in 1926. With these and similar additions to the local scene, the free-for-all spirit of the New Orleans style, the form and pathos of the blues, and the careful orchestrations of trained musicians merged. They produced an approach that persisted well into the 1940s.

At first the financial depression of 1929 almost wiped out the jobs these musicians depended upon for sustenance. But the fresh vitality of a new style rapidly won an audience, in spite of economic bad times. By the time the song "Happy Days are Here Again" was more than a hopeful political slogan, jazz was solidly entrenched as *the American Music.*

The Taming of Jazz

Duke Ellington was only one of many who contributed to the jazz amalgam of the 1930's called *swing*; there were scores of white and black instrumentalists and singers who singly and collectively added their unique touches. Brilliant composer-arrangers Don Redman, Fletcher Henderson, and Benny Carter were critical members of the cast. Their compositions, along with Ellington's, set the pace for this more tightly reined, carefully plotted jazz. It was during this period that the "arrangement" (which means merely the written-out, as opposed to improvised, aspects of the music) established itself as the basis of the jazz repertory. In this alone is evidence of the growing bulk, precision, and complexity of the jazz sound.

Big Band Era

By the time the United States entered World War II (December of 1941), no metropolitan area of the country lacked a spacious ballroom where the the "Big Bands" played. The reference here is not to the military-type bands that had graced the town squares of America earlier with Sousa marches and von-Suppé overtures. "Big Bands" in this case refers to the swing bands of Tommy Dorsey, Bunny Berrigan, Benny Goodman, Count Basie, Glen Miller, Duke Ellington, Artie Shaw, Stan Kenton, Charlie Barnet, Woody Herman, Gus Arnheim, Jimmie Lunceford, Cab Calloway, Clyde McCoy, Ben Pollack, Harry James—a representative listing would fill pages.*

These traveling jazz outfits were relatively uniform in instrumentation and musical style, yet each fiercely cultivated some distinctive trait as its identifying feature for the listening public. The identifying sound most frequently originated with the leader, who "fronted" his band as featured soloist and occasional conductor. Ellington's and Basie's pianos, Berrigan's and James's trumpets, Shaw's and Goodman's clarinets provided just these kinds of idiomatic trademarks.

Most of the ensembles were populated with from thirteen to eighteen performers of the following divisions of labor:

Saxophones (alto, tenor and baritone), 4–5
Trumpets, 3–4
Trombones, 2–3

---

*An entertaining survey of this colorful era, heavily documented with photographs, can be found in Les Walker's *Great Dance Bands* (Berkeley, Calif.: Howell-North Books, 1964).

Rhythm: Piano, bass, drums, and sometimes guitar
Vocalist: male, female, or both. (With more prosperous bands a vocal trio or quartet of mixed voices.)

The music played by these formidable collections of sound-makers was a curious blend of real jazz, improvised within carefully charted scores, and special arrangements of popular songs. This was the day of the "hit song," when announcements of the "most popular song of the week" were awaited in some quarters with as much anxiety as reports of the New York Stock Exchange. The hit song was the popularity base of the big band, a layer of commercialism superimposed on the traditional jazz from which it sprang. The result was the full flowering of swing music.

Thorough coverage of the period would at least recognize the names of its most venerable masters. But our goals lead us to only two musicians. With the hindsight of several decades, they appear to portray the spirit and substance of the dozen years of the most creative and enduring swing music: Duke Ellington and Benny Goodman.

Ellington helped to solidify this second wave of jazz as a pianist, band leader, and composer. Goodman, widely touted as the "King of Swing," was a brilliant clarinet soloist and leader who, unlike many of the jazz musicians of the 1930s, also cultivated the chamber music of classical composers.

HARLEM SPEAKS: THE DUKE ELLINGTON BAND OF 1933

Since jazz is largely an art of improvisation, its singers and instrumentalists play more creative roles than do performers of classical operas or symphonies. The trumpet player in Beethoven's Symphony No. 5 exercises precious little invention when playing his part; playing a solo in an Ellington composition, he would share equal responsibility with the composer for what comes out. So listeners who search for the kinds of thematic exposition and development they can hear in a movement by the great German symphonist search in vain.

And thus improvisation is jazz's most severe limitation, as well as its main source of excitement and surprise. Its dependence on spontaneous creation—as opposed to carefully planned and reworked creation—yields a quite different object for the listener's enjoyment. It also demands a somewhat different creative approach from the composer, who establishes the skeletal outlines of harmony and melody that must channel performers' improvisatory creations.

The composer of jazz is a miniaturist. Much like the great pianist-composer Frédéric Chopin, he founders when confronted with the over-large canvas of the symphony orchestra, with its traditional forms of extended length.

Illustration 36.2
Duke Ellington

Ellington's Career

Duke Ellington (1899–1974) was just this kind of musical miniaturist.*
His total development as a pianist and composer was dominated by the
act of an individual's improvising within the formal and emotional
schemes set by the blues and the popular tunes of the day. (And all of this
had to happen within the three minutes available on one side of the ten-
inch disk recordings that prevailed until the advent of the long-playing
record in the 1950s.)

Ellington's early career included the music lessons and adolescent
dance bands common to most American composers who grew up during
the same era. He was born in the northwest section of Washington,
D.C.—the "colored section," as it was known by whites then—in 1899.

---

*Ellington produced multi-movement jazz works of considerable length, including film
scores, Broadway shows, and background music for plays. These have not been wholly
successful; the composer even removed some to make them unavailable for performance.

His first strong musical enthusiasm was kindled by local ragtime pianists who helped brighten the festive scene of the capital city in the years immediately following World War I. His most potent musical influence was the great rag pianist James P. Johnson, whom he mimicked by using piano rolls on his parents' player piano. He sometimes played these at half speed in order to duplicate exactly the fingering and pedaling of his unseen master.

Duke's first band was a neighborhood ensemble, congregated within walking distance of his home at the True Reformers Hall in 1917. In spite of easy success that came his way from local jobbing with this group, he moved to New York City in 1922 in search of a greater challenge.

In the Prohibition speakeasies, Harlem dance halls, and private parties of the big city Ellington was introduced to the piano styles of the pop artists of the day. His own musical instincts were touched by the delicately rapid runs over the keyboard of Willie the Lion Smith and the aggressive rhythms of Fats Waller. He could have pursued a celebrated career as solo pianist. Instead, he furthered his musical aims as a composer and leader by once again forming his own band, many of its sidemen his youthful friends from the earlier Washington band.

Ellington's initial years as a band leader in New York were beset by the usual problems any organization has when several human beings must work together for a narrow common goal. But the biggest obstacle of the group to commercial success, and one that would remain an obstacle for thirty years, was the racial bias that controlled the music business of Manhattan just as certainly as it controlled the cotton business of Memphis. This bias dictated that Negro bands could not play the most elegant hotels; and wherever they did play, they rarely were granted radio time, which, prior to the advent of television, was the path to public glory in America.

IMPACT OF NEO-AFRICAN MOVEMENT   But one social fashion of the twenties favored Ellington's music and his band. America's search for its own national identity, following the cultural and human carnage of World War I, led to a sudden zealous devotion among white intellectuals for Negroes and black culture. A swelling "neo-African" movement was in the making. There was a sudden consciousness that the hitherto disenfranchised black possessed a potent cultural heritage of his own.

Ellington was touched by this interest in Negro culture in two main ways. Since his band consisted of blacks, it provided a natural basis for commercial exploitation. Of more lasting import, it sparked in the Ellington psyche a keen interest in developing a musical style that could be identified as black in origins. From this time on, we hear from his band the growls of trumpet and trombone, barrages of frenzied drums, and sliding saxophone cries. At the time of their inception these were widely regarded as "echoes of the African jungle." (The average American of 1925 thought that the whole of the African continent was an impenetrable jungle darkness.)

The band made its first recordings in 1926, just six years after Mamie Smith's blues recordings jolted the black ghettos. The titles of some of those early works reflect a consciousness of the black's remote and more recent cultural past. They include *Alabama Bound* (1926), *Song of the Cottonfields* (1927), *Black and Tan Fantasy* (1927), *Jungle Jamboree* (1928), and *Mississippi Moan* (1929).

WEAKENING PREJUDICE TOWARD BLACK MUSICIANS A continuing stream of recordings and public appearances in and around New York soon made black and white America aware of the band and its leader. By 1931 racial bigotry had been overcome to the extent that the group was broadcast from Harlem's Cotton Club, where the band had opened in late 1927.* In spite of the deep economic depression of 1931, the band traveled to the West Coast for public performances and to film a short movie in Hollywood. In 1933 it even shipped off on a tour of England and France; its arrival was announced in one London headline as "Duke Ellington, 'Hot Gospeller' of Crazy Music and Haarlem [sic] Rhythm."

Racial prejudice was not absent in England, yet the band initiated an aroused British public to a kind of music that it found fresh and stimulating, if at times bewilderingly different. Their appearances in Paris brought enthusiasts from all over Europe to behold this exotic music of America's blacks.

Perhaps of even greater sociological impact, the band broke the "color line" of the heavily prejudiced South in the same year. Attendance records were broken at theaters of Dallas and Fort Worth, Texas, where the band played in 1933. The same public acclaim followed them in Louisiana, when the band appeared in New Orleans in 1934. Clearly, America was responding to something this group had to offer, in spite of the frequent disclaimers made by established music critics. (The American critic Paul Rosenfield wrote in 1929 that "Jazz is not music. Jazz remains a striking indigenous product, a small-sounding folk chaos. . . ")

The "Swing" Controversy

By the time the word *swing* entered America's musical vocabulary in the 1930s, Duke Ellington's compositions and band were recognized as established traditions of the national scene. The swing category was itself just a new way of identifying jazz, as it was played by bands larger than the five- to seven-piece ensembles of its New Orleans origins.

---

*Although the entertainers of the Cotton Club were black, it catered to a white patronage.

Ellington objected to the word *swing* used as a noun. He once remarked, with his typical elegance, that "Swing is not a kind of music; it is that part of rhythm that causes a bouncing, buoyant, terpsichorean urge." In other words, for Ellington *swing* was a verb, referring to a kind of musical motion rather than a thing. For his own music he preferred the term "Negro music." If one listens to recordings made during those times by the gargantuan swing orchestras of conductors like Paul Whiteman or Raymond Scott, it is much easier to appreciate Ellington's distinction. In the music of those overinflated ensembles one hears only the polite, insipid imitations of the real thing.

Harlem Speaks

This piece reveals little of the melodic gift of Duke Ellington the composer. It is a "head arrangement," meaning that it consists of a brief introduction, background figures for improvised solos, a basic theme,* directions for the order of soloists, and an ensemble finale. It is the kind of "composition-by-committee" that was so vital to the ensemble jazz of the Big Band Era, composer and soloists acting together as a creative force.

Harlem Speaks was recorded twice during 1933, once in New York and later in London during the band's first tour of England.† It is scored for a fourteen-piece group consisting of four saxophones, three trumpets, three trombones, piano, bass, guitar, and drums. The soloists on both recordings are men who, as much as Ellington, were responsible for the band's fame as a swinging jazz ensemble; with the leader they were the creators of the Ellington style.

The work is shaped by a succession of jazz solos and ensemble figures based on a thirty-two-bar song form. With the twelve-bar blues pattern, this longer form dominated American popular music and jazz for three decades (1920–1950). Its organization is a simple *A A B A* plan, each sub-unit a phrase of eight measures.** *Harlem Speaks* uses the plan as the basis for an overall form of six choruses.

Introduction (four bars)
Chorus 1: Open trumpet solo (Freddie Jenkins);
Chorus 2: Alto saxophone (Johnny Hodges);
Chorus 3: Muted trumpet (Cootie Williams) for the *A A B* parts, the baritone Sax (Harry Carney) on the break and final *A*;

---

*Simple themes of this kind are called *riffs* in the jargon of jazz musicians. A riff also is any figure repeated several times to form a longer passage.

†According to the discography in Barry Ulanov, *Duke Ellington* (New York: Creative Age Press, Inc., 1946).

**The *B* phrase of this form is called *bridge*; it "bridges" the two initial *A* statements with its recurrence at the end.

Chorus 4: Trombone with growl mute ("Tricky Sam" Nanton);

Chorus 5: Sax ensemble for *A A*, then trombone (Lawrence Brown) on *B* and the final *A*;

Chorus 6: Full band (*tutti*) with interpolations by growl trombone (Nanton) and clarinet (Barney Bigard).

This succession of improvised choruses incorporates the same variation principle found in Louis Armstrong's *Gut Bucket Blues*, even to the final "hot" chorus. But in other respects the two compositions are miles apart. The instrumentation of Ellington's piece is much larger and richer, and the scoring ensures precise ensemble playing. Even the background riffs are carefully planned, probably written down, and played with obvious respect for corporate precision.

The soloists in *Harlem Speaks* do not stray far from the simple theme established by the solo trumpet in the first chorus. Here is a good example of the somewhat restrained improvisation that crept into jazz during the Big Band Era. The soloist frequently begins his chorus by playing the first phrase relatively "straight." With the second phrase his version of the theme is freer or completely loses contact with its basic contour and rhythm. (It still corresponds with the established harmony.)

One jazz trait that comes through clearly in this piece is the use of timbre and texture as main agents of formal contrast. Within the strait-jacket of the six-chorus form, each chorus of the same *A A B A* pattern, the danger of monotony is awesome. Yet solo timbres and background textures change in ways that topple this restrictive scheme, particularly in choruses three, five, and six.

The "stop-break" at the end of each *B* phrase, or "bridge," links it with the New Orleans style of Armstrong's *Gut Bucket Blues*. At these points the rhythm stops, the background texture disappears, and the soloist soars for one fleeting moment of musical weightlessness. For the listener of 1933 this brief solo cadenza must have been ultimate proof of the genuine Southland article, *hot jazz*.

The parts played by the rhythm section (piano, drums, guitar, and bass) date this piece as somewhat later than the early Chicago or New Orleans styles. Although the bass frequently plays a two-beat pattern, drums and guitar bear down at the rate of four per bar, thereby creating the more driving pulse that characterizes later swing styles. There is none of the "boom-chick, boom-chick" two-beat sound of the Delta-land blues in this music.

When the Ellington band visited Paris in 1933, the most frequent reaction from French musicians was their astonishment at the band's instrumentation and the exotic sounds coaxed from some of the horns. *Harlem Speaks* manifests some of these sounds, which to an audience almost a half-century later may again sound exotic.

The growling trombone of Joe "Tricky Sam" Nanton dominates choruses four and six. This is one of the "jungle" sounds linked with the Ellington neo-African consciousness of the late 1920s, although it can be heard in some of the earlier recordings of blues singers like Bessie Smith. Since the technique was difficult, it wasn't duplicated often by other trombonists. Adopted by the more agile trumpet players of the band (in later years, Rex Stewart in particular), it was one of those identifying trademarks that made the Ellington sound unique in those glorious days of the American jazz band.*

STOMPIN' AT THE SAVOY: THE BENNY GOODMAN ORCHESTRA (1936)

As we suggested earlier, the Big Band Era sprang from the union of jazz—the improvised hot music of the black South—and the popular song of white Broadway. For some musicians of the decade 1936–1945 the two musical streams joined, producing a genuinely fresh branch of jazz. For others the intermingling was shaky from the beginning, many bands opting for one style in preference to the other. During this period the official news magazine of the American jazz world, *Downbeat*, recognized this stylistic schizophrenia by including two separate categories in its annual "best band" poll: one award was for "swing bands," the other for "sweet bands."

Jazz Versus the Pop Song

Benny Goodman managed to retain enough of the improvisatory approach in his orchestra's repertory to dam the flood of supersentimental ballads that swept the country during the 1930s. This was not an easy line to take. Although jazz was its manna of the day, a band's path to commercial success was paved with the frivolous lyrics and insipid tunes of a thousand pop songs.

The protest song, the revived folk song, and the culture-conscious song of the 1960s were far in the future. The decades of the thirties and forties were laced with the empty-headed musical likes of "I've Got a Date With an Angel," "This Love of Mine," "One-Two-Three Kick," "Boo-Hoo," "Racing With the Moon," "When My Dreamboat Comes Home," and "Mares Eat Oats and Does Eat Oats and Little Lambs Eat Ivy" (or "Mairzeedoats'n'doeseedoats'n'liddlelamzeedivee!"). Seen from the vantage point of over three decades later, it was an embarrassing chapter in American popular art, saved only by the integrity of bands, like Ellington's, Basie's, and Goodman's, that preserved the jazz spirit in their music.

---

*To produce these strangely human cries, the player first fixes a straight mute within the bell of his horn. He then alternately opens and shuts the horn's bell chamber with the rubber cup removed from a "plumber's friend" that is used around the home to clear stopped drains.

Goodman's Band

The Benny Goodman Orchestra, featuring Goodman as leader and clarinet soloist, achieved national prominence first in late 1935. The group endured none of the racial barriers thrust before the black bands of the times; its free access to the country's most elegant dance palaces and hotel clubs lent an aura of new respectability to jazz that it had not enjoyed before.

Goodman was himself a product of careful musical training of the "traditional" kind. He was one of those first in jazz who, although tutored in the classical heritage, had learned to improvise hot music with a fluency heretofore experienced by few white musicians. Born on Chicago's West Side, he was studying clarinet at ten. By twelve he was a featured performer with the Ben Pollack Orchestra.

His music admirably represents the subtle shifts of emphasis that attended the emergence of the swing era. The band played with the same impeccable taste and flawless precision that characterized its leader's clarinet playing.

The "clean" approach to performance was a result of Goodman's personal desire for a new kind of excellence. As he wrote in 1939, ". . . that's why I am such a bug on accuracy . . . in the written parts, I wanted it to sound as exact as the band possibly could make it."* The band could make it exact, for its members were products of training foreign to the largely self-taught musicians of earlier bands. Their style suggested an artfulness and control that calmed the fears of some who had envisioned moral anarchy as the result of listening to this uncouth music. For the time being, at least, the earthy emotion of hot music was to be sublimated in favor of a neater, more ordered, more "polite" version of jazz.

Public Acclaim for Goodman

By 1936 the Goodman band met frantic enthusiasm wherever it played. Its popularity was not unique for bands of that time, although one can compare the tumult that accompanied its public appearances only to the bedlam of today's largest rock concerts. In March of 1937 the band began a series of "concert" performances at the Paramount Theater in New York City, where the drawing power of jazz orchestras recently had been discovered. Patrons lined up for tickets at six in the morning. They danced in the aisles all day, greeting the opening strains of their favorite pieces with wild cheers. Many remained in the theater until late night, leaving only after the band's final sounds had decayed to their natural end.

A not too different scene prevailed when the band played the first formal concert by a jazz group in New York's hallowed home of art music, Carnegie Hall. The Depression years were now behind. The reigning economic and political optimism of Roosevelt's New Deal seemed to

---

*In *The Kingdom of Swing*, New York: F. Ungar Pub. Co., 1939, pp. 241–42.

be right for the massive acceptance of this new art for the common man that had been brewing in the underground of black America for three decades.

Stompin' at the Savoy

Like many of Ellington's works, this title reflects the dance origins of jazz as well as one of its performance sites.* The Savoy Ballroom was one of Harlem's famous clubs, where jazz had served the demands of a crushing tide of listening and dancing fans. *Stompin'* is a "medium swing" piece, a kind of fence-sitter between the two extremes of the era, the dreamy pulse of a romantic ballad and the pressing frenzy of "jitterbug music." It is a relatively sedate riff piece. Its main theme is a simple alternation of melodic motifs (or riffs) between brass and saxophones, a call-and-response texture couched in the rhythms and harmonies of American pop music of its time. Its layered texture is easily seen in the simplified score of Example 36.1.

Example 36.1 Texture at the beginning of *Stompin' at the Savoy*

As in Ellington's *Harlem Speaks*, a four-phrase *A A B A* form of thirty-two bars provides the strophic basis for the entire piece. (The four-phrase pattern is slightly abbreviated in Chorus 4.)

It is symptomatic of the jazz metamorphosis wrought by Goodman and his contemporaries that a new ratio of "composed" and "improvised" passages make up a work's total form. Of the fifteen phrases that shape *Stompin'*, only six contain improvised solos. This suggests the principal innovation of swing: the encroachment of the arranger or composer into the territory of the improvising soloist. (In *Harlem Speaks* twenty-two of the twenty-four phrases contain improvised passages of some kind.)

The rhythm section in *Stompin' at the Savoy* performs the background function that was its almost exclusive role during this period of jazz: it is the steady heartbeat over which every other musical event is super-imposed. Note that in performing this function the two-beat past and the four-beat future of jazz are intermixed. In the beginning and ending choruses the bass, drums, piano, and guitar share a *strong-weak-strong-*

---

*The Savoy Ballroom was not a site of Goodman performances, for it was in black Harlem.

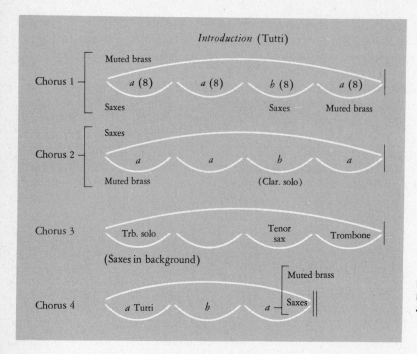

Introduction (Tutti)

Chorus 1
Muted brass
a (8)   *a* (8)   *b* (8)   *a* (8)
Saxes   Saxes   Muted brass

Chorus 2
Saxes
a   *a*   *b*   *a*
Muted brass   (Clar. solo)

Chorus 3
Trb. solo   Tenor sax   Trombone
(Saxes in background)

Chorus 4
a Tutti   *b*   *a*   Muted brass / Saxes

Example 36.2
Mapping of the overall form,
Stompin' at the Savoy

weak pattern that projects quite a different feeling from the steady *one-two-three-four* articulations that dominate Choruses 2 and 3. And just as the melody, timbre, and texture of Chorus 1 return at the end of Chorus 4, so does the more lilting two-beat meter of the rhythm section.

The differences of the Goodman and Ellington pieces—obviously a too limited sampling for conclusive generalizations—are symptomatic of jazz as it yielded to the changing fashions of its broadening audience.

Perhaps most evident is the more fully orchestrated sound of Goodman's music, its more extensive use of composed passages as opposed to the considerable reliance on solo improvisations in the Ellington band. The result in *Stompin' at the Savoy* is an uncluttered, more homogeneous sound that makes up in refinement for what it loses in spontaneity. Much of the credit for this composed swinging goes to one of Goodman's chief arrangers, Fletcher Henderson. This is the same man who accompanies Bessie Smith on *Midnight Blues* (Chapter 35) and who exerted á powerful influence on big band jazz well into mid-century.

Another contrast lies in the more venturesome timbres of the Ellington style. In *Harlem Speaks* the growls of the brass soloists, and even the solo role played briefly by the bumptious baritone sax of Harry Carney, add a dimension that is absent in the Goodman band. It is interesting that Goodman transplanted some of these "African" sounds into his orchestra in later years, breaking the unwritten "color code" of music by hiring Negro performers like the great trumpet soloist Cootie Williams. Williams had played with Ellington, specializing in the kind of brassy growls that had been the province of Buber Miley and Joe "Tricky Sam" Nanton in the pioneering Ellington band.

Illustration 36.3 A few small ensembles—or *combos*—preserved the raw spirit of earlier jazz during the swing era. Artie Shaw's "Gramercy Five" sometimes alternated in ballrooms with his much larger orchestra. This early 1940s photograph shows Dodo Marmarosa (piano), Roy Eldridge (trumpet), Shaw (clarinet), Barney Kessell (guitar), and an unidentified bass player.

37

VIRTUOSO JAZZ:
THE BOP OF CHARLIE PARKER
AND DIZZY GILLESPIE

BACKGROUND: CHARACTERISTICS OF BOP

The bountiful flowers of big band swing began to fade just after World War II ended in 1945. A sobered America settled into a promised post-war peace and prosperity. For some reason, discharged hordes of war veterans did not return to the Saturday night dance. Once proud ballrooms—the Baroque palaces of pop America—nailed up their doors or added refrigeration for ice skating. By 1950 the glorious Big Band Era was a nostalgic memory for all but a handful of the itinerants who had bused across the country on the one-night stands of the thirties and forties.

Characteristics
of Bop

As frequently occurs in the final stages of any large-scale human movement, the seeds it has sown earlier spring up to replace it. Such was the case with Big Band jazz, which now gave way to a new style called *bop*. Known also as *bebop* and *rebop*, it derived its enigmatic name from attempts to sing the rhythms that identify it. These vocal imitations of instrumental riffs used nonsense syllables for words, much like the earlier scat singing of Louis Armstrong. The result was a vibrant phrase, usually coming out something like "Ah–boo–bu–da–bee'–bop," or, equally onomatopoetic, "Ooh–bop–shee–bam'–, ah–kluga-mop." So why not just call it *bop*!

This post-war stylistic shift was distinguished by three main characteristics, any one of which could lead some of the more traditional swing musicians to disclaimers of "Noise!" or "Idiot-music!" Perhaps most

Illustration 37.1
Charlie Parker

Illustration 37.2
John Burks ("Dizzy")
Gillespie

evident to the uninitiated was bop's sometimes frantic rhythms, a trait in part supplied by the drummer. While the drums of swing bands were mainly a source of steady pulse, bop drums provided a continuing solo-istic commentary on the musical flow set by the lead solo instruments. The bop drummer kept the crucial jazz beat, but he sometimes incorporated a flailing, virtuosic stream of overlaid rhythms as well. This new percussive sound-dimension was one cause of the nervous drive this music projects.

A second characteristic was provided by the rhythms played by the lead instruments—usually piano, trumpet, or sax. They too were more elaborate. In fact, the rhythmic density* of a solo played by a bop musician is two to three times greater than its swing-era counterpart. There are also a certain agitation and angularity in the lines that immediately stamp them as bop. Someone coined the expression "sheets of sound" for this trait, and the spasms of cascading tones played by Charlie Parker or Dizzy Gillespie and their followers are just that.

As Leroi Jones describes the bop style, "It was perhaps the most legitimately complex, emotionally rich music to come out of this country." A major part of its complexity was a new rhythmic freedom, sometimes near chaos, sometimes bordering on the sterile, but often emotionally penetrating in a way that music of more relaxed rhythms could not be.

Still another aspect of bop's complexity was harmonic. Music of the swing era was concocted with a chordal vocabulary of late nineteenth and early twentieth-century European music—the sweetness of Tchaikovsky and Puccini. Bop enriched this vocabulary. Harmonic density increased from a norm of three to four pitch classes to five or six, and fresh chord relationships developed that gave old pop tunes a new color and vibrancy. Even the basic blues progression was overhauled in bop hands, through intricate embroideries around its traditional three-chord basis. It was all a part of a new sound, a break with the standardized (and thus bland) harmonies of a past that had become less than adventuresome.

Origins

Although the roots of bop are impossible to trace with precision, they were centered in New York City. If one location can be singled out, it would be a small nightclub called "Minton's" that was located in Harlem on 118th Street. The manager at Minton's was a former band leader named Teddy Hill, whose tastes for music drew young musicians to the club for late-night jam sessions. These seminal gropings for a new kind of jazz spread downtown rapidly; a circle of clubs such as Kelly's Stable, the Three Deuces, the Downbeat Club, and the Onyx Club became the epicenter of bop's rumblings. Before long the quake had spread all the way to

*Rhythmic density is discussed in Chapter 3.

the West Coast. By 1946 bop clearly represented the wave of the future, not as a replacement for older styles but more as an added ply in the thickening laminate of jazz.

CHARLIE PARKER (1920–1955) AND DIZZY GILLESPIE (1917–––)

A thorough unearthing of bop's foundation would reveal many jazz musicians who were prominent before 1945, a date we can posit with some justification as the conspicuous beginning of "modern jazz." Hovering in the background of Gillespie's extroverted trumpet phrases are both Louis Armstrong and Roy Eldridge. The same lurching rhythm and ringing tone tie the playing of all three, even though each represents a style of three separate decades in the period 1925–1955.

In Parker there are frequent reminders of the great tenor sax players Lester Young and Coleman Hawkins. There is an occasional dim echo of the alto soloist who led the Ellington sax section for over thirty years, Johnny Hodges. And along with Gillespie, Parker also clearly owed a debt to the enormous harmonic and melodic inventiveness of the great pianist Art Tatum.

But these connective tissues with a past cannot hide the obvious: "Diz" and "Bird," as they were known by their intimates, played a distinctive kind of jazz. Its newness was self-devised, but it was compounded from a host of earlier jazz practices and some borrowing from the art music of the times. Just as Armstrong had revitalized the New York jazz scene of the 1920s with a transfusion of Southland blues, Gillespie and Parker found a way forward for the over-distilled jazz of the forties.

There were attempts to accommodate the bop style in a few large bands after 1945. But the affinity of its foremost soloists clearly lay with the small combo of five to seven pieces. Their choice was not influenced solely by economic pressures: the virtuosic character of the new style dictated a smaller group, in which players could respond directly to one another. In this rather important sense, bop was a wholesome attempt to recapture the spirit of its chamber music origins.

Parker and Gillespie   Although linked together in history as the two most influential musicians of modern jazz, Gillespie and Parker were quite different personalities. Each embodied the traits shared by those who play their respective instruments. Trumpeter Gillespie, the gregarious showman, frequently wavered on the narrow line that separates the profound artist from the clown who plays to the gallery. He was a balancing foil for the brooding introvert Parker, whose frantic playing reflected his frantic insides.

Most jazz critics tout Parker as the more inventive, the more "important" of the two. His early death in 1955 (at thirty-four) perhaps fed the myths that grew up around his playing, overshadowing the contributions made by Gillespie. But what frequently is viewed as an artistic inequality of the pair also can be seen as the contrasting modes of expression forced upon each by the horn he played. A part of the trumpet's emotional power lies in its highest pitches, where the player clearly works harder to play. This inherent quality influences *what* the trumpet player plays and *how* it is played. A vital part of the intrument's potential message resides in the telegraphic punching of screaming high notes, a technique that can create boredom when played on a saxophone. As a result, Gillespie and Parker do not cultivate the same kind of musical excitement for their listeners. The saxophonist's approach is more subtle, less dependent on sheer brute force, as befits the very nature of his instrument.*

Parker's Innovations

Parker came from Kansas City, where jazz had enjoyed a healthy life from its infancy. The Count Basie band had played a significant role in the city's rich jazz background. It was a blues-based group whose driving style survived the swing era intact. This blues birthright is persistently evident in Parker's playing, even when what he is playing has no direct connection with the twelve-bar blues. His phrasing suggests some of the feeling of abandon, his notes some of the "off-key" wailing of the great blues singers who preceded him.

On the blues basis Parker overlaid an incredibly fluent saxophone technique and an unparalleled rhythmic creativity. The notes stampede from his horn at times, yet always form a meaningful pattern, a progression of developing peaks and valleys within the vaporous flow. His genius was the ability to sculpt a full solo chorus from a single melodic motif, the metamorphosis arising from continual shifts of accent, shadings of timbre, and added or subtracted notes.

Perhaps most crucial to his playing was a harmonic sensibility that enabled him to create vibrant new melodies from the faded harmonies of the swing era's most vacuous ballads. It proved to be the "Eureka!" experience of all modern jazz.

He was playing in a small club on Seventh Avenue, depressed by the impasse he seemed to have reached in his own style and bored with the apparent dead end of current jazz. (This was 1939.) Experimenting with the old Ray Noble tune *Cherokee*, he discovered that he could create new relationships between the melodies he improvised and the harmonies of the piece. In describing his reaction, Parker once said "I came alive!"

---

*It is interesting that recent sax players have cultivated a "screaming" sound as a part of the Afro-jazz movement.

It was these "new relationships" that led many traditional jazz musicians to charge Parker and Gillespie with playing "wrong notes." Just as Debussy's contemporaries mistook *different form* for *formlessness*, anti-bop factions concluded that *new notes* were in fact *inharmoniousness*.

Parker met Gillespie in 1941 when they both played with Cab Calloway's big band. By 1942, now back in New York, the pair became regular fixtures in Harlem's clubs, especially Mintons's and Monroe's Uptown House, where the aggressive bop style was incubating. In 1942 and 1943 he and Gillespie again played together, first in the Earl Hines band and later in Billy Eckstine's, both of which tested the developing new sounds. Tiring of big bands and road dates, Parker returned to New York in 1944, shifting his territory to downtown Manhattan to play with Gillespie and others of the youthful bop clan. In late 1945 he joined Gillespie in an historic quintet on the West Coast, playing briefly in Billy Berg's club just off the Sunset Strip in Los Angeles.

Shortly after this historic teaming of the two principal founders of modern jazz, Parker succumbed to the deterioration brought on by his indomitable drug habit. He was broken, capable of survival only in a hospital. Inactive for two years, he became publicly prominent once more in 1948. When he died in 1955, again reduced to emotional and musical instability, friends collected money to finance his burial and care for his wife and children. He died the tragic victim of poverty, artistic disregard, drugs, and perhaps most poignant of all, his own passionate frustration. And yet his recorded legacy survived him to become the New Testament for the serious jazz musicians who came after him.

GROOVIN' HIGH: GILLESPIE (1945)

This piece illustrates three dominant features of the early bop style. It shows how harmonic, rhythmic, and melodic invention can transform a hackneyed pop ballad into a fresh jazz utterance. Second, it displays the fantastic virtuosity of its performers, who create spontaneous streams of melody within the harmonic progression that is their chosen reference. In this second quality *Groovin' High* reveals how far the jazz improviser had left behind references to the precomposed melodies of an arranger or composer, who were the ruling forces of the swing era. And last, this short riff-piece shows how rhythm instruments, formerly assigned only the menial background roles, have now risen to soloistic status.

The song *Whispering*, of which *Groovin' High* is an ornate variant, consists of a thirty-two-bar chorus. Its phrase plan is not the same, however, as the *A A B A* plan of *Harlem Speaks* and *Stompin' at the Savoy*. Its plan consists of two halves of sixteen bars each, the second half a near-duplicate of the first. This 1920 song so completely reflects the banal girl-boy ballads of its era that we reproduce it here.

Example 37.1 *Whispering* (Schonberger)

(chords): Eb   Cdim   Eb

Whis - per - ing while you cud-dle near me, Whis - per - ing so no one can

C7   F7   Bb7

hear me, Each lit - tle whis - per seems to cheer me;

Eb   Bb7   Bb+ Eb

I know its true there's no one dear but you; You're whis - per - ing why you'll nev - er

Cdim   Eb   C7

leave me, Whis - per - ing why you'll nev - er grieve me;

F7   Bb7   Fm   Abm   Eb

Whis - per and say that you be - lieve me, Whis-per-ing out I love you.

Groovin' High uses only the basic chord progression of one sixteen-bar half of the song, treating its chords as furrows in which to plant the soloists' improvisations. The original chords are themselves garnished with the kinds of "higher intervals" Parker favored. A few are even replaced by typical bop variants, but enough of the original remains to be detected by the forewarned ear. (Try humming or whistling the tune *Whispering* during the alto sax or trumpet solos.)

Example 37.2 Mapping of *Groovin' High*

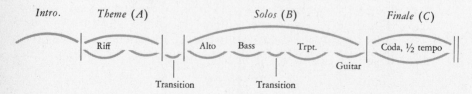

Intro.   *Theme (A)*   *Solos (B)*   *Finale (C)*

Riff   Alto Bass   Trpt.   Coda, ½ tempo

Guitar

Transition   Transition

This practice of overlaying—or "parodying," as it would have been called in the sixteenth century—was applied to many other familiar songs of the swing era by bop performers. They probably took their cue from the way the blues was subjected to thousands of improvised "re-creations." In this they revealed a disinterest in melodic references. Their strength lay rather in devising new melodic strands over an established harmonic background. Less than earlier musicians, they felt no compulsion to quote the actual melody of a song in their improvisations. Note how the riff-theme of *Groovin' High* is an overlay to the original chord relationship of the first few bars of *Whispering*. Not a hint remains of the original tune.

Example 37.3   Riff-theme and chords of *Groovin' High*, first five measures

The closing half-time (or half as fast) passage of this piece is a rare departure from the usual layout of a jazz form. It bypasses the conventional closing gesture, the return of the opening riff and texture. This particular coda-cadenza ends the piece effectively, but it also provides a showcase for Gillespie's biting high notes, now with open horn rather than the cup mute of the beginning.

Aside from the brilliant playing of the two main soloists, there are other highlights in this piece that merit our attention. One is the colorful bass playing of Slam Stewart, who provides occasional bottom notes for ensemble harmonies, plays a solo chorus, and also sustains the four-beat pulse with drummer Cozy Cole. That the bass plays a solo chorus at all is uncommon (although the swing era had advanced the cause of rhythm instruments as soloists). That Stewart plays his solo with a bow rather than in the usual plucked style of the jazz bassist is even stranger. But that he also *sings* a precise duplication of his bass's tones while he plays them creates one of the most startling timbres in the history of any musical idiom.* He does this with the same swinging fluency we hear from the

---

*Stewart had used the same technique much earlier, particularly in his recordings with pianist Art Tatum and guitarist Tiny Grimes.

horns of the other solo artists, indicating how at least one bass player had liberated his instrument from the "beat holder" role it formerly had.

A less obvious departure from jazz tradition can be heard in the background piano of Clyde Hart. In a technique developed earlier by pianists like Ellington and Basie, he jabs out syncopated chords behind soloists instead of holding to the sterile *one-two-three-four* pulsations expected of pianists of times past. The total result is a coordination of bass, drums, and piano rhythms that forms a rich body rather than a uniform, blunt-edged beat.

One trait usually found in fully developed bop ensembles is missing in *Groovin' High*. The drummer on this recording, Cozy Cole, matured during the early days of jazz, along with Armstrong and Ellington. His firm drumming provides the steady pace expected of the drummer, but the difference is vast between what he plays and the backgrounds provided by bop drummers such as Kenny Clark and Max Roach. In this respect, *Groovin' High* is a mixture of old and new.

A NIGHT IN TUNISIA: GILLESPIE (1953)

This recording presents bop eight years later than *Groovin' High*. Here it is played in full bloom by its most polished exponents. A more sympathetic roster of jazz musicians could not have been collected in one five-piece ensemble. Bud Powell plays piano the way Parker blew alto sax; Charlie Mingus and Max Roach play bass and drums as though rhythm sections were never meant for supporting roles. Except for the still steady pulsing of the bass, the thudding mechanical beat of the swing era has been replaced by scattered bursts of sound. Here the piano's chords and the drum's shifting timbres have replaced the background figurations of the swing "arrangement." Even the bass, which remains as the vestigial pillar of rhythm, frequently dispenses with the simple beat in favor of its own "melodies."

Although considerably longer than *Groovin' High*, the form of *A Night In Tunisia* is not more complicated. It retains the basic *A B A* outline of Riff-theme–Solo Improvisations–Riff-theme that had been institutionalized much earlier. (The resemblance of this ternary plan to Exposition–Development–Recapitulation of sonata form should not be ignored.) Within this overall return form lie some musical ideas of compelling force, some jazz playing of unsurpassed excitement. The mapping of Example 37.4 can serve as a reference for our discussion.

The listener does not wait long to hear differences between mature bop and jazz of the thirties and early forties. The introductory measures provide overwhelming proof that this is more complex music, its harmonic and melodic character decades removed from homespun early jazz or polite showbiz music of the thirties.

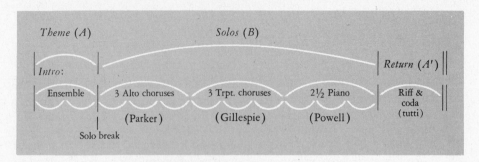

Example 37.4 Overall mapping of *A Night in Tunisia*

The formidable introduction grows as a piling-on of ostinatos, drums, bass, piano, and alto saxophone establishing a rich web of sound within which Gillespie's trumpet will expose the riff-theme. The rhythmic and tonal characteristics of this opening texture mark a radical departure from the simple foreground–background combinations one hears in jazz ensembles prior to 1945. Only the most daring jazz arranger of late swing could have conceived this five-ply texture that is an on-the-spot creation by these five superb instrumentalists.

The three long solos (Parker, Gillespie, Powell) provide an audible encyclopedia of bop style. The harmonic basis of Gillespie's piece itself offers a comfortable mold for their special kinds of melodic probings. The piece's *A* phrases revolve around a change of two chords a half step apart, a *tonic–non-tonic* relationship that suggests the *Phrygian* mode.*

Example 37.5 Harmonic basis of the main motif

This single tiny harmonic event is a strong bit of evidence of the gulf between bop and swing. Swing era arrangers had gradually obliterated the richness of pitch shadings—the so-called "bluenotes"—of the classic blues. Their passion for clarity and "singableness" had boxed jazz into the tight corner of the major scale. A part of the strange tonality of *A Night*

---

*See Glossary, *Modes*, "Phrygian."

In Tunisia is its exploitation of this simple harmonic relationship that suggests a departure from the homogenized tonal colors of swing.

The solo break, which we have observed in earlier jazz, crops up here too. The beginning of Parker's solo (just following the riff statements) makes evident the remaining vitality of this simple procedure for ushering a hot soloist into his chorus.

Solos of Parker, Gillespie, and Powell

The galloping virtuosity of Parker's three solo choruses manifests those "sheets of sound" we mentioned earlier as a hallmark of the bop style. It seems at times that he has saved up a storehouse of notes from which to build his solo, squeezing them, finally, into the few remaining beats of a phrase. In this solo there are occasional allusions to the riff-motif of the piece. These are only fleeting glances, but they help to remind us that the cascading patterns retain some kinship with the immediate business at hand, which is *A Night In Tunisia*.

Gillespie's solo, also three choruses long, reveals his bop traits too. His trumpet's machine gun fusillades link his playing with Parker's; they are identical twins whose mirror images are distorted only by the different timbres of their respective instruments. But this solo also exemplifies a sometimes simpler, more driving and emotional kind of bop improvisation. Here Gillespie's playing suggests more openly its paternity by the biting high-note style of Roy Eldridge, who after Louis Armstrong had been the most respected jazz trumpet player of the big bands. The style is direct. It has nothing of the covert ingeniousness we might associate with playing that seeks complexity for its own sake. It is as much the punching *Hallelujiah!* of a Southland prayer meeting as it is the facile *Go!Go!Go!* of a northern jazz hall.

And last, Bud Powell's piano solo shows how the Parker-Gillespie breathlessness had rubbed off on other instrumentalists by the 1950s. His left hand no longer plays the beat-by-beat accompaniment, the "stride style" bass of practically every jazz pianist from Fats Waller through Teddy Wilson and Art Tatum. Instead, it flails spasmodic chords as a foil for the racing right hand, consistent with the new rhythmic freedom of the bop style.

38

MID-CENTURY SYNTHESIS:
NIGHT MUSIC

Gunther Schuller (1926————)

BACKGROUND: JAZZ INFLUENCE ON CONCERT MUSIC

The swing era—whose broad sociological product was the white man's acceptance of the black man's music—brought hot music to the attention of a broad population base. But it was bop, with its spectacular new resources, that aligned jazz with the technical finesse of classical art music. The harmonies, rhythms, and textures of this grassroots music had now grown to the level of Haydn, Ravel, and Bartók, yet retaining the unique emotional genes its ancestry provided at its conception. If Charlie Parker's alto sax can speak with the technical wizardry and emotional fervor of Heifetz's violin, then jazz must be reckoned with. It has surpassed its folk origins.

Few American composers born after 1925 have escaped some direct and enduring scrape with jazz. Composers born before, like Aaron Copland (1900————) or Leonard Bernstein (1917————), have been marginally influenced; but their jazz involvements were more of the bland cocktail piano variety than of the raw blues style that nourished the jazz professionals of the same generation. Younger American composers matured when jazz was a national celebration, and those who played it, studied its artists, and made its features a part of their musical instincts could come to grips with its artistic potentialities in ways composers of earlier generations could not.

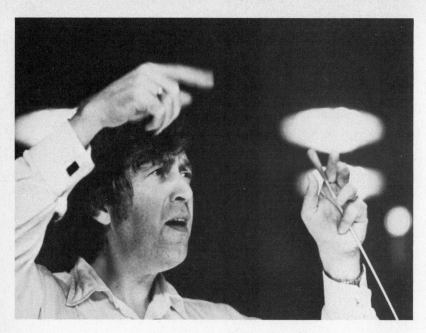

Illustration 38.1
Gunther Schuller

Since 1946 jazz has even been granted academic respectability, courses in jazz history gradually emerging in colleges to join the jazz ensembles that began to appear on campuses after World War II.* In many schools today, future professional musicians can study jazz along with Palestrina's masses and Mozart's symphonies.†

A number of composers have attempted to close the breach that has separated jazz and classical music. This was precisely the aim of George Gershwin and Paul Whiteman during the 1930s. Works like *Rhapsody in Blue, Concerto in F, An American in Paris,* and the opera *Porgy and Bess* all reveal a composer treading the deep waters of classical idioms muddied by jazz colors and phrasings. But any composer who tries blending the two kinds of music faces inevitable criticism. From "classical" quarters he hears cries of "commercialism"; from jazz quarters he is reproached for pandering to "sterility."

And yet a number of younger composers have successfully merged aspects of both musical traditions. Rather than treat jazz as an artistic stepchild, they have adapted its most durable aspects to classical skills and procedures, achieving a healthy synthesis rather than a cheap alteration. The term *Third Stream Music* was coined by Gunther Schuller some years ago. It aptly describes the fresh kind of synthesis some composers have sought. Accepting west European art music as a "first stream" and jazz as a "second stream," the "third stream" is the separate lively branch that can be the union of both.

---

*Academe's coy acceptance of jazz is indicated by the bland euphemism normally given jazz bands in schools. They are called "laboratory bands," or just "lab bands."

†The first jazz degree was established at North Texas State University in 1946.

NIGHT MUSIC (1962)

Schuller was born in 1926. Trained in the traditions of classical music, he once played French horn in the Cincinnati Symphony and the Metropolitan Opera Orchestra. For a number of years he was President of the New England Conservatory of Music in Boston. He grew up during that period of American history we mentioned earlier, when many serious young musicians responded to jazz more directly than schooled musicians could before 1925. An established composer of symphonies and operas, Schuller nonetheless shares an enthusiasm and understanding of jazz that is peculiar to many musicians of his generation.

The jazz critic Martin Williams once defined Schuller's fitness for creating music that combines the forms and skills of European traditions with the emotional overtones of jazz. He observed that Schuller's "... knowledge of jazz is not only sympathetic but historically authentic and penetrating—'knowledge' is not the right word: let's call it love."*

Night Music has formal similarities with the "head scores" of Ellington and the riff pieces of Gillespie and Parker. Its composed elements form a skeleton within which improvisations flesh out the musical substance. The composer has provided rather specific directions (in addition to scored passages) which the performers follow in exercising their own creativity.

The form of this work is remarkably similar to that of Samuel Barber's *Adagio for Strings*, which we discussed in Chapter 2. Its quiet opening, gradual growth to fervent climax, and sudden decay are represented by the mapping of Example 38.1.

---

*In *Evergreen Review* Vol, 7, No. 30. (May-June, 1963), p. 119.

Example 38.1   Overall shape of *Night Music*

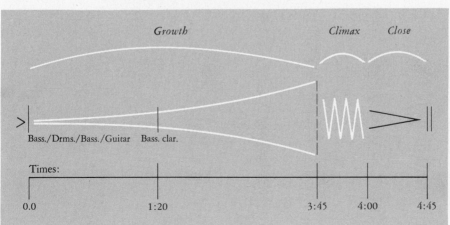

Clearly, Schuller's work draws upon the timbres associated with jazz. It uses two basses, guitar, drums, and a bass clarinet to replace the more strident tones of the saxophone. There are other, somewhat less evident differences. Unlike Barber's work, *Night Music's* growth is based on a strophic pattern of six measures, whose repetitions form a ground for its tonal and rhythmic flow. This melodic ground has strong ties with both the traditional twelve-bar blues and techniques of European art music.

Marriage of Blues and Serial Technique

You will remember that the structural basis of the blues is a twelve-bar pattern of three phrases (4 + 4 + 4). If we add two of Schuller's six-bar grounds together, we get twelve bars, which accounts for some of the blues atmosphere that dominates the piece. Careful study also reveals that the six-bar ground is based on a twelve-pitch series, of the kind developed in the 1920s by Arnold Schoenberg. This same "serial method" of composition is an important element in Alban Berg's Violin Concerto (Chapter 26), and it was used extensively by most modern composers during the period 1930–1965. The pitch series of *Night Music* is reproduced in the next example.

Example 38.2 The twelve-pitch series used in *Night Music*

The persistent growth of this piece is undergirded by fifteen soundings of its six-bar ground pattern, which is lost to the ear in the thickening texture soon after the entrance of the bass clarinet. The next mapping shows how the terraced entries of instruments build a texture during the growth

Example 38.3 Strophic basis of the "Growth" section

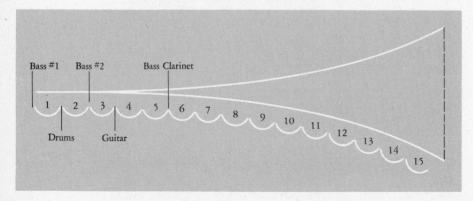

section. (Numbers denote successive statements of the six-bar pitch series.) And so this work boasts rich parentage. It is rooted in the chaconne and passacaglia of Bach's time and the serial method of twentieth-century art music, and it also bears potent reminders of the blues of Bessie Smith and Louis Armstrong.

Emotional Power in *Night Music*

Lacking prior warning, a listener might assume that *Night Music* is no more than a carefully planned and brilliantly executed piece of strong blues character. But this would describe only the tip of the iceberg. Fascinating qualities are to be found below the surface.

In addition to its twelve-pitch ostinato, Schuller's framework provides other examples of skillful organization that help this piece grab our attention and reward us for the trouble. One is the compelling nature of its long growth to climax. Terraced texture is not the only way growth is suggested. The instrumentalists also increase the rhythmic density of the patterns they play, they stretch the high-low range of their tones, and the bass clarinetist (William O. Smith) even slips into a raucous, squealing timbre that directly projects mounting tension. In all, then, loudness, pitch range, texture, rhythm, and even timbre combine to create this prolonged passage of rising turbulence.

At the very point of climax, rhythmic density increases radically. The formerly steady pulse dissolves and the five instrumentalists improvise a simultaneous "solo break" that sustains the climactic peak.

Once ended, this stirring climax reverberates within a prolonged silence, a pause that introduces the quiet ending passage. Schuller ensures maximum musical interest in these final rustles of sound. Here the timbres of the beginning texture are turned upside down. The guitar plays low pitches against the very high bowed sounds of the two basses, a haunting quiet within which the bass clarinet can reflect upon the principal motifs of his preceding solo.

As an ultimate stroke of musical coherence, the last four notes played by the bass clarinet are a spatial reordering of the first four notes played by the solo bass in the opening measures of the piece.

Example 38.4 Opening and closing pitches, bass and bass clarinet

bass at opening

(*Db*   *G*   *Ab*   *B*)

bass clar. at end

(*Db   G   Ab   B*)

As if to flaunt its "third stream" ties, this final bass clarinet motif clinches its ties with the blues tradition. Its notes form a trademark of all

Illustration 38.2 Leading jazz musicians since the bop era have performed more for formal concerts and recordings than for dancing patrons in smoke-filled clubs. Gerry Mulligan (above) and Stan Getz (right) matured during the Parker/Gillespie days of change; their music is wholly jazz in feeling and substance, yet technically as complex and immaculate as a performance by an Isaac Stern or a Vladimir Horowitz.

blues, emphasizing the "blue seventh" note of the scale that dominates every blues rendition from Ma Rainey to John Coltrane.*

Night Music is a treasure of jazz and classical techniques. But most important for the listener, it is convincing music, expressing feeling with the same intensity one might expect from Bessie Smith or Richard Wagner. That it effectively combines techniques of both traditions makes it a convincing example of the best sense of a musical third stream. Here jazz is an inherent part of the expression.

---

*This "blue seventh" also is the final pitch of the old phrase "Good evening friends," which provides an easy reference to what it sounds like in context.

PART **VII**

ART MUSIC OF TWO OTHER CULTURES: JAPAN AND INDIA

INTRODUCTION

An unfortunate product of modern technology has been its leveling effect on the rich and colorful varieties of human cultures. Even within our own country, radio, television, and movies are slowly eroding regional speech patterns. By the end of this century the "Southerner" and the "Yankee"— once readily distinguished by their speech—may remain only as quaint memories of an American past.

Wars, jet travel, and instant communication effect greater cultural similarities. Arabian monarchs travel their deserts in Cadillacs; Japanese magnates wheel and deal in Hart Schaffner and Marx suits; and African generals light their Havana cigars with Cricket lighters. Our world seems bent on achieving a uniculture, erasing those very marks of individuality that make something special of being human. While we can, we must enjoy what is left of the unique traces of the earth's cultures. They are the endangered species of a shrinking world.

Among these unique traces are musics of other peoples, which provide us with experiences that are unavailable from our own culture. Just as the study of a foreign language often provides us with a more secure grasp of our native tongue, some understanding of another culture's music can enhance and deepen our responses to the music we call our own.

As a gesture to this end, we shall take a brief look at some aspects of the traditional art music of Japan and India. These cultures have produced musical systems as powerfully equipped to yield deep and sustaining musical responses as those that engendered a Mozart and a Debussy.

FEATURES OF JAPANESE AND INDIAN MUSIC

The musics of these two countries rubbed elbows early in their development; they thus share some common structural traits and aesthetic motivations. Like most non-Western musics, their essence is melody. Harmony and texture are mere "accidental" properties, arising mainly as by-products of the melodic forces at play.

For the Westerner, music of the East is indeed different. But it is by no means unapproachable. Its timbres are at first strange for ears weaned on the lush harmonies of pianos, violins, and clarinets, for its native instruments are an integral part of its authenticity.

On the other hand, those who know the popular music of the West since 1965 can at times discover brief but striking resemblances. Few pop groups, from the Beatles to some of the more enterprising of today, have not tinkered with the sounds and processes of Indian music. And as we observed in George Crumb's *Ancient Voices of Children* (Chapter 23), composers of art music have on occasion blended their works with Oriental touches.

Music's Function The uninitiated listener must first acknowledge and accept the function assumed by the Japanese or Indian for his art music. This function is in fact many-faceted, as it is for our own art music, and yet one of its critical aims is to lead the listener into a contemplation of and "connection" with that which is beyond the common affairs of life. Japanese *gagaku*, for example, has been associated with the ceremonials of royalty and religion since its earliest development. Its primary function is thus to reinforce conditions that will lift man above his daily humdrum. The Buddhist traditions of both India and Japan are rich in the kinds of ritual and abstract precepts that form any religion's base. These traditions affect the music of believers, just as Judaism, Catholicism, and Protestantism developed musical embellishments peculiar to their own theological tenets and practices.

Even in concerts of Indian and Japanese music today, certain ritualistic features remain as adjuncts to the music-making. Wafting incense during an Indian raga performance, like the humble bows of the Japanese koto player to her instrument, are both vestiges of the ceremonial traditions of their music. Clearly neither incense nor bows can exert an *auditory* influence on the music; both are nonetheless crucial aspects of the atmosphere within which their respective cultures expect worthwhile music to take place. Even the visual effect of the Japanese gagaku orchestra is carefully controlled so that no blemish will weaken the ceremonial elegance of a performance. Refinement and tradition extend to the elaborate costuming of the performers, the seating arrangement of the group, and even the design and adornment of each instrument.

The Westerner who has not heard Japanese music within a Shinto shrine or Buddhist temple, a Kabuki theater or an imperial court cannot fully plumb the depths of its impact. But this is nothing new to us. Neither can we fully appreciate some of the music of the American composer Charles Ives unless we have heard the cacophony of a rural congregation singing "Nearer My God to Thee."

THE VIRTUOSO'S VENERATION OF TRADITION

As in cultures of the West, the performer's virtuosity is much esteemed in the East. A part of the listener's pleasure derives from the realization that what is heard is the result of mastery. But there is a subtle difference. In Japanese and Indian music the performer ultimately is regarded as more an intermediary between the listener and a state of heightened awareness. The performer is a midwife who eases the birth of the listener's consciousness. He or she is not a final object of veneration.

This hastens our mention of the sanctity of tradition in the music of both cultures. We have mentioned in earlier chapters the various historical periods of Western music, those pigeonholes of centuries and half-centuries that mark off musical styles of our past, like *Renaissance, Baroque* and *Classical*. Our acceptance of change in art is not so readily shared by the musicians of Japan and India.

The traditional musician of India and Japan venerates his past. He acknowledges that hard-won skill is best displayed within the frames of reference bequeathed him by ancestors, frames to be filled in with only scant attempts to express individuality. The performer's aim is to refine skills within tightly prescribed limits rather than to expand them to a point where they might lose contact with the past. For this reason, there are few really "new" compositions in the art music of either country. Creativity is channeled into the reworking of melodies and forms passed on from previous centuries.

39

TRADITIONAL
MUSIC OF JAPAN

BACKGROUND

You could visit Tokyo today and hear no music you would not hear in New York, Cleveland, or Los Angeles. At an opera house you might hear *Carmen* or in a concert hall Schubert's *Unfinished Symphony*, and you might well hear Dixieland jazz in any number of clubs on the Ginza, which is Tokyo's version of Los Angeles's Sunset Strip. Since Commodore Matthew Perry's liberating overtures of the nineteenth century, and with an accelerated pace since World War II, Japanese population centers have adopted Western dress, habits, and commodities, music included.

Traditional Japanese music is not extinct, but it also is not conspicuously accessible. It is not a part of the music studies at Tokyo University, where Steinway's piano is better known (and more revered) than a koto. Except for performances at major Shinto shrines, Buddhist temples, the Imperial palaces, and as a part of Japanese drama (*noh* plays and *kabuki*), its presence in a large Japanese city is easily overlooked.

It is called *hogaku* (*ho-gah-koo'*). It can be traced to Chinese and Indian origins of the eighth century, but hogaku as we know it today developed most extensively during a period of over two centuries (1615–1868), during which the city of Tokyo (then called *Edo*) became the industrial

Ryuteki　**Hichiriki**　**Sho**

Shoko　**Tsuri-Daiko**　**Kakko**

Koto　**Biwa**

and cultural hub of the country. It enjoyed a stirring rebirth during Japan's surge of militarism that led to the bombing of Pearl Harbor in 1941. The rampant nationalism of those times nourished an enthusiasm for everything that could be regarded as distinctly Japanese. Even the concerts of the Emperor's court were opened to the public during those years, as a gesture to this infatuation with the past.

As an introduction to only two kinds of Japanese traditional music, let us examine two characteristic types. We shall use these as our guides and points of reference, deriving as much general understanding and insight as they can provide.

GAGAKU MUSIC

The art music of the Japanese Imperial Court—its "elegant" or "correct" music—is called *gagaku* (*gah-gah-koo'*). We shall discuss only the purely instrumental concert music of this tradition, which is known as *kangen*

442

(*kahng'-gen*). Two other branches of gagaku are *seigaku* (*say-gah-koo'*), or vocal music, and *bugaku* (*boo-gah-koo'*), or dance music.

The Western listener receives the first shock from the mere sounds of this music. They come from an ensemble that, like its Mozartian counterpart, the symphony orchestra, is comprised of a body of winds, strings, and percussion. But there close similarities end. Among the winds are three instruments, the *hichiriki* (*heech-ee-ree'-kee*), the *ryuteki* (*ry-oo-tay'-kee*), and the *sho*.

The hichiriki is most like an oboe, a short tube with finger holes that is blown through a mouthpiece housing a double reed. Its blatant, sometimes screaming timbre is unique among the world's sounds.

The ryuteki is a flute made of bamboo. Seven finger holes provide its pitch control. This instrument's breathy tone has a softening effect in combination with the more strident tone of the hichiriki.

The third member of the wind section, the sho, is an elaborate mouth organ that looks like the partially spread tail feathers of a small peacock. The "feathers" are actually seventeen pitch pipes. When

Illustration 39.2 (Left) Small but piercing, the hichiriki's whistle-sound is one of the unique tones of all music.

Illustration 39.3 (Right) Like the folded feathers of a miniature peacock, the sho's cylindrical pipes provide the chordal background heard in Gagaku music.

played as a chord, these provide a continuing web of background sound for the melodic figurations of the hichiriki and ryuteki. (Only fifteen of the pipes actually sound; the remaining two fill out the shape of the instrument!) The gagaku ensemble normally uses three of each of these instruments.

In the gagaku string section the *biwa* (*bee'-wah*) and *koto* provide highly distilled versions of the melodic patterns played by the winds, marking off phrases and other formal junctures of the continuing texture. A typical ensemble will contain two of each instrument, seated between winds and percussion. The biwa is like a lute (or overgrown mandolin), its four strings played with a wooden plectrum that produces a slightly raspy tone. The koto is the more elaborate of the two, a long instrument of thirteen strings, which produce sounds very much like those of the harp. The koto player sits on folded legs while plucking this zither-like instrument, which itself rests horizontally on the floor.

The third orchestral group, the percussion, performs much the same function in gagaku as it performs in Western music: its players help the ensemble keep a stable rhythm, their taps and rolls reinforcing points

Illustration 39.4   (Left) This gracefully elaborate lute, the biwa, is one of the most beautiful instruments of any culture. Evident in this picture are its rear-thrusting scroll and the triangular plectrum used to pluck its strings.

Illustration 39.5   (Right) For westerners the koto is probably the best known Japanese instrument. An authentic performance is as much a social ritual as a musical performance.

within the phrases of a composition.* The section consists of three percussion types. The largest is the *daiko* (*tah-ee'-ko*), a drum whose deep resonance marks the main accents of the melody's phrases, once the composition is underway. The *kakko* (*kah'-ko*) is a smaller drum with elaborate rigging between its two skin heads. (It rests horizontally on a special cradle.) It is the most active voice of the section, but it usually plays in phase with the *shoko*, a small bronze gong, filling in some of the silences between markings of the taiko.

---

*This "marking off" function is sometimes called *colotomic*.

Illustration 39.6 Kakko

Illustration 39.8 (Below) Shoko

Illustration 39.7
(Left) Daiko (Tsuri-Daiko)

Gagaku texture

The essence of any gagaku composition is its underlying melody. We say *underlying* because a performance consists of simultaneous interpretations by multiple players of the single melody. In gagaku each instrument provides not just its singular timbre: it offers its own special version of the melody as well.

The result, of course, it a heterophonic texture, which we first described and illustrated in Chapter 6. It is the counterpart, in music of the Orient, of the homophony and polyphony of Western music, in which harmony plays such a distinctive role. Harmony in gagaku is only a residue of melodies, those points wherein separate strands of melodic elaboration happen to produce different pitches at the same time. Even the chords sounded by the sho are frozen compounds of the pitches winds and strings play successively as melody. This fortuitous but static harmony of Japanese gagaku is another of its fundamental contrasts with traditional music of the West. It also is a major part of its fascination for us.

Scales

The pitches of Japanese melody were formalized long ago into collections of scales. Lacking a true system of harmony, the music is nonetheless organized around a tonic pitch in a way that is reminiscent of Gregorian Chant.* Even the scales that provide the pitch collections for particular melodies are divided into two basic types. This two-fold grouping seems to be characteristic of all scale systems of man's past: it holds for the modes of the Christian era in the West (*authentic* and *plagal* modes) and the scales of later European music (*major* and *minor* scales).

The two scales used in gagaku—and they hold generally for other types of Japanese music as well—bear striking resemblances to the major-minor types of our tradition. The *ryo* scales have five primary and four secondary pitches. The scale shown in Example 39.1 is the *ryo* scale based on *D*. (The same pattern is used with *E* or *G* as tonic.) The five primary members (which alone would form a pentatonic scale) are shown here as open note heads.

Example 39.1   The *ryo* scale with *D* as tonic note

The "minor" scale type of the Japanese system is called *ritsu*. Its pattern is shown next as it would appear with the note *E* as tonic. (The same scale is used with the tonic notes *B* or *A* as well.) Again, the scale's five primary pitches are shown as open note heads.

---

*See Chapter 16.

Example 39.2 The *ritsu* scale with *E* as tonic note

As in Western music theory, these scales must be viewed only as generalizations of what happens in particular pieces of music. Players frequently "shade" the pitches they play to heighten expression. In some performances the secondary notes of a scale turn out to be just as prominent as some of the primary notes. So Japanese scales, like any theoretical abstraction, cannot be understood as the total representations of pitch content in actual music. Instead, they are approximations of "most probable" elements.

Form

The aesthetic goal of gagaku is typically Japanese: unique individual beauty within the highly prescribed bounds of a conventionalized structure. Like Japanese prints, rock gardens, and haiku poetry, each work is marked by its singular nature; it is not exactly like any other. At the same time, in its basic features it is a carbon copy of all other examples of its kind. Its tradition-bound delicacy has been described best by those who refer to it as "the art of little things."

A gagaku performance follows a predetermined order, although parts can be omitted, repeated, or not repeated, as willed by the leader of the ensemble (who usually plays the kakko). In an actual concert, the body of a piece is preceded by a brief "warming up" prelude, the *netori*. This tentative laying out of the sounds establishes the mood and pitch content for the work that is to follow. In the netori the individual wind and string instruments perform snatches of prefatory patterns within a free-moving rhythm. Percussion is absent from this musical foreword, entering the texture only toward the beginning of the composition's main body. They always play on the odd-numbered beats of the duple meter, which is conceived by the musicians in two, four, or eight beats, depending upon the tempo. (Very slow tempos are counted in eight, very fast in two.)

In the main body of the composition a three-part scheme outlines the standard process of performance. (A standard that is not always followed, we might add.) It is a simple plan that moves through three states which are reflected in the following descriptive terms:

> Section I: *jo* ("prelude")
> Section II: *ha* ("breaking away")
> Section III: *kyu* ("hurried")

These terms suggest an acceleration of tempos, but this is not necessarily the case. The progression from beginning to end sometimes is effected more by increasing rhythmic density than by a quickened pulse.

Etenraku:
Nippon Gagaku Kai

This work is probably the most revered of the entire gagaku repertory. It is widely known outside Japan, and some attempts have even been made to transfer its melody to the sounds of a Western orchestra. The composition is based on a melody of three phrases, only two of which are played in the recording by the Nippon Gagaku Kai. Example 39.3 shows only those first two phrases heard in this performance. The slanted lines that connect or precede some of the notes represent pitch slides, which are significant in the expressive style of playing by both the ryuteki and the hichiriki.

Example 39.3 Melodic phrases of *Etenraku* as performed by the Nippon Gagaku Kai (transcribed by the author.)

In a complete performance of this piece a third phrase, *C*, would be joined to the *A* and *B* phrases shown here. The conventional ordering would be *AA BB CC AA BB*, thus creating a basic return form. In the performance we are discussing, only phrases *A* and *B* are used (both are repeated), and the work is not prefaced by the customary netori. If you do not read notation fluently you will find that you still can follow the score most of the time by tapping a pattern of eight rapid pulses for each measure. This may be difficult at first because a gagaku ensemble "stretches" beats to its collective will. (Though vastly different, this waxing and waning is reminiscent of Chopin's *tempo rubato.*)

True to gagaku tradition, the ryuteki begins the piece, playing the first two notes of the melody alone. Remaining instruments fill in the texture gradually while the tempo stabilizes. Kakko and shoko join first followed by the taiko. Toward the end of the first phrase (*A*), the sho begins its unearthly chord and the hichiriki's nasal twang merges with the flute. Example 39.4 shows the entrances of these instruments as they relate to the melody played by the ryuteki. Note that strings join the ensemble only at the beginning of the repeat of phrase *A*.

Example 39.4 Cumulative texture, opening of *Etenraku*

etc.

{
1 = *kakko* and *shoko*
2 = *daiko*
3 = *sho* and *hichiriki*
4 = *biwa* and *koto*
}

The main body of a gagaku composition lacks strong contrasts. Its winding melodies, isolated drumbeats, and spasmodic string pluckings edge forward to an end that is faintly reminiscent of a jazz man's solo break. This standardized gesture is called the *tomede* (*to-may'-day*). At this point the lead players of each section of the orchestra perform brief solo passages. The sho's chord dissolves, the winds finish their fragmentary solos, and then the biwa and koto strum their dramatic final pitches. In the Nippon Gagaku Kai performance of *Etenraku*, the tomede finale is abbreviated. Momentum abruptly wanes with the last pitch of phrase *B*, the kakko taps a closing roll, and then come the ultimate plucked tones of biwa and koto.

Those final tones of the strings are the main pitches of *Etenraku*, the first and fifth notes of the ritsu scale on which the melody is based. (In this case the scale's tonic note is *E*.)* Look back to Example 39.3 and you will find in the melody the notes of the scale shown in Example 39.2, except for the sixth note. The final pitches played by the biwa and koto are notes one and five in that scale.

You may at first react to gagaku with a feeling of boredom laced with mild humor. Its raucous timbres, the sense of near immobility it projects, and its sliding melodies run counter to the foot-tapping pleasure we usually expect from music. But hear the work several times. You may find its archaic charm preying on your memory. It is subtle music, the

---

*In Japanese theory this ritsu scale on *E* is called *hyogo*.

delicate reincarnation of an ancient past. Its carefully wrought and exquisitely controlled sounds are not easy to forget, once they have been heard
for their own sake. A part of this music's appeal is our realization that its
tradition has survived relatively intact. What we hear today is reasonably
like what we might have heard in the Imperial palace of Kyoto in the
twelfth century.

KOTO ENSEMBLE MUSIC: SAN-KYOKU

Complementary to the "orchestral" music of gagaku, there is also a vast
repertory of "chamber music" in the Japanese art tradition. One particularly effective chamber combination is called *san-kyoku*, which quite appropriately means "music for three." The conventional instrumentation for
this form of Oriental salon music is koto, *shakuhachi* (*shock-oo-hot'-chee*),
and *shamisen* (*shom'-ee-sin*). The music of this genre is not strikingly different
from gagaku. In fact, both underwent their most productive periods of
development at about the same time, during the Edo period of Japan's
history.

The koto represents in Japanese music what the piano represents in
Western music. At first it played an important role only in music of the
Emperor's court, accompanying songs and dances as well as performing
solo. Established in those roles, it gradually entered the homes of well-to-
do families, becoming a badge of culture among the urban Japanese.
Like the parlor piano of middleclass America in the nineteenth century,
it became the proper mode of artistic achievement for the "nice young
ladies" of prospering families.

It is a lovely instrument to hear and to see. A flattened cigar-shaped
box of about six feet, its hollow cavity acts as a resonator for the thirteen
strings of starched silk that are fixed over its top.*

Unlike the harp and piano, all of the koto's strings are the same
length. The instrument's different pitches are controlled by movable
bridges, whose placement along the length of each string affects tension
(and thus pitch). The player also can alter pitch during performances by
pressing a string down with the left hand, usually to achieve a fleeting
pitch slide. But the instrument's standard sound is produced by plucking
open strings with ivory (or plastic!) picks that are attached to three fingers
of the right hand. (The koto is shown in Illustration 39.5)

The shakuhachi is a flute like the ryuteki, except that it is held verti-
cally and end-blown. The picture in Illustration 39.9 can clarify this
distinction more clearly than words.

---

*Some modern versions of the koto have seventeen strings, and plastic strings often
replace starched silk.

Illustration 39.9 (Left) This player's wristwatch is modern, but his shakuhachi is as ancient as its bamboo body suggests. The instrument's breathy tone provides one of the unmistakable sounds of traditional Japanese music.

Illustration 39.10 (Above) With a plectrum plucking its strings the shamisen's twangy timbre compliments the harplike quality of the koto in ensemble performances.

The tone of the shakuhachi is considerably softer and breathier than the tone of the Western flute or the Japanese ryuteki. Its air column is activated in exactly the same fashion as one blows a pop bottle to produce a tone. Its pitches are controlled by four finger holes on the top and one on the underside of its bamboo body, but the skilled player can produce a multitude of pitches and pitch shadings far in excess of what those five holes might suggest.

The shamisen (sometimes spelled *samisen*) enjoys the same widespread popularity in Japan that the guitar holds in most Western countries. Its traditional uses are many, from accompanying folk songs and general party merriment to its more sedate role in various art music ensembles. It is even the principal voice in the background music of kabuki plays.

Like the shakuhachi, the shamisen's origins are Chinese. It looks like an underfed banjo, the extended, slender body bearing only three strings of twisted silk. Even its sharp-edged timbre is not unlike that of the banjo, a similarity that is reinforced by the large plectrum used to pluck its strings. (The playing styles of the two are so different in other respects, however, that one rarely would be mistaken for the other.)

When the koto, shakuhachi, and shamisen are combined as an ensemble, the koto is the principal instrument, the melodic spine to which the other two add embellishment. As in gagaku, each instrument plays about the same melody as the others, but their singular interpretations lead to the simultaneous variations that make a heterophonic texture. A second koto or shamisen is sometimes added to the standard three parts of the koto ensemble, thus producing an even richer body of intertwining melodies.

Rokudan no Shirabe ("Variations on Rokudan")

This performance follows the standard scheme of koto ensemble music, which is the statement of a well-known theme and subsequent variations. The melody *Rokudan,* which literally means "six sections," is played by the ensemble in an ordering of sections that suggests the plan of *jo, ha, kyu* we mentioned earlier in our discussion of gagaku.

It is not difficult to follow the overall form. The melody is dominated by a motif of a falling skip. This pattern begins the melody in long tones, ends the melody, and recurs periodically through middle phrases. (It is marked by a bracket where it occurs in Example 39.6.)

At about one minute and fifty seconds into the piece, a brief interlude introduces an accelerated pace, and slightly more elaborate melodic action forms a first variation of the theme. After little more than a minute, another tiny interlude announces a still more rapid tempo; then a second variation is played. This variation dissolves subsequently into the solo gestures of a slow *tomede* that ends the work. The result is a simple processive form of *A A' A''.*

The scale we can extract from the melody of *Rokudan* is interesting because two different notes occur at various times as its sixth member. As Example 39.5 shows, the first of these two notes (B♭) fits the ritsu scale-type we showed in Example 39.2 The second (B♮) forms with the other notes a pattern corresponding to the first six notes of the Dorian mode.*

Example 39.5   The scale basis of *Rokudan no Shirabe*

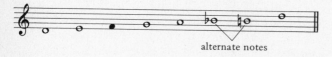

alternate notes

Note in Example 39.6 how two melodic excerpts from *Rokudan* correspond to the notes of the scale shown in Example 39.5.

---

*See the Glossary, *Church modes.*

Example 39.6   Melodic patterns from the beginning of the melody

You may notice that the pulse of *Rokudan no Shirabe* is far steadier, once the tempo has settled in, than the pulse heard in *Etenraku*. It is not at all difficult to tap a steady four beats to its three large sections, although each is progressively faster than the one before. As you will hear, the music of the koto ensemble tradition does not possess the kind of elastic rhythms we observed in *gagaku*.

40

TRADITIONAL MUSIC
OF NORTH INDIA

BACKGROUND

Most Westerners find Indian traditional music less strange than Japanese. The reasons are simple and few: Indian rhythms seem more akin to those of our own heritage, and the instrumental sounds are not far different from those we hear in our own pop music.

While Japanese gagaku and san-kyoku ensembles perform relatively fixed music—compositions that sound much as they did centuries ago—Indian music thrives on improvisation. Most of the melodic substance in a particular Indian performance will be unlike any other performance of before or after. As we noted in Chapter 39, Japanese performers are handed down actual melodies which, except for "interpretive" alterations and embellishments, they strive to reproduce with accuracy. Indian performers are bequeathed only a set of "game rules"; these form the basis for spontaneous creations.

The ceremonial elegance of Japanese gagaku gives that music a sound of remoteness that harks back to its role in an imperial court. Although Indian music of past centuries was cultivated and enriched by members of the courts of sultans and maharajas, its flavor is decidedly more democratic. It is music of warmth, conveying a spirit of human interaction rather than separation.

Illustration 40.1
Although the microphones are 20th century additions, the seated positions for a raga performance by tabla, tanbura, and sitar are as old as the musical style itself.

Our classification of the art music of India as "Northern" or "Southern" is consistent with real cultural boundaries of that country. The musical division of North and South in this case refers to an imaginary line that would cut through Hyderabad, which lies in the central lower region of the country. And thus, for musical purposes, Bombay and Calcutta, as well as Delhi, are "North Indian." The music of this area is the focus of our discussion.

The reasons for this national split was the Muslim domination of North India during the thirteenth century. A rich Indian traditional music had flowered as early as the seventh century. Its performance style and theoretical basis were formulated as elegantly as those of Greek and Chinese music. The Muslim subjugation of provinces in the North forced Hindu artists and intellectuals to flee southward when they could not accept the compromises of Islamic rule.

The relevance to our study of this invasion by another culture is twofold: (1) Traditional Indian music remained relatively intact and pure in the South; and (2) there was an intermixing of Hindu and Muslim concepts and practices in the North. And so today we can have Karnatic music (from the South) or Hindustani music (from the North). In some respects they are alike; in numerous details they are quite different. We shall touch upon some of their differences in our discussions of Hindustani music.

455

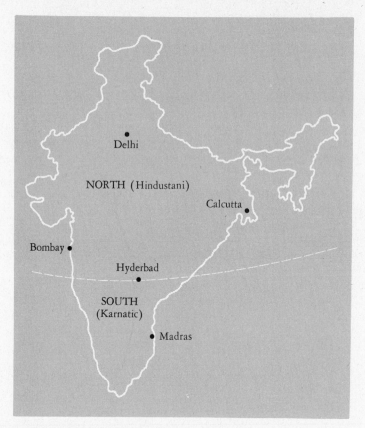

Delhi

NORTH (Hindustani)

Calcutta

Bombay

Hyderbad

SOUTH
(Karnatic)

Madras

Illustration 40.2 Map of India

THE CHAIN OF TRADITION IN INDIAN MUSIC

The master Indian musician learns his trade through a long and arduous system of apprenticeship. The system's demands on the apprentice are strenuous enough to make a religious monastic feel liberated. The musician's skill must be great, and thus training is no light matter. The master teacher (*guru*) must be chosen with uncompromising care. As one who knows the process admits, "The choice of the guru is even more important than choosing a husband or a wife."* The novice is as much servant as student. Paying nothing for his lessons, he is expected to be at the command of the teacher, to perform the most menial as well as more musical tasks.

---

*Ravi Shankar, *My Music, My Life*, New York: Simon and Schuster, 1968, p. 11.

Until a master is convinced that the student has achieved a minimal level of artistry, the latter must remain in a pupil role or ultimately relinquish all hopes of an esteemed musical career. The teacher passes on knowledge and skill by rote instruction. The pupil listens, sings back, plays back, memorizes, and practices in a way that seems light years removed from the conventions of our modern conservatories.

Musical Origins

As with most art music of the world, Indian music originated in religion. The Vedic hymns, counterparts of early Hebraic chants and Christian songs, are probably the oldest song tradition of the world. An art song type emerged from these ceremonial melodies over a period of several centuries. This artistic offspring shaped the vocal traditions that dominate all Indian music today, instrumental as well as vocal.

The more "modern" tradition we shall focus upon is called *khyal* ("*kee'-all*"). It is the most important form used in performances of North Indian art songs and instrumental pieces today, replacing the older *dhrupad* in an evolution that began in the fifteenth century.* As we shall see, the khyal bears some resemblance to the return form we know as the rondo. As a musical type, however, khyal implies more than just a form. It also suggests a kind of instrumentation and a process of performance.

---

*The dhrupad is a more inflexible musical form than *khyal*, involving considerably less real improvisation. It can be heard more in the South than in the North.

Illustration 40.3
Ravi Shankar, shown here playing sitar with drummer Chatur Lal, was largely responsible for making the music of India known throughout the world.

PITCH BASIS OF INDIAN MUSIC

Most Americans who have heard Indian music also have heard the word *rāga*, and this is a good point of departure for our discussion of the substance of Indian music. A rāga is an exacting pattern of pitches. It is more than a scale, yet it is less than a full-fledged melody. Let us say that it is the melodic list of materials from which the Indian performer creates, in spontaneous improvisation, a musical composition.

There are hundreds of known rāgas. They have multiplied, they have been combined, and they have been altered and refined over an evolution of centuries. The accomplished Indian musician must have memorized between fifty and one hundred of these pitch patterns before achieving professional status. And yet the most renowned masters of North Indian music rely on only a dozen or so rāgas for their performances.

The pitches of a rāga can be represented as a scale, but one must keep in mind that a scale cannot wholly represent what an Indian understands by the term rāga. There are melodic turns, ornaments, and pitch shadings that also contribute to the character of any particular rāga. In fact, some rāgas can be reduced to the same scale, but the way a performer executes the notes of that scale within his improvisation determines which rāga he plays. Even the scale itself is often different going down from what it is going up.

For example, the scale of rāga *Tilang* has five principal notes in its ascending and five in its descending forms. But one of the principal notes is different in the two, and an additional secondary note occurs in the descending pattern. Example 40.1 shows (1) the complete scale for rāga *Tilang*, (2) the notes that are emphasized most in performance (called *vadis* and *samvadis*), and (3) a melodic pattern that occurs frequently in any performance of this rāga.*

Example 40.1   Pitch details of raga *Tilang*

one characteristic melodic pattern of the rāga

---

*For a more complete discussion of rāga *Tilang*, see Walter Kaufmann, *The Ragas of North India*, Bloomington: Indiana University Press, pp. 207–8.

The meaning of a rāga's scale to a performer is simple. When playing a melody whose contour goes up, the performer uses only the pitches of the ascending scale. When the melody moves downward, the pattern must be confined to notes of the descending scale. Observance of this practice is one crucial aspect of the rāga's mood, or what Indians call its *rasa*.

Rasa

This word *rasa* is significant for all Indian art. It refers to the primary emotion, or "sentiment," projected by the artist in his creation, whether it be a poem, a painting, a play, or a musical composition. In music, each rāga supports a particular rasa and that one only. The possible rasas of Indian lore are classified as nine, the *Nava Rasa*. They are the following:

Shringāra:	romantic, erotic
Hāsya:	funny, amusing
Karun:	pitiful, lonely
Raudra:	angry, furious
Veera:	majestic, brave
Bhayānaka:	fearful, disturbing
Vibhatsa:	disgusting, repellent
Abdhuta:	strange, amazing
Shānta:	tranquil, peaceful

If you are not immersed in Indian music and lore, don't become disheartened if you cannot sense one of these "feelings" when listening to a particular rāga. Like the existence of unicorns, the direct relationship of rāga to rasa is not easily demonstrated. Indian lore is filled with stories of miraculous feats performed by revered musicians, who, once in perfect control of their art, could bring rain, make flowers bloom, or even melt stones through the intense projection of an appropriate rasa. (The frequency of such feats appears to have subsided in recent decades.)

Rāga and function

Since each rāga is possessed of its own rasa, or mood, it is supposed to be performed only at particular times. There are rāgas for special seasons of the year, and there are rāgas deemed appropriate only for a special time of the day or night. Rāga *Tilang*, which we illustrated in Example 40.1, is a "light" rāga (meaning less than profound in nature); its proper performance time is evening.

In spite of these traditional controls on rāga performance, however, corruption has come with modern times. The rising popularity of large public concerts has led to the decay of this long-imbedded convention. Even in the Karnatic music of the tradition-prone South, ragas intended for specific parts of the day or night are played at any time, except by those performers who most carefully guard the purity of their tradition.

RHYTHMIC ORGANIZATION

In addition to the rāga, which determines the pitch content of a performance, there is also a rhythmic component for guidance. Called *tala* ("tah'-lah"), this rhythmic component amounts to a precise way of organizing melodic phrases and their beats within an extended composition. A tala (which in Sanskrit means "palm of hand") is a time-unit that is divided in a special way to make a rhythm. When used, the tala, chosen from a number of such patterns by the performer, is repeated over and over again until the end of the composition.

In discussing the blues tradition of jazz in Chapter 5, we noted that a scheme of three phrases underlies most blues songs and improvisations. We also noted that each phrase contains four measures (or bars) of four beats. It is helpful to recall this characteristic of the blues—its overall "phrase rhythm"—in discussing the tala of Indian music.

Example 40.2   The three-phrase rhythm of the standard blues verse

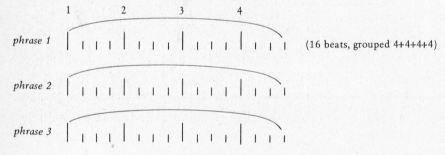

Blues performers must have this elemental rhythm of forty-eight beats as a part of their subconscious to perform a convincing blues verse. Its beat-groupings of $16 + 16 + 16$, each phrase itself composed of $4 + 4 + 4 + 4$ beats, is the rhythmic groundwork of the form.

The Indian tala serves the same kind of shaping function. Lacking harmony as a component of improvisation, Indian musicians nonetheless control the ebb and flow of their improvisations by following precisely the beat order of a single tala. One may play patterns that are at odds with the tala, just as a jazz performer plays syncopations that momentarily contradict a prevailing meter. But one must always return to patterns that comply with the accent structure of the chosen tala or risk losing the underlying unity of the composition.

Like rāgas, there are many talas. The lengths of particular talas extend from only three beats to one hundred and eight beats. But, again as with rāgas, the practicing Indian musician favors only a sampling of the talas the tradition provides. Most of the talas used today in North Indian music consist of from six to sixteen beats.

Unlike the measures of blues phrase-rhythms, talas do not always consist of units of equal length. Some do, like tala *Tintal* ("Teen'-tall"). Although its whole pattern is comparable to only one phrase of a blues verse, *Tintal* contains beats grouped in fours, and its pattern is sixteen beats long. Our next example shows its structure.

Example 40.3   The beat structure of tala *Tintal*

The "accent" numbers at the bottom of Example 40.3 bear some explanation. The X at the beginning is called *sam*.* It is the downbeat for the full phase of sixteen beats, the rallying point for all musical forces engaged in an improvisation. The *2* in the example refers to the second accent of the tala, and the *0* marks an "open accent," which is more felt than real. And *3* is the stress that is preparation for the following *sam*, which will occur upon the repetition of the complete pattern.

To understand better what tala *Tintal* is really like for the Indian musician, count out, *in fours*, the pattern shown in Example 40.3, taking care that each successive number is uniform with all others. As you follow the diagram in your recitation, clap and stomp on *sam* to repeat the cycle. Once you can perform the cycle seven or eight times without missing a clap (or stomp!), you have a fundamental notion of what tala *Tintal* means for an Indian drummer.

Many talas possess more engaging patterns than *Tintal*. Tala *Dhamar-tal*, for instance, consists of fourteen beats grouped as a pattern of $5 + 2 + 3 + 4$. Its accent groupings are shown in Example 40.4. You may find its uneven units a bit harder to perform than the simple fours of tala *Tintal*.

Example 40.4   The beat structure of tala *Dhamar-tal*

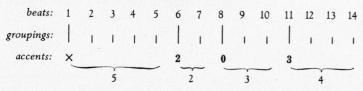

---

*The word *sam*, in Sanskrit, means "with" or "together."

Whatever the length or complexity of any tala's pattern, it is the Indian performer's artistic responsibility to control the rhythmic life of his music by it, in those portions of works where tala is appropriate. Performers choose the rāga and tala they will incorporate within a given performance. In combination with the pitch basis provided by the chosen rāga, the tala is the skeletal time-frame within which a work is created.

INSTRUMENTS OF KHYAL

The generating force of all Indian music is the human voice. From the ancient Vedic hymns to the contemporary rāga concert, musical styles of Hindustani and Karnatic musics have been modeled after the styles of traditional Indian singers. Even the ornamentation and rapid runs played by solo string instruments or flutes have their counterparts in singing. The Indian vocalist, who is as much a creative improviser as the instrumentalist, is esteemed as much for *what* is sung as for *how* it is sung. Thus he or she cannot be judged only in terms of sheer vocal beauty.

As for instruments, the favored instruments in recent centuries have been plucked strings, particularly those of the *sitar* and the *vina*. The sitar is favored in North India, although master performers play both instruments. Both are fretted, like the guitar, and both are played by plucking the metal strings, usually with a plectrum, sometimes with bare fingers.

The sitar is a beautiful lute-type, with a large gourd attached behind and at the end of its fingerboard.* Its long body accommodates seven strings, five of which are used by the player for melody notes, the other two for the accompanying "drone" sounds that abound in all Indian music. The sitar body also harbors thirteen extra strings that are not plucked. They are carefully tuned so that they will "whir" in response to the sounds of those played by the performer. These sympathetic strings are a major source of the unique timbre of the sitar, making it sound quite different from a guitar.

The sitar is always accompanied in ensembles by the *tanbura* ("tah-boo'-rah").† This is a drone instrument that provides only the main pitches of the rāga as a continuous background. The tanbura normally plays three different pitches (all open strings), most often only the first and fifth notes of the rāga's scale. This incessant pattern helps to remind the performer (and the listener too) of the foundation of the rāga, as it progresses within an improvisation.

---

*The hollow cavity of the gourd once provided a resonator for the sitar's tone. It is decorative rather than functional on modern sitars, except as a handy prop for the body when the instrument is set down. The vina has two gourds.

†Spellings of Indian concepts and instruments vary. I have chosen those used by Walter Kaufmann.

Illustration 40.4
The sitar's metal frets, used to control pitches, and decorative gourd are evident in this photograph of virtuoso player Nikhil Banerjee.

Illustration 40.5
Tabla drum under right hand, banya under left, the skilled tabla performer produces some of the most intricately compelling rhythms imaginable.

Illustration 40.6 The tanbura's four strings furnish the steady pulse for improvisations within some sections of a rāga. This instrument's rounded body—derived from the shape of a gourd—makes it one of the most beautiful of the lute types.

Next to the sitar in importance in the Indian *khyal* performance are two small drums played by one performer. The two are collectively called *tabla* ("*tah'-blah*"). The left-hand drum, called *banya*, is slightly larger than that for the right hand, which by itself is called *tabla*. The smaller drum is tunable; the player adjusts its pitch to sound the principal note of the rāga in use. Under the hands of a master player, the tabla become solo instruments on a par with the sitar, and many exciting "battles" occur when two players of comparable skill perform together.

Within a rāga performance the tabla are played only during sections of the improvisation where a tala is incorporated. We shall discuss this peculiarity of *khyal* music presently, noting for the present that the preservation of a tala's integrity is a major responsibility for the tabla player, just as the tanbura must provide the unceasing drone composed of the rāga's principal pitches.

RĀGA PERFORMANCE

Like the formal processes of Japanese gagaku, a rāga performance is based on conventions that are followed as closely as its performers choose. A true Indian concert is an interesting play of responses between artists and listeners. As in most genuinely improvised music, the performers determine how long their spontaneous creation will go on, and this demands on-the-spot decisions that rule out rigid forms. As Ravi Shankar so fluently states, "The miracle of our music is in the beautiful rapport that occurs when a deeply spiritual musician performs for a receptive and sympathetic group of listeners."* When this happens, a rāga may last hours. When it does not happen, the performance may be brief and perfunctory.

There are, nonetheless, at least two formal principles that hold in an ensemble performance of a Hindustani rāga. They are the *alap* and *gat*, which occur in that order. These two large divisions of the performance can themselves be divided into a multitude of smaller parts, some of which are frequently deleted in current practice.

The alap lasts just as long as the soloist feels it should. Its function is similar to that of the prelude in Western music, or what the Japanese gagaku tradition calls the *netori*. Accompanied only by the tanbura's drone, the solo's rhythms are free, creating a rhapsodic "invocation" in which the pitches and characteristic melodic turns of the chosen rāga are divulged. The soloist fights a series of fanciful skirmishes around the principal notes (*tonic*, *vadis*, and *samvadis*), ever careful to observe the allowable notes of the rāga's up-and-down scale forms.

Once content that the rāga's characteristics have been exposed adequately, and a foundation for the appropriate rasa laid, the ensemble then proceeds to the next large section, the gat. Here for the first time the tabla enters. Now begins the first sounding of the tala cycle. If in a broad sense we view the alap as a distinct Exposition of the rāga, then the gat is its Development.

With the beginning of the gat and its tala, a steady pulse is introduced. The initial pulse-rate may continue to the end of the work or it may quicken considerably as tension mounts. Whether it remains or changes depends upon the rāga employed and the rasa it is intended to suggest. But the whole gat is itself conceived as a section of several parts. These smaller parts offer soloist and accompanists alternative ways for

---

*In *My Music, My Life*, p. 58.

extending a performance that is going well (or abbreviating one that is going badly!). The gat's extensity varies from one performance to another, but its conventional parts are the following:*

1	*Asthayi:*	tabla enters; soloist stresses notes in lower part of the rāga's scale;
2	*Antara:*	soloist stresses upper notes of rāga's scale;
3	*Asthayi:*	one full tala statement, *sam* to *sam*;
4	*Alap:*	now accompanied;
5	*Tans:*	rapid figurations based on patterns heard earlier;
6	*Proper* (or "*big*") *tans:*	still more complex figurations usually rising to a climax;
7	*Asthayi* (or *abhoga*):	brief return to the first *asthayi*; ensemble ends together on a final sam of the tala.

As itemized here, with its two returns of the asthayi, the layout of khyal resembles a rondo form. But the novice listener must be warned that *hearing* distinct returns in the improvisations of a rāga is quite another matter. Don't be alarmed if you do not recognize any returns to earlier melodic patterns as you listen to your first rāga performances.

Rāga Maru-Hihag:
Ravi Shankar,
sitar; Chatur Lal,
tabla; N.C.
Mullick, tanbura

This performance† contains a relatively brief alap. Sitar and tanbura slowly unfold the full range of tonal characteristics of *Maru-Bihag*, an evening rāga. The scale of this rāga is shown in Example 40.5, its most important notes (*vadis* and *samvadis*) appropriately marked. Some notes are shown in parentheses. Although they occur in the rāga within melodies, they are decidedly ornamental. The exotic sound of this rāga results in part from use of *F♯* (degree #3 in the ascending scale) as one of its primary notes. This single pitch makes the tonal material contrast sharply with the scales of most Western music, which would contain *F♮* in this position.

Example 40.5   The scale of rāga *Maru-Bihag*

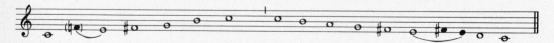

The melodic figures shown in Example 40.6 are typical of some you will hear, in both the alap and the later gat. Listen to them played on

---

*This listing is most consistent with Kaufmann's in *The Rāgas of North India*. A different set of names, based mainly on Karnatic practices, can be found in Malm's *Music Cultures of the Pacific, the Near East, and Asia*, 2nd Edition (Englewood Cliffs, N.J.: Prentice-Hall, Inc., 1977) pp. 103–4.

†The same performance can be heard on Columbia WL 119, Band 3 of Side 1.

a piano for a better grasp of the tone relations of the rāga. (Note also, as you listen, what a poor substitute for a sitar the piano makes!)

Example 40.6   Two characteristic melodic patterns of *Maru-Bihag*

The whole gat of this performance is based on a tala called *Jhaptal*. Its ten-beat structure is shown in Example 40.7.

Example 40.7   Beat structure of tala *Jhaptal*

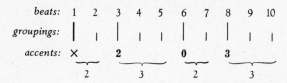

It is not difficult to follow the tala of this performance. Listen through the gat several times. During a later hearing pay special attention to just what the tabla player is doing with his separate drums. The sam is most often stressed in a special way on the lower drum (*banya*). In almost every cycle no other articulation follows that beat immediately, so that it seems isolated within the whole pattern. The second "measure," beginning with accent *2*, contains strokes on both high and low drums. Then the "open," or *0* accent, invariably contains only the higher drum, with the banya emerging for the beats of the last grouping, accent *3*.

One way to "get into" the tala of this piece is to listen for the "open beats," each of which is followed by the three beats of accent *3*. Once you have located this "bare spot," the following sam seems obvious, and you will be able to follow the continuation of the pattern.

Although sitar and tabla gradually increase the intensity of their patterns, the beats of the tala are kept in order at the same slow tempo. And—as befits the integrity of any master of the rāga—the three performers end together, precisely on the final sam. They have completed a total of sixty-three cycles of tala *Jhaptal* in the process.

GLOSSARY

An italicized word within a definition can be found defined within the Glossary. References in parentheses at the end of some entries are to Chapters in which the topic is treated in depth.

A CAPELLA   Choral music without instrumental accompaniment

ACCELERANDO   To grow faster, accellerate

ACCENT   Greater emphasis on a tone within a group of tones, often through stress by playing it louder

ACCIDENTAL   Notation signs such as sharp (♯), flat (♭), or natural (♮), which indicate a change of pitch by one half-step

ADDITIVE FORM   Formal scheme in which the large sections contain different thematic material, such as $ABCD\ldots$

AIR, AYRE   Archaic terms for relatively simple songs, usually of *Strophic form*

ALEATORY   A process involving chance. Aleatory music is not wholly controlled by the composer but allows chance events a central role in producing the piece

ALLEGRO   Fast tempo (ALLEGRETTO: Moderately fast)

ALTO   Low female voice

AMPLIFIER   Mechanism that increases the loudness of a sound. The hollow body of a violin is an amplifier as is the electronic device called "amplifier" in any audio system.

ANDANTE   Moderately slow tempo

ANTHEM   Modest sacred work for choir performed within the Anglican or Protestant service

ANTIPHONY, ANTIPHONAL   Musical texture in which two or more separated bodies of sound (such as two choirs) alternate

ARIA   Song for solo singer accompanied by orchestra within an opera, an oratoria, or a cantata

ART SONG   Solo song, intended for concert performance, that is a careful combination of words, melody and accompaniment

ARPEGGIO   Successive rather than simultaneous sounding of the tones of a chord

A TEMPO   Return to the preceding or to an earlier main tempo

ATONAL, ATONALITY   Absence of tonality; no sense of tones related to a single pitch class or chord

AUGMENTATION   Stretching out the durations of a rhythm heard previously. Usual rate is a doubling of durations, so that ♩ ♫♩♫ ♩ would become 𝅝 ♩. ♫♩ ♩. Opposite of *Diminution*

AVANT GARDE   Latest thing; most recent style; most advanced

BAGATELLE   Brief, unpretentious piece, usually for piano although sometimes for small chamber group

BALLAD   Poem or song that relates a story

BALLETT   English song of the Renaissance period. Dance-like in character, the ballett usually contains a *fa-la* segment within its text.

BAR, BARLINE   Vertical lines in musical notation that divide the staff into measures

BARITONE   Mature male voice whose pitch range lies between tenor (high) and bass (low)

BAROQUE PERIOD   Musical era that begins with early opera around 1600 and ends with the death of J. S. Bach in 1750

BASS   (1) Low male voice;
(2) Lowest sounding part in a musical texture, whether sung or played by an instrument

BASSO CONTINUO   See *Continuo*

BEAT   Regular pulse in music, the "count"

BEBOP   See *Bop*

BEL CANTO   Style of singing that emphasizes beautiful tone and brilliant performance technique rather than the expression of dramatic emotion

BINARY FORM   Any form that contains only two large sections, such as *A B*

BLUES   Type of musical expression and form of Negro origins. Originally sung, the characteristics of the blues were early transferred to purely instrumental performance. (Chapters 5 and 35)

BOP   Complex jazz style of the period 1945–1960, developed by such performers as Charlie Parker and Dizzy Gillespie. (Chapter 37)

BRASS   Any of the instruments such as trumpet, trombone, tuba, and horn that are made of brass, with the exception of the saxophone (a *woodwind* because of its reed mouthpiece). The term is often used to denote the section in an orchestra or band that consists of the brass instruments

BRIDGE   Musical passage that links two other passages of thematic importance. In *Sonata Form* such a passage usually connects the first and second thematic sections

CADENCE   Event in any musical passage that suggests momentary or permanent conclusion. The cadence is the ending event of phrases, sections, and whole compositions

CADENZA   Elaborate passage of improvisatory style played by a soloist, usually in a *Concerto*. The *cadenza* is an opportunity for the soloist to reveal extraordinary technical skill within the thematic content of the composition.

CANON   (1) Polyphonic texture in which voices perform the same melody but starting at different times;
(2) A whole composition that incorporates the canonic process

CANTATA   Composition for solo voice or a combination of solo voices, instrumental accompaniment, and, usually, a chorus. Depending on the subject matter of its text, a cantata can be sacred or secular.

CANTUS FIRMUS   Literally, "fixed melody." Refers to a melody that is used as the basis for a composition for several voices. In such a work the *cantus firmus* melody usually occurs without changes that might reduce its identity. (See *Passacaglia*)

CHACONNE   Composition in which a repeated chord series provides the basis for variations

CHAMBER MUSIC   Music intended for performance by a small group of instruments (or voices and instruments) within relatively intimate surroundings

CHANCE MUSIC   Music in which the composer allows chance or accident to play a role in determining the final result. (See *Aleatory*)

CHANSON   French for song

CHANT   (1) In general, a singing style that is rhythmically free and similar to recitation;

(2) The monophonic songs of the early Christian church. (See *Gregorian Chant*)

CHOIR   Usually refers to the group of singers in a church, but also to instrumental groups of the same family, such as string choir, brass choir, woodwind choir

CHORALE   Hymn melody of the German Protestant church, usually harmonized for singing by a congregation. (Chapter 19)

CHORD   Collection of tones of different pitch sounding together as a unit

CHORUS   Body of singers outside a church

CHROMATIC   (1) Set of two or more pitches that are separated by successive half-steps (such as *c—c♯—d—e♭*); (2) a single note whose pitch is raised or lowered by an *Accidental* (such as *G♭* or *C♯*)

CHURCH MODES   Collection of scales that provided the tonal basis of early Western music (before 1600). The four basic modes were Dorian, Phrygian, Lydian, and Mixolydian; late additions were Ionian and Aeolian

CLASSICAL PERIOD   Musical era that began around the time of J. S. Bach's death (1750) and extended to the eruption of Romanticism around 1810

CLAVICHORD   Early keyboard instrument whose strings are struck by small metal wedges, or tangents. Somewhat quieter than the harpsichord, whose strings are plucked

CLEF   Sign of musical notation which, when placed on a staff, indicates the pitches of notes. Most common clef signs are treble, or *G* clef ( ) and bass, or *F* clef ( )

CLOSING THEME   Melodic event whose main function is to suggest the imminent conclusion of a large musical section

CODA   The "tail" or concluding passage of a whole composition

COLORATURA   Elaborate singing style consisting of rapid rhythms, florid ornamentation (such as trills), and generally virtuoso character

COMBO   Small collection of instruments—usually no more than five or six—used in performing jazz

COMPOSITE METER   Meter in which basic pulses are of unequal durations, such as in $\frac{5}{8}$, $\frac{7}{4}$, or $\frac{8}{8}$ ($\frac{3}{8}$ + $\frac{3}{8}$ + $\frac{2}{8}$). Usually identifiable as combinations of duple and triple meters.

COMPOUND METER   Meter whose basic pulse is normally divided into threes, such as $\frac{6}{8}$, $\frac{9}{8}$, and $\frac{6}{4}$. Opposite of *Simple* meter

CON BRIO   With spirit

CONCERTINO   Group of soloists in a *Concerto Grosso*

CONCERTO   Large work that combines a solo player (sometimes players) and orchestra as equal rivals. The standard concerto consists of three *Movements*

CONCERTO GROSSO   Favored concerto type of the Baroque period, combining a small group of soloists (the *Concertino*) with a supporting orchestra of strings and harpsichord (the *Ripieno*)

CON MOTO   With motion—moving onward

CONSONANCE   Property of pitch combinations—intervals or chords—of relatively low tension. Consonant chords usually contain no more than three different pitch classes (low *Harmonic density*)

CONTINUO   (1) Bass part of Baroque compositions that included harpsichord or organ. This part consisted of a melody and sets of numbers which denoted chords to be sounded by the keyboard player; (2) the group of instruments that play the continuo part

CONTRALTO   Same as *Alto*

COUNTERPOINT   Technique of combining melodies that create a *Polyphonic* texture

COUNTERSUBJECT   Secondary melodic pattern used in continuing association with a principal theme or subject. Many fugues contain countersubjects which provide a constant foil for the fugue's main subject

COUNTERTENOR Name frequently used for the mature male voice that sings within the female pitch range

CRESCENDO Growing louder

CYCLE One complete oscillation of a vibrating body (string or reed)

CYCLIC FORM Composition of several movements in which a theme from an early movement returns in one or more later movements. (See Beethoven's *Symphony No. 5*, Chapter 8)

DECRESCENDO Growing softer, less loud

DEVELOPMENT (1) Process of reworking or varying melodic patterns that have appeared earlier in expository statements; (2) a separate section of *Sonata form* in which thematic reworkings and modifications occur

DIATONIC Collection of pitches that corresponds to the notes of a major or minor scale or a mode. Adjacent notes in these scales may contain half-steps or whole steps.

DIMINUENDO Same as *Decrescendo*

DIMINUTION Reducing the durations of tones in a rhythm heard previously. The usual rate is a halving of durations, so that ♩. ♩ ♪♩ ♪♩

becomes ♩. ♪♫♫♩. The opposite of *Augmentation*

DISCORD A pejorative term sometimes used to describe a dissonant chord

DISSONANCE Property of pitch combinations —intervals or chords—of relatively high tension. Dissonant chords contain intervals of high *Sonance* rating, such as seconds and sevenths

DOMINANT (1) Fifth degree of a major or minor scale; (2) the chord based on the fifth scale degree

DOTTED NOTE A note whose duration is increased by a dot, thus making it half again greater. Thus a dotted half note (♩.) is equal in duration to three quarter notes

(♩ ♩ ♩)

DOUBLE EXPOSITION Procedure of many classical concertos in which both orchestra and soloist successively expose thematic material (Chapter 25)

DUET A composition for two equally prominent performers (with or without accompaniment)

DUPLE METER Meter whose pulses are grouped in units of equal twos, such as $\frac{2}{4}, c, \phi, \frac{4}{8}, \frac{6}{8}, \frac{2}{2}$ or $\frac{12}{8}$

DYNAMICS Loud/soft property of musical sounds

ELECTRONIC MUSIC Music created with electronic sound generators rather than with acoustical instruments such as violins, drums, clarinets, or voices

EPISODE Brief section of secondary formal significance, usually devoid of statements of main theme patterns

ÉTUDE Composition whose substance is largely derived from patterns that provide technical development for the performer. French word for "Study"

EXPOSITION Section of a composition—at or quite near the beginning—in which main thematic patterns are first exposed

EXTRAMUSICAL Ideas which although relevant to a composition are not themselves musical. For example, the image of a sailboat in the wind is relevant to Debussy's *Voile*, but it is hardly a musical object as such

EXPRESSIONISM Artistic movement of the early 20th century that stressed the artist's expression of inner feelings about things rather than the images of those things. (Berg's *Violin Concerto*, Chapter 26)

FERMATA Sign of musical notation (⌢) indicating that durations of a note are to be extended

FIGURED BASS Shorthand system of numbers and signs used in keyboard parts of the late Baroque period. The numbers—or figures— appear below the bass line, indicating to the player what chords should be played above the bass

FLAT Sign of musical notation (♭) that indicates the lowering of a natural note by one half-step

FORM The ordering of large musical events according to some principle such as *Return, Strophic, Additive,* or *Processive*

FORTE (*f*); FORTISSIMO (*ff*) Loud (or strong); very loud

FREQUENCY Rate at which a vibrating body completes its *Cycle* of vibration. The frequency of the pitch *a* at the middle of the piano keyboard is 440 cycles per second

FUGATO Brief passage, within a larger composition, whose texture is that of the *Fugue*

FUGUE *Processive form* in which imitative polyphony is the exclusive texture. A fugue begins with the exposition of its subject (or principal theme) and continues through successive developments of that subject, all of which rely on imitation as a textural course of action

GENERATOR Device that electronically produces a sound wave

GENRE General musical type according to medium of performance, purpose of the performance (church, concert hall, football game), and to style. Opera, jazz, urban blues, bluegrass, and symphony are each examples of a different genre

GIGUE Brisk dance in compound meter that sometimes contains fugal textures

GLISSANDO Smooth slide from one pitch to another without resting on pitches of arrival in between

GREGORIAN CHANT Collection of sacred monophonic songs of the Roman Catholic Church. Named for Pope Gregory I (540–604)

GROUND, GROUND BASS Short melody repeated continually in the bass of a texture whose upper parts unfold varied patterns

HALF-TONE Smallest pitch interval on the piano and in conventional Western scales. Also called semitone and half-step

HARMONIC DENSITY Refers to the number of different pitch classes contained within a single chord

HARMONICS (1) Less prominent higher pitches that accompany most tones produced by musical instruments (synonomous with "overtones");

(2) pitches playable on a string or wind instrument by dividing the open string or the total air column into equal segments (same as "partial")

HARMONY In a narrow sense, synonomous with *Chord*. In a broader sense, the total pattern of chords within a musical passage

HETEROPHONIC, HETEROPHONY Musical texture in which two or more parts perform slight variants of the same melody at the same time (Chapter 39)

HOMOPHONIC, HOMOPHONY Musical texture dominated by a single melody, all other parts secondary

HYMN *Strophic* song sung within a religious service by the congregation

IDÉE FIXE Recurring melody or motif of extramusical reference that provides unity between sections or movements of a large composition. The term Berlioz used to define the melodic basis of his *Symphonie Fantastique*

IMITATION Restatement in succession of a melodic pattern by another voice or other voices. Usually, though not always, produces a polyphonic texture

IMPRESSIONISM Brief artistic movement during the late 19th and early 20th centuries, represented in music by such composers as Claude Debussy, Maurice Ravel, and Charles Griffes. (Chapters 11 and 32)

IMPROVISATION Spontaneous rather than carefully pre-planned creation. Jazz musicians play largely through improvisation rather than from composed parts

INTERVAL Distance between any two pitches, usually named according to the line-space distances of the musical staff. For example, a

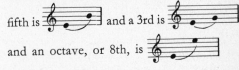

fifth is [musical notation] and a 3rd is [musical notation] and an octave, or 8th, is [musical notation]

INTERMEZZO Relatively light entertainment placed between the acts of more serious entertainment. In music the title usually refers to a brief, lightweight movement between more profound movements.

INTRODUCTION Opening gesture of some compositions, often without thematic bearing on what follows

INVERSION (1) MELODIC: Turning a melody upside down so that its former rises in contour fall, and vice versa;

(2) INTERVAL: subtraction of an interval from the octave produces that interval's inversion; thus the inversion of a fifth is a fourth;

(3) TEXTURAL: Melody of the bass is changed to the top of the texture and the melody formerly on top becomes the bass

JAZZ Music of Negro origins and development that is wholly or partially improvised, of strong rhythmic drive, and performed by particular kinds of instruments such as percussion, trumpets and trombones, saxophones and clarinets

K Abbreviation for K.V., which refers to the numbering system for the compositions of Mozart that was published by L. von Köchel in 1862. (Köchel-Verzeichnis = K.V.)

KEY SIGNATURE Notational code at the beginning of a staff line that shows which pitch classes are to be sharped or flatted (if any), unless otherwise specified by *accidentals*. The key signature for Bb major consists of two flats, while the key signature for A major consists of three sharps

LARGO Extremely slow tempo

LEDGER LINE Notational lines used above or below regular staff lines for note placement

LEGATO Smooth articulation of a series of tones, each connected closely with the next rather than separated

LENTO Very slow tempo

LIBRETTO Text of an opera or oratorio

LIED German for song, frequently used to mean *Art Song* as opposed to popular or folk song

LINE Distinct part in a texture, whether genuinely melodic or wholly accompanimental in character and function

LUTE Generic name for several different instruments that have strings, are plucked by the hand, have rounded bodies similar to a turtle shell, and contain frets for producing different pitches. Lute was most popular in Western music during the late Renaissance period (Chapter 18)

MADRIGAL Popular choral type of the Renaissance period. Secular counterpart of the motet, the madrigal flourished among art composers in England and Italy.

MAJOR (1) Diatonic scale whose 1st and 3rd degrees are separated by the interval of a major third (four semitones);

(2) a Harmonic triad whose three members correspond with the 1, 3, and 5 degrees of a major scale;

(3) music that makes use of the major scale and whose *tonic* chord is a major triad

MANUAL The keyboards of an organ or harpsichord, as distinguished from any pedal mechanism operated by the performer's feet

MASS Primary liturgical service of the Roman Catholic church and the music written for it. This rite represents the central belief of the Catholic faith, which is the sacrifice of Christ through crucifixion

MAZURKA Polish dance in triple meter. The mazurka varies from slow to fast, but its rhythm usually contains accents on the second and third beats rather than on the first beat, as in the *waltz* and *minuet*

MEASURE Unit in musical notation that represents the meter. A triple meter, for instance, is notated so that each three-beat span is contained within a single measure

MEASURE LINE See *Bar*

MEDIUM Forces used to perform a composition

MELODY Succession of pitches that establishes a sense of continuity, of line

MELISMATIC Setting of words to music in which one syllable is stretched out over several (or many) different pitches, (majority of popular and communal songs are set with one syllable to each pitch)

METER   Pattern of accented and unaccented pulses that provides the time-track on which rhythms flow

METRONOME   Clocklike device that produces audible pulses at a variety of precisely controlled tempos

MEZZO   "Medium" or "between." A Mezzo-soprano voice is half-way between alto and soprano in pitch. The indication mezzo forte (or *mf*) means a loudness level between piano (soft) and forte (loud)

MINIATURE   Popular title during the Romantic period for a brief composition for solo piano or for piano and vocal or instrumental solo

MINOR   (1) Diatonic scale whose first and third degrees are separated by the interval of a minor 3rd (three semitones); (2) a harmonic triad whose three members correspond to the 1, 3, and 5 degrees of a minor scale; (3) music that makes use of the notes of a minor scale and whose *tonic* chord is a minor triad

MINUET   Dance in triple meter popular in royal courts and transferred to concert music during the 17th and 18th centuries. The minuet is of moderate tempo, its main accent on the first beat

MODAL   (1) Music that does not correspond to major or minor key systems yet is not *Chromatic*; (2) any work that uses pitches best represented by one of the *church modes*

MODE   (1) Synonomous with scale; (2) any one of the church modes

MODERATO   Moderate temp

MODULATION   Change of *tonic* or keynote from one pitch class to another

MOLTO   Very (Molto *Allegro* = very fast)

MONODY   Although it should refer to solo song, actually refers to a type of accompanied solo song that was the precursor of early opera

MONOPHONY   Texture created by several different parts singing the same melody

MOTET   Sacred choral composition, usually polyphonic

MOTIVE, MOTIF   Brief melodic pattern, longer than one articulation yet not as long as a phrase. Opening pattern of Beethoven's *Symphony No. 5* is the archetype of a musical motif

MOVEMENT   Complete, separate, and relatively independent large unit within a longer composition, usually separated by silence from other movements

MUSIQUE CONCRETE   Early form of tape music whose sounds were produced by natural sources—people, trains, wind, and the like—rather than by electronic devices

MUTE   Device applied to a musical instrument to reduce its loudness and alter its timbre. A violin mute is a small clamp attached to the instrument's bridge; a trumpet mute is a cone-shaped plug inserted in the horn's bell

NATIONALISM   Artistic movement of the late 19th century that emphasized national elements such as folk heroes, folk songs, and other symbols of cultural identity

NATURAL   Sign of musical notation (♮) that denotes the pitch of a natural note rather than a flatted or sharped note. The seven "natural" notes are represented by the white keys of the piano, *A B C D E F G*

NEOCLASSICISM   Reaction of the early 20th century to the super emotionalism of the late 19th century. Neoclassic music self-consciously returned to ideals and stylistic traits of some 18th century composers such as Bach, Haydn, and Mozart

NOCTURNE   "Night piece." One of many fanciful titles attached to little piano pieces composed during the second half of the 19th century

NON TROPPO   Not too much. (Adagio non troppo = slow, but not too slow)

NOTE   Notational equivalent of any musical sound, representing only the duration and pitch of that sound

OCTAVE   The "eighth note," in terms of any 7-note diatonic scale, and thus the interval between notes of the same name, such as g^1 and g^2, C and c

OPERA   Drama set to music that includes acting, costumes, staging, and, of course, singing accompanied by an instrumental ensemble

OPERA BUFFA   Italian opera type that stresses comedy (buffoons)

OPERA SERIA   Italian opera that stresses tragic, heroic events and characters

OPUS   Refers to the numbering of a composition within a composer's total output. Beethoven composed his Opus 1 at the age of seventeen

ORATORIO   Dramatic work of serious tone—usually religious—for solo voices, chorus, and orchestra, but produced in concert version without costumes, staging, or acting

ORCHESTRATION   Act of mixing instruments together into textures that produce a successful ensemble sound

ORDINARY   Portion of the Roman Catholic Mass whose parts (*Kyrie, Gloria, Credo, Sanctus, Agnus Dei*) remain the same, regardless of the day within the Church Year.

OSTINATO   Relatively short pattern—rhythm or melody—that is repeated many times in succession while other musical events unfold within the remaining texture

OVERTURE   Introductory piece for instruments that opens an opera or other dramatic presentation. In the 19th century independent compositions of a programmatic nature were sometimes called Overture, even though they were openings to nothing

PART   (1) A separate voice or line within a texture;
(2) Segment within a musical form

PASSACAGLIA   *Processive form* in which variations unfold in conjunction with a persistently repeated (and thus strophic) melody that remains in the bass through most of the composition

PASSION   Large concert work similar to an *Oratorio* yet whose text is based on the final tragic days of Christ, as related in the New Testament Bible

PEDAL POINT   Texture in which a single pitch is sustained or rearticulated while motion occurs within other parts

PENTATONIC   Five note scale, as opposed to the seven-note scales of the major, minor, and modal systems

PERCUSSION   Instruments whose sounds are produced by striking membranes, metal or wooden objects

PHRASE   Meaningful unit of a musical passage that is similar to a sentence or complete clause in language. Longer than a motif, a phrase is more easily heard than defined

PIANO (*p*); PIANISSIMO (*pp*)   Soft (or quiet;) very soft

PITCH   High/low aspect of sound

PITCH CLASS   The collection of all pitches of the same note name. For example, all pitches called E♭—in whatever *register*—are members of the E♭ pitch class.

PIZZICATO   Act of plucking strings with the fingers as opposed to bowing

PLAINSONG   Religious melody of early Christianity. *Gregorian Chant* is one kind of plainsong

POCO   Little, somewhat (Poco allegro = slightly fast)

POLONAISE   Courtly dance of Polish origins in triple meter. Somewhat stiffer and statlier in tone than the mazurka

POLYPHONY, POLYPHONIC   Texture in which two or more imposing melodies are blended together

POLYMETER   Combinations of rhythms that project different meters

PRELUDE   (1) Originally a short work which, though separate and independent, served as an introductory composition for another (usually longer) work;
(2) In the 19th century the title was used indiscriminately for compositions that were to stand alone (the preludes for piano of Debussy and Chopin, Debussy's *Prelude to the Afternoon of a Faun*)

PROCESSIVE FORM   Form in which extension is achieved when a process of *development* is applied to a musical theme. Fugue and Theme and Variations are two rather different examples of this form type. A processive form projects a scheme of $A \ A^1 \ A^2 \ A^3 \ A^4 \ldots$

PROGRAM MUSIC   Composition whose title or accompanying remarks link it with a story, idea, or emotion. Program music covers a broad spectrum, from the detailed events portrayed in Richard Strauss's *Til Eulenspiegel* to the vague suggestiveness of Debussy's *La Mer* or Ives' *The Unanswered Question* (Chapters 11, 12, 15, 32)

PROPER   Portion of the Roman Catholic Mass whose parts change, unlike those of the Ordinary, with the day and service during which they are performed

QUARTER TONE   Pitch interval smaller by half than the semitone. Unacknowledged in Western scales, it nonetheless occurs in much of the music we hear played by instruments (including the voice) which can control an infinite range of pitch shadings. Some composers of the 20th century have used quarter tones in planned ways (Carillo, Xenakis, Haba, Penderecki)

QUARTET   (1) Combination of four voices or instruments
(2) composition for four singers or players

QUINTET, QUINTETTE   See *Quartet* and add one!

RAGTIME   Musical style of highly syncopated rhythms and percussive articulation that followed the 19th century minstrel music and preceded jazz. Although developed by pianists such as Scott Joplin and T. M. Turpin, the style was early transferred to instrumental ensembles

RANGE   The limits of pitch extension for an instrument or voice, from highest to lowest

RECAPITULATION   Return section in a form. Usually applied to *Sonata form*, in which the recapitulation is the third (and final) large section

RECITATIVE   Singing style that preserves the natural rhythms of words and cuts a less active melodic contour than a typical melody. Used in operas to provide information about characters or events in a way less time consuming than the usual song

REED   Vibrating element (in clarinets, bassoons, etc.) that is set into motion by the player's breath and in turn activates the instrument's air column. Oboes, bassoons, and English horns use two reeds that are coupled together, while clarinets and saxophones have a single reed

REGISTER   Level or span of pitch, such as high register, low register

RENAISSANCE PERIOD   Musical era that dates roughly from the music of Josquin des Prez (around 1500) and extends to the advent of opera around 1600

REST   Sign of musical notation that indicates the absence of sound. Like notes, rests represent different durations, such as 𝄽 (quarter-note rest) and ▬ (half-note rest)

RETROGRADE   Reversal of any musical pattern so that its beginning becomes its end and vice versa

RETURN FORM   Form in which a musical pattern returns after contrasting event or events have been established. The scheme can include one or several returns, such as *ABA*, *ABACA*, or *ABCA*

RHYTHM   Articulation of time by sound. We usually reserve the term for relatively brief series of articulations that project a sense of pattern, of several tones hanging together as a unit

RHYTHMIC DENSITY   Relative rate of sound articulations per time period

RIPIENO   Larger body of instruments in the 17th and 18th century *Concerto grosso*, as distinguished from the smaller soloistic group, the *Concertino*

RITARDANDO   To slow the tempo gradually

RITORNELLO   Returning material in compositions of the late 17th and early 18th centuries. Similar to the returns within a rondo form

ROMANTIC PERIOD   Difficult to pin down to a neat period of years, the most likely span musicians might agree upon is the era that separates the final decade of Beethoven's life (1817–27) from the end of World War I (1918)

RONDO   *Return* form of bouyant character in which at least two returns to an initial theme occur. Most rondos are in a triple meter.

ROW   Series of musical elements (pitch classes, durations, timbres) that is used as a fixed element in composing a piece. The term is most often associated with music composed within the twelvetone method developed by Arnold Schoenberg (Chapter 26)

RUBATO Style of performing in which the pulse is treated somewhat flexibly but the meter is kept intact. The result is a flow of speeding up and slowing down within very brief time spans. Wholly appropriate in some music of the late 19th century, especially the music of Chopin

SCALE Ordered display of notes that represent the pitches used in a composition. Scales normally are notated beginning with the *tonic* as the lowest note and ending with its *octave* equivalent

SCHERZO Dancelike movement in triple meter that Beethoven cultivated as a replacement for the statelier *Minuet* in the symphony and the sonata. A return form, sometimes with the multiple returns of the rondo

SCORE Notated document for any musical composition, the written music used by the conductor in directing an ensemble.

SECCO RECITATIVE *Recitative* that is accompanied by only a keyboard instrument and a bass part. Its counterpart, the accompanied recitative, is supported by the full ensemble or one of its sections

SECOND GROUP Sometimes applied to the themes that follow the principal theme or themes in a sonata form

SEMITONE See *Half-tone*

SEQUENCE Succession of a pattern (melodic or chordal) by its *repetition* at a different pitch level. The duplication can continue beyond one instance, although more than twice can bring boredom

SERIAL Composing process that incorporates a series of elements—a *series*—as a structural basis. Most often applied with a series of twelve pitch classes (Chapter 26)

SERIES See *Row*

SHARP Sign of musical notation that indicates the raising of a natural note by one half-tone (♯)

SIMPLE METER Meter whose pulse is normally divided by rhythms in twos, such as $\frac{3}{4}$, $\frac{2}{4}$, $\frac{4}{8}$, C and ¢

SINGSPIEL German opera of comic intent in which considerable spoken dialogue occurs

SLUR (1) Two different pitches played in succession without a rearticulation between; (2) notated as a curved line that connects the notes to be played without a break (⌒)

SONATA Instrumental work for solo or for no more than three instruments. The typical sonata contains three separate movements

SONATA FORM, SONATA-ALLEGRO FORM *Processive-return* form developed by composers of the classic period, especially in the first movements of sonatas, symphonies, and concertos. Large scheme is that of *Exposition, Development,* and *Recapitulation*

SONG CYCLE Collection of songs related by poetic theme and intended to be performed as a group rather than as separate compositions

SONORITY Literally "sound," though often used to refer to complex chords or timbres that defy easy classification

SOPRANO (1) High female (or boy) voice; (2) highest part in a texture, whether sung or played by an instrument

STACCATO Articulation of a series of sounds with brief silences in between, thus a detached, crisp effect

STAFF, STAVE Notational grid of five lines on which notes play

STANZA Return unit in many songs, usually consisting of the same text as well as music. Sometimes called Verse

STRETTO Imitative texture in which the imitating voice overlaps with its leader. The musical product is compression, a sense of events crowding together

STRINGS (1) Violins, violas, cellos, and double basses of the orchestra; (2) Any instrument whose sounds are produced by vibrating strings (guitar, mandolin, biwa, piano, harp, as well as those of (1) above

STROPHIC   Form in which one musical pattern is repeated to produce musical extension, thus *A A A A* . . .

STYLE   The total collection of characteristics—emotional as well as technical—that make a musical culture, a historical period, or the compositions of a single composer distinctive and unique

SUBDOMINANT   Fourth degree of a diatonic scale or the chord based on that note

SUBJECT   Principal thematic element, synonomous with *theme* but usually applied only to the main melody of a fugue

SUITE   Collection of movements, often relatively light in character and of dance origins. The orchestral suite of Bach's time consisted of five movements, four of which were stylized dances. (See Persichetti's *Divertimento for Band*, Chapter 14, for a modern example of the Suite)

SWING   Period and style of jazz that blended improvisation with popular song and dance music, roughly extending from 1930 to 1945 (Chapter 36)

SYLLABIC   Setting of words to music in which single syllables are attached to single tones

SYMBOLISM   Suggestion in music of a non-musical object or idea

SYMPHONIC POEM   One-movement orchestral work accompanied by a suggestive title or detailed story line (Debussy's *Prelude*, Chapter 11, Ives' *The Unanswered Question*, Chapter 12, Penderecki's *Threnody*, Chapter 15)

SYMPHONY   Extended work for large instrumental ensemble, usually orchestra. Most symphonies contain four movements, although some contain more, some less (Chapters 7 and 8)

SYNCOPATION   Rhythm whose accents do not correspond with the established *meter* accents

SYNTHESIZER   Electronic instrument that produces musical sounds which can be manipulated and controlled in ways unavailable on traditional acoustic instruments

TAPE MUSIC   Music that is composed directly on audio tape, usually using electronically produced sounds.

TEMPO   Rate at which music unfolds in time

TENOR   Mature male voice that is higher in pitch than the baritone and bass

TERNARY FORM   Simple *return form* in which large sections produce an *A B A* scheme

TERRACED DYNAMICS   Alternation of loudness levels without gradual changes from one to another. Typical of orchestral music during the Baroque period before *crescendo* and *diminuendo* were used

TEXTURE   Total mixture of sound patterns as they are intermeshed in time

TEXTURAL DENSITY   Relative number of different tones that sound simultaneously

THEME   Topic or subject of a musical section or whole composition. Usually refers to a most prominent melodic pattern, although some compositions use a rhythm, a texture, or even a particular timbre as their primary themes

THOROUGHBASS   See *Continuo*

THROUGH-COMPOSED   *Additive form*—usually a song—in which different themes succeed one another without returns or without variation. Large sections produce a scheme such as *A B C D* . . . .

TIMBRE   Quality or "color" property of sound

TIME SIGNATURE   See *Meter Signature*

TONALITY, TONAL   Pitch organization in which a single pitch class, or the chord based on it, acts as a point of reference. In most Western music the term *key* is synonomous with tonality

TONE   (1) Sound that has identifiable pitch, timbre, duration, and loudness; (2) same as *whole-tone*

TONE COLOR   See *timbre*

TONE PAINTING   See *Symbolism*

TONE POEM   See *Symphonic Poem*

TONIC   Pitch class that acts as reference point ("home base") in music that has tonality

TRANSITION   Passage whose function is to move from one formal section to another

TRANSPOSE   To move a collection of pitches—

melody, chord, or entire texture—from one pitch level to another

TRIAD   Chord consisting of three different *pitch classes*. Often used to mean only a major, a minor, a diminished, or an augmented triad

TRILL   Rapid alternation between two tones that are adjacent in pitch

TRIPLE METER   Meter whose pulses are grouped in units of equal threes, such as $\frac{3}{4}$, $\frac{9}{8}$, $\frac{3}{2}$ and $\frac{3}{8}$

TRIPLET   Rhythm of threes that occurs in meters for which a division of twos is normal. In notation the triplet is usually designated as such:

TUNE   Melody, usually one that is easily sung or well known

TWELVE-TONE SERIES   Ordering of the twelve pitch classes that is used as a fixed series in a composition

UPBEAT   Beat, or pulse, that comes just before a downbeat (first beat of a measure)

VARIATION   (1) Pattern that is a modification of another pattern yet retains its identity with the pattern previously heard; (2) musical section based on a *Theme* but modified and presented as a separate musical statement, such as in a Theme and Variation

VERISMO   Style of late 19th century Italian opera that concentrated on the realism of everyday life rather than on events of history or mythology

VIBRATO   Slight undulation of a tone's pitch that increases the emotional quality of the sound, creates greater warmth of tone

VIRTUOSO   Performing in a way that reveals the consumate mastery of an instrument or voice, complete control of its expressive potential

VOCALISE   Melody sung without words

VOICE   (1) Throat sound of humans; (2) a distinct line or melody within a texture, whether sung or played by an instrument

WALTZ   Dance in triple meter with strong accent on the first beat, popular in Europe of the 19th century

WHITE NOISE   Sound made prominent in *electronic music* that contains a wide band of frequencies that are close together and of the same loudness. The *sh* sound, as in the word shine, is a reputable example of white noise

WHOLE TONE   Musical interval whose size is equal to two *half-steps*. Also called "Major Second"

WHOLE TONE SCALE   Six-note scale whose successive pitches are a whole tone apart

WOODWINDS   Instruments whose sounds are produced by a reed (as with the clarinet) or by blowing over an open hole (as with a flute). The family of woodwinds comprises piccolo, flute, oboe, English horn, bassoon, recorder, and saxophone

WORD PAINTING   Musical projection of the meaning of a word or word phrase (Chapter 18)

INDEXES

NAME INDEX

Numbers in boldface represent extended coverage of a topic.

SUBJECT INDEX

Numbers in boldface represent extended discussion of the topic.